3000 800054 53909
St. Louis Community College

Florissant Valley Library
St. Louis Community College
3400 Pershall Road
Ferguson, MO 63135-1499
314-595-4514

Lacrosse

Lacrosse

A History of the Game

Donald M. Fisher

The Johns Hopkins University Press

Baltimore and London

© 2002 The Johns Hopkins University Press

All rights reserved. Published 2002

Printed in the United States of America on acid-free paper

9 8 7 6 5 4 3 2 1

The Johns Hopkins University Press
2715 North Charles Street
Baltimore, Maryland 21218-4363
www.press.jhu.edu

Library of Congress Cataloging-in-Publication Data

Fisher, Donald M., 1967–
    Lacrosse: a history of the game
        p.   cm.
    Includes bibliographical references (p.) and index.
    ISBN 0-8018-6938-2 (hardcover : alk. paper)
    1. Lacrosse—North America—History.   I. Title.
  GV989 .F56 2002
  796.34′7′09—dc21   2001005690

A catalog record for this book is available from the British Library.

For my parents

The late Donald A. Fisher
and
Patricia A. Fisher

Contents

Preface and Acknowledgments   *ix*

Prologue   **Contested Ground**   1
An Introduction to the History of Lacrosse

Chapter 1   **Learning from the "Sons of the Forest"**   10
The Birth of Modern Lacrosse in Canada, 1860–1914

Chapter 2   **"King of the Field Games"**   64
Lacrosse in the United States, 1879–1919

Chapter 3   **"What Are a Few Cuts . . . ?"**   120
Defining and Defending Lacrosse, 1920–1945

Chapter 4   **"Mayhem on the Lawn"**   189
Lacrosse in the United States and Canada, 1945–1970

Chapter 5   **The End of "The Lords of Lacrosse"?**   243
The Creator's Game in the Late Twentieth Century

Epilogue   **Ground Still Contested**   308
North American Cultures and the Meaning of
Lacrosse

Appendix: All-Time Great Lacrosse Players   *315*
Notes   *319*
An Essay on Sources   *349*
Index   *355*

Preface and Acknowledgments

WHEN I WAS IN HIGH SCHOOL, a fellow student made a very bold comment: if there was a professional lacrosse league, it would outdraw major league baseball by a landslide. At the time, the statement struck me as odd. But the reader should understand that the school was LaFayette High School, which sits beside Route 11 just south of Syracuse, New York. The school's population included a mixture of children from the town's white- and blue-collar middle class, agricultural families, the rural poor, and the Native American residents of the adjacent Onondaga Reservation. It was a small school, graduating fewer than a hundred students per year. In the spring, lacrosse was king. I was intrigued by the fact that so many sons of middle-class families regarded as their own what everyone knew was "an Indian game." Some walked the halls of the school carrying their lacrosse sticks. Many lacrosse players seemed to take a very negative stance toward baseball. How, I wondered, could so many boys turn their backs on the national pastime?

Many years later, I enrolled in graduate school at the State University of New York at Buffalo. I had always been interested in the history of North America's native people, but, like so many other youngsters, I had been exposed only to the military history of the western frontier. I began to recall the sociocultural milieu of life in high school. My thoughts also turned to my maternal grandfather. He had died a bitter man. During his final days, he spoke about how his Indian mother had not been allowed to be buried in the "white cemetery." My general interest in the historical relationship between Native Americans and mainstream "white society" led me to search for an original, unconventional research topic for a history dissertation. Instead of delving into the history of white stereotypes of Indians or the history of the western frontier, I preferred to walk on less explored ground.

In April 1993 I proposed the idea of a cultural history of lacrosse to Professor Norman Baker. His faith in the project proved instrumental. With the exception of the endless days sitting in front of a microfilm reader, which often left me bug-eyed, I thoroughly enjoyed every aspect of the researching, writing, and editing of this book. For the next several years my research took me from the Library of Congress to the Akwesasne Reservation, from southern Ontario to suburban Maryland, from the dusty attic in the U.S. Lacrosse Hall of Fame to the basement of the home of former coach Roy Simmons, Sr., and from watching professional indoor lacrosse games with sixteen thousand screaming fans to playing catch with my ten-year-old niece. The more I learned about the history of lacrosse as a contested cultural battleground, the more determined I was to share what I had discovered with others.

Several months before I defended my thesis, I was hired for a tenure-track job teaching at a nearby community college. My new heavy teaching load—and the purchase of a mountain bicycle—led me to set the manuscript aside after graduation. Occasionally I was able to conduct further research as well as revise and restructure chapters. During the summer of 2000, time permitted me to finish the book and forward it to the Johns Hopkins University Press. I owe thanks to Bob Brugger and Melody Herr at the Press for their patience in waiting for the manuscript over the past few years.

MANY INDIVIDUALS AND INSTITUTIONS deserve recognition both for assisting me in this project and for shaping me as a historian over the past decade or more. My early development as a historian took place mainly in western New York, but it all began an hour and a half to the east, at Saint John Fisher College in Rochester, New York. Mieczslaw Biskupski and Donald Bain were the two historians who set me on the path on which I find myself today. Many thanks go to those who served on my dissertation committee: Norman Baker, Michael Frisch, Susan Cahn, and Donald Fixico. Professor Baker was especially helpful as a mentor and a friend. He read and critiqued more than one version of my work. He reinforced my understanding of a very simple but valuable lesson: ultimately, history is about flesh-and-blood people. Professor Frisch served as the chairman of the committee and helped me to see the forest when I could find only trees.

Other people helped me make this book a reality in disparate ways by offering their insightful comments, reading sections of the manuscript, pointing me toward source materials, and providing moral support or even a spare bed or couch. These people include John Hajduk, Donald Fritz, Alan Stafford, Bill Tanton, Stan Shillington, Robert Wright, Lars Tiffany, Todd Phillips, Barbara Landis, Tom Vennum, and Karen and Rich Hilchey, plus Jennifer and Christopher, my aunt Dee Preston-Dillon, John and Joan Kumor, and even Bart. Steve Stenersen and his staff at the U.S. Lacrosse Hall of Fame were especially helpful in providing information and photocopying services during my numerous research trips to Baltimore. I found very helpful the interviews and conversations I had with Oren Lyons, Jr., Wes Patterson, Roy Simmons, Sr., Emil Budnitz, Caleb Kelly, Bob Scott, Barb and Ken Van Every, Lilly Benedict, Peter Burns, Charles Perkins, Allan Blair, Ken Drum, Al Paige, Ken Croft, and William G. Hersperger. I must also offer thanks to the many friends, acquaintances, colleagues, and students who have listened to me talk about my research over the past few years.

Just days before Christmas 1996, I was offered my job at Niagara County Community College. I especially thank Tim Tomsen for the opportunity to start my career as a professional historian. He gave me the chance to teach U.S. and world history survey courses and a Native American history course that has been particularly helpful. The latter allowed me to develop a more sophisticated understanding of the important historical patterns that have unfolded throughout eastern North America during the past millennium. Our division's office staff—Anna Petroziello, Beth Mayer, and Lucy Boehnke—have been very patient with my requests to use office computers to print documents.

Also providing valuable help were the librarians, curators, archivists, and other staff members at numerous institutions, including Syracuse University and the Onondaga Historical Association in Syracuse, New York; Hobart College in Geneva, New York; the Akwesasne Cultural Center in Hogansburg, New York; the U.S. Military Academy at West Point, New York; the Johns Hopkins University, Enoch Pratt Free Library, Maryland Historical Society, and U.S. Lacrosse Hall of Fame in Baltimore, Maryland; the National Archives and Library of Congress in Washington, D.C.; the U.S. Naval Academy at Annapolis, Maryland; the Canadian Sports Hall of Fame and University of Toronto in Toronto, Ontario; the State University of New York at Buffalo in Amherst, New York; the Buffalo and Erie County Historical

Society in Buffalo, New York; and Niagara County Community College in Sanborn, New York. Also helpful were Michael Lachappelle of the Canadian Lacrosse Association in Ottawa, Ontario; Rochelle Winterton of the British Columbia Lacrosse Association in New Westminster, British Columbia; and Arden Phair of the Saint Catharines Museum in Saint Catharines, Ontario.

The man most deserving of my gratitude is my father, Donald A. Fisher. When I was a young boy he reluctantly told me of his experiences as a forward observer in the First Infantry Division during the Second World War. He and all of his stories inspired me to go to college and earn bachelor's, master's and doctoral degrees in history. My dad was very proud to see me receive my Ph.D. in 1997, but I know in my heart that no degree can begin to compare with the Bronze Star he earned at Omaha Beach in 1944. Like so many men of that generation who actually saw front-line combat, he was extremely humble about his wartime heroism. On August 22, 2001, just thirty-nine days after he watched me receive the sacrament of marriage, my father passed away. I shall always miss him terribly.

My mother, Patricia A. Fisher, deserves much recognition for offering me her unconditional love and support throughout my life, but especially over the past decade. Together with my father, my mom was very patient in watching me pursue the path of higher education.

To my best friend—my wife, Christine—I offer thanks for her love and companionship. During the final stages of this project, she helped me numerous times by solving my computer problems, bringing me coffee late at night, and offering me moral support. I am forever in her debt for her selflessness. I will always be grateful that she is on my team in the game of life.

Lacrosse

Prologue **Contested Ground**

An Introduction to the History
of Lacrosse

ON JUNE 4, 1763, a group of Ojibwa and Sauk Indians staged a stick-and-ball game outside Fort Michilimackinac, in what later became the state of Michigan, as part of a celebration of the English king's birthday. Once occupied by the French, the fortification had been garrisoned by British troops as a result of the Seven Years' War. The general roughness of the activity, the ebb and flow of the contest, and the exotic thrill of witnessing Indians engage in mass recreation captivated many of the soldiers. Suddenly the two teams of Indians dropped their playing sticks, grabbed their weapons, and killed the onlooking troops. Such was the remote incident that took place during Pontiac's Rebellion. A century later, the Iroquoian version of this game had become a sporting activity among affluent white men in the United States, Canada, and eventually England and Australia. Despite the insignificance of the Fort Michilimackinac incident in the evolution of the actual modern sport of lacrosse, the event was incorporated into the lore of white lacrosse enthusiasts—sportswriters, officials, coaches, and athletes alike—throughout the nineteenth and twentieth centuries. In 1870 even historian Francis Parkman provided readers with his own version of the incident.[1] No doubt the game and the attack promoted different views of lacrosse that reinforced each other. For many generations of white devotees, the contest between the two groups of Indians symbolized this fast-paced, roughneck athletic activity indigenous to eastern North America. At the same time, however, enthusiasts remained fascinated with the brave, mythical "noble savage" who had carried out the attack.

The relationship between real and romanticized Indians lies at the core of the history of lacrosse. This book is an attempt to understand how and why various peoples transformed a traditional Native American ball game played centuries earlier by disparate Indian tribes in eastern North America into a modern sport played at universities, secondary schools, commercial arenas, and Indian reservations across the United States and Canada. By pointing to the character-building qualities of the modernized game of the "noble savage," amateur sportsmen in Canada and the United States created an exclusive athletic world for themselves and a periodically accepted minority of native participants that existed throughout most of the nineteenth and twentieth centuries. These amateur sportsmen generally had little toleration for the excesses of commercialism or social democracy that were sometimes imposed on their sport. Not until the 1970s, when mass-produced synthetic sticks challenged and quickly displaced the sticks made by native craftsmen, did lacrosse attract significantly larger numbers of athletes. Essentially, the sticks produced in limited volumes by native stick makers were nearly made obsolete by modern factories armed with research and development dollars and the ability to increase production rapidly when necessary. Besides examining who were actually enthusiasts and why, this narrative explores how the modern progeny of English settlers and Iroquois Indians utilized lacrosse as an extraordinary domain of cultural struggle well after white men had established political and economic dominance over the continent.

As a way of introducing the reader to the subject, it is necessary to refer briefly to previous, but limited, scholarship. A more comprehensive bibliographic listing of scholarly studies on lacrosse can be found in the notes and in the "Essay on Sources" following the notes. Because Native American culture was transmitted from generation to generation through an oral tradition, the very first histories of the game went unrecorded. By listening to tribal elders, the young learned the stories of the origins of the game and the importance of playing for the Creator. During the second half of the nineteenth century, white propagandists, journalists, and athletes compiled their own salutary histories. Building on these efforts, coaches and players in both Canada and the United States wrote short histories in newspapers, magazines, and instructional books. Not until well after the Second World War did anyone take much of a serious interest in the history of lacrosse. In 1965 and again in 1977, former player and coach Milton Roberts published two books, but preoccupation with athletic minutiae guaranteed a readership confined only to the zealous. Physical education students, anthropologists, and historians produced a number of studies during the 1970s and

1980s. Much of this work addressed either traditional Native American ball games or the nineteenth-century Canadian sport. In 1994 Thomas Vennum published *American Indian Lacrosse*. Building upon numerous previous studies, Vennum's work is the most thorough account of the native ball games of eastern North America as interpreted by academicians and Native American "traditionalists."[2] Vennum's topically oriented study is informed by anthropological methods rather than historical questions, and it includes several chapters of historical fiction. Unlike other modern sports, especially English soccer and American baseball, lacrosse has lacked a comprehensive and scholarly presentation of its past. The vast academic and journalistic literatures of these other sports clearly indicate the important functions people have attached to them. All of the books on those sports have helped generate and guarantee present and future interest. Until the publication of this volume by the Johns Hopkins University Press, lacrosse has had no such tradition or record.

Lacrosse: A History of the Game attempts to present the history of lacrosse within broad cultural and social contexts. Besides highlighting the development of the sport as a formal part of the surrounding culture, this book examines the game as a unique venue wherein which native people and European newcomers experienced everything from cooperation and tolerance to outright hostility and confrontation. An important concept expressed in this book is that lacrosse must be viewed as a "contested ground." The term implies a duality. Obviously it refers to the combative, potentially violent nature of the game. Lacrosse has provided a setting in which athletes have competed for possession of balls, scored points and defended goals, achieved victories and avenged defeats, and given and taken lumps. Lacrosse can also be scrutinized as having provided a means whereby competing groups have contested cultural meaning. During the most recent century and a half, enthusiasts have included whites and Indians, amateurs and professionals, hometowners and nationalists, gamblers and social reformers, Irishmen and Anglos, Canadians and Americans, collegians and manual laborers, men and women, New Yorkers and Baltimoreans, preppies and public schoolboys, field and box lacrosse proponents, eastern and western Canadians, "progressives" and "traditionalists," talented players and goons. In this sense, studying lacrosse allows for an investigation of how and why people reach consensus or conflict, the changing meaning of culture, and the social, economic, political, racial, geographic, and technological factors shaping the contestation of culture. The book also points to the continuity of Native American tradition as negotiated through the parameters of a world governed by capitalism and "progress." This history asks the reader to consider the survival of native culture in the contemporary consumerist world of North America. Although scholars have emphasized the demographic disaster among native peoples after 1492 and subsequent nation building by the descendants of the European colonizers in their many tomes on North America, the history of lacrosse serves as a vivid reminder that the long-term consequences of the Columbian Exchange are diverse in scope and complex in significance.

Unlike the enthusiasts of other, more prominent, team sports that have appealed to larger, more diverse groups of people, those who have called lacrosse their game of choice have tended not to chronicle, much less analyze, their sport. With a few exceptions, scholars have also remained disinterested. The problem has been compounded by the actual devotees of the game. Because sport was not supposed to be taken seriously, some socially elite sporting organizations did not leave behind meticulous records of their activities. And because native enthusiasts emphasized cultural continuity through oral history, the preservation of detail was lost at the expense of timeless truths. The paucity of materials has created a quandary and makes reconstruction of the history of the game a most arduous task. Regardless, such a history can be forged, and it is one that includes many viewpoints. City and campus newspapers, periodical literature, and publications of national and local athletics organizations reveal the institutional structure of the game as well as ideological postures taken by different people regarding the game. Dominating and dissenting views can indeed be found. Even though most source material was generated by white observers, the Native American side of the story has not necessarily been lost, slighted, or suppressed. Evaluating press coverage of native lacrosse can be eye-opening. By employing methods of inquiry used to examine the cultural and historical significance of newspaper and magazine advertisements, readers can account for distortions in white accounts and achieve glimpses of reality.[3] What readers might misconstrue as the simple fictions of white men can actually be useful indicators of a native worldview. Archival materials including personal correspondence, administrative records, newspaper clippings, and scrapbooks enhance this narrative by allowing us to listen to the candid voices of coaches, players, and officials who shaped the game.

Although portions of this book rest upon previous research, most materials utilized were generated not by scholars, but rather by coaches, journalists, players, officials, and fans, who tell the story themselves in their own voices. For over a century the world of lacrosse remained confined to university playing fields and locker rooms, intercollegiate conventions, Indian reservations, private athletic clubs, and ice hockey arenas converted for summer play of other games, but perhaps now this history can be explored. The positions taken by proponents lead the reader to examine historical issues beyond the realm of sport. This volume offers opportunities to scrutinize the social and cultural characteristics of elite education and athletics, the forces of change and continuity within social systems, elite attitudes toward socioeconomically marginal peoples and vice versa, cross-cultural relations between native and non-native communities, definitions of masculinity, the cultural and social significance of the Canadian-American border, allusions to cultural imperialism and hegemony, and the relationships among technology, democracy, and the capitalist marketplace.

Several recurring themes have permeated the history of lacrosse. Among the more significant has been the emergence and dominance of a socially elite conception of lacrosse as a "gentleman's game." Created by nationalist George Beers for nineteenth-century Canadians, this ethos of lacrosse as an elite sporting element of culture was transplanted to the United States by Canadian immigrants and germinated in private athletic clubs as well as prestigious institutions of higher and secondary education. A second theme points to the relationship between lacrosse and its Native American originators in the eyes of white enthusiasts of the game. White proponents often conceptualized the Indian athlete as the "noble savage" first identified by Jean-Jacques Rousseau. This fictional icon of the Enlightenment not only survived well into the twentieth century, as affluent white athletes saw themselves as the symbolic descendants of romanticized Indian warriors of old, but it helped to justify rough, physical, but not excessively violent activity among collegians and schoolboys. Together, these dual images of the gentleman's game and the noble savage functioned as the basis for interest in lacrosse among many socially elite sportsmen and -women. A third theme revolves around the rise of commercial interests confronting the dominant amateur conception of the game by challenging the cultural authority of the socially elite field lacrosse community first in Canada and then in the United States. While commercialism and professionalism triumphed over Beers's gentlemanly conception of lacrosse as Canada's "national game" during the late nineteenth century, only to collapse under the weight of a marketplace unsuited to these forces by the era of the First World War, such challenges failed to decenter the amateur game in the United States. Only at the end of the twentieth century did a fully commercialized version of lacrosse have any success. Finally, no comprehensive narrative of lacrosse would be complete without an evaluation of the game's originators: Iroquois Indians. Although they realized that nonnative enthusiasts were restructuring their game and imposing administrative control over it, the Indians offered both accommodation and resistance to white governing bodies.

The intersection of these several themes makes the history of lacrosse a complex tale. The Iroquois Indians who originated the sport and manufactured the playing sticks of all participants conveniently doubled as the "noble savages" who stimulated interest in the game among many nonnatives. The limited appeal of this romantic image concocted by affluent sportsmen and the limitations of the native stick industry ensured that the North American lacrosse community would be relatively small. The tensions between the forces of amateurism and commercialism also affected the evolution of the sport. The commercial threat reinforced a gentlemanly backlash, attracted new affluent enthusiasts, and eventually pushed the amateur community to become more inclusive. Together, these two broader cultural contests—the contest between real and imagined Indians and that between amateurism and commercialism—provide the broad contours of the history of lacrosse during the nineteenth and twentieth centuries.

The comprehensive nature of this chronicle calls for both narration and analysis. The five chapters of this book flow chronologically, but sometimes take diversions to explore other topics. Chapter 1, "Learning from the 'Sons of the Forest,'" examines the native origins of lacrosse as well as its appropriation by middle-class English sportsmen around the time of the confederation of Canada. It shows how Canadian clubs paid lip service to amateur ideals while covertly paying players. The second chapter, "'King of the Field Games,'" covers the rise of American lacrosse as a phenomenon among club and collegian athletes, especially at institutions such as the

Johns Hopkins University. Not only did the former "national game" of Canada take on a new tone in New York, New England, and Baltimore, but Native American players adopted modern versions of the Creator's Game. The next chapter, "'What Are a Few Cuts . . . ?,'" examines how defenders of amateur sport in the United States fought off a variety of challenges, including problems posed by the Great Depression, the Second World War, and Canadian "box" lacrosse. Meanwhile, by turning to England for an amateur sporting model, Americans recommitted themselves to sport for sport's sake. Chapter 4, "'Mayhem on the Lawn,'" tells how a more democratic American field lacrosse community began to emerge during the quarter-century after the war. Canadian lacrosse enthusiasts completely embraced box lacrosse, but found themselves geographically isolated. Finally, the chapter entitled "The End of 'The Lords of Lacrosse'?" examines the proliferation and diffusion of different versions of the game since 1970 throughout North America and overseas. Besides exploring the decline of aristocratic pretensions, the emergence of the mass-produced synthetic stick, and the rise of a professional game, the chapter surveys the emergence of the Iroquois Nationals, the first native sport organization permitted to participate in international competition.

The cultural geography of this book requires some clarification. The peoples of three places and cultures dominate this study: Iroquoia, Canada, and America (see map on page 8). Among the Native American originators of lacrosse and their nineteenth- and twentieth-century descendants a variety of terms are used to refer to specific tribes and reservation communities. The most prominent people with active roles in the history of the game include those of the Mohawk reserves near Montreal: Saint Regis/ Akwesasne and Caughnawaga/Kahnawake; the Six Nations Reserve near Brantford, Ontario; the Cattaraugus, Alleghany, and Akron Reservations of Seneca Indians in western New York; the Onondaga Reservation near Syracuse, New York; and urban native communities in Buffalo and Rochester, New York. Because the game learned by white Canada was Mohawk in origin, the earliest play took place in Montreal and nearby Cornwall. Other important areas include communities in and around Toronto and the rest of southern Ontario, such as Peterborough, Hamilton, and Saint Catharines and in southwestern British Columbia, such as Vancouver, Victoria, New Westminster, and Coquitlam. The most prominent lacrosse communities in the United States could be found in and around New York

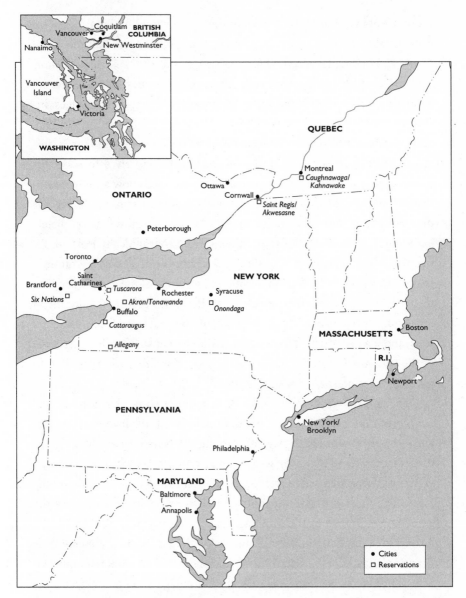

Iroquoia, Canada, America. Indian reservations, small cities in Canada, and sub-urban communities in the American Northeast are the geographic focal points of the cultural history of lacrosse.

City, especially Brooklyn, Westchester County, and suburban Long Island; in Boston and nearby New England towns; in upstate New York and Philadelphia; and in Maryland, especially Baltimore and Annapolis.

A few words should be said about what *Lacrosse: A History of the Game* is *not*. Because this book is a theme-oriented cultural study, readers will not find detailed examinations of the rules of the game, narratives of contests, or celebrations of the sport's various great players, coaches, or championship teams. It is unnecessary for anyone to be familiar with the sport's on-field legends and heroes to appreciate its cultural history. However, if the reader wishes to consult lists of some of the greatest lacrosse players ever, they can be found in the appendix at the end of the book. In addition, although the subjects of primary concern are men's field lacrosse in the United States and relations between native and non-native communities, this book also addresses, on a smaller scale, the significance of the Canadian box game and women's lacrosse in the United States.

Chapter 1

**Learning from
the "Sons of the Forest"**
The Birth of Modern Lacrosse in Canada,
1860–1914

A VARIETY OF Native American ball games may have been common throughout eastern North America prior to European contact, but middle-class anglophone Canadians created modern lacrosse during the years surrounding the confederation of Canada in 1867, when they adopted and then adapted the Mohawk ball game *tewaarathon*. The transformation of this element of native culture into a modern sport was made possible by the convergence of several historical developments in mid-nineteenth-century Canada, including the marginalization of the Iroquois Confederacy, the formation of a Victorian sporting culture, and the birth of Canadian nationalism. The Anglo-Canadian appropriation of Mohawk lacrosse was a peculiar event in the history of the New World, because usually it was the colonizers who were seeking to force the Indians to accept *their* culture. Affluent athletes in Great Britain had adopted medieval folk football from rural peasant culture, transformed it into several modern team sports, and championed the cultural values of amateurism. Similarly, Canadian gentlemen believed the "primitive" native game could be sanitized and made to serve young men facing the challenges brought on by industrialization and urbanization through the development of character and manliness. The birth of modern lacrosse reflected the construction of a transcontinental Canadian national identity rooted in imperialistic Anglo-Canadian attitudes toward the New World environment and its native inhabitants. Essentially, virile Canadian national manhood could be made possible through the modernization of the white conception of the "noble savage." By applying the forces of "progress"—rationalism, secularism, and bureaucracy—to a traditional folk culture, Canadians could create a vehicle through which they could invigorate themselves as a new nationality.

Despite the wishes of many of the earliest advocates of the amateur Canadian "national game," the game's organizers quickly accepted the values of commercialism and a covert form of professionalism. Many lacrosse enthusiasts may have paid lip service to nationalism, but the rise of inter-club disputes, gambling, and organizational fragmentation during the late nineteenth century and the early twentieth century signaled a sport world unable or unwilling to confront problems with a unified front. Ultimately, even though the fully professional version of Canadian lacrosse began to collapse under the weight of the commercial marketplace, the amateur version of the game survived among Canadian immigrants living in the northeastern cities of the United States.

Natives and Newcomers: Ball Games and the Collision of Cultures during the Colonial and Early National Eras

By the time European explorers first set foot in the Western Hemisphere, ball games in the so-called New World were very old.[1] They are best understood against broad political, economic, and cultural developments during the half millennium prior to the arrival of Christopher Columbus. Whether they arrived at the islands of the Caribbean or the eastern coastline of North America, Europeans did not realize they were entering the "back door" of a world far removed from the Old World of Europe, Asia, and Africa. Over two decades would pass before the Spanish would discover an urban civilization in Mesoamerica. To the north, Native American life was concentrated around a massive river drainage system centering around the mighty Mississippi. Other waterways, such as the Ohio, Arkansas, and Missouri Rivers and the numerous creeks feeding into them, facilitated the movement of peoples, crops, and ideas over many hundreds of miles. Consequently, the many tribes occupying eastern North America had much in common culturally.

Between roughly A.D. 800 and 1100, a maize revolution had occurred. As Indian corn had spread north from Mesoamerica into the rest of North America, local populations mixed with peoples from other regions to produce a different world as new trends began to reshape native life. With the emergence of corn came a new mixed economy based on horticulture, hunting, fishing, and foraging; a population boom; and new political pres-

sures. Growing populations produced fewer but larger towns with a growing emphasis on extended families and multifamily dwellings at the expense of a way of life once dominated by small villages and nuclear families. Many of these new towns moved away from river- and lakefronts to
elevated, more easily defensible positions. Townspeople surrounded their
communities with palisaded walls and cornfields to protect and feed themselves. The new defensive posture of settlements led to the formation of
multitown alliances, and linguistic kin formed even larger intertribal confederations. For instance, five Iroquoian-speaking peoples—the Mohawk,
Cayuga, Onondaga, Oneida, and Seneca nations—established an alliance
sometime between 1450 and 1525 in what later became the English colony
of New York. They were called Iroquois by the French, the Five (and later
Six) Nations by the English, but they referred to themselves as the Ho-
denosaunee, or "the People of the Longhouse." By using their type of
dwelling as a metaphor for self-identification, they made the alliance a per-
sonification of their family-structured society.

Native people had played a variety of ball games throughout the continent prior to the appearance of the Europeans. By the time Spanish
conquistadores first landed in Mexico during the early sixteenth century,
the cities of Mesoamerica already had an ancient tradition of playing elaborate games symbolizing the movements of celestial bodies on courts made
of stone. The Olmec, Maya, and, most recently, the Aztec empire had all
practiced these games. This tradition moved north to what would later become the southwestern United States. Game traditions involving the carrying, hitting, or kicking of a ball could be found elsewhere throughout North
America, but without the elaborate stone court surface. The characteristics
of a particular game were often related to a tribe's subsistence. Among the
tribes of the desolate and flat Great Plains and the mountainous and coastal
Far West, where hunting and foraging were common, native people played
"shinny." The game's playing stick resembled a digging tool. In the continent's vast eastern woodlands, where people placed a greater emphasis on
agriculture, Indians played "racket." In a world where population growth
produced hostilities, rivalries, and alliances, this game's stick resembled a
war club. Whether there was any connection between the diverse ball games
of the Mississippi River drainage system and those of urban Mesoamerica
is unclear. The tradition of the Mesoamerican court game did diffuse to the
Southwest, but whether the game eventually spread west, north, and east

and was distilled into distinct games through the continent's extensive trade network is a subject of speculation. If this premise is correct, the lack of large city-states akin to those found in Mesoamerica may explain why the ball games of eastern North America morphed into games with many different forms and the elaborate Mesoamerican game did not remain intact.

Regardless of any connection between Mesoamerica and North America's eastern woodlands, the widespread similarity of the games throughout the settlements of the Mississippi drainage system shows the importance of long-distance trade relationships among Native American peoples. Regardless of region, all ball games took place on irregular playing surfaces, sometimes over a mile long. Each of these contests involved players' carrying and passing a ball in a webbed pocket mounted on a stick to a goal. All game sticks in this area possessed stringed pockets, but the shapes and sizes of the sticks reflected at least three broad clusters of games. Iroquoian tribes in the Northeast, especially those in the Iroquois Confederacy, played a game utilizing a single stick, four to five feet long, with an unenclosed pocket in which to carry the ball. Around the Great Lakes and upper Mississippi River valley region, a single stick, two to three feet long with an enclosed wooden pocket, was used by Algonquian and Siouian tribes. In the Southeast, Muskhogean nations such as the Chickasaw and Choctaw, as well as the Iroquoian-speaking Cherokee, played a game featuring a pair of sticks, one to two feet long, with enclosed pockets. Even though each tribe's game had unique features, it is possible to make generalizations about the gaming tradition in the eastern woodlands. Unfortunately, however, the primary sources of these ball games—reports by European explorers and missionaries as well as native oral traditions—come to modern readers from the era of colonization. The lack of evidence unaffected by colonization makes any comments about the games prior to the colonists' contact with the natives very tentative. Regardless, most ball games served practical and symbolic purposes, promoting military preparedness, diplomatic conciliation, social conformity, religious continuity, and economic equality.

Because war was a constant threat, native people placed a great emphasis on military power and diplomacy. The most obvious purpose of a ball game was to sustain a nation by keeping its men strong and healthy for war and hunting. The constant running, rough play, and stick skills needed to play the game conditioned men for combat. Even the names employed by Indians revealed the game's violent nature. Although some Native Americans used some form of the conjugate "to hit" in the name itself, one of the "Five Civilized Tribes," the Creek of the Southeast, even named their game the "younger brother of war." In many instances, the rituals of a ball game were the same as the rituals of warfare. Pre- and postgame activities were associated with victory, scalp, and war dances. Injuries during play surely occurred, but early European observers tended to exaggerate their claims of players' dying on the field. After all, the men who played against one another closed ranks when facing a military foe.

Aside from training individual warriors, the ball game served as an instrument of diplomacy that was used to avert war with neighbors. Since a ball game was usually played by nations that had achieved a significant level of population concentration and extratribal affiliation, a contest permitted tribes to reinforce political fellowship while solving territorial disputes within the context of an alliance. The maize revolution that created the population boom and a greater need for political leagues essentially changed the map of North America and the pattern of intertribal war. Tribes could no longer afford to be in a constant state of petty war with nearby nations over hunting grounds when other more distant peoples posed greater threats. Confederacies allowed tribes to protect one another's interests and project their collective might against enemies. Playing a ball game facilitated and reinforced these bonds. It should be no surprise that one group of Native Americans with a rich tradition of ball play, the Iroquois Confederacy, became a major military power during the seventeenth century and the early eighteenth century, usually at the expense of other native peoples on their own frontiers. Not ironically, it was also their game that evolved into modern lacrosse.

Even though ball games served practical diplomatic and military purposes, they were also steeped in spirituality and served as agents of socialization. They promoted community stability among individuals and between generations by fostering religious continuity, social conformity, and economic equality. According to the oral traditions of many tribes, a primeval game had been played either between quadrupeds and birds or between creatures with teeth and those with feathers. Other mythologies declared that a god or spirit had given the games to humans, sometimes through dreams. Articles of faith, these stories explained Nature and served as allegories about the importance of the individual to the tribe. Ball games reinforced each nation's unique relationship with the Creator and embodied Man's relationship with Nature. The animal and historical legends about games played a significant role in the cultural coherence of a nation. Moreover, ceremonial ball games involved intratribal competition, included fewer contestants than intertribal contests, and deemphasized rough play. The ball game functioned as a cultural stabilizer and reinforced the power of spiritual authorities. Tribal religious leaders called for the playing of ritual games to alter the weather, cure the sick, or honor the dead. Games were played under the watchful eyes of conjurers and medicine men. Since these shamans scheduled contests according to seasonal rhythms, ball games reinforced holistic thinking and a cyclical conception of time. The games helped bind the present with the past. After all, not only might a game take place in conjunction with an annual celestial or agrarian event, but through it old-timers could nostalgically recall their heroic deeds as younger men.

Ball games also ensured the survival of a nation by reinforcing communalism, chieftain authority, and gender roles. From the beginning of an encounter, men paired off with opponents and pursued the ball in large clusters. The character of play allowed for significant latitude in individual performance. With little specialization of playing roles on the field aside from general attacking or defending responsibilities, the games encouraged conformity and an egalitarian social order. Since individual players did not have predetermined roles in any stratified social hierarchy on or off the field, they were given leeway in how they played. As a consequence, spontaneous fights and wrestling matches broke out on the field of play. These sparring matches may seem to have been counterproductive to the group's aim of winning the contest, but the fights demonstrated the game's function as a rite of passage to manhood. In addition to guaranteeing community stability through the acknowledgment of the power of shamans, ball play reinforced the separate male and female spheres of life. To achieve purity before a contest, for instance, men segregated themselves from women, especially those experiencing menstruation. In many eastern woodlands communities, men and women provided a family with different types of nutrients. Because men were the hunters and warriors, they provided protein and fat. As the community's farmers, women provided carbohydrates by growing and harvesting the "three sisters": corn, beans, and squash. Although men and women occasionally played ball games with or against one another, most games were male activities, with women serving as vociferous spectators, encouraging or chastising their men according to performance.

Gambling on a ball game stabilized social life by promoting economic equality. Every time people wagered, they facilitated the redistribution of wealth and material between or within tribes. Hunting rights to disputed territory might be the prize in an intertribal match, but individuals also wagered on articles of personal value, items made by human hands and others found in nature. Over the course of years, the parity of talent and the frequency of play ensured stability both within and between tribes. Although a man might lose possessions after betting on one contest, for example, he stood a good chance to recover his losses later. Regardless, even if someone did lose a favorite tool, weapon, or article of clothing, it could be replaced. Gambling simply prevented anyone from permanently holding onto personal property. Prior to the intrusion of the European material culture, no significant technological gap existed among natives in an area. The results of a wager reinforced technological similarity among neighboring nations. The winner of a bet might learn a better way of making something by examining an item he had won, but the loser would have to work hard to replace it.

The European invasion of eastern North America affected not only the balance of power among tribes and confederations, but the ball games as well. A familiar pattern of intrusion by Spanish, French, Dutch, and English interests reshaped the Native American world. European microbes penetrated interior trade routes well in advance of any colonial army. Moreover, any native nation incurring the wrath of a European colonizer faced extermination; others who had access to European firearms became powerful at the expense of those who did not have such access. During the seventeenth and eighteenth centuries, warfare became more common, more destructive, and more geographically diffuse. Even though the ball games continued to serve their traditional purposes, they could not help but be affected by the European presence. Whether serving as ceremonial ritual, conditioner of the physique, instrument of diplomacy, unifier of Man with Nature and the Creator, or reinforcer of tradition, ball play functioned as a binding force within Native American nations. Any changes in tribal life brought on by contact with Europeans were reflected in the playing of the games.

During the era of French and English colonization, from the early seventeenth century through the mid-eighteenth century, intense warfare pressed many Indian men into military service to the colonizers. Prior to contact with Europeans, for many natives war was a means to acquire captives and achieve individual prestige. In the age of European empires, war took on commercial and genocidal overtones. The introduction of firearms into the Native American world forever altered the traditional balance of power among tribes and confederacies. With the advent of the gun, participation in a ball game no longer gave a man all the training he needed for combat. Also, any time a native accepted Christianity, the traditional belief in a holistic understanding of Man, Nature, and the Creator was called into question. The mere presence of Christian missionaries caused tensions with native shamans, who felt threatened. And finally, the introduction of factory-made goods from Europe fundamentally altered the consequences of gambling. The repercussions of winning or losing an iron tool or a musket were far greater than those of winning a stone-gouger or a longbow.

The most detailed transcribed accounts of native ball games were produced by European explorers and missionaries during the sixteenth and seventeenth centuries. The Jesuit priests of New France were among the earliest European game chroniclers. In the wake of the Protestant Reformation, these Roman Catholic missionaries practiced a zealous form of proselytization in the New World. Known to Indians as the "Black Robes," the members of the Society of Jesus tried to create a biracial theocracy in New France by grafting Roman Catholicism onto the traditional beliefs of the Indians. In their effort to reconcile native culture with Roman Catholicism, the Jesuits highlighted what they saw as the positive qualities of Indian life in their *Jesuit Relations* reports to authorities and mission financiers in France. In 1637 Father Jean de Brébeuf described the power of dreams in native life, friction between Jesuits and shamans, and gambling:

> There is a poor sick man, fevered of body and almost dying, and a miserable Sorcerer will order for him, as a cooling remedy, a game of crosse. Or the sick man himself, sometimes, will have dreamed that he must die unless the whole country shall play crosse for his health; and, no matter how little may be his credit, you will see then in a beautiful field, Village contending against Village, as to who will play crosse the better, and betting against one another Beaver robes and Porcelain collars, so as to excite greater interest.

Sometimes, also, one of these Jugglers will say that the whole Country is sick, and he asks a game of crosse to heal it; no more needs to be said, it is published immediately everywhere; and all the Captains of each Village give orders that all the young men do their duty in this respect, otherwise some great misfortune would befall the whole Country.[2]

Ball games gave Indians opportunities to carry out their responsibilities as members of a village. Playing a ball game for a sick man helped the community and pleased the Creator.

Even though many ball games were played throughout the eastern woodlands before and during European colonization, modern lacrosse is a direct descendent of only one of the many "traditional" ball games. It was middle-class Anglo-Canadians from Montreal and Mohawk Indians from the nearby Caughnawaga reserve whose cultural exchange led to the birth of modern lacrosse. The place of origin is significant given the history of war along the eastern Great Lakes frontier and in the Ohio River valley. Although contact between native peoples and the kingdoms of western Europe ranged from conflict to cooperation during the three centuries after 1492, the latter usually won, extracting raw materials, converting "heathen savages," and establishing permanent settlements. Spanish conquistadores, French fur traders, and English tobacco farmers all measured Indians against the yardsticks of Christianity and European civilization. These colonizers judged native peoples as either inferior or subhuman, and often determined their fate: extermination, slavery, removal, or assimilation. However, since some European newcomers perceived the Old World as crowded and diseased, with a greedy society ruled by a constrictive church and a corrupt state, they often viewed the New World as a life-giving Paradise occupied by a free and innocent people. Intellectuals of the eighteenth-century Enlightenment viewed the contemporary Indian as a mirror image of the primitive European of centuries past, giving rise to a romantic conception of the "noble savage." Regardless, most Europeans saw the rational and industrious world of Christian civilization as superior to the licentious, pagan world of the Indians.

France and England struggled for empire through the middle of the eighteenth century, and their respective Indian policies differed greatly. After establishing a foothold in the Saint Lawrence River valley, the French created a network of trading posts to engage with natives in a mutually beneficial fur trade. Permanent French settlements usually took root in areas sparsely populated by Indians, preempting the recurring pattern of territorial struggles that was a common feature of Anglo-Indian relations. The small number of French colonists minimized the potential threat to Indians, and French exploration into the continent's interior took place with the consent and cooperation of natives. When the French crown tried to maintain strategic and commercial interests, it usually recognized native rights of self-determination. French colonists enjoyed favorable relations with the Indians, becoming their trading partners and military allies and practicing intermarriage and miscegenation. Even if many Frenchmen conceived of Indians as unpolished, primitive wild men and women, they also saw them as worthy companions. The combination of French adjustment to the native cultures and their cooperative economic and military ties with natives made Franco-Indian relations distinct from those between natives and Englishmen.

Permanent English colonization in North America spread from the Jamestown and Plymouth settlements. Compared to French fur trappers and priests, Chesapeake tobacco planters and New England Puritans expressed less interest in missionary work, cultural exchange, or intermarriage with natives. Most Englishmen wanted either to transform the American wilderness into land for cash crops or to recreate an Old World society adjusted to Calvinist ideals. The implicit requirement of land by colonists called for the English to push the Indians out of the way. These colonists emphasized agriculture and the extraction of raw materials to fuel England's colonial economy. They often viewed their Indian frontier as a barrier to expansion inland. When Englishmen permitted native peoples to live near them, it was only within the context of a Protestant "praying town" where Indians experienced anglicization. As a result of the differences between English and French attitudes, most native nations, except some such as the Iroquois Confederacy, allied with the French through the 1750s. French employment of Indian auxiliaries to harass Britain's colonies reinforced a durable and mutual hatred between anglophones and Native Americans.

After four major wars between 1689 and 1760, the Anglo-French confrontation concluded with a British victory in the Seven Years' War, the Peace of 1763, and the French surrender of Canada. The immediate consequences for native peoples were devastating. Not only did England cut off the Indian supply of firearms, but pitting one European power against another for trade was no longer a diplomatic option for the natives. Once the

Six Nations lost this ability after the war, everything about Iroquois life became more vulnerable to the whims of the English colonists and the policies of the British Empire. By recasting French territory as their own, the English inherited a francophone Canadian population as well as what they believed to be Indian subjects. However, because the native nations had viewed the French not as masters, but as partners, England was unable to reproduce in the former New France the system of imperial dominance of Indians that stretched from Massachusetts to Georgia. Beginning in the spring of 1763, the Ottawa war chief Pontiac assembled an alliance of tribes from the Ohio River valley and the Great Lakes to attack the old French forts now occupied by the British. The phony ball game, described in the prologue, that resulted in the surprise seizure of Fort Michilimackinac was but one of many such operations carried out during the rebellion against England. In October the British government demonstrated its wish to maintain temporary peace between the natives and the land-hungry English colonists by officially separating them by means of the Proclamation of 1763, drawing a boundary along the Appalachian frontier. Because many colonists ignored London's decision, the frontier problem remained.

With the balance of power between white men and Indians already disrupted, the American Revolution promised to make life worse for the natives. Because an independent America threatened to push farther west into native territories, most Indians found themselves ironically allied with the interests of the British crown. This should be no surprise; the real enemy of Indians was not the English king, but his subjects who lived to their east. The eventual Patriot victory over Britain signaled a diplomatic and military disaster for all native peoples, especially for the several Iroquois nations that gave their wartime support to Britain. In 1779 a Patriot invasion of Iroquois country resulted in the destruction of most of their towns and crops and their flight as refugees into Canada. After the war most Iroquois peoples lived either along the Saint Lawrence River near Montreal or beside the Grand River in Ontario. But even in the aftermath of defeat, the Iroquois nations preserved their traditional ball game. In both 1794 and 1797, for example, Seneca and Mohawk teams staged matches in southern Ontario to reaffirm political ties.[3]

Devastated by the American Revolution, Iroquois society experienced cultural decay and social anomie. Alcoholism and accusations of witchcraft became common. Military subjugation forced Indian men to learn women's traditional work: farming. Among the Seneca, the prophet Handsome Lake called for spiritual renewal to avert the disintegration of tribal life. Blending traditional native faith with Protestant disdain for intemperance, Lake began his ministry in 1799. Although Lake's efforts met with mixed results, the new economic, social, and political order of Iroquoia reached critical proportions in the years following the revolution. Meanwhile, the Iroquois ball game endured great pressures. The developments of the previous hundred or more years had challenged the very nature and purposes of the traditional game. With the military defeats of the late eighteenth century, the military preparation function of the game had become archaic. By the early nineteenth century, the military power of the Iroquois nations was a relic of the past. Moreover, for the geographically dispersed and reservation-bound nations of the Iroquois Confederacy, it became more difficult to maintain intertribal ties. No longer would ball games be used to settle territorial disputes among people confined on smaller and smaller tracts of land dictated by the governments of white men. Even though natives continued playing games out of respect for the past, the new realities that confronted them in the nineteenth century implicitly changed their game.

When most native peoples became either dependent upon the European colonial economy or culturally infected by the new order, the economic function of ball games began to alter significantly. Once Indians had engaged in trade with Europeans, they incorporated non-native items such as firearms, blankets, horses, and utensils into their system of gambling, substituting them for more traditional hand-crafted tools, clothing, and ornamental items. Since the new European items were technologically superior to traditional native tools, the consequences of Indian gambling became acute. Traditional Native American economic egalitarianism became obsolete. Moreover, as the European material culture undermined the economic purpose of ball play, Christian missionary work reinforced the secularization of the game. The salvation offered by the white man's Jesus Christ often came at the expense of the authority of conjurers and honoring the Indian concept of the Creator. The priests who fought against the old native religious beliefs also affected the economic dimensions of ball play. Their prohibitions on gambling among natives contributed to a decline in wealth redistribution.

The deadly events of the last quarter of the eighteenth century politically emasculated the Iroquois Confederacy and severely diminished the diplomatic and military functions of the ball game. Now defeated and divided, the Iroquois nations could not hope to achieve military victory. When they adopted farming, the ball game no longer served as a mechanism for reinforcement of their military might. When they became economically dependent on whites, militarily and politically weakened, and partially assimilated into European culture through Christianity and sedentary agriculture, ball play ceased to function as a means of maintaining traditional notions of tribal integrity, autonomy, and survival. Yet despite the emergence of a new order in North America, the Iroquois kept some traditions alive. Even though the economic, political, military, diplomatic, and religious parameters of the ball game had been modified, the activity was still a part of native culture. It changed right along with other aspects of native life. Such was also the case in spiritual matters. The faith articulated by Handsome Lake was a reaffirmation of old beliefs mixed with a Christian agenda to bring salvation to Iroquoia. Before Lake died in 1815 at the Onondaga Reservation near Syracuse, local men honored him with a ball game.[4]

Throughout the wars for eastern North America during the seventeenth and eighteenth centuries, the Mohawks had been the most pro-British of the Iroquois, mainly because of that nation's lucrative position as middleman between Albany fur purchasers and inland suppliers. However, with the Patriot victory over Britain during the War for American Independence, many Mohawk people fled New York to traditional hunting grounds at Akwesasne along the Saint Lawrence River under the leadership of the Jesuit mission at Saint Regis. Similar to the Caughnawaga Iroquois mission settlement near Montreal, which had been established by Jesuits in 1667, the community of Mohawks at Saint Regis blended Iroquois culture with Roman Catholicism. Later joined by people from the Abenaki, Onondaga, Oneida, Cayuga, and Huron nations, the Mohawks tried to recover from the devastation of the colonial and revolutionary eras. In this dependent environment, a more secular and recreational form of ball play developed, which Jesuit fathers still found an obstacle to Christian life. In 1808 one Saint Regis missionary complained to church authorities that ball games interfered with Sunday church attendance.[5] But they were allowed to continue. During the 1830s, visiting Englishmen from Montreal noticed the game. In hindsight it is clear that the resulting potential for cultural exchange was made possible because of the earlier French partnership with the Indians and the Roman Catholic tolerance for native culture, a relationship and attitude inherited by the English in Quebec after the Seven Years' War. Had the French treated native peoples as had the English in Massachusetts or Virginia, the Iroquois ball game would have been expunged.

Much of the early cultural development of the United States discouraged interest in any Native American ball game. Traditional games were played in the territories west of the new United States, but the unfriendly relations between Anglo-American society and Indian tribes thwarted any possible appropriation of native ball games by white America. The Five Civilized Tribes of the Southeast engaged in mass ball play, but hostile white attitudes punctuated by the Indian Removal of 1830–38 highlighted malevolent racial attitudes toward Native Americans as well as southern white efforts to appropriate fertile Indian lands. Besides, the impetus for organized team sport in mid-nineteenth-century America came not from western frontiersmen, but from the affluent ranks of the urban Northeast, who were physically distant from native peoples. In Canada Mohawk Indians lived near a big city. Moreover, white men in Canada and America did not look at Indians exactly the same way. While some Anglo-Canadians began to conceptualize Indians as their civilizational forebears, white Americans understood the natives within the context of a mythological western frontier, usually as savages hindering Manifest Destiny.

Even though Anglo-Americans viewed native culture with contempt and condescension, they were not oblivious to the ball games. When the painter George Catlin traveled through Indian country during the early 1830s, he captured a Choctaw match on his canvas, and he showed off his work in New York City in 1837. Three years after the American Civil War ended, native ball teams toured midwestern states such as Kentucky, Ohio, and Missouri. Many of these Indians came from tribes who had lived in the Southeast prior to the Indian Removal. Naturally, white citizens in those states had especially benefited from the seizure of native land. In May of 1868, an exhibition of the two-stick southeastern ball game at the Union Grounds in Covington, Kentucky, featuring Comanche, Choctaw, Osage, and Creek Indians generated amusement from white spectators. The conduct of the match led one correspondent to suggest that Indians preferred lice to cleanliness: "Whatever romance attaches to the Indian character exists only in the schoolboy's brain; for civilization has so effectually torn

away the veil which beclouded and obscured the vision that the noble savage is now seen just as he is—a rude, cruel, treacherous biped, as ignorant
of the commonest commodity, soap, as though *pediculi* were a blessing and
the former a curse."[6] Two squads of Choctaws played a game in June at the
Union Grounds in Cincinnati. Not surprisingly, spectators greeted the
native athletes with laughter.[7] In July, a former Confederate Army colonel
led teams of Choctaw and Chickasaw players who had fought for the South
during the Civil War to Saint Louis for a match.[8]

For the white American spectators who attended these matches, the Indian game legitimated popular views of Native Americans as primitive and
violent, but now only a remote threat to the survival of the young republic.
Even with the Civil War recently ended, they realized, sectionalism still
posed more of a danger than any Indian frontier. Besides, the racially
charged world of postwar politics made the southern "Negro question" a
national issue. If white Americans concerned themselves with any racial
"other," it was going to be not reservation-bound Indians, but rather the
millions of freed black slaves. Individuals might find amusement with native peoples, but white America's faith in Manifest Destiny dictated intolerance of Indian "savagery" in any form. Not surprisingly, the only local
Native American ball game with any significant level of interest and support among white patrons could be found in the former French colony of
Quebec. Middle-class Englishmen who lived in and around Montreal
forged relationships with the nearby Mohawks and learned to play the game
Frenchmen had been calling *lacrosse*. This French name for the Indian game
was actually a general term for any game played using a curved stick. Even
though the game they adopted had already experienced a fair amount of
cultural change due to Christianization, military defeats, and the entrance
of Indians into the industrial economy, lacrosse was still native.

George Beers, Canadian Nationalism, and the Modernization of Lacrosse

Although European missionaries and explorers had commented on Native
American ball games since the sixteenth century, the first recorded match
between Mohawk Indians and white men took place in Montreal on August
29, 1844.[9] Six decades had passed since the collapse of the Iroquois Confederacy. With the end of the War of 1812, any serious resistance to white
military power was out of the question. The United States and Britain had

been seizing Indian land for decades. With the earliest lacrosse matches between whites and Indians, this encroachment moved into the cultural arena. White involvement in lacrosse remained sporadic until the formation of the Montreal Lacrosse Club in 1856. The actual game as played by these anglophone Montreal gentlemen was the secularized game played at Saint Regis and Caughnawaga. However, these middle-class athletes encouraged the development of sticks with larger taut-stringed hoops that placed a greater accent on passing and teamwork. Despite this technological innovation, white players employed the "bunching" and "mass play" tactics they had learned from the Mohawks. Regardless of the style of stick used during play, they chased after the ball on the ground en massed.[10] Along with the Hochelaga and Beaver clubs, the Montreal Lacrosse Club (L.C.) provided social occasions for sportsmen to engage in physical exercise either among themselves or with their nearby Mohawk neighbors. During the 1860s and 1870s, these and other Canadians played lacrosse and attached Victorian sporting values to the game.

Native dominance of these early contests with white men occasionally led to frustration and violence on the part of the Montreal men. In July 1860 the *Montreal Gazette* commented on one such incident: "We are sorry to see one of the Montreal players strike one of the Indians with his crosse. Doubtless the gentleman lost his temper in a rough tumble, but nevertheless it was not the fault of the Indian."[11] With a lack of written regulations governing play, gentlemen negotiated rules prior to every contest among themselves or against Indian squads from the Mohawk reserves. Due to a visit by the Prince of Wales to Montreal in August, local patrons sponsored a "Grand Display of Indian Games" that featured a contest between thirty-man Iroquois and Algonkian teams and a second match pitting twenty-five Indians against twenty-five local gentlemen.[12]

After the royal visit, an ardent student of the native game called for the standardization and popularization of lacrosse. Shortly before the end of his four-year dental apprenticeship, in September 1860 a teenage William George Beers wrote a pamphlet of rules and instructions, noting that field lengths should not exceed one-half mile. The irregular Indian fields were usually much longer.[13] In his spare time, this "father of modern lacrosse" authored several articles on the game and other aspects of Canadian life.[14] He crowned his early proselytizing by publishing a book, *Lacrosse: The National Game of Canada,* in 1869.[15] Along with other enthusiasts, Beers zealously promoted the game by pointing to the virtues of its indigenous origins. "This game, being now purely Canadian, is likely to become the *National Game of Canada,*" Beers claimed in 1860. "Long, long after the romantic 'sons of the forest' have passed away, long, long after their sun sinks in the west to rise no more, Lacrosse will remind the pale-faces of Canada of the noble Indians that once lorded it over this continent."[16] According to Beers, lacrosse should be viewed as a symbolic torch passed from the noble savages of primitive Canada to modern progressive gentlemen of a nation-state.

Besides being an impassioned lacrosse advocate, Beers championed Canadian nationalism by helping to found the volunteer Victoria Rifles, with which he served during the Fenian Raids of 1866 and 1870.[17] In the months following the birth of the Dominion of Canada on July 1, 1867, Beers campaigned to have lacrosse proclaimed Canada's national game. He alleged that the new Parliament had made the title official, even though it did not convene until November. Many Canadians accepted as fact this fabrication, which remained part of Canada's national folklore until disproved in the 1960s.[18] Regardless of the fiction that became national myth, Beers's initial efforts to popularize lacrosse succeeded. Canadians quickly adopted lacrosse as the national game, partially because it functioned as a unifying symbol for the emerging Canadian nationality, right along with the beaver.[19] Only two days before the dominion's creation, Beers expressed much optimism about the future of the sport: "There is such unanimity of feeling with regard to the acceptance of Lacrosse as Our National field Game, that not only should players use the present season to secure its permanency but lovers of sports who believe in the mental and moral as well as the physical utility of these exercises should support us in our efforts to spread and nationalize this fine field game of Lacrosse."[20]

Much of the enthusiasm of nationalist and sportsman Beers came from his experience as a lacrosse goalkeeper. Having played in numerous contests against the Mohawks, Beers believed that by appropriating and then transforming the Mohawk ball game into a "rational" sport, distinct "primitive" qualities could be made to benefit the "civilized" white Canadian. By modernizing the native game, Beers furthered the cause of a Canadian national identity aimed at respectable gentlemen: "If our National game, while exercising the manly virtues, also trains [them in] the national and the moral [virtues], it will, undoubtedly, help to make us better men; and genuine 'pluck' will never go out of fashion in Canada."[21] Pointing to the role of sport in ancient Greece and contemporary England, he claimed that the beneficial exercise gained through lacrosse had "done more than anything else to invoke the sentiment of patriotism among the young men in Canada."[22] The Canadian nation with which he was preoccupied, however, was always defined in middle-class terms.

Beers lamented what he saw as the inevitable passing of Canada's "noble savage" into history. Although the Indian faced extinction because of his barbarism, the Montreal dentist thought, Canadian civilization could help itself by learning from him. White enthusiasts often measured their play according to Indian standards. In commending the performance of the Montreal L.C. against the Ottawa L.C., the Montreal press noted that the play of the former "could not be excelled by the most practiced Indians."[23] Beers also celebrated lacrosse as "an *invigorating* game"[24] that aided the muscular development of Victorian sportsmen. Since brute strength alone was not a sufficient gauge of manliness, Beers argued that the Indian's reliance on the body had accounted for his demise: "In every tribe [the ball game] developed an amount of splendid physical energy sufficient to have made their race masters of this continent for ever, had mind not been so subservient to body, nor destiny so inevitably pointed against them."[25] However, Beers conceded what he viewed as the physical superiority of Indian athletes. To compensate, he advocated the development of a "scientific" version of the game, complete with rationalized playing space, standardized rules, designated player roles, and the implementation of "civilized" strategy and tactics. For Beers, the superiority of Canadian civilization, masculinity, and science would be guaranteed, rather ironically, by turning to what gentlemen athletes believed to be the noble qualities of a "savage" ball game.

Club fields in Montreal were much smaller than those used in traditional Native American ball games, with the agreed-upon size dictated by the distance between the goals. Not only was the traditional native lacrosse field incompatible with modern urbanization, but the smaller fields better suited white "science" over Indian "wind." Beers admitted that a club of gentlemen could not defeat a native team in a contest played on the latter's terms: "The whites have only ever beaten the Indians because they played on smaller fields than the latter are accustomed to; and there is no doubt but that if the red skins had goals half a mile apart, the whites would seldom, if ever, get a chance to touch the ball."[26] Shorter fields facilitated the coming of modern lacrosse, in which "civilized" team play and finesse replaced "savage" mass play and brute force. Beers tried to make it easier for whites to win games by making the fields smaller to negate native running tactics. The way Beers refined the game ironically paralleled government policies toward Indians; governments in both Canada and America limited native autonomy by confining Indians onto reservations.

Beers believed his adopted game improved not only the white man's nutrition and appetite, circulation, and respiratory and digestive systems, but also his relations with other middle-class men. The game, he thought, especially benefited the mind and soul: "It develops judgment and calculation, promptness and decision; destroys conventionality, and creates a sort of freemasonry which draws men of the same tastes and sympathies together." Having achieved a balance between mind and body in his "civilized" version of the Iroquois game, Beers believed it affirmed the supremacy of the modern Canadian over the "savage" Indian: "The present game, improved and reduced to rule by the whites, employs the greatest combination of physical and mental activity white men can sustain in recreation and is as much superior to the original as civilization is to barbarism, base ball to its old English parent of rounders, or a pretty Canadian girl to any uncultivated squaw."[27] Lacrosse not only animated Canadian men, Beers believed, but it fortified women's role in Victorian society. But the way he viewed their relationship to the game changed over time. In 1860 he wrote that the playing of lacrosse by girls would benefit these "future mothers of a manly race,"[28] but by 1869 he relegated women to the margins. Fairly knowledgeable of Indian lacrosse folklore, Beers explained to readers the pregame Indian custom of women's running onto the field "to give beaded and other tokens of favoritism to their dusky gallants, which these savage lovers wore during the game as faithfully as the most chivalrous knight of the 12th century ever carried his lady's glove in combat." Encouraging the appropriation of the "noble" qualities of Indians, he wrote: "What an incentive to first twelves if Canada's fair daughters would revive the fashion! How it would put one on one's mettle to be a crack player!"[29]

Much of the philosophy behind Beers's attempts to modernize native lacrosse was reflected in his career as a professional dentist. From the end of his apprenticeship in 1860 until a diseased heart killed him in 1900, Beers labored to make dentistry a fully rationalized, scientific profession in

Canada.[30] In June 1868 he began publishing his privately financed *Canada Journal of Dental Science*, arguing that dialogue among educated peers improved dental care and increased practitioners' income. Beers later served as editor of the *Dominion Dental Journal*, secretary and president of the Provincial Dental Board of Examiners, and dean of the Dental College of the Province of Quebec.[31] The year after Beers published his book on lacrosse, he addressed the Quebec Dental Society. He outlined a philosophy intended to bring order to dentistry and praised protective legislation and the merits of "progress" in science. Echoing the ideas of other proponents of evolutionary thinking, Beers claimed that the natural development of all science and art led the ideal to triumph over the deficient: "As in the animal kingdom, genera and families disappear after having fulfilled their time, and become transmuted and further developed in others called more perfect, so through a series of progressive developments, an imperfect principle in science is the forerunner of one of perfection and truth, and scarcely leaves a vestige by which we can detect its origin."[32] These evolutionist views on dentistry and science were similar to those on his favorite pastime. His comments about life forms' eventually disappearing were certainly consistent with Beers's belief in the inevitable passing of the "noble savage" into oblivion.

Beers's conception of the "national game" was aided by the publication of a second, more precise, set of rules he had written by the *Montreal Gazette* in July 1867. He fixed the number of players at twelve, established the authority of umpires, and stated that the winning team would be the first to score three goals.[33] Besides standardizing the Indian game, this revision of the rules he had previously promulgated served as the first step in the formalization of lacrosse by outlining a regulatory body: "Any amendment, revision or alteration proposed to be made in any part of these laws shall be made only to a Committee of the MONTREAL LACROSSE CLUB, specially appointed and a delegate from every other club in Canada."[34] The anglicization of the Mohawk ball game continued with the formation of the National Lacrosse Association (NLA), the first national governing body for sport in Canada, at a convention held in Kingston, Ontario, in September 1867. Maintaining its leading role in organized lacrosse, the Montreal L.C. had provided the impetus for the creation of the NLA: "It now devolves upon the educated and civilized white man to systematize and subject to laws this hereditary but hitherto traditional sport of the sons of the forest," the Montreal Gazette reported. "To this end a general convention composed of delegates or representatives from the numerous clubs now existing as well as from the native originators of the game is both requisite and necessary."[35] Although the NLA adopted Beers's rules and standardized the minimum length of fields at 150 yards, Beers clearly acknowledged a role, however limited, for Native Americans in the organization as athletes. Native delegates were welcome, but marginal.

Within only a decade, George Beers—nationalist, dentist, and gentleman athlete—had created a cultural mythology and a tough game for thousands of young Canadians. Beers's "national game" provided these middle-class men with the means to create an Anglo-Saxon civilization distinct from that of mother England, their unruly American cousins to the south, and the Native Americans perceived to be Canada's civilizational forbears. The advent of lacrosse coincided with the emergence of other Victorian team sports that were serving as vehicles for British imperialism. Throughout the second half of the nineteenth century, England exported cricket throughout the empire to foster goodwill among the ruling classes. In a gesture reflecting both an indigenous nationalism and loyalty to the crown, Canada added lacrosse to this imperial dialogue by sending three lacrosse tours to the British Isles between 1867 and 1883.[36]

For the second tour, in 1876, the Montreal L.C.'s Committee of Management conceived and implemented a not-for-profit plan to send a squad of white Canadian "gentlemen amateurs" and a squad of Caughnawaga Indians to Britain, supported by private funds and gate receipts. Showcasing the supposedly exotic and primitive qualities of the Indians, the tour's promoters created a distinct image of Canada for English spectators. The Caughnawaga dressed in red and white stripes, complete with blue caps, beadwork, feathers, and jewelry; in sharp contrast, the Montreal club wore white, gray, and dark brown. By making natives a tour focal point, the promoters hoped to cement cultural ties between England and Canada. Watching white and Indian athletes battle one another in lacrosse allowed English spectators to see a symbolic representation of Britain's New World conquests. Prior to a private game for Queen Victoria at Windsor Castle, Caughnawaga chief and team captain Keraronwe exchanged a public pledge of Native Americans' loyalty to the British crown for autographed pictures of the monarch.[37] The Caughnawaga also performed caricatured exhibitions of elements of native ceremonies, including "war dances" and "pow-wows." Despite this obvious self-lampooning by the Indians, one London newspaper cried fraud: "At home they are staunch Conservatives, devout Roman Catholics, sit on Windsor chairs, and are more addicted to smoking bird's eye tobacco than to brandishing tomahawks."[38] The correspondent's comments highlight the difficulty of accurately assessing the Indians on the tour. After all, these Mohawks had willingly participated in the pageantry of the matches and helped to construct the tour promoters' desired image of the "noble savage." The natives' public pledges to Victoria reveal the motivations of the Iroquois team. After the Mohawks defeated the gentlemen, 3–1, before seven thousand paying spectators at Glasgow, a reporter from the *Montreal Gazette* interviewed the chief. When he asked the team leader if victory accounted for his excitement, the Indian replied, "No, ... Canadians more goods than my boys. They [Mohawks] young, weak, no breath. What make me happy, much people—much money I see our good father, Dr. Beers, have."[39] The organizers had hoped that the tour would not only encourage the playing of lacrosse in the British Isles, but present a positive image of North America to foster emigration to Canada. The tour became an advertising vehicle in this intense era of Canadian competition with the United States, Australia, and Africa for British immigrants. According to a Montreal newspaper, promoters hoped to dispel misconceptions about Canada held by English emigrants.[40]

Building on the interest generated in 1876, the Canadian Department of Agriculture sponsored another trip in 1883. Playing a rigorous schedule of sixty-two contests in forty-one Scottish, English, and Irish cities in two months, participants in this tour included another Caughnawaga Indian team and a squad of gentlemen from the Montreal and Toronto Lacrosse Clubs. Like the 1876 tour, this more extensive promotional campaign had no commercial objectives. Gate receipts financed two-thirds of the trip, with the balance paid for by team members and public subscriptions. However, when the trip became an inadvertent commercial success for its sponsors, the tour promoters refunded one-third of members' money. The tour's participants—Native Americans decked out in scarlet, Anglos in blue with white maple leaf crests—operated as active immigration salesmen. Besides staging contests, players distributed about 150,000 government-certified immigration flyers and 36,000 pounds of special *Canadian Illustrated News* supplements.[41] Clearly, the tours attempted to promote immigration to North America by catering to the English enchantment with native peoples. Once again, the Indians reminded British citizens of their imperial history.

The tours of 1876 and 1883 contributed to a permanent lacrosse beach-head overseas; affluent English sportsmen established northern and southern associations in 1879 and 1880, respectively. Meanwhile, the scheme to promote immigration achieved only moderate success. It is nearly impossible to gauge the impact of these exhibitions on immigration decisions among contest spectators. After all, British citizens were bombarded with many forms of immigration propaganda during the 1880s, including post office advertisements, press reports, and incentives offered by many railroad and steamship companies throughout the Americas. A lacrosse contest perhaps reaffirmed an individual's choice of staying home, heading for Canada, or opting for somewhere else. Unfortunately for Canadian immigration propagandists, the years immediately after 1883 witnessed a significant decline in the number of Britons moving to Canada, as well as a decline relative to other destinations.[42] Nevertheless, the introduction of lacrosse to the British Isles and even the game's colonization in Australia in 1874 confirmed Canada's rather peripheral cultural position within the British Empire. The limited growth of the game throughout the empire underscored the confines of Canadian cultural imperialism as well as the relationship between dominion and empire in the late nineteenth century. Regardless of the success or failure of Canada's "national game" abroad, however, this "modernized" element of Iroquois culture helped define the postconfederation Canadian national identity.

Although George Beers left his personal mark on the early history of modern lacrosse, larger cultural developments accounted for the widespread popularity of Canada's "national game" in Ontario and Quebec. The creation of modern lacrosse expressed an imperialistic New World English nationalism rooted in a popular middle-class faith in science and the idea of "progress." For instance, scientific knowledge gained from inventory sciences such as geology and botany contributed significantly to a spirit of possession of the environment that strengthened the impulse toward Canadian nation building. Many middle-class Canadians believed that the conquest and cultivation of nature was necessary for the development of a Canadian national identity. Although many Canadians emphasized the need to subjugate the environment, others outlined what they perceived to be a close relationship between the invigorating qualities of the cold North and the racial character of Canadian nationalism. Victorian Canadian men achieved the conquest of their harsh climate in part by turning to their Native American neighbors. According to contemporary theories of social evolution popular among the middle class, the Indians existed in a state of barbarism that was far below the state of Anglo-Saxon civilization. One such evolutionist, railroad attorney Lewis Henry Morgan, conducted an anthropological survey of Iroquois Indians. In 1877 his research led him to elaborate on the prevalent model of human social development by which societies were seen to progress from savagery to barbarism to civilization.[43] When juxtaposed against white Canadian civilization, reservation-bound Indians helped to define where "primitive" Canada had been, and where "civilized" Canada would go.

Morgan's anthropology had much in common with the nation-building goals of George Beers.[44] Often referred to as the "father of anthropology," Morgan not only urged the study of Native American cultures to validate a monogenist, progressive view of humanity, but he also advocated intermarriage as a way to acculturate Indians and invigorate whites. Less than three hundred miles from Morgan's home in Rochester, New York, the "father of lacrosse" went further, actually appropriating and manipulating Iroquois culture for the benefit of white Canadian civilization. Although some Canadians believed in the inevitability of the passing into extinction of the "noble savage," Beers wanted to learn from the Indian ball game before the death of native culture. Through a modernized, scientific form of native culture, along with a constant influx of new Anglo-Saxon blood from the British Isles, Canada would adjust to the cold northern climate and conquer the "wilderness." By breathing fresh Canadian air and playing a modernized version of an old Mohawk game, young Canadian men would achieve national and patriotic manliness through the development of strength, self-reliance, and moral purity.

The modernization of a rough-and-tumble gaming activity taken from a people Canadians perceived as part of nature and at a lower stage of social development than themselves reflected a self-conception of Canada as an evolutionary and counter-revolutionary society developing within the British Empire.[45] This elite North American form of English nationalism stood in contrast to what many Canadians discerned as a more rowdy, revolutionary American folkway to the south. Canada's myth of the North may have mourned the passing of the Indian into history, but the American myth of the frontier applauded Indian extinction as necessary for the conversion of the savage frontier to civilization. Americans were hardly alone in demonizing, expelling, confining, assimilating, and killing native peoples, but Canadians illustrated their lamentation of the fall of the sons of the forest by adopting and modernizing a Mohawk ball game. Unfortunately for advocates of modern lacrosse such as George Beers, their new "national game" would not survive intact for very long. In the decades following the confederation of Canada, the growing specters of commercialism, professionalism, and American cultural imperialism altered the road Beers had paved for his "national game" for gentlemen.

From Gentleman's Game to Commercial Sport: The Transformation of Canada's "National Game"

George Beers's conception of lacrosse as an amateur, patriotic, and manly activity remained an ideal that was not always practiced with the spread of the game from Montreal to other cities, from Quebec to Ontario and other provinces, and from the middle class to the working class during the late 1860s. As a governing body, the NLA encouraged and regulated this process. From only a small handful of clubs in Canada in the spring of 1867, the game spread rapidly; there were thirty-five clubs with 1,380 players by late September and eighty clubs with some 2,000 members by mid-November.[46] As each club grew in size, so did the range of skill within the club. Eventually clubs fielded teams at a variety of levels, ranging from adults to schoolboys. In October of 1867 the Montreal press commented on the broad appeal of the game: "Every Saturday afternoon particularly, the Parks and Commons are crowded with Lacrosse players, from the Professor who doffs the gown for the occasion, to the little urchin who can barely scrape together 50¢ to purchase a crosse."[47] Organized lacrosse also took hold in Winnipeg, Manitoba, with the formation of the Prince Rupert Lacrosse Club in 1871. The growth of interest in lacrosse could best be seen in the city of its origin, Montreal. In 1861 there had been nine clubs. The number of clubs had risen rapidly during the next quarter century, to fifteen in 1871, thirty-one in 1877, twenty-five in 1881, and forty-five in 1887.[48]

Despite its aura as the "national game" of Canada, lacrosse remained confined to the southern portions of Ontario and Quebec throughout the 1870s and 1880s. Proponents championed the game's alleged health and social benefits. But the growth in the numbers of clubs and registered athletes gave rise to a desire for interclub competition, because the most skilled athletes wanted to test their abilities. It became necessary for clubs to have administrative secretaries to negotiate with other clubs and make travel arrangements. Seeing the potential for prestige derived from victory, a club's more affluent members provided some of the capital to pay for club expenses. Unfortunately for the clubs, however, costly railway trips for away-from-home games made it difficult for all players to defray their own expenses. Consequently, the need for gate revenue quickly became an issue. By the middle of the 1870s, clubs openly negotiated as to what portion of gate revenues visiting teams would receive. Most opposition to these arrangements by idealistic club members receded into the background when they realized that intercity contests could not be staged without the gate money. Not surprisingly, clubs began to place a greater emphasis on pleasing paying crowds. As crowds of thousands flocked to playing fields, the attention paid to gate revenue intensified further. Clubs catered to spectator interests by having regimental bands perform during match intervals, establishing reserved seating for holders of more expensive tickets, selling refreshments, and even wiring telegraph lines to provide fans back home with out-of-town results.[49]

The emerging competitive ethos was best reflected by many clubs' decisions to take championship games more seriously. As early as October 13, 1866, the newly organized lacrosse community awarded its first Championship of Canada when the Caughnawaga Indians defeated the Montreal L.C.[50] In November of 1867, Montreal merchant T. James Claxton donated a set of four championship goal flags and flagpoles, valued at over $250, to the Montreal L.C., and Beers took this to signify "the appreciation of the mercantile community" for the efforts of the club to promote the sport.[51] With the support of local businessmen, lacrosse appeared to have become a "respectable" activity for the whole city. Ironically, sponsorship by businessmen underscored the game's place within the capitalist marketplace. Claxton's gesture cemented ties among the middle-class Protestant citizens of Montreal, but also contributed to increased competitiveness among clubs. The combination of Claxton's gift and the growth in the number of clubs made interclub matches more common, and secretaries scheduled "challenge matches" with other clubs. In 1871 Toronto politicians representing the national Parliament and the Ontario legislature provided a gold medal for competition. Besides crossed lacrosse sticks and a ball, the medal bore images that reflected both Canadian nationalism and British imperialism: Canadian maple leaves, a beaver, and the English crown.[52] Subsequently, businessmen, politicians, and newspapers offered a slew of medals and trophies for competition in Ontario and Quebec. These awards inspired a club's players and fans to place their own personal interests in victory ahead of idealistic notions of nationalism and manliness.

By endorsing the irregular challenge system, the NLA crowned national champions until the implementation of a league system in 1885. Six clubs monopolized the championships, including the dominating Montreal Shamrock L.C., which won thirty-nine of seventy-five title matches from 1866 to 1884.[53] Since the club represented the interests of Montreal's Irish Roman Catholic population, it did not totally accept the elite Anglo values of George Beers. Most of the players were from the working class (mechanics and clerks, but not manual laborers), and the club relied upon affluent local Irish citizens for support, including the mayor, James McShane.[54] The Shamrocks' steadfast commitment to on-field success conflicted with the amateur ethos of George Beers, in that players often played for pay and pushed Beers's rules of play to the limit. Shamrock fans inverted respectable forms of public behavior by being generally boisterous and verbally offensive to achieve temporary victory over the Anglos who were their socioeconomic superiors. The Irish repudiated Anglo "character" in favor of victory over their Protestant rivals. For example, in a hotly contested match between the Montreal and Shamrock clubs for possession of the Claxton flags in June 1870, Irish fans assaulted a Montreal player and intimidated the rest of the Anglos into not resuming the match.[55] This general Shamrock attitude toward winning, eventually adopted by most other clubs, represented the beginning of a significant paradigm shift away from an ethos of Victorian amateurism and toward a more competitive cultural model embracing professionalism and commercialism.[56]

The trend toward greater competitiveness embodied in the dominance of the Shamrocks resulted in developments not planned by the founding fathers of modern lacrosse: gambling, interclub disputes, covert player recruitment, and athletes' not living up to the spirit of the rules. Though officially banned by the NLA in 1870, gambling became fairly common at lacrosse grounds, and some taverns even established betting pools. With the belief that championships brought higher gate revenue, many clubs filed protests with the NLA over disputed championship claims and resorted to acquiring the best talent by offering jobs or cash. Moreover, with the outcomes of matches taking on larger roles in attracting future spectators or even determining championships, players increasingly resorted to foul play.[57] As early as September of 1868, the NLA outlined several prohibitions on violence: no lacrosse player was permitted to clutch either an opponent's stick or his body with his own stick, and no player was permitted to push, hit, trip, or shoulder an opponent.[58] The specificity of the prohibitions demonstrates the types of infractions being committed in a sport once touted as promoting respectability. Only a few months before, a Caughnawaga chief had told Beers that white athletes could not control their roughness as well as Indians could: "You smash heads, cut hands, make blood. We play all day; *no hurt, except when drunk.*"[59]

The commercialization of the "national game" profoundly influenced organizers' attitudes toward Indians and distinctions between amateur and professional athletes. Prior to the formation of the NLA in 1867, the main professed differences between white and Indian players were social class and skill level. Gentlemen acknowledged the superior play of Indians, but this did not preclude competition between middle-class amateurs and professionals from the Caughnawaga and Saint Regis reserves.[60] White athletes certainly grumbled about what they assumed to be the inherent physical advantage of Indians, but criticized the Indian playing style. By "bunching" around the ball instead of adopting positional play, whites argued, Indians held back scientific progress. Because middle-class Anglos originally regarded Indians as professional ball players because of their lower socioeconomic status as manual laborers, pay for play was not an issue. After all, even gentlemanly clubs accepted money to defray the costs of out-of-town trips. Because gentlemen regarded Indians as the best players, in September of 1868 organizers decreed that no white club could feature an Indian unless the opposition agreed.[61] Despite this race-based discrimination, the NLA permitted professional Indian clubs to hold association memberships and compete in championship play.[62] During these early years of organized lacrosse, clubs dominated administratively by gentlemen athletes rarely felt threatened by native victories. Loss of an athletic contest to Indians did not signify a loss of social status. What bothered gentlemen was the hiring by other white clubs of Indian "ringers." Apparently clubs did not trust one another about hiring native talent, but allowing all-Indian teams to compete was not a problem. Eventually, however, the new competitive ethos led organizers to move away from viewing the game as a respectable recreational activity that tolerated Indian participation and toward seeing it as a more diverse, multiclass sport that was hostile to Indians. The NLA soon adopted rigid distinctions between amateur and professional, praising the former and attacking the latter. In May of 1876 the NLA revised its constitution to read: "No club in the Association shall play for a money challenge except with Indians. Any club playing for money (except as aforesaid) shall be suspended from membership in the Association."[63]

Despite this official ban on playing for pay, commercial concerns made professionalism a permanent feature of organized lacrosse, whether club officials cared to admit it or not. A championship controversy between the Toronto and Shamrock clubs during the summer of 1877 demonstrated this reality. The interclub dispute resulted from Toronto's unwillingness to take the field against a recently released convict playing for the Shamrocks. When the association voted 35–13 to give the Shamrocks the title, middle-class purists perceived it as a victory for crass professionalism.[64] According to one member of the Tecumseh L.C., "The vote, which has caused so much interest, has taken the championship from a gentleman twelve and given it to a professional twelve."[65] The growing on-field success of clubs that were covertly paying players inspired national organizers to condemn open professionalism. In June 1880, the NLA changed its name to the National Amateur Lacrosse Association (NALA) and banned the most visible professionals (i.e., Indian teams) from membership in the association and from competing for championships.[66] Apparently middle-class amateur sportsmen had grown tired of the movement away from the principles outlined by men like George Beers during the 1860s. Club administrators blamed gambling, on-field fistfights, fan rowdyism, and petty interclub disputes on the presence of men who were not true gentlemen. Instead of attacking the more authentic causes—unenforced rules, biased referees, powerless officials, and an inefficient bureaucracy—promoters made scapegoats of professionalism in general and of native clubs in particular.[67] Apparently some middle-class sportsmen believed the commercialization of lacrosse could take place without endorsing professionalism.

The middle-class Protestant men of the Montreal L.C. chose to remain outside the NALA for a while to protest the professionalism of the Shamrock L.C. By refusing to play the Shamrocks, the Montreal gentlemen essentially condemned the commercial excesses of lacrosse. However, when they agreed to play the Irishmen in exhibition contests and split the gate receipts, the press shouted hypocrisy.[68] In June of 1881 the *Toronto Mail* wondered why all of a sudden the Montreal L.C. did not mind mixing with "the Shamrock element" on the field: "If this is correct and the statement [was] made on the authority of some of their principal officers, it seems strange that they should be willing to play and divide the gate money with a club they don't think good enough to meet in the Association. If they are good enough to go halves with in money affairs, they surely can't be very much worse when their delegates are met in the Association. Consistency? Thou art a jewel!"[69] Widespread disagreement over commercialism and professionalism dominated the "national game." Although everyone publicly praised amateurism and accepted commercial practices, the organized lacrosse community reached no consensus on pay for play. Evidently, the Anglos of the Montreal L.C. had no problem with charging entrance fees for contests, but they were apprehensive about the working-class professionalism of the Irishmen from Montreal's Griffintown.

The geographic and social expansion of lacrosse led the "national game" in unintended directions as the cultural meaning of the game became a contested issue. Conflicts over professionalism, Indian athletes, on-field violence, and playing rules pointed to a growing fissure. George Beers may have spelled out a very specific vision for the game, but the many constituents of lacrosse had different, competing interests. At the top of the lacrosse world were the organizers. In most clubs, these executives and officials came from the local community's affluent leadership class. They included bankers, attorneys, and businessmen. Most educators and clergy supported their efforts to promote a game that invigorated the community with middle-class notions of character, manliness, and respectability. For example, in 1871 when reform-minded organizers introduced the "national game" to the Ontario cities of Ingersoll and Woodstock as an antidote to a variety of social problems facing youth, they believed urbanization and an increasingly sedentary education system had brought about moral and physical degeneracy. They thought their Shamrock (Ingersoll) and Beaver (Woodstock) clubs would stimulate town pride and deter destructive impulses among the young.[70] As supporters of urban boosterism, the organizers believed getting residents to support the home team would minimize class and ethnic differences and teach people to accept the authority of the mercantile class. By calling for community solidarity and pride in the home

town, they celebrated the community's growth. However, many of the local businessmen who supported clubs had other priorities. Because they offered awards and recruited talented athletes by offering them jobs or paid
them under the table, these businessmen ironically undermined the efforts
of social reformers and nationalists. After all, because of them players pursued an idol instead of an ideal. The competition between these two brands
of boosterism—urban versus capitalist—was not always obvious.

Meanwhile, many of the men actually taking the field were disinterested in lofty ideals and instead just wanted to win. Making money on the
side made the game even more attractive. In terms of social class, the players were usually dissimilar both from the men who organized the sport and
from the general workforce. In Ingersoll and Woodstock, for instance, the
breakdown of the male workforce during the 1870s and 1880s was roughly
one-fourth nonmanual workers, one-half manual skilled workers, and one-
fourth manual unskilled workers. The executives were drawn overwhelm-
ingly from the affluent class of nonmanual workers. The lacrosse players,
on the other hand, came from the nonmanual and manual skilled classes of
workers in equal proportions.[71] Essentially, they were less affluent than the
club organizers, but more so than the general labor pool. Players could
make money by accepting payments from gamblers to fix or throw games.
The pursuit of money by these speculators placed them at the opposite end
of the spectrum from the middle-class organizers. However, since they conceptualized the game in economic terms, they had something in common
with the businessmen who lent their financial support to the game.

Finally, a growing number of spectators utilized lacrosse to express beliefs inconsistent with organizer/reformers' ideal of sport for sport's sake.
They preferred victorious competition over character development. They
transformed the hometown pride celebrated by the organizers into a rowdy
brand of hometown chauvinism. The many essentially co-opted and redefined the culture of the few. Reformers especially hated gamblers. "Unless betting and the influence of betting men is stamped out," the *Woodstock
Sentinel* asserted, "amateur lacrosse is dead—in fact it don't deserve to
live."[72] But there were many ways to subvert the ideals of the game. For instance, in 1885 some Woodstock residents evaded the payment of gate fees
by watching games from the elevated cemetery overlooking the local
lacrosse field. Sitting on tombstones drinking alcohol, they could watch
games without having to conform to the middle-class organizers' wishes.[73]

Moreover, the thousands of paying spectators who provided clubs with the fiscal sources to fund a team's expenses lent support to the capitalist view of sport. Consequently, lacrosse became more popular, but home-team chauvinism undermined reformers' efforts to inculcate manliness, character, and nationalism.

The problems noted at Ingersoll and Woodstock often occurred wherever reformers introduced their game. Although the resulting dilemmas gave organizers headaches, they remained nominally in control. Following the lead of George Beers's Montreal L.C., most of the earliest clubs originated in Montreal and Toronto, and clubs from these cities dominated organized lacrosse both on and off the field through the 1870s. However, with the geographic and social expansion of the game these big-city gentleman's clubs became a minority by the mid-1880s. Clubs based in Montreal and Toronto comprised only fourteen of the NALA's fifty-four clubs by 1884, compared to the thirty-two clubs from small cities and towns in Ontario. Despite this shift from big cities to less populated areas, both the Montreal L.C. and the Toronto L.C. maintained administrative control and moral authority in organized lacrosse.[74] Even though the game spread to other towns and social classes, the gentlemanly amateur vision prevailed, if only as a stated principle. The Montreal L.C.'s powerful influence among organizers allowed it to serve as a champion of amateurism in the face of rising competitiveness, on-the-field violence, commercialism, and accusations of professionalism during the 1870s and 1880s.[75] Many clubs discreetly hired professional athletes to improve their chances at victory, but publicly applauded the acknowledged primary purpose of the game: instilling character. The Montreal L.C. sustained a prominent, influential position primarily because of its vocal support of amateurism. Its members came from the city's anglophone Protestant middle class and allegedly played the game to inculcate manliness, character, and patriotism. The club's image as a bastion of all that was proper and gentlemanly about lacrosse—and hence what everyone else praised publicly—allowed it to wield moral power in administrative matters against clubs covertly paying athletes. Other clubs simply acquiesced in the face of the Montreal L.C.'s defense of gentlemanly purity while quietly accepting professionalism as a necessary means to their own prosperity.[76] This dualism on the part of many rank-and-file clubs— public exaltation of amateurism, but private exercise of professionalism— resulted in a dilemma for officials. The essential problem was the need to

find a way to prevent clubs from using money from gate fees (an openly accepted practice) to pay working-class professional athletes who served as
trained ringers to win games (a disreputable but common custom).

To bring order to the world of lacrosse, beginning in April of 1885 the
NALA replaced the informal challenge system with a series or league system that crowned as champion the club with the best overall record among
an elite echelon of association teams. Unfortunately, however, the guide-
lines for the new system proved confusing and subject to interpretive differences. For example, the association called for the Shamrock, Montreal,
Toronto, and Ontario Lacrosse Clubs to play each other three times apiece;
the team with most victories would be declared the winner of the 1885 campaign. After disqualifying the Ontario and Toronto clubs for missing scheduled contests, the association declared Montreal the victor in a rather contentious season. Controversy continued into the next season, when the
association once again declared Montreal champion in 1886 after a dispute
with Toronto over regulations governing title play. The Toronto men carried their bureaucratic fight into the following year, losing a 46–14 vote
among association delegates. As a result, the Toronto L.C. led an exodus of
Ontario-based clubs from the NALA in April of 1887. Once independent,
the Toronto men created a rival Canadian Lacrosse Association (CLA) for
clubs in western Ontario, thus making the NALA an organization of Quebec and eastern Ontario clubs.[77] This first step in organizational fragmentation highlighted the inability or even the unwillingness of many administrators to face problems in their sport with one voice. Propagandists still
conceived of lacrosse as the "national game," but the trend toward organizational fragmentation demonstrated a lack of consensus. The real problem revolved around the tendency to attach price tags to everything—gate
admissions, travel accommodations, lacrosse sticks and balls, trophies and
medals, and playing facilities—to everything, that is, except the relationship between clubs and athletes. Club officials did not want to admit publicly that some athletes either needed money to compensate for lost wages
or should be paid for their talent.

After the collapse of the NALA championship series system in 1888, the
association's top four teams—those of the Montreal, Shamrock, Cornwall,
and Ottawa Lacrosse Clubs—reunited with the Toronto L.C. to form a new
organization in April of 1889. The membership of this new Senior League
fluctuated periodically as clubs tried to further their own gate-taking com-

mercial interests.[78] For better or worse, the game George Beers had designed during the 1860s had changed significantly within only two decades.

"They Are Only Killing the Game": The Decline and Fall of Canada's "National Game"

From the 1890s through the era of the Great War, a fierce competitive ethos dominated Canada's "national game." Contrary to the wishes of men like George Beers, most lacrosse players and spectators preferred victory over character. Clubs fought for championships and, when necessary, jumped to a rival circuit if conditions suited them better there. Three leagues dominated the highest levels of play during the late nineteenth century and the early twentieth century: the National Amateur Lacrosse Association, with clubs mainly in Quebec and southeastern Ontario; the Canadian Lacrosse Association, with clubs in the western and central areas of southern Ontario; and the British Columbia Amateur Lacrosse Association (BCALA) on the West Coast. Some clubs, such as the Toronto L.C., jumped back and forth between the two eastern leagues. In Montreal, clubs represented distinct ethnic and religious communities: the Amateur Athletic Association (the old Montreal L.C.) drew support from Anglo Protestants, the Shamrocks from the Irish, and the Nationals from the French. Other prominent eastern clubs included the Ottawa Capitals and the Cornwall Colts. Compared to the league membership of the NALA, that of the Ontario-based CLA fluctuated from year to year, including clubs scattered across the province's many towns and cities, such as Brantford, Paris, Saint Catharines, Orillia, Niagara Falls, Brampton, and Orangeville. On occasion a club from Buffalo, New York, competed in the CLA. In British Columbia three cities contested for league honors: Vancouver, New Westminster, and Victoria.

Unfortunately for organizers, the pursuit of championships led to increasing levels of on-field violence. A brief comparison of rule books across Canada during the late nineteenth century illustrates how organizers tried to keep the game clean. Every time a governing body adopted a new rule prohibiting player misbehavior, it was trying to curb excessively rough play. In 1879, for instance, players were not allowed to wear spiked shoes; touch the ball with their hands; throw their sticks; grab an opponent or his stick; hit, punch, or threaten anyone; interfere with an opponent pursuing a ball; or charge into an opponent with both hands on the stick. Over the next two decades, however, the prohibitions multiplied. By the 1889 season, players could not kick the ball, move when the referee called a time-out, stand in the goal tender's crease, hit the goal tender, hit an opponent from behind, push him into a fence, or kneel down in front of an opponent pursuing a ball. Apparently behavior in the 1890s was even more unsportsmanlike. According to a rule book published in 1899, new rules included restrictions on delaying a game by throwing the ball out of bounds, knocking the stick out of an opponent's hands, influencing or threatening the on-field official, and using foul language.[79] The growing seriousness with which clubs approached the game made George Beers's values seem archaic. By the first decade of the twentieth century, newspapers were filled with stories of fistfights between players, brawls involving crowds, assaults against referees, and arrests by policemen. For example, during a June 1911 contest between the Vancouver L.C. and the New Westminster Salmonbellies, a crowd of ten thousand fans watched each team accumulate seventy-seven minutes in penalties. Not only did a Salmonbelly break an opponent's stick across his knee, but police had to break up a fight. Angry fans questioned penalties called by the referee. According to the *Vancouver Daily Province,* "Some of his rulings did not suit the crowd who could not understand why Lalonde was benched for twenty minutes for receiving a wallop from Galbraith, nor why Fitzgerald got ten minutes for hitting Gifford after Tommy had assaulted him and Tommy only got five."[80]

Meanwhile, clubs continued to negotiate a path between the two sets of values tugging at them from earlier decades: amateurism, urban boosterism, patriotism, and manly sport versus professionalism, hometown chauvinism, commercialism, and sport as spectacle. The lure of the latter set of values grew even stronger as the nineteenth century drew to a close and a new century began. Organizers promoted clubs as extensions of their communities. Many cities had nicknames identifying their unique character. Cornwall was the "Factory Town," while Brantford was known as the "Telephone City." Residents called Saint Catharines the "Garden City." In the West, New Westminster's nickname was the "Royal City." Not only did officials stage matches in conjunction with community picnics, but lacrosse seasons now included games on Victoria, Dominion, and Labour Days. Underneath the obvious façade of a civic-minded appreciation for the "national game" lay commercial concerns. Club officials became ever more sensitive to spectator interests to ensure a steady stream of revenue to cover operating expenses. Rising costs of traveling, equipment, advertising, league membership, and facility leasing and maintenance guaranteed that staging contests would not be cheap. Clubs tried to appeal to spectator interests by standardizing the length of contests, creating goal nets to end scoring disputes, and enhancing the theatricality of the game. Many fans grew restless with having a victory awarded to the first team to score three goals. After all, a match could be over in minutes or go on for hours until called by darkness. Although organizers had employed time limits for exhibitions from the 1870s to the early 1880s, most governing bodies approved them for regular play by the 1890s. To end controversies over disputed goals, British Columbia enthusiasts established a dominion precedent by introducing goal nets in 1897. By the first decade of the next century, organizations divided playing time into two forty-five-minute halves or four twenty-minute quarters with brief intermissions. No longer did teams take a break after each goal scored. Catering to fans, clubs continued to hire marching bands to play between periods, but now they also made players don jersey numerals for personal identification.[81]

During the late nineteenth century, organizers found it increasingly difficult to retain amateurism as a guiding value system the more they embraced commercialism and a multiclass clientele. Even when politicians and other prominent citizens donated expensive trophies to reward amateur championship play, they unwittingly contributed to the emphasis on intense competition. In 1901, for instance, the governor general of Canada, the Earl of Minto, donated a cup for the national championship of Canada's senior leagues. Meanwhile, the Toronto Globe Publishing Company introduced a Globe Shield trophy for the CLA senior championship. And then in 1910, railroad builder Sir Donald Mann donated another cup for championship play. Although a winning ball club could be a great drawing card, many administrators realized that sufficient gate receipts could be ensured by securing the services of the most skilled players, who were usually "imported" from other cities. Consequently, they circumvented the amateur principle by tendering cash or jobs to players to win matches and attract crowds. As clubs transgressed the letter and spirit of lacrosse constitutions by hiring professionals, the athletes further muddied the pristine waters of amateur play by selling their services to the highest bidder on a season-by-season basis. These "ringers-turned-tourists" exacerbated the dilemma over professionalism by contributing to the escalation of player pay, which strained a very delicate fiscal balance among club expenses, gate receipts,

and on-field performance. The lure of Iroquois athletic talent only complicated matters. Even though most officials agreed Indians should not be allowed to play organized lacrosse, clubs circumvented these prohibitions.
They turned to nearby reservations and hired light-skinned native "ringers"
who spoke fluent English and passed for Anglo.[82]

The inability to choose a coherent set of values proved to be the critical problem facing club officials. And the problem was worsened by the lack
of an umbrella organization governing the entire sport. Unfortunately for
purists, spectator cries for championships drowned out applause for amateurism. Earlier solutions, including the NLA's formal prohibition of pay
for play in 1876, along with its name change to the National Amateur
Lacrosse Association and the expulsion of native clubs, both in 1880, proved
futile. The Toronto L.C.'s secession from the NALA in 1887 and the ensuing
formation of the CLA only complicated matters. If clubs openly ratified
professionalism, which they publicly criticized but privately practiced, the
link between pay-for-play and commercialism could be acknowledged.
Ironically, the men who voiced the loudest opposition to professionalism
were the same men who enjoyed the fruits of a white-collar, middle-class
lifestyle. Club administrators may have juggled between their belief in sport
for sport's sake and the commercial necessities of the emerging capitalist
marketplace, but the growing mass of spectators pressured clubs to abandon their aristocratic pretensions in favor of winning at any cost.

Unable to settle the debate over amateurism versus professionalism,
lacrosse organizers turned to outside assistance. Beginning in 1890, the
NALA affiliated with the Amateur Athletic Association of Canada (AAAC),
which evolved into the Canadian Amateur Athletic Union (CAAU) by
1898.[83] As an outside and impartial arbiter, the AAAC pointed to the heart
of the problem: the unwillingness of clubs to engage in hypocrisy by ac-
cusing rivals of professionalism. The AAAC executive outlined its view of
the state of lacrosse in 1892: "The people living in glass houses exhibited an
extraordinary amount of discretion in throwing stones at their neigh-
bours."[84] A club might be angry over another club's success in acquiring a
gifted athlete, but it knew it did the same. Moreover, identified pay-for-play
infractions usually resulted in the punishment of athletes rather than clubs.
Because players could be replaced, the real culprits remained in power. The
crisis reached its zenith during the first decade of the twentieth century. In
contrast to the experience of American baseball, which had openly adopted

professionalism by the 1870s, the Canadian controversy resembled crises in England over professionalism in soccer and rugby. After decades of pairing commercial practices with amateur ideals, some lacrosse organizers called for a more complete economic modernization of their game by openly accepting professionalism. In April of 1903 both the CLA and the National Amateur Lacrosse Union (NALU) debated the issue of allowing amateur and professional players to compete together, but in September the CAAU defended amateurism and struck down the NALU request for mixed or "open" play. Clubs defied this legislative roadblock and continued to pay players, which eventually resulted in a confrontation.[85] The CAAU's declaration in June 1904 that many CLA teams were professional soon led to open disobedience. At its annual convention in April 1905, the CLA unilaterally decreed: "Amateur athletes shall not lose their amateur status by competing with or against professionals in lacrosse matches, for which no prizes are given, or in championship competitions permitted by any lacrosse association."[86]

The CLA's sanction of open play backed the CAAU into an administrative corner. The national governing body realized that rigid adherence to amateurism could result in its own alienation from a lacrosse world increasingly receptive to outright professionalism. In 1906 the NALU dissociated itself from the CAAU when the national governing body tried to nullify "open" play for its league. When the NALU embraced professionalism, it also dropped "Amateur" from its name, becoming simply the NLU. In the West, when the Souris L.C. played the NLU's Montreal Shamrocks for the Minto Cup in July 1906, the CAAU suspended the club and declared its players professional. Although Souris lost its official status as an amateur club, the national governing body of Canadian amateur lacrosse succeeded in distancing itself from yet another organization in the lacrosse world.[87] Apparently, with many club officials championships and gate receipts took precedence over any stamp of approval from a national organization stuck on glorifying the middle-class virtues of amateurism.

An all-out administrative "athletic war" began in February 1907 when the Montreal Amateur Athletic Association helped to create the Amateur Athletic Federation of Canada. The new AAFC challenged the CAAU's right to claim jurisdiction over not only lacrosse, but all Canadian sport. By functioning as an alternative to the CAAU, this new governing body gave leverage to lacrosse clubs and associations embracing "open" play. Although

Quebec and Ontario served as battlegrounds in the war between the proponents of amateurism and those of professionalism, the pivotal confrontation in the crisis over professionalism occurred in British Columbia.
Big-city clubs from Toronto and Montreal dominated organized lacrosse
through the 1890s, but the rise of the game on the West Coast added a new
dimension to the battle between amateurism and professionalism. The New
Westminster Salmonbellies' undefeated record against top eastern clubs in
a tour of Ontario and Quebec in 1900 symbolized the national coming of
age of lacrosse in British Columbia. Throughout the first decade of the century, western clubs tested the CAAU's authority by practicing professionalism. In September 1907, for instance, the Vancouver L.C. threatened to
ignore the CAAU if it did not consent to its match against the NLU's professional Tecumseh L.C. of Toronto. Annoyed by such forthrightness, the
CAAU denied Vancouver's request, but the club defiantly engaged in the
contest in October anyway. Similarly, when New Westminster defeated the
NLU's Montreal Shamrocks for the Minto Cup in July 1908, the CAAU declared that any cup defense against professional clubs would result in sus-
pension. As a result, the BCALA seceded from the British Columbia Amateur Athletic Union, the CAAU's regional affiliate, and adopted "open" play
in March 1909.[88] With this move, the CAAU lost further ground.

The CAAU-AAFC war over professionalism finally ended in September 1909. The two organizations merged in November, forming the Amateur Athletic Union of Canada (AAUC). It endorsed amateurism by pre-
cluding pay for play, accepting payment above traveling and hotel expenses,
and pursuing athletics as a livelihood. The union also unofficially condoned
professionalism by providing opportunities for amateur reinstatement.
Moreover, to promote amateur play, the AAUC established a new organization, the Canadian Amateur Lacrosse Association (CALA), in November
1912. The original ideals of George Beers had once again been reaffirmed,
but national sport administrators effectively proclaimed tolerance for regulated professional lacrosse. Many spectators, athletes, and administrators
favored commercialism and professionalism, but prominent organizers
chose to retain amateurism as a guiding principle. Club officials basically
institutionalized their hypocritical views toward amateurism and professionalism. Even with the end of the war among governing bodies, the "national game" remained organizationally fragmented. The CALA governed
amateur lacrosse on a national level, but the sport lacked a central govern-

ing body with a single guiding philosophy. After all, the CLA had functioned professionally from 1904 to 1910, and the NLU and BCLA had begun operating on a professional basis in 1906 and 1909, respectively. When Toronto and Montreal clubs seceded from the NLU over traveling expense disagreements, they had formed yet another organization, the Dominion Lacrosse Association (DLA), in November 1911.[89] Now even the professional leagues pursued different paths. This development set the stage for an interleague business war, which was not unlike the ones that faced professional baseball in the United States during the late nineteenth century and the early twentieth century.

Once the BCLA joined the ranks of professional lacrosse, club organizer Con Jones initiated a player salary bidding war by luring the best eastern players, such as Eduoard "Newsy" Lalonde, from the NLU to join his Vancouver L.C. By boosting player salaries, Jones also encouraged the trend of players' jumping from one club to another in a rival league. Jones actually embodied many of the dominant themes of Canadian lacrosse. Hometown pride and the quest for victories motivated him, but his hefty contract obligations showed the role of capitalism within organized lacrosse. He paid players whatever it took to lure them west, but did not have an easy time collecting enough revenue to meet expenses. His Vancouver team attracted crowds of eight thousand to twelve thousand, but many spectators received free passes. After all, Jones wanted a packed house. To promote the sport, he even gave away over a thousand free lacrosse sticks to young boys at one match in 1911.[90] Men like Jones enticed players to abandon one club for another, but in 1912 the president of the NLU put all of the blame on players' shoulders. "They are only killing the game," he said. "They are taking the shortest and quickest route. This war will only result in everyone becoming dissatisfied. All these players should realize that the high salaries cannot be kept up for any considerable length of time. The clubs cannot afford it."[91] Apparently he tried to make readers believe that players somehow forced clubs to pay high wages. The bidding war elevated salaries, but gate receipts failed to keep pace. The DLA and BCLA agreed to a cease-fire in April 1913, approving a national commission akin to the system employed by professional baseball in the United States, with each club retaining exclusive contract rights to twenty players. Unfortunately for club officials, the 1913 season resulted in a financial bust. Snubbed by the new DLA-BCLA cartel, the NLU abandoned professionalism and returned to amateur competition in April 1914.[92] These developments mattered little, because the interruption caused by the First World War brought a temporary end to bitter disputes over lacrosse. Play continued during the war, though on a smaller scale.

Canadian lacrosse never regained the relative level of popularity it had enjoyed during the late nineteenth century. When lacrosse players returned home from service in Europe, the old "national game" survived on the sporting landscape of Canada as a regionally bound amateur sport, confined chiefly to southwestern British Columbia and southern Ontario. Contemporary explanations of the demise of lacrosse often pointed to professionalism and the increasing amount of on-the-field violence by players.[93] In 1929 H. H. Roxborough recalled Canadian newspaper headlines from the decade prior to the Great War: "weekly row in National Lacrosse Union," "mounted police assist in quelling lacrosse riot in Toronto," or "players carried off unconscious and others run up in stand and assault spectators."[94] But the increase in violence had been only the symptom, not the cause, of the decline of Canada's "national game." Club and league officials had almost never faced issues such as professionalism with either conviction or a united front. Too many clubs had hypocritically championed amateurism as a public ideal while paying players covertly. Although they charged admission to the games, they did not dare admit to paying athletes.

Moreover, the organizational fragmentation of professional lacrosse had certainly guaranteed the long-term financial demise of the game, as competing leagues had caused player salaries to spiral out of control. The lack of a powerful national governing body that was willing to establish uniform policy had encouraged backroom squabbling between clubs over game officials, which had periodically caused games to be canceled and forced the refunding of ticket money. These frequent occurrences had soured fans. Furthermore, since interest in lacrosse had been strongest in small urban areas, organized lacrosse lacked the mass fan base to sustain a professional operation. In communities such as New Westminster and Cornwall, crowds had simply not been able to provide the consistent revenue clubs needed to survive as commercial enterprises, especially if clubs from British Columbia and Ontario were going to play one another and raid each other's rosters by offering lots of cash. By comparison, major league baseball clubs in the United Stated operated in far larger cities. Trips from Boston to Saint Louis were shorter than those between Vancouver to Montreal. And all pro baseball teams employed a "reserve clause" to respect each club owner's rights over labor. The rising level of violence by lacrosse players throughout the late nineteenth century and the early twentieth century had merely served to alienate the one group of enthusiasts clubs needed most as patrons: the "respectable" middle class. Because the affluent middle class believed fistfights and violent play did not belong in a sport promoting character, they had began spending weekends going for car rides or camping. In addition, the geographically isolated pockets of enthusiastic support spanning the vast two-thousand-mile Canadian landscape had also made the patriotic and nationalistic rhetoric associated with lacrosse seem hollow.[95]

The increasing interest in America's "national pastime" in Canada also hindered interest in the mythical "national game." Baseball gradually dethroned lacrosse as the primary spring-summer sport in Canada and solidified a cultural link with the United States. By the 1920s, baseball and softball dominated the sporting world in Canada. In May 1914, magazine writer Fred Jacob had made an appeal to Canadian sports fans to give lacrosse a fair trial. He thought it puzzling that his countrymen would adopt a fully professional American sport, yet reject the professional version of Canada's "national game." Baseball captured the hearts of North American sports fans, Jacob argued, because it embodied the mechanical "efficiency" of modern life,[96] but also because its daily playing schedule gave it "a natural advertising value" that weekly lacrosse could never achieve. Most important, baseball's honesty as a commercial venture employing professional athletes contrasted with the hypocrisy of lacrosse: "The game that has both professionals and amateurs, with a very hard and fast line between them, is much more likely to be in a healthy condition than the sport that tolerates pseudo-professionalism."[97] American baseball included separate amateur and professional spheres, along with a gray area for collegians who played professionally in the summer, but Canadian lacrosse did not.

During the 1920s, lacrosse remained limited primarily to small pockets of support in southern Ontario and southwestern British Columbia, but advocates such as Roxborough remained optimistic about a possible revival. "Lacrosse will become an instrument of international goodwill wherever our national game is played," wrote Roxborough. "Lacrosse deserves to come back, and every Canadian sportsman wishes it good luck." Thankfully, this partisan argued, Canada's "national game" survived and even thrived in contemporary England, Australia, and, most important, the United States: "If Canada has rejected its offspring, the sportsmen of the United States have generously afforded it board and lodging and a chance to grow."[98] Unwilling to abandon his favorite sport, Fred Jacob also lamented over dissenting retired lacrosse players who compared the dilapidated contemporary state of the sport with a romanticized view of the game they had played as youth, "when the men who played it were giants with the prowess of giants."[99] Regardless of the nostalgic attitudes of former or current players, Canada's "national game" was a minor sport by the 1920s, as professional and amateur baseball overshadowed lacrosse on both sides of the Canadian-American border. This development highlighted the slow but steady growth of the cultural influence of the United States on its northern neighbor.

From Canada to America: Transferring the Gentleman's Game to the United States

The image of George Beers's "national game" suffered greatly during the five decades after the birth of modern lacrosse, but many of his Victorian values did not expire with the advent of a commercialized professional game in Canada. As lacrosse took hold in Ontario and Quebec during the late 1860s and early 1870s, some Canadians emigrated to the United States. Their movement to cities such as New York and Boston increased rapidly during the late nineteenth century as the Canadian-born population of the United States grew from a quarter million in 1860 to over 700,000 by 1880.[100] Although Canadians of different social classes and ethnic groups moved across the border, the rise of the dynamic American industrial economy especially attracted middle-class and skilled working-class Canadians who shared some of the values of George Beers.[101] Motivated by economic interests, they were assimilated into American society. As part of this migration, pockets of Anglo-Canadians brought their "national game" to the United States. Although in Canada lacrosse developed into a contested cultural battleground pitting supporters of amateurism and professionalism against one another throughout the country, the same protracted dilemma did not occur in the United States. Despite temporary problems associated with professionalism, the amateur game reigned supreme.

Throughout the 1870s and 1880s, Canadian immigrants established clubs in the greater New York City area, in Boston and Baltimore, and in other cities in the Northeast, the Midwest, and California. As early as 1867, newcomers organized clubs in Manhattan and Brooklyn, but they disbanded them within two years.[102] In contrast to the situation in Canada, where lacrosse enjoyed a multiclass clientele, in the United States lacrosse attracted few followers from outside the affluent classes. The strong identification of lacrosse as an amateur sport probably ensured that support for the game would be confined to the elite. Moreover, although the rhetoric of lacrosse as Canada's "national game" may have appealed to Canadians of different social classes, this identification did not interest most working-class Americans. Furthermore, since everyone bought their lacrosse sticks directly from Indian reservations or through a limited number of retailers, the acquisition of a hand-crafted stick proved far more difficult for Americans than did the purchase of a mass-produced baseball glove.

Mohawk Indians from Caughnawaga and Saint Regis also played a role in generating interest in lacrosse among Americans. These Mohawks created a mobile entertainment industry based on the exhibition of "Indian shows," lacrosse contests, and traditional dancing as well as the sale of baskets, beadwork, and carvings.[103] Saint Regis Indians demonstrated lacrosse in Brooklyn as early as 1863, but the game did not catch on.[104] When two teams of Canadian Indians visited Williamsburg, Long Island, in September 1869, one correspondent noted: "[This] lacrosse raid is more novel than dangerous, we are informed, and if a battle should take place between the belligerents it will be fought with lacrosses and not with tomahawks." The exhibition inspired local gentlemen to form the Knickerbocker L.C. of New York in October. To establish ties with the Canadian lacrosse community, the Knickerbockers traveled north and lost to the hosting Toronto L.C. in August 1870. Later that fall, former Canadian residents of the greater New York City area joined on Thanksgiving Day at Paterson, New Jersey, for dinner and contests among the Prescott (Brooklyn), Knickerbocker, Manhattan, and Paterson clubs. In 1871 the Montreal Shamrocks and the Caughnawaga Indians toured New York, Brooklyn, Saratoga, and Troy.[105]

Not only did Canadian immigrants and Iroquois travelers promote the game around eastern New York state, but the emerging summer haven for the social elite, Newport, Rhode Island, provided another setting for some of the earliest American lacrosse contests. Inhabited by Boston intellectuals, aristocratic New England Yankee "nobs," and nouveau riche "swells" from New York, this resort area played host to an influential sporting subculture. Besides mingling with prostitutes and Broadway chorus girls, these sportsmen occupied their time with polo, yachting, lawn tennis, foxhunting, horse racing, and lacrosse.[106] Like their counterparts in New York City, they had developed an interest in lacrosse in response to visiting Iroquois teams. In August 1876, for instance, several thousand "fashionable" people, including the foreign ministers of Italy, Austria, and Spain, witnessed the Montreal L.C. defeat the Caughnawaga Indians in two exhibitions.[107] Although summer lacrosse eventually faded at Newport, the resort's sportsmen learned to associate gentlemanly sport for sport's sake with the "savage" nobility of lacrosse. In the future, this combination dominated the thinking of early enthusiasts.

Canada's "national game" became a permanent fixture in metropolitan New York by the late 1870s. The large membership of the Canadian immigrant Ravenswood Club allowed for the formation of a second team, the New York L.C.[108] Contests among these two teams and the Prospect Park (Brooklyn) and New York University clubs became more common by the spring of 1878. Meanwhile, Newport provided a home for "championship" matches. For example, Ravenswood defeated both the Union Athletic Club (A.C.) of Boston and the New York L.C. to win a championship cup presented by New York Herald publisher and Westchester Polo Club President James Gordon Bennett in August 1878.[109] Considering Bennett's views on the Indian frontier, his role in fostering lacrosse was ironic. Not only did this former associate of George Custer perpetuate the image of the "vanishing American"—that is, the vanishing Indian—in his pro–Democratic Party newspaper, but he defended the seizure of the Black Hills and advocated the extermination of native peoples. During the mid-1870s, Bennett made frequent connections among the country's various "dangerous classes," including blacks in the South, radical workers in the North, and Indians in the West.[110]

As lacrosse slowly expanded in New York with the aid of visits by teams from Ontario and Quebec, Canadian immigrants founded clubs in other cities wherever they settled. In May 1884, for instance, Harper's Weekly reported that clubs formed "wherever the Canadian element is present."[111] In his survey of the growth of lacrosse in the United States by 1886, New

York University player J. A. Hodge, Jr., observed that although there had been only "six or seven clubs" in the United States in 1878, there were more than 150 by 1885, including more than 12 in New York City and between 25 and 30 in Boston. By 1885, clubs highlighted middle-class Canadian settlement in San Francisco, Saint Paul, Milwaukee, Saint Louis, Chicago, Detroit, Cleveland, and even LaCrosse, Wisconsin.[112] Canadians and their new American friends dominated these local organizations, but the elite aura pervading clubs annoyed some municipal officials. When the city of Boston denied the Independent L.C.'s request to play on Boston Common, one alderman declared: "Some of these organizations are made up of people who do not care to associate with some people who [would] like to be members and take part in the exercises of the organizations."[113]

The New York-based *Spirit of the Times,* a national gentleman's weekly paper devoted to horse racing, theater, and sports, published reports of lacrosse practices, exhibitions, games, tournaments, club formations, meetings, and announcements. It serves as a useful indicator of the presence of the game throughout the United States. Based on the periodical's references to lacrosse, the Canadian sport took on prominence in the late 1870s, but declined rapidly by the early 1890s. In 1882 the *Spirit* began publishing match results in a separate column. Lacrosse activity seems to have been most common in the greater New York City area, including Brooklyn, Long Island, Staten Island, and eastern New Jersey; Boston and surrounding towns; and other sites in New England, Pennsylvania, Maryland, California, and the Midwest. Later dubbed the "father of American lacrosse," Irish-Canadian immigrant John R. Flannery tried to coordinate this emerging national lacrosse community. After playing for the Montreal Shamrocks, he moved to Boston in January 1875. When a young Caughnawaga chief visited him in 1878 and convinced him to start a club, Flannery and fellow Montreal expatriate Samuel McDonald formed a team for the Union A.C. When Flannery discovered Canadians in New York City playing the game, he invited them to Boston for a match. This "amateur championship" resulted in a July 4 victory for the home club against the Ravenswood Club on the parade grounds of Boston Common, thereby establishing Boston gentlemen as the first victors in intercity lacrosse in the United States.[114] After Flannery moved to New York in early 1879, he remained active as a player and became secretary of the new United States National Amateur Lacrosse Association.[115]

Immigrant Canadian businessman Erastus Wiman also performed an early and conspicuous role as a lacrosse promoter in the United States. Born in Churchville, Ontario, in 1834, he had reported for Toronto and Montreal newspapers before becoming a partner in the New York City branch of the R. G. Dun and Company mercantile reporting agency in 1867. Wiman also organized and presided over the Great North-Western Telegraph Company of Canada beginning in 1881. His development of a railroad and ferry rapid transportation system, an amusement park, and an industrial energy supply company in New York earned him the title "Duke of Staten Island." Wiman chastised Britain for its imperialism; proclaimed loyalty to Anglo-Saxon institutions and the ideas of liberty, justice, and equality; and praised the ideal of a commercial union between Canada and America.[116] He promoted the culture of his homeland by forming the Canadian Club of New York and served as its first president.[117] Wiman's inaugural-dinner speech on July 1, 1885, offers insight into the city's Canadian population, the club's membership, and his own views on Canadian-American relations. Club ranks included prominent leaders from New York's journalism, insurance, legal, and banking communities. Wiman stressed the club's role as a cultural oasis for the approximately six thousand Canadians living in New York, many of whom worked as clerks and mechanics. Inexpensive initiation fees and annual dues ensured that downtown club life would "provide for those who, in the proverbial boarding house, find scant comfort in narrow rooms, isolated and alone; or who wander aimlessly through the streets of this great city, tempted at every turn to some departure from the rigid paths of rectitude." Wiman also wanted to provide "good books, newspapers, innocent games, and good companionship, free from vice or temptation." Moreover, Wiman emphasized the shared American and Canadian desire to solve "the noble problem of self government,"[118] the importance of hospitable Canadian-American relations, and the club's function in maintaining ties between New York Canadians and their home country.

The clubhouse included a library complete with Canadian newspapers, portraits of Queen Victoria and prominent Canadians, a British flag, a salmon trophy, and symbols of Canada's seasons: snowshoes and toboggans for the winter, lacrosse sticks for the summer. Unfortunately for Wiman, overextended investment on Staten Island, the Panic of 1893, and the two years it took to be cleared of forgery charges combined to topple him from his commercial empire and his role as an advocate of Canadian culture in

New York. When the Canadian government continued with the protectionist National Policy, Wiman abandoned the cause of commercial union and became a U.S. citizen in July 1897.[119] His decision to accept U.S. citizenship symbolized the acculturation of many Canadians living in America. In retrospect, the implication of this trend for lacrosse seems clear. If Canada's "national game" was going to survive in the United States, it could not remain an immigrant's game with patriotic overtones. Pioneers such as Flannery and Wiman would have to give way to men who would emphasize the class-based values of amateurism and celebration of the "noble savage."

Canadian immigrants played a major role in establishing lacrosse clubs in the United States, but touring Iroquois teams continued to aid the spread of the game south. After trips to New York in 1867 and 1869 and to Newport in 1876, Iroquois teams visited Oswego, Buffalo, Boston, several sites around New York City, and other cities in the Northeast. Not surprisingly, the number of Indian visits to these cities increased just after Canadian lacrosse organizations began banning native participation. Besides Mohawk teams from Saint Regis and Caughnawaga, teams representing the Tuscarora and Onondaga reservations took to the road as well. Besides the national press, local newspapers reported on Indian matches involving white clubs. In July 1875 the *Syracuse Journal* claimed that a Canadian "tutor" had given the local Onondaga natives "instruction in this favorite game among the aborigines." This reference provides few clues about the diffusion of the modern Canadian version of lacrosse from Montreal and its nearby Mohawk Indians to Iroquois reservations in New York and Ontario. The anonymous colonizer had perhaps come from the Caughnawaga reserve and taught the Onondaga the new version of the traditional game. Other evidence suggests that natives played exhibition matches serving commercial, social, and cultural purposes. During the 1870s the Onondaga, Oneida, and Seneca nations staged all-native contests, with admission and rail or horse fare ranging from 10 to 35 cents at the Lakeside Park in the Town of Geddes.[120] In March 1878 Syracuse newspapers published Captain Tallchief's announcements that his club was willing to play any team in the country.[121] Expecting a large crowd at Newell Park in May, a local paper advertised that an Onondaga-Oneida match would include other festivities: "There will be a green corn and war dance, with the Indians in paint and feathers, and with all the paraphernalia that belongs to such exhibitions. They will perform the dances strictly according to ancient custom."[122]

Such events illustrate a native attempt to capitalize on white interest in the "primitive," as well as an effort to show off Iroquois culture to their white neighbors. Furthermore, reservation lacrosse near Syracuse served as a medium for community diplomacy. In late August 1875, white residents from the Town of South Onondaga joined on the farm of L. P. Field to watch a game between Onondaga and Oneida Indians. After the contest, native women treated the spectators to dinner and a chief bestowed upon Mr. Field an Onondaga name that translated as "Helper." According to a local resident, "The chief then took him by the arm and promenaded for a time, going through their accustomed manner of initiating others into the tribe, and others shaking hands to show their approval. Mr. Field replied to them, saying he hoped a friendly feeling would always exist between them hereafter, as had always been before."[123] For the Onondaga and nearby white residents, lacrosse might alleviate conflict.

Iroquois lacrosse teams made several trips to New York and Boston between 1878 and 1891. The Indians benefited financially from the tour in exchange for providing a "primitive" image they believed white people wanted to see. Their own curiosity to see the world beyond the reservation probably combined with a desire to maintain authority over lacrosse. For white athletes and spectators, these contests provided the affluent with the opportunity to witness a flesh-and-blood version of the noble savage before the disappearance of the "vanishing American." New York's mayor welcomed a team of Caughnawaga Indians accompanied by George Beers in early March 1878. Preceding a carriage bearing a brass band, the Indian squad arrived at City Hall in a four-horse wagon with advertisements hanging from its sides. Not only did the Caughnawaga team include several players of mixed race, but many wore their hair as did white men. Despite this evidence of acculturation and miscegenation, the *New York World* noted that the Indians played up to the primitive expectations of white audiences: "All had their faces streaked with blue or red paint or spotted with black patches." When the Caughnawaga entered City Hall, a sarcastic employee "gave a loud Tammany war whoop, which caused the Iroquois to start and look nervously around." After the mayor condescendingly said "he was pleased to see before him men who were so simple, innocent and strong" and that "the Indians in Canada were much better off now that they had been adopted by the whites of Canada," the Caughnawaga began a tour of the city to promote their upcoming matches.[124]

These Mohawks joined Onondaga Indians and three white lacrosse clubs in a tournament at Gilmore's Garden, which later became the original Madison Square Garden, before a crowd of about eight hundred people. Aside from the display of all-native lacrosse, the Indians entertained the audience with a seventy-yard snowshoe race. After the Ravenswood Club defeated both the Elmira (New York) club and the club from New York University to conclude the tournament, the two Indian squads remained in New York for a few days for more lacrosse, snowshoe races, and dancing. According to the *Spirit of the Times,* white audiences apparently judged their visitors in terms of their ability to amuse: "The Syracuse Indians are third-class lacrosse players," it reported, "but the most grotesque and entertaining song-and-dance men ever seen in New York City." Fascinated with the Native American game, the New York Athletic Club invited and played host to the Caughnawaga. In front of two hundred spectators, five Indians defeated fifteen gentlemen. With the Mohawks serving as coaches and instructors, club members then played a match among themselves. Eventually three Indians joined each side, and the day concluded with a one-mile race between two natives.[125] This unusual example of Indians' tutoring white men inspired the formation of local clubs.

Other Iroquois matches during the late 1870s and the 1880s further illustrate the motives of Iroquois lacrosse teams and their gentleman hosts. For example, press coverage of a Caughnawaga tour of New York City in July 1884 highlights the dominant themes of Iroquois travelers. Dubbed "Royal" by the New York press after their visit to England one year earlier, the Caughnawaga attracted much interest from local sportsmen and ladies. One correspondent noted the white reaction to a change in tactics by the visitors in a Caughnawaga victory over the New York L.C. at the Polo Grounds. With the Indians trailing, the *New York Times* reported, "they brought out all their clever tricks of dodging, passing, bumping, and knocking, which were applauded."[126] During the tour's second contest, the frustrated athletes of the Independent L.C. resorted to violence, but the Mohawks hesitated to retaliate. According to the press, "The bare brown legs of the Indians mangled in confusion with the white trousers of the Independents, and several of the latter became excited and whacked their opponents over the head. The Indians took the blows with smiles and perfect good nature." Violence directed at the Caughnawaga hardly went unnoticed. After a gentleman hit a Mohawk in the head, a burly Irish-

American policeman interrupted the game, raised his billy club, and yelled: "If yez don't stop this . . . begorra I'll stop the game."[127] As during previous visits, the Caughnawaga also "loaned" players to local gentlemen during the tour to make play more competitive, but also for instruction.[128] On July 29 the Caughnawaga "Northern men" concluded their visit to New York City by defeating the "city men" of the New York L.C. at the Staten Island Cricket Club grounds before "a large number of spectators, including at least 300 ladies, whose bright-colored costumes were plentiful on the grand stand and terraces."[129]

Not to be outdone by their Quebec counterparts, the Saint Regis Indians journeyed to New York for a series hosted by Erasmus Wiman in September 1885. At the Camp Washington Ground on Staten Island, Saint Regis mastered the New York L.C., despite playing with one to two fewer men throughout the match. The generally affluent crowds who witnessed the Indians win four of their next five matches often had to contend with the lack of field boundaries. In their final match in New York, the Saint Regis squad quickly scored four goals in thirty-seven minutes against the host Williamsburgh A.C. so they could keep their rail schedule. "As soon as the game was over," the New York Times reported, "the black and red suits of the Indians were just discernible as their wearers flew down to the elevated railroad intent on getting their train."[130] Indian awareness of time restrictions highlights their accommodation to limitations placed on their periodic visits to gentlemen's clubs. In Boston, for example, in November 1878 the Caughnawaga had unsuccessfully tried to end their match with the Union A.C. early so they could catch the return train to Montreal. However, after missing their train, the Indians remained in Boston for the weekend and played a Monday afternoon contest before returning to Canada.[131] Iroquois teams surely treated matches as calculated exhibitions, but the tours also demonstrated their personal devotion to the game.

The visiting Iroquois provided white fans in New York with the opportunity to observe "primitives," but these natives also served as objects of violence. Although white enthusiasts north and south of the Canadian-American border advocated a "scientific" and "civilized" form of play, they often did not live up to this view. In a feature story on the recent history of lacrosse, one commentator wrote: "When the whites began the game and faced the Indians their more civilized souls revolted against cold-blooded attempts to maim and hurt." However, this writer apparently accepted an

Irish resort to violence. After being defeated once by the Caughnawaga in a fierce contest, the Montreal Shamrocks challenged the Indians to a rematch, while selecting "12 of the choicest rough-and-tumble fighters in the club." The ensuing battle was physically lopsided: "the Irishman met the Indian on his own ground and gave him all the rough play he wanted." The Shamrocks were ruthless: "They opened the heads of Fenimore Cooper's gentle friends and jumped on their backs and body-checked them against trees and blackened their eyes and made their noses bleed, and did so thoroughly maul and pommel them that they furnished a horrible example to all Indians in the future."[132]

The curiosity of white crowds and the enthusiasm of affluent athletes to learn lacrosse from their Indian guests reveal some of the prevailing attitudes among many northeastern sportsmen toward native peoples. This view dictated that the extinction of the primitive and unrefined Indians was inevitable. The quest to subjugate the Far West and integrate it into the American republic had to proceed, especially after Custer's Last Stand in 1876.[133] Though far from the western frontier, Iroquois Indian lacrosse offered eastern whites a brief opportunity to witness the last vestiges of "primitive" life. That young white gentlemen willingly adopted the modern version of an old Indian game demonstrated a belief that there was some practical value in native culture. Surely the perceived "nobility" of lacrosse could reinforce the class status of affluent athletes. Some gentlemen openly acknowledged the place modern lacrosse took alongside other character-building sports such as football, cricket, and baseball. In 1886 J. A. Hodge provided an inaccurate depiction of the origins of his adopted game. "It is the offspring of the American savage," Hodge wrote. "It was born and bred upon the plains of the South and West, cherished and nurtured by a race of barbarous but most truly professional sportsmen, men who not only sported to live,—which is our definition of 'professionals,'—but who lived to sport."[134] Despite the negative association of professionalism with the lower classes, Hodge's views reflected a sense of adventure other gentlemen may have idealized.

Any conclusions on nineteenth-century native views toward modern lacrosse must be full of conjecture. Although white officials served as mediators and tour organizers, Natives administered their own clubs. Regardless of whether elite amateur clubs or Indian reservations initiated negotiations to have a native squad make a public appearance, the Iroquois played for pay. If white gentlemen and their ladies agreed to pay the expenses of traveling Mohawk teams to demonstrate their "noble" skills, then these Iroquois were willing accomplices by capitalizing on white misconceptions of their people. The Iroquois' desire to travel hundreds of miles to play signals their own attempt to thwart the complete white takeover of their ancestors' game. The Indians realized that if they were to participate in lacrosse and retain any personal authority over their sport, they would have to do so in a manner that affluent white athletes and audiences would accept.

Traveling Indian lacrosse teams occupied a fairly unique position as an entertainment commodity in the commercial marketplace of the late nineteenth century, but they were not alone. White entrepreneurs competed for entertainment dollars with these lacrosse-playing Indians. As early as 1869, Sidney Barnett's Grand Buffalo Hunt, a show based in Niagara Falls, New York, featured not only gun-toting Wild Bill Hickock, but lacrosse matches between Cayuga and Tuscarora Indians.[135] Although independent Mohawk entertainment excursions continued into the early twentieth century, commercial enterprises such as Buffalo Bill Cody's Wild West show (1882–1913) dominated the market for white Americans interested in Indians. Instead of authentic dances and lacrosse matches, Cody's program included horse and foot races, shooting exhibitions, and bison riding and roping. Playing up to eastern interest in the "wild" frontier, white and Indian actors depicted hand-to-hand combat and attacks on settlements and stagecoaches. Wild West productions sometimes concluded with a white victory to reaffirm the triumph of civilization over barbarism. Otherwise, shows ended with a mythical recreation of Custer's Last Stand. White audiences were expected to reflect on the sacrifices of George Custer and his men. The show employed Indians from several tribes, including Mohawks, who played not only noble and ignoble savages, but antagonists from China, Mexico, and the Philippines when Cody adapted Custer's Last Stand to current events such as the Boxer Rebellion.[136]

Cody's show visited Staten Island just one month after an appearance by an Indian lacrosse team in New York City. Catering to a more general, multiclass audience, Cody promised something to audiences that native lacrosse clubs could not: "wild, picturesque life to be seen without the confines of civilization."[137] The show celebrated not gentlemanly virtue or the noble savage, but rather the triumph of civilization over savagery. Inevitably, the rise of Wild West shows contributed to the decline of interest in touring Indian lacrosse teams. By the early 1890s, northeastern interest in the distant mythical frontier came at the expense of the cultural ventures of Mohawk lacrosse clubs. Banned by Canadian athletic organizations and now undercut by Buffalo Bill Cody, Iroquois athletes retreated to their reservations. With the alleged end of the frontier in 1890 and the Depression of the mid-1890s, the only reason natives wandered off their reservations was to look for industrial jobs at construction sites. Regardless, although many Canadians were abandoning lacrosse, the Mohawks did not.

Chapter 2 **"King of the Field Games"**
Lacrosse in the United States, 1879–1919

CANADIANS MIGHT HAVE regarded lacrosse as their national game during the late nineteenth century, but it took a long time for a stable American lacrosse community to be established. The first seeds of lacrosse successfully germinated in the New York City area, especially Brooklyn, as well as in Baltimore and Boston. Even though some eastern colleges adopted lacrosse as a spring-semester sport, private athletic clubs provided much of the moral and organizational leadership. Organized competition among clubs and universities was sporadic until the first decade of the twentieth century. Besides cultivating the game in nearby preparatory schools, early collegian and club sportsmen constructed an ideology for their adopted game based on a variety of ideas, including the Victorian notions of "character development" and "fair play"; the amateur ideal of a game played for its own sake, uncontaminated by professionalism; and an emphasis on rough, manly sport. The focus on gentlemanly self-control prevented serious problems from arising as a result of playing a game with a lethal implement such as a wooden lacrosse stick. However much this value system resembled the ideology of those who supported football, it contrasted greatly with the culture of the country's fully commercialized and democratic "national pastime," baseball.

Tolerant of rough play, early twentieth-century proponents of lacrosse also saw themselves as the symbolic descendants of the "noble savage" of antiquity. Sportswriters and college alumni played an important role in creating and perpetuating these traditions. Meanwhile, because enthusiasts based many of their presumptions about their game on a somewhat authentic but ultimately romanticized conception of Native American peoples, many collegian and club sportsmen played against Indian lacrosse

teams throughout the first two decades of the twentieth century. White athletes and coaches alike may have looked down upon native peoples as their
social and racial inferiors, but they also believed crossing sticks with reservation Indians would provide modern athletes with a useful indicator of
their own skills. However, native lacrosse teams held different assumptions
about cross-cultural contests. Aside from recognizing the potential economic benefits of play, many Indian athletes played the modernized version of lacrosse precisely because of its native origin. Victorious or not, Indians participated in the world of intercollegiate athletics in order to assert
their cultural authority.

Keeping Out the "Rowdy Element": Early Amateur Lacrosse in New York, New England, and Baltimore

Through the efforts of Canadian immigrants who had organized clubs and
institutionalized their national game in America, and the efforts of Iroquois
Indians who had piqued the interest of affluent sportsmen, lacrosse had
gained a permanent foothold in the United States by the end of the 1870s.
Club officials squabbled over the amateur status of athletes, rough play and
on-field violence, and whether or not they should create systems in nearby
preparatory schools to feed players to the clubs. But they agreed to recast
their northern neighbors' national game into a game acceptable to American sportsmen. The first formal lacrosse organization in America was created through the efforts of private athletic clubs. In June 1879 delegates
from eleven clubs in New York City, Brooklyn, and Boston, as well as
Elmira, New York, and Bradford, Pennsylvania, met in New York City at the
Astor House and formed the United States National Amateur Lacrosse Association (USNALA). The new organization elected shipping merchant
Herman Oelrichs of the New York Lacrosse Club as president.[1] Oelrichs,
who had been born in Baltimore in 1850, was the son of a German immigrant businessman. He had completed his education in Germany, then returned to the United States in 1871 and assumed control of his family's
shipping business, Oelrichs and Company, in 1887. Aside from involvement
with the Democratic Party, his participation in New York City's elite social
life included membership in twenty-two private clubs.[2]

After the formation of the USNALA, the development of collegian organizations followed. Established in April 1883, the Intercollegiate Association had members that included prestigious eastern universities: Harvard,

Yale, Princeton, New York, and Lehigh Universities and Stevens Institute. Clubs and colleges in the New York City area formed the Metropolitan Lacrosse Association in March 1885, and clubs based in Baltimore, Philadelphia, and Brooklyn formed the Eastern Association in April 1889.[3] To generate interest in the sport, Erastus Wiman and Herman Oelrichs sponsored an American all-star team's trip to England during May and June of 1884 by underwriting the $5,000 cost.[4] Captained by *New York Tribune* writer H. H. Balch, the team included athletes from Harvard, New York University, Princeton, and Yale. These collegians combined with gentlemen athletes from the New York, Union (Boston), Druid (Baltimore), and Calumet (Chicago) clubs to form the first national lacrosse team and the first-ever "All-America" squad in any sport. It won nine of its ten matches in Britain. During the trip the team dined with American diplomats and Canadian government officials. Upon returning home, the U.S. team lost twice to the Toronto L.C. on Staten Island in July. Gate receipts were used to help defray the expenses of the base of the new Statue of Liberty.[5]

Erastus Wiman consciously made Canada's national game part of the leisure landscape on Staten Island during the 1880s. According to the *New York Times*, it was Wiman's intent "to give lacrosse a boom such as it never had before." Wiman not only paid the traveling and dining expenses of anyone willing to come to Staten Island and practice lacrosse, but helped pay for an Irish team to come to America. His financial sponsorship suggests that not all enthusiasts—especially less affluent Canadian immigrants—had the money or time to participate without assistance. Regardless, as a colonizer of the sport Wiman made the game a permanent activity in New York. Exaggerating the popularity of lacrosse in the summer of 1886, the New York press emphasized the importance of cultural exchange between North America's anglophone nations: "It is comparatively a few years since lacrosse, brought to us from Canada in fair exchange for the transplanting of American baseball in the Dominion, bespoke a place in popular favor, and the grace, skill, and excitement that belong to it have easily conquered this place, especially since the main points of the game can be comprehended at once by all spectators." As president of the USNALA, Wiman also maintained ties with the lacrosse communities of the British Isles by welcoming Irish gentlemen from Belfast in 1886. Entertained by their hosts, the New York L.C., the Irishmen witnessed cricket and lacrosse matches at the Staten Island Cricket Club.[6] After losing to an "All-America" team, these

Protestant Irishmen traveled to Montreal and competed against teams representing that province's distinct ethnic communities: the Montreal L.C. (middle-class Anglo Protestants), the Shamrock L.C. (working-class Irish Catholics), and the Caughnawaga Indians (reservation Native American Catholics). The men from Ireland concluded their trip with stops in Toronto, Niagara Falls, Saint Catharines, Richmond Hill, Ottawa, and Brockville.[7]

Many American players adhered to the amateur code, regarding sport as pastime, not profession. However, not all supporters followed the letter or spirit of this ethos. Just as in Canada some clubs resorted to paying especially good players for play and emphasized victorious competition over character development. Consequently, club administrators felt obligated to defend their teams' integrity. For example, in September 1882 the captain of the Calumet L.C. of Chicago denied an Associated Press report that four former players of the Louisville L.C. had signed with his club. A. G. Goldsmith contended, "There is not a player in the Calumets who is not a regular member in good standing," arguing that the "Club is made up of young men who have taken to the game as a means of recreation, and victory to them is nothing if it cannot be attained honorably." Regardless of the authenticity of the wire service report, Goldsmith assured readers of the *Spirit of the Times* that Calumet included only gentlemen who played the game for the game's sake. Sometimes rough play called into question the gentlemanly status of athletes. In 1886, roughness by a Stevens Institute player compelled one writer to comment that "collegiate culture sometimes develops bullies and cowards." Meanwhile, an "unruly" crowd caused a match between the New York L.C. and the Brooklyn Athletic Association to be suspended early.[8]

Similar controversy surrounded a July 1886 championship contest between the New York L.C. and the Saint Paul club of Minnesota. Emulating the Montreal L.C., which tended to take the moral high ground, the New York gentlemen alleged that Saint Paul had imported two professional players from Winnipeg. Not only off-field bickering, but also violence marred the match. A supposedly inadvertent blow by a Saint Paul player to the face of a New Yorker resulted in immediate retaliation by New York's captain and eventually created a general brawl involving spectators. Even though the New York team walked away with the victory, club secretary T. M. Marson decried the behavior of Saint Paul's players and spectators: "Our team, made up entirely of gentleman amateurs, went 1,400 miles to win a cup, as they expected, under conditions of fair play and gentlemanly treatment. Instead, as soon as there were any signs of their success, some of the St. Paul players resorted to the most ferocious form of play, in which they were encouraged and abetted by the plaudits of a rowdy element among the spectators." His reference to "a rowdy element" implied the presence of working-class spectators with little interest in gentlemanly sport for sport's sake. Marson further alleged, "The truth puts the St. Paul players in the position of men who sought to avert by physical violence a defeat achieved at their expense by the superior skill and sportsmanlike behavior of our own club."[9]

Later that month, Saint Paul club secretary Ralph Martin exonerated his club's "gentlemen spectators," yet refrained from arguing that its players were amateur. Although he criticized the "ungentlemanly" conduct of the New York captain, he did not censure on-field violence. Referring to the rough play that had led to the fight, Martin wrote: "We looked on the blows that were distributed to our players simply as accidents, and made no remarks, and, had it not been for the pugilistic interference of Captain Cluff, the blow received by Popham would have passed unnoticed and the game would never have given Mr. Marson a chance to exhibit his defamatory talents in the choice selection of standard epithets that characterises his production."[10] Essentially, both teams tried to control the terms of the argument, the New Yorkers by emphasizing gentlemanly sport for sport's sake, the Minnesota club with its competitive ethos of the commercial marketplace.

Increasing numbers of incidents of player violence, spectator rowdiness, and covert professionalism—all common themes in late nineteenth-century Canadian lacrosse—coincided with efforts to commercialize lacrosse in the United States. One effort to stage lacrosse as a spectacle occurred in New York City in 1891. The Madison Square Garden Company held a two-day exhibition tournament of eight-man indoor lacrosse before fifteen hundred spectators at the amphitheater in January. The program featured the professional Caughnawaga Indians and five amateur clubs: the Montreal L.C., the Staten Island Athletic Club (A.C.), the Corinthian A.C., the Jersey City L.C., and the Druids of Baltimore. As in previous appearances, the Caughnawaga Indians catered to white stereotypes of native peoples by also staging three half-mile snowshoe races on dirt. *The Week's Sport* criticized the affair, calling for the U.S. Amateur Athletic Union (AAU) to take action: "This tournament is given by the management of the

Madison Square Garden Company, not in the interests of amateur sport, not for the pecuniary benefit of any of the athletic clubs, but solely and purely to put dollars into the treasury of the company." The periodical asserted that amateur sportsmen could be "hired by professional theatrical managers to disport themselves for the public gaze at so much per head."[11]

The tournament promoters paired match opponents with caution. The three amateur American clubs played either among themselves or against Montreal. The professional Indian team played contests only with Montreal. However, the Caughnawaga also played a match against a selected team of amateurs representing the United States, and this match forced the AAU to take action. About three weeks after the tournament, the AAU suspended the amateurs who had competed against the Caughnawaga. The decision shocked the four Druids from Baltimore who were affected by the decree. According to one suspended player, Yates Penniman, the decision was inconsistent with the AAU's inaction related to the actions of players of other sports. Amateur tennis players and college baseball teams routinely played against professionals and received no AAU condemnation. "There was no prize offered in the game with the Indians," Penniman asserted. "If to play with a professional in an exhibition lacrosse match makes all who take part professionals, why should not the same rule apply to other games? And yet we know that the gentlemen of Philadelphia play right along on the cricket elevens with professionals and nothing is said about it. The board seems to have ignored entirely the fact that none of the Baltimore players knew the Indians were paid until after the game."[12] Although organizers had permitted American lacrosse clubs to compete with Mohawk Indians during earlier visits, the AAU suspensions reflected a growing hostility to both professionalism and native players.

Allegations of professionalism and of "importing" players from Canada plagued officials of amateur clubs. Accusations of player ineligibility surrounded an 1892 AAU tournament featuring the Lorillard, Manhattan, New York, and Staten Island clubs. Lorillard and Staten Island both had former New York players who had never received permission to play with another club. To increase the likelihood of victory, Manhattan acquired two Canadian "imports," while New York sent "recruiting agents" north to enlist six Canadian "ringers." Although Staten Island played the tournament under protest, team captain Cyrus C. Miller criticized New York's recruitment tactics: "When a club deliberately imports six or eight of the best players in Canada, feeds them like fighting cocks, keeps them with nothing to do from one week's end to another but play lacrosse, and then plays them against a team composed of business men who don't get a chance to practice more than three or four hours a week, I think it's about time to stop it." Miller emphasized the local origins of his athletes and directed his anger at the secret nature of efforts to recruit Canadians: "Although we are not afraid to take a beating from a Canadian team as such, we don't care to be beaten by Canadians and have a New York club get the credit of it."[13]

Because most U.S. athletic clubs had abandoned lacrosse by the 1890s, clashes over professionalism mattered little. But the game survived on eastern university campuses. By the turn of the century, the American version of lacrosse took a path quite different from that taken by the game north of the border. Not only was professionalism a dead issue after 1900, but the American game lacked the rhetoric of social reform and patriotism prevalent in Canada. Whereas Canadian lacrosse was imbedded in local clubs, its American counterpart was found within institutions of higher education. Lacrosse allowed sportsmen to engage in a spirited and manly activity removed from the realm of their socioeconomic inferiors. The lack of working-class interest in lacrosse also explains why the American game never emulated major- and minor-league baseball. Recasting Canada's national game in terms acceptable to affluent Americans, lacrosse partisans created a self-contained athletic environment that was untainted by contact with working-class sportsmen. Flesh-and-blood Iroquois Indians had played an important role in the early years of organized play in Canada, but American organizers reserved a very marginal place for native peoples. Like the country as a whole, the Indian frontier in American lacrosse seemed to be closing by the 1890s.

Lacrosse proponents cultivated their game among other collegians in Baltimore, the New York City area, and New England from the 1890s through the first two decades of the next century. They constantly fought against the lukewarm support of undergraduate students, persevering in the promotion of their game. Organizers also spread their game to nearby secondary schools, creating local feeder systems. Regardless of whether play took place at a private club, on a university campus, or in a prep-school yard, lacrosse allowed the sons of affluent families to participate in an elite springtime alternative to the democratic and commercialized national pastime, baseball. While baseball evangelists believed their game integrated all members of society into a larger whole, lacrosse advocates focused on an exclusive body of athletes at the elite levels of higher and secondary education. At campuses such as that of the Johns Hopkins University in Baltimore and at private clubs such as the Crescent Athletic Club in Brooklyn, enthusiasts articulated what they believed to be the special cultural, social, historical, intellectual, and health qualities of their adopted game. Regardless of whether these athletes were businessmen who played at private clubs or undergraduate students who crossed sticks on campus, they competed in a friendly, "gentlemanly" environment with and against members of the same affluent social class.

The institutional development of intercollegiate lacrosse was slow. In 1888 the Intercollegiate Lacrosse Association (ILA) included Princeton, Johns Hopkins, and Stevens, with Lehigh joining the following season. With the withdrawal of Princeton in 1891, the ILA became a three-school association, and it remained so until Swarthmore College joined in 1902. Renewed interest on some campuses resulted in the formation of a second association, the United States Inter-University Lacrosse League (USIULL), in 1894, with Harvard, Columbia, and Cornell as charter members. The league's ranks expanded when the University of Pennsylvania joined in 1899. USIULL president Cyrus C. Miller's effort to centralize college lacrosse resulted in a merger when a new eight-school United States Intercollegiate Lacrosse League (USILL) replaced the older associations in December 1905. Over the next fifteen years, USILL membership expanded very slowly. Although Penn and Columbia both dropped out temporarily, the association grew with the reentry of Penn and the addition of newcomers Yale and Syracuse University. The growth of the collegiate game included not only institutions unaffiliated with the association, but schools with a less affluent social composition. Prior to the First World War, teams represented the U.S. Naval Academy, Maryland Agricultural College, the University of Maryland, Springfield Manual Training College, the City College of New York, the U.S. Military Academy, Carlisle Indian Industrial School, Pennsylvania State University, and the University of Virginia. Contrasting lacrosse on both sides of the Canadian-American border, the campus press at Johns Hopkins painted an optimistic view of the American game in May 1914: "Lacrosse may be losing ground as the Canadian national game, but no close observer of college sports would care to be credited as saying that the game was becoming less popular in America."[14]

The Rise of Lacrosse in the Northeast

After the demise of most amateur lacrosse clubs during the late 1880s and the early 1890s, a second but smaller wave of club formation began. The new clubs played against colleges and participated on intercollegiate governing bodies. By the beginning of the Great War in 1914, fourteen clubs were operating in Baltimore, Philadelphia, Pittsburgh, Boston, Hartford, New York City, Syracuse, Rochester, and Buffalo. Unlike the lacrosse community of the 1870s and 1880s, where play had been more multiregional (with clubs even in California and the Midwest) and Canadian in character, the new lacrosse community of the 1890s and 1900s was geographically limited to the Northeast. For example, Maryland's first contact with lacrosse occurred the day after gentlemen from the Baltimore A.C. competed in a track meet at Newport, Rhode Island, on August 22, 1878. After witnessing their first match of Canada's national game, the gentlemen returned home with newly purchased lacrosse sticks. The group began practice in mid-September and played its first intraclub match before several hundred spectators at Newington Park on November 23. The following spring, the club lost its first intercity match against the Ravenswood Club of New York on May 29. Over the next few years, the Baltimore A.C. crossed sticks with clubs from Baltimore, Washington, and Philadelphia, but then disbanded in March 1882. Students at Baltimore City College began play in the fall of 1879 as the Monumentals club, but renamed themselves the Druid L.C. in 1883 after their Druid Hill Park practice site.[15]

The earliest supporters in Maryland were from the affluent old families of Baltimore. In 1879 the imported Canadian coach of the new Baltimore A.C. lacrosse team characterized his players to the *Montreal Evening Post* as elite: "The members are principally sons of wealthy merchants, with a good sprinkling of merchants themselves."[16] Many of these gentlemen also fostered their adopted game among local schoolboys. Some of these converts then went on to introduce or encourage the game at Princeton, Harvard, Lehigh, Pennsylvania, and Stevens during the 1880s. For example, six grandnephews of author Edgar Allen Poe built up the game at Princeton. They included S. Johnson Poe, a member of the class of 1884 who later became a Baltimore attorney, and Edgar Allan Poe, a namesake of his granduncle, who graduated in 1891 and later served as attorney general of Maryland.[17] When *Baltimore Sun* journalist W. Wilson Wingate wrote a history of lacrosse for his paper in 1930, he relied on the memories of lacrosse veterans who said they had "trained in the sport the young scions of many of the oldest Baltimore families."[18]

Despite the general decline in lacrosse on campuses throughout the late 1880s, students at Johns Hopkins embraced the game.[19] The administrators channeled all financial resources into the construction of new academic buildings after the founding of the university in 1876,[20] and they did not deem either an indoor gymnasium or an outdoor playing field a priority. However, the Baltimore A.C. admitted Johns Hopkins students for a $1 monthly fee beginning in 1880,[21] and other students of the university played for the local Druid lacrosse team.[22] Some of these undergraduates later formed their own Johns Hopkins squad in 1883, but the university team went defunct after playing the Druids.[23] A few years later, in the fall of 1887, the Druids encouraged three Johns Hopkins freshmen to start a campus team. Sustaining long-term interest among students seemed to be very difficult. "It was slow work getting recruits," one member of the class of 1890 recalled in 1903, because "the baseball men tried in every way to discourage us."[24] Beginning formal play in 1888, the Johns Hopkins team played against ILA opponents and other intercollegiate teams, as well as the Druids, the Maryland A.C., and the A.C. of the Schuylkill Navy in Philadelphia.[25]

Collegians' regular play against club sportsmen and other undergraduates led to influential socio-occupational networks that proved useful upon graduation, especially considering the lines of work of most alumni. According to a survey undertaken in 1912 of 920 students who had graduated from Johns Hopkins from June 1879 to June 1906, the professions they most commonly entered included law (22.5 percent), academia and education (22.3 percent), medicine (17.5 percent), and science (9.2 percent). These men achieved prominence in their fields throughout Maryland and the South. Many believed their university's production of intellectual leaders had redefined the leadership not only of Baltimore, but of Maryland and the whole New South. "Johns Hopkins will be such a factor as was the University of Berlin in the reconstruction of Prussia," James Curtis Ballagh argued in 1902. "But national and international as the fame of the University has become, it still maintains a peculiarly close relation to this locality and its future." Convinced of the importance of their university, the student editors at Johns Hopkins underscored "a reliance upon the vital and essential, youth, vigor, enthusiasm, reality and the present, rather than upon dim tradition and authority."[26] Lacrosse enthusiasts in particular romanticized their sport by comparing the game's heroes with historical figures. Pointing to star athlete William Harvey Maddren, the 1899 yearbook said, "Rome had its Cæsar, Carthage its Hannibal, Russia its Peter the Great, and our Lacrosse Team its Maddren."[27]

A succession of national championships prodded Johns Hopkins alumni to create athletic traditions promoting continuity and permanency at the university. After graduation, many alumni returned to cheer on the varsity twelve and encourage undergraduates to support lacrosse. For example, members of the class of 1902 offered a cup to the winner of an intra-class competition between the freshmen and the juniors in April 1906 to develop talent for the varsity. The classes accepted the challenge, but many apparently lost interest after winning the cup. Realizing that some students had competed merely to win rather than for sport's sake, the alumni sponsored another cup competition in 1909, but stipulated that students had to enroll on their class teams and practice rather than just showing up on the day of the competition. Apparently the alumni and current students had very different agendas. The alumni were promoting a gentlemanly conception of sport among undergraduates, while the campus youth seemed disinterested in perpetuating the university's invented tradition.

Aside from crusading on the Johns Hopkins campus, alumni created their own lacrosse team, but undergraduates disagreed over its merits. In April 1909, one adversary insisted that an alumni squad would draw spectators and quality opposition away from the varsity. "The enrollment of a college or university depends largely upon the advertisement it receives through a medium of its athletic teams," this critic wrote. "The average preparatory school boy judges an institution solely by the success of its athletic teams. If by any inadvertent means the interest of Hopkins athletics is decreased, I think the undergraduate department of the University is to be the sufferer." The previous season's team manager disagreed: "Such a team . . . has the effect of stimulating lacrosse interest in larger circles, and thus tending to increase the interest of the public generally, with the corresponding result that all audiences will be larger and more enthusiastic."[28]

A Johns Hopkins alumni team also strained relations between the university and nearby clubs. For instance, many alumni played for the Mount Washington Lacrosse Club, located in a northwestern suburb of Baltimore. Formed in January 1904, the club played on the former grounds of the Baltimore Cricket Club, which had sold the land and consolidated with the Baltimore Country Club.[29] Armed with the motto "Fair play, clean sport," Mount Washington's team participated in competitive athletics untainted by professionalism, commercialism, or contact with Baltimore's working class.[30] The new club quickly became a focal point in the social life of "attractive looking gatherings of men and women from the best families of the city." In July 1905 the *Baltimore Sun* noted that the club had quelled members' anxieties: "Among the dwellers in the beautiful cottages clustered about the hills of Mount Washington the suburban spirit of sociability is seen at its best. The families got together as soon as the Cricket Club at Mount Washington consolidated with the Baltimore Country Club and secured an option on the old quarters of the cricketers for fear the property might be devoted to some undesirable amusement enterprise."[31] The possibility that a commercial venture might attract working-class patrons into the affluent neighborhood had caused great concerns among club members. Membership in the club swelled to about four hundred by May 1906. Club officials were sensitive to the occupational demands of their men. For example, the club scheduled its match with the University of Toronto in May 1915 to begin at 5 P.M., the *Baltimore Sun* reported, "in order that the business men and people in the offices will have an opportunity to get out to see the match."[32] Mount Washington eventually developed a friendly rivalry with Johns Hopkins undergraduates. However, fearing the dispute they thought would inevitably arise if Mount Washington and a Johns Hopkins alumni team were to draw from the same talent pool, the university temporarily abandoned the idea of an alumni team in 1911. Instead of antagonizing one another, the organizations avoided an unnecessary confrontation that might impair existing social ties.[33]

Lacrosse in New York State

While enthusiasts at Johns Hopkins and Mount Washington were cultivating lacrosse as an elite sport in Baltimore, the Crescent A.C. of Brooklyn was the trailblazer in the greater New York City area during the 1890s and throughout the first third of the twentieth century. Originally founded as a football club in November 1884, this Brooklyn club reorganized as an athletic club in January 1886 with Walter Camp as president,[34] and it fielded a lacrosse team beginning in 1893. The club operated a summer country clubhouse at Bay Ridge in Brooklyn until 1931, when the Crescents abandoned

it in favor of a new facility at Huntington, Long Island. Because the Brooklyn elite regarded the club's annual formal opening as the social occasion of
the year, the Brooklyn press noted that "a girl who hadn't been able to wrangle a Crescent Club date on the seasonal Decoration Day opening of the Bay
Ridge Country House was the town's No. 1 social flop."[35] Club members
participated in many sports, but believed the lacrosse team was their biggest
source of athletic pride. Stocked with Canadian immigrants and former
American collegians, the "New Moons" usually defeated all opponents and
attracted large crowds of club members and their guests. In contrast to "the
crack team of the New York Athletic Club . . . composed for the most part
of Canadians and star men who received compensation in more ways than
one," in 1896 the Crescents were praised by *Leslie's Weekly* as "a first class
team of *bona fide* amateurs" who deserved "great credit and praise for the
good turn they do the cause of amateur sport." Although many Canadians
played for the Crescents, the periodical claimed, "All of them have profitable
business interests and play the game for the love of it."[36]

Relatively early in the Crescent club's existence, members discussed the
possibility of sending their lacrosse team to visit Great Britain. Such a trip
was not out of the ordinary for affluent athletes in England and America
during the late nineteenth century. Anxieties among the ruling classes in
both countries gave rise to the doctrine of "Anglo-Saxonism," the belief in
the racial superiority of anglophones. Although many British citizens felt
threatened by the rising strength of other European Great Powers and the
so-called Slavic and Oriental perils, older-stock Americans feared immigration from eastern and southern Europe and debated fiercely the benefits
and drawbacks of newfound spheres of influence overseas. The sporting
elite in England and America responded to these issues by celebrating a
common sense of superiority.[37] Cordial relations among diplomats and intellectuals also coincided with more hospitable Anglo-American sporting
relations. Although the athletic teams of American and English universities
had competed against one another as early as August 1869, when Harvard
had squared off with Oxford in rowing, that event had been a rarity. However, after track men from Yale and Oxford raced one another in July 1894,[38]
lacrosse players from Brooklyn reestablished transatlantic ties that had
been severed since 1884. In August 1896, the editors of the Brooklyn club's
magazine gave moral support to those contemplating a tour of England: "If
. . . the members of the team are men so connected in business that they can

afford to take six weeks or so off without a thought of recompense outside of glory won on the field of play, then we can not see why they should not be permitted to make the trip in the name of the Crescent Club." Praising the team as champions of "fair play and courtly demeanor," the *Crescent* editors believed the tour could avenge the customary losses to the English: "It would be indeed refreshing to see a Crescent A.C. team beard the lion in his den and start the ball of foreign victories a rolling."[39] Citing the Yale rowing team's recent failure to capture the Grand Challenge Cup at Henley, the *Crescent* editors said their lacrosse team would invade the British Isles and triumph over the English.[40]

By early December, officials announced that the club would send a team to England in the spring of 1897, with each player paying his own expenses to show the club's commitment to uncontaminated amateurism. The North of England Lacrosse Association, the South of England Lacrosse Association, and the Irish Lacrosse Union agreed to serve as hosts. Of the men on the regular squad, only three said occupational duties overruled their desire to play for the tour team.[41] Lionel Moses praised teammate John Curry's efforts to convince employers to grant six-week leaves of absence to players: "We all know with what diplomacy Curry interviewed Bishops and presidents of companies, and so strengthened our team by the addition of several members." Moses went out of his way to note the sacrifices of some members: "It is reported that when one of the players applied for leave of absence his principals answered that they thought the office could be closed for six weeks or so. And rumor has it that work aggregating millions of dollars a year is done in this office, which of course goes to show how valuable are the services of this man in business as well as play." Apparently other men did not even bother to seek permission, as one "did not want to know whether he could 'get off,' but if he could 'get on' again upon his return."[42] Moses also admitted that while the lacrosse team wanted to return victorious, they also yearned to meet the English on their own social terms.

The Crescents departed from New York in March after defeating several universities and clubs in an abbreviated domestic season.[43] Aside from noting the different playing seasons in America (spring and early summer), Canada (summer and early fall), and Britain (fall to spring), post-tour commentators highlighted other distinctive characteristics. Although American sportswriter Caspar Whitney pointed to inferior British stick skills and the

English tendency to "bunch" their attackmen,[44] an Englishman noted that British lacrosse was far less violent than either the American or the Canadian game: "While there can be no doubt that Lacrosse brings out all the best points of a player's pluck and determination, there is no reason to believe that it may ultimately become a rough or brutal game."[45] Compiling a record of 7–5–2 against the British clubs, the Brooklyn gentlemen believed the tour had accomplished several tasks. Besides validating the elite social status of the Crescent men, the tour had demonstrated the club's athletic competitiveness, if not its superiority. In a June summary of the tour, Moses wrote: "The number of dinners and other entertainments tendered to the team may lead some to believe that this trip was more of an event socially than athletically, but this view is absurdly erroneous."[46]

The tour team held a return banquet, and later held annual reunion dinners to reminisce. Emphasizing Anglo-American unity, they decorated the banquet room of the 1905 reunion with menu cards featuring intertwined English and American flags.[47] By their twenty-fifth anniversary meeting, most of the former players had established careers in law, politics, education, business, and medicine. The team's lone attorney, New York University graduate Cyrus C. Miller, was serving on the United States Intercollegiate Lacrosse League executive board and was a former borough president of the Bronx. The club also included the founder of the lacrosse club at Hobart College in Geneva, New York, the Reverend Joseph A. Leighten, a graduate of Harvard who was then a professor of philosophy at Ohio State University. Other former squad members included Charles H. Roberts, a graduate of New York University, and John P. Curry, an alumnus of City College of New York, who had developed a business as construction contractors; Cincinnati broker H. L. Parsons; Persian Rug Manufacturing Company executive Giles Whiting, a graduate of City College of New York and Columbia; stockbroker Edward H. Jewell; and real estate dealer Charles F. De Casanova. While Dr. Malcolm Rose, a Columbia graduate, practiced medicine in New York City, two other New Yorkers with professional careers included mechanical engineer Embury McLean, a Stevens alumnus who had recently lived in Russia and France, and architect and art director Lionel Moses, a graduate of Brooklyn Polytechnic. Unfortunately, the two Canadians—team captain James S. Garvin and H. McConaghy of Toronto—had not lived to see the silver anniversary of the tour.[48] In 1934 McLean recalled the physical demands of the tour. "After every game we were entertained royally and they saw to it that our glasses were never empty," McLean said. "But I guess it kept us going or we wouldn't have been able to play so many games in such a short time."[49]

After the Crescents' tour in 1897, transatlantic lacrosse was played infrequently during the first decade of the new century. Although the sports committee of the Paris Exhibition sought lacrosse competition in 1900, English and American clubs failed to schedule an international championship.[50] A joint Oxford-Cambridge team toured the American Northeast in 1903, but interest remained confined to about a dozen colleges. "It was distinctly a 'society' event, and reminded me, on a smaller scale, of Harvard, Yale or Princeton events," Leighten later recalled about the visit to Hobart. "A number of prominent people from out of town were present as well as the cream of Geneva."[51] Even though "national" lacrosse teams crossed sticks at the 1904 Saint Louis and 1908 London Olympics, interest remained confined to the few.[52] The great expense of extended transatlantic trips precluded frequent international engagements.

Striving to make amateur sport "not an idea but a reality," the editors of the Crescent A.C.'s official magazine took a stand against professionalism: "We banish from our dictionary the term 'paid,' whether it means actual money disbursed or pleasant quarters and free meals." Allegedly, the Crescent athlete competed "from pure motives of interest and ambition." Moreover, the editors hoped to make an effective public statement defending the interests of the sporting elite: "Long may the Crescent flag wave for such a reform, and may its fluttering in the breeze bring a change in the present translation of the word 'amateur.'"[53] According to former player and member of the board of governors Carroll J. Post, the Crescent club accepted a missionary role in the world of organized lacrosse: "With the idea of developing the game among the Colleges, we encouraged them to come to Bay Ridge by paying their expenses, and when this was not possible, by going to their grounds." Moreover, Post continued, "Attendance at the games increased from about fifty to nearly two thousand."[54]

Because the Crescents usually defeated American opponents, the club often invited Canadian teams to Brooklyn. To complete the 1900 season, the Crescents scheduled matches with the Capital and Markham clubs of Toronto, the University of Toronto, and the Montreal Amateur Athletic Association. When the Crescents played the University of Toronto in May 1910, the *Brooklyn Daily Eagle* reported: "The teams played real Canadian lacrosse and to the uninitiated this game is no parlor entertainment. As a matter of fact, there were several calls for physicians and there were teeth lost in the encounter, while several players sustained lacerations and cuts."[55] Season-ending matches with Canadian clubs in June usually inaugurated the summer social season at Bay Ridge. The Crescents incurred great expense in playing weekend host to visiting Canadian and American teams, paying part or all of their traveling costs. Although the Crescents played most of their contests at their luxurious country clubhouse, their yearly excursions to Ontario and Quebec added to the team's expenses. As a result, the club allocated the largest portion of its athletics budget to lacrosse. For example, during the period from 1912 through 1919, excluding 1913, the club spent $57,127.37 on eighteen different sports. Lacrosse led all sports in funding, receiving 25.7 percent of all athletics funding, followed by baseball (21.3 percent) and golf (19.6 percent).[56]

The Crescents' athletic prowess inadvertently attracted the general public to Bay Ridge. As the center of attention during the spring, its lacrosse matches often attracted several thousand spectators. The presence of members of other social clubs and curious working-class patrons compromised the club's desire to remain socially exclusive. To curtail the unwanted visitors, in June 1900 officials notified members that future guests would have to be escorted. According to the chairman of the club's athletics committee, too many loud strangers donning "wheeling costumes" visited club grounds, taking all the good seats and forcing members to stand during play. Regardless, strangers still flocked to the Crescent grounds. At the annual formal May opening of the country club in 1905, some six thousand people—including many of "Brooklyn's most fashionable people"—gathered to watch a thirty-six-hole golf tournament, the Brooklyn interscholastic lacrosse championship between Poly Prep and Boys' High, and two lacrosse matches involving the Crescents' senior and junior squads. "The quaint little grand stand was crowded" for the senior team's victory over the University of Toronto, the Brooklyn Daily Eagle reported, and "the terraces were thronged and the south side of the emerald field was lined five deep with enthusiastic spectators."[57] In early June the Crescents drew crowds of four thousand each to matches against two Canadian clubs and another crowd of twelve thousand for a contest against Mount Washington.

Despite the proximity of collegians and schoolboys to Indian reservations in upstate New York, the institutional development of lacrosse was slower there than in the New York City area. Originally from Orangeville, Ontario, Dr. Joseph A. Leighten introduced the game to Hobart College in the fall of 1897. Educated at Trinity College in Toronto, the Sage School of Philosophy at Cornell, and the Episcopal Theological School of Harvard University, Leighten served as chaplain and professor of philosophy at Hobart from 1897 through 1910. Although Hobart's lacrosse team played collegian squads, their most frequent foe was a collection of former college players and Canadian immigrants living in Rochester, who called themselves the Rangers. Occasionally these teams played one another indoors at armories in Geneva and Rochester.[58] Students of Syracuse University may have encountered lacrosse as played by local Onondaga Indians at some earlier date, but official play began in November 1906. With only a handful of experienced students on campus, writers of the *Syracuse Daily Orange* hoped a team would increase Canadian enrollment. After erratic play on campus in 1906 and 1907, club leaders formed a team around a nucleus of varsity football and basketball athletes, former Hobart players, and Canadian students.[59] This Syracuse squad, also called the Rangers, played other varsity and club teams around the state. Hockey coach Robert Hilliard and other city residents served as mentors. With only mild interest, the team disbanded at the end of the campaign. However, Laurie D. Cox, a former Harvard player and professor of landscape engineering at the State College of Forestry on the university campus, recruited enough forestry students to start a new team in the spring of 1916. Cox's missionary work paid dividends when the university officially made lacrosse a "minor sport" in October 1916. War interrupted the athletics schedule at Syracuse throughout 1917, but the following year it played the local Syracuse L.C., Hobart, and the Onondaga Reservation all twice each, plus Stevens, Carlisle, Pennsylvania, and the Crescent A.C.

Lacrosse Goes to School

During the first two decades of the twentieth century, intercollegiate and club lacrosse grew very slowly among well-to-do sportsmen in Baltimore, New York and Brooklyn, upstate New York, and elite universities and colleges throughout the Northeast. Because most young men learned lacrosse as college students, coaches complained if they had to spend too much time on basic skills rather than strategy and tactics. The solution to the problem of inadequate development of talent in college, many university athletics

officials believed, was to promote lacrosse at local preparatory and secondary schools. Athletes from many eastern universities targeted preparatory
schools and created a system to feed talent to college campuses. Not only
might the scheme ensure future college victories, but, more important, a
direct relationship would benefit the university community by enrolling
enthusiastic new lacrosse-playing students from prep schools. In Baltimore,
Johns Hopkins actively fostered schoolboy lacrosse by targeting nearby
prep schools. In March 1900, the *Baltimore Sun* reported that Johns Hopkins was encouraging lacrosse among local schoolboys so "early training
may produce more athletes than heretofore who will be able to compete
with the cracks from the great universities. The schoolboys, however, want
it fully understood that they are primarily 'in it' for themselves."[60] As when
the alumni had encouraged undergraduates to play, the young athletes simply wanted to play the game for their own personal reasons. At the beginning of the season, Johns Hopkins enthusiasts acknowledged the continual
problem of having to train yet another batch of freshman athletes. The university's *News-Letter* attributed the poor quality of new talent to the lack of
local interscholastic lacrosse: "With so many efficient schools in Baltimore,
there is no reason why such a state of affairs should exist; no reason why
men entering Hopkins should not be able immediately to play on teams."
Johns Hopkins captain Ronald Abercrombie gave schoolboys at Marston's
University School their first lacrosse lesson in March 1900. The university's
student press believed the new Inter-scholastic League would not only aid
future Johns Hopkins teams, but strengthen the university's relationship
with area schools: "As most of the Baltimore preparatory school students
will enter Hopkins in future years, this year's practice will be of inestimable
benefit both to them and to our future athletics."[61] Near the end of the season, Marston's School evidently acknowledged its role in the emerging
"feeder system" by sending a "delegation" of student rooters to support
Johns Hopkins against Lehigh.[62]

The playing of lacrosse at the public Baltimore City College was sporadic until Johns Hopkins developed an informal relationship with the college. Although schoolboys fielded their own teams from 1879 until 1891 and
again in 1896, proselytizing Johns Hopkins students made lacrosse a permanent part of the college's athletics program. "In 1902 the spirit of lacrosse
took a mighty hold on about twenty boys. The City College must have a
lacrosse team," City's *Green Bag* editors wrote. "Several of the Hopkins

team, hearing that and being influenced by the same spirit, came over and made many eloquent speeches. The thing was settled, the aforesaid boys by many devious ways secured the great sum necessary to purchase a stick." Practices at the Druid Hill Park were particularly rough: "One after another was knocked across the head. All hit each other sometimes, but one boy seemed especially fitted for the slugging part, so much so that in the game with the Hopkins Scrubs the loyal City College rooters termed him the 'slugger.'" However, students weighed injuries against the social benefits of playing: "Notwithstanding all these troubles, many happy days were spent at the Park, for all feminine beauty of the city went to the lacrosse grounds to see the team practice."[63] Members of the Johns Hopkins team of 1906 also sought to ensure the survival of the game at nearby prep schools such as City College: "Shall we give up this valuable training school for our teams of the future? We ask that you do all in your power to foster this year's team at the College; 'we need its members in our business.'"[64]

Lacrosse enthusiasts at Johns Hopkins clearly played an active role in promoting the game around the city. For instance, the university's students convinced Baltimore Polytechnic Institute boys to begin practice at the Druid park in 1906. However, the institute did not officially adopt lacrosse until 1912, when history and civics teacher and former Johns Hopkins player Charles F. Ranft agreed to coach the boys. According to the 1912 *Poly's Cracker*, "This fascinating game has spread through our Colleges and High Schools 'til we humbly have taken to it. After patient striving we have launched the sport and arranged a promising schedule of which we hope to render an agreeable account."[65] Over the next two decades, the local interscholastic league in Baltimore usually included the freshmen or reserve teams from Johns Hopkins, the Mount Washington club's junior squad, and teams from the city's two prestigious public schools: City College and Poly. The efforts of the university men, and the support they received from the press, reveals much about the ambitions and resources of these men to ensure the continuity of lacrosse at the university. The names and faces would change every four years, but Johns Hopkins would retain a championship program.

Although schoolboys in the greater New York City and Boston areas learned lacrosse during the 1880s and 1890s from local club men, formal interscholastic play began after the turn of the century. As early as 1905, probably even earlier, the Crescents allowed boys from the Brooklyn Polytechnic Preparatory School to use their lacrosse field, and several members volunteered to "instruct the youths in the mysteries of the grand old Indian game."[66] Over the next three decades club members colonized the local high schools with the game and provided the Bay Ridge club grounds for many interscholastic matches. By 1917 New York's new Metropolitan Interscholastic Lacrosse League included Manual Training, Erasmus Hall, Flushing, and Boy's High Schools; Saint John's Prep; and Stevens Preparatory School (from Hoboken, New Jersey), with matches played at Crescent A.C., Prospect Park, and Flushing in novice and veteran divisions.

Schoolboy lacrosse got its start in and around Boston as a result of proselytizing club and university athletes as well. As early as 1881, students at the Phillips Academy in Andover, Massachusetts, began to dabble with lacrosse and continued for a few years because of the efforts of a Canadian immigrant who lived in Boston. However, financial pressures led to an early demise of the game. "Combining the speed of a greyhound, the cunning of a fox, the heart of a lion, and the strength of a prize fighter, the game demands all the spirit of manhood," the school's *Phillipian* declared in April 1884 in a last-ditch appeal to retain the game. "Popular in Canada, it has taken a firm foothold in this country," the paper proclaimed. "It is truly the game of the future. Try it!"[67] Students revived informal play in the fall of 1906, and lacrosse received official Athletic Association support from the academy in 1912.[68] In an early inter-regional high school match, the academy hosted Curtis High School of Staten Island in May 1913.[69] Eventually, however, the school gave only a half-hearted endorsement to the team, and once again abandoned the game in 1917 to give students more time for military training.[70]

The demise of lacrosse at Phillips did not come without opposition. In April 1915 a Phillips graduate then attending Yale implored the Academy's Athletic Department to retain the team, because Andover boys comprised most of the Yale squad.[71] Lacrosse players at New England universities appreciated the importance of prep schools to their programs. As captain of the Harvard lacrosse team, F. C. Alexander observed in 1910: "[The] chief obstacle to the development of the sport is the lack of experienced men on whom to draw for material, a difficulty that exists because of the fact that until this year lacrosse has been played in the preparatory schools only about New York." However, he hoped secondary schools around Boston would serve as a system to feed talent to Harvard and stimulate interest in the game among other colleges and universities in New England: "It is only by thus beginning at the bottom that the college teams can be permanently strengthened; and the college that draws most upon experienced men from the preparatory schools will have a decided advantage in the Intercollegiate League."[72] By 1913 the Harvard freshmen began regular play against Phillips Academy. In the end, many universities and colleges seemed as much concerned about winning games as they were about bringing future generations of young affluent students onto their campuses. Collegian sportsmen claimed to engage in sport for sport's sake, but defeating an Ivy League rival was just as important.

The slow institutional and organizational development of lacrosse—whether club, intercollegiate, or interscholastic—from New England to Maryland highlights the uphill struggle advocates faced during the early twentieth century. However, sportsmen of Johns Hopkins, Mount Washington, the Crescent A.C., and the Ivy League all remained committed to the survival and propagation of the game. Early interscholastic play reflected the degree to which university and club sportsmen believed a modern version of an old Indian game strengthened ties between prep schools and major centers of higher education. In fact, USILL officials made the introduction of lacrosse to prep schools a league objective at the organization's yearly meetings in 1914, 1917, and 1919. This desire to establish a feeder system definitely suggests an overemphasis on winning that is usually associated with professionalized athletics. However, intercollegiate programs did not turn to lower-class "ringers" from rural farms and coal mines as their football counterparts often did.[73] Instead they turned to the affluent prep-school boys with whom they had so much in common.

College Spirit and Gentlemanly Sport: The Formation of an American Lacrosse Ethos

The anxieties of many older-stock Americans over urbanization, immigration, and "race suicide" during the Progressive Era led to the creation of a new definition of masculinity through the cult of team sports. By living Theodore Roosevelt's "strenuous life," modern man could allegedly combat the harmful effects of effete civilization. This antimodern reaction to the maturation of capitalism led many men to seek physical, intellectual, and moral strength through the cultivation of virile character. Although the Boy Scouts and adventure literature proved sufficient for some young men, team games such as baseball and football made character development a physical reality. Factors influencing the reception and retention of particular sports included equipment and facility expense, the ease or difficulty of creating playing surfaces, and competition with other forms of culture. However, because men regarded sport as a metaphor for modern life, the constructed set of attitudes toward a sport dictated the extent of its popularity. Scholars such as Steven Riess and Michael Oriard have documented well the allure of baseball and football, respectively, around the turn of the century.[74] The particular appeal of lacrosse is especially made clear when it is juxtaposed with these sports in terms of cultural values and temporal space. Although lacrosse shared values with the fall sport of football, it contrasted greatly with baseball, its late spring and early summer competitor.

During the late nineteenth century and the early twentieth century, football was primarily the preserve of the northeastern elite. Although the big-city press popularized the game nationally in terms of geography and social class, the upper class and upper middle class regarded football as their fall sporting activity. These Americans considered the game a reflection of corporate culture and scientific management and a tactical equivalent of war. Despite general consensus, competing views of football within these affluent sporting circles emerged. National sportswriter and lacrosse commentator Caspar Whitney presented an elite, old-family, anglophilic conception of football as an amateur game for gentlemen. Yale coach Walter Camp articulated a Yankee entrepreneurial notion of football as a hierarchical, pragmatic, competitive sport for the ruling class. Attitudes toward controversial issues such as violence and player death reflected differing worldviews of the aristocracy and the nouveaux riches. Although muscular Christians and gentleman sportsmen viewed rough play as a brutal, but requisite, part of instilling virile masculinity and gentlemanly stoicism, Social Darwinists and advocates of the new corporate managerial class saw violence as merely the consequence of scientific strategy and a necessary means to ensure the racial potency of the Anglo-Saxon elite. Lacrosse advocates agreed with many of these principles. By the 1920s the similarity of their ideologies helped to seal ties between many campus football and lacrosse teams, with crossover athletes even wearing the garb of both.

From openly professional leagues to sandlot teams across the country, baseball represented cultural impulses different from those of the elite, violent game of football. The national pastime owed much of its popularity to its tendency to "touch base" with Progressive Era themes that illuminated the nation's deep-rooted anxieties. Those who held a stake in baseball's economic success—mainly club owners and sportswriters—perpetuated widely held beliefs about baseball, some based in fact, others the product of popular folklore. To make baseball an important cultural device in the "search for order," baseball proponents created cultural myths to serve symbolic functions for a distended society. These doctrines included mythologies of agrarianism, an ideology that appropriated a Protestant work ethic from an arcadian past for the replication of rural Jeffersonian values in cities; social integration, which taught people from disparate origins a system of respectable behavior rooted in traditional values to encourage civic pride; and social democracy, which instilled the notion that baseball was open to all Americans regardless of race, class, ethnicity, or place of origin. Enthusiasts used these beliefs to promote character development and community pride, acculturate newcomers to the urban world, and idealize the social mobility ethic.

Like proponents of baseball and football, lacrosse supporters professed an ideology revealing the instrumental and symbolic functions they believed their game served. When enthusiasts in New York, New England, and Baltimore assessed lacrosse, they underscored a commitment to Victorian amateurism and the manly character-building qualities the sport allegedly inculcated. Although enthusiasts elsewhere certainly contributed to the formation of an American lacrosse ethos, the students, coaches, and alumni at Johns Hopkins hold special historical significance for their role in ensuring the prominence of lacrosse at the university, as well as its subsequent fame, fortune, and cultural leadership throughout the rest of the century. These advocates believed their game deserved to be as popular as baseball, but they selectively targeted future novices. Moreover, because American society regarded American Indians as savages who entertained white audiences in mass spectacles, lacrosse enthusiasts' public celebration of their game as native probably undermined any potential for multiclass support. After all, only well-to-do sportsmen felt secure enough about the alleged superiority of their race and class to associate themselves with Native Americans in any way.

Although lacrosse shared some basic mechanical characteristics with other team games, it differed greatly from baseball and football. A lacrosse team possessed five offensive players, five defensive players, and a center man, all covering the entire field, and a goal tender. Somewhat akin to basketball, lacrosse lacked the clearly distinguished player roles found in baseball and football. Lacrosse may have had different positions, but the variance in playing roles was hardly as pronounced as in other sports. According to Standard Oil's John R. Flannery, whose roles as "the father of lacrosse in the United States" was discussed in chapter 1, "Lacrosse is democratic. Every player has his innings all the time while the game is proceeding. . . . Wherever the ball goes the battle for it rages, and every man who can get to the spot can dig in and do his prettiest for his side."[75] Heralding lacrosse as the "King of the Field Games" in July 1911, Flannery praised the positional egalitarianism of the game. To lacrosse proponents, the distinctions between right fielder and third baseman or between defensive lineman and quarterback were far greater than those between first attackman and cover point. With the exception of the goal tender, every player—and hence, every gentleman—was an equal. Whereas the differing player roles of baseball and football reflected the job specialization of the Taylorized industrial workplace, lacrosse mirrored the homogeneous social class of men who professed expertise to earn a living. As "all-rounders" rather than specialists, they displayed their status as amateur sportsmen.

Proponents of team sports all championed the notion of character development. The elite Anglo-Saxon philosophy of amateurism embodied a belief that sport improved the moral integrity of the young. Proponents of amateurism argued that team sports taught boys and young men to be aggressive, hardworking individuals who functioned within a group environment according to accepted norms. The complexity and pace of team play also necessitated the development of crisis-conditioned thinking skills. Lacrosse men certainly agreed with these notions. Yet while baseball advocates openly accepted professionalism and commercialism alongside the values of Victorian sport, lacrosse coaches and players chose to adhere to the value of sport for sport's sake. The latter group believed lacrosse could teach men that the fairness learned on the field through competition was more valuable to everyday life than the brief feeling of success achieved upon victory. Furthermore, competition in a contact sport played by men armed with wooden sticks required self-control, a quality affluent sportsmen believed necessary to prevent the demise of their race and class. Because many lacrosse players enjoyed lengthy careers in business, law, and medicine, the irony of the values of their sport becomes clear when these values are placed against the backdrop of broader cultural anxieties. While a businessman had to emphasize success at any cost over "fairness," bodily self-control led to the ill-desired trend toward Anglo-Saxon "race suicide."

During the 1890s many collegians professed faith in the alleged amateurism of the ancient Greeks. Despite the widespread practice of professionalism in the ancient Greek Olympics, American and English athletes iconized a Hellenic culture that had called for balance between body and mind. Arguing that university athletics are as legitimate as formal education, the 1893 Johns Hopkins yearbook declared that leadership learned through sport increased one's status within the academic class. Eventually this experience could enable former student sportsmen to fulfill leadership roles in the city of Baltimore.[76] In June 1903 a member of the class of 1890 offered this simple advice to all lacrosse players at Johns Hopkins: "Play fast, play hard, play to win, but over and above all these PLAY FAIR."[77] At Hobart the student press also praised amateurism: "Let's have an ideal in sport. We want to win: but above all we want to be gentlemen. Let's make Hobart's hospitality and fair play a by-word. We encounter only gentlemen on the campus and we must meet them as gentlemen."[78] Surrounded by an increasingly bifurcated world, young men at Johns Hopkins, Hobart, and other colleges justified their advantageous social status by claiming to be hardworking, fair-minded "gentlemen." Ideally these men would go on to participate in the upper echelon of an economy where the fittest survived and prospered, while the unfit did not.

American lacrosse commentators from 1890 to the Great War usually pointed to the importance of the mental development to be gained through "science" and stick skills. Reflecting the middle-class emphasis on character and expertise, in June 1892 one Philadelphia-based periodical outlined the essence of modern lacrosse: "A fair and scientific style of play should be cultivated, confidence in one another encouraged, and *skill* substituted for *brute force*."[79] Labeling lacrosse "a game for gentlemen," in 1892 the *New York Times* claimed that the game developed arm, leg, and back muscles, but also fortified useful mental skills for public life: "A lacrosse man learns to be cool and collected, to take in the situations at a glance, and act with rapidity and precision during most exciting moments."[80] At Johns Hopkins proponents believed lacrosse required brains and hand-eye coordination skills rather than brawn and sheer body mass. In 1899 medical student and athlete William H. Maddren argued that "the man who carefully thinks over and *understands* each play is the man who in the end will be master of the game." Another student surmised that lacrosse required "the elements of endurance, keen judgment, quick eye and the peculiar ability of appreciating and solving complicated conditions."[81]

While contemporary baseball men called for an inclusive, public display of urban pride—in part to lessen class tensions and ethnic rivalries, prevent social radicalism, and reinforce the political status quo—lacrosse proponents chose to recruit support from a more exclusive population of university students and their affluent families. At Johns Hopkins, for example, intercollegiate lacrosse enthusiasts promoted the socialization of young men who would one day be part of Baltimore's ruling class by attacking student apathy, advocating "college spirit," binding alumni with undergraduates, inventing traditions, and promoting rough and socially exclusive sport.[82] They articulated the community, social, and health benefits of a lacrosse team. Student editors, coaches, and alumni at Johns Hopkins urged undergraduates to support organized sports teams. Regardless of whether they were athletes or eyewitnesses, they collectively argued, their patronage was a must. In April 1898, for instance, the campus *News-Letter* criticized the five-sixths of the student body who did not attend athletic events: "Let us be willing to make some sacrifice, to give up some other pleasure, for the sake of supporting our athletics."[83] Students should be willing to make sacrifices, without public recognition, that would generate pride in the university and, by default, the institution's social position within the city.

In their efforts to create a cohesive elite community through sport, enthusiasts often encountered students generally disinterested in athletics. Student indifference and the scornful editorials at Johns Hopkins showed that loyalty and mass campus support for the lacrosse team did not come easily or quickly. Lauding the Protestant work ethic, in January 1900 the *News-Letter* pleaded for participation by graduate and medical students, noting that "a lacrosse championship does not come to him who waits, but to him who works." Although apathy was derived from the lack of what student leaders generically termed "college spirit," they argued that the athletics program could reinvigorate the campus. In October 1900 one member of the campus community surmised that fervor for the school required both "college fun" and "college worship." The former "is the emblem of free, independent minds enjoying the fullest extent of straightforward, high-minded pleasures; it is the incentive and producer of those enjoyments which college life offers, and which no other branch of life affords," while the latter "implies willingness for self sacrifice, and readiness for the resolute denial of personal advantage if necessary to further the interests of college." According to this proponent of college spirit, everyone should accept the motto "My college, my class, and then myself." True "college spirit" could best be found in sports such as football and lacrosse. Athletes and spectators alike played important roles in developing these pseudo-religious qualities that could be retained throughout a man's life, well after graduation. According to the student press, "The practice of such college spirit will produce infinite pleasure in college and in after life, present tangible enjoyments, and future recollections."[84] Benefits to be derived from this invented tradition included access to advantageous social networks, a sense of attachment to the university long after graduation, and confidence in the quality of the education received in the face of competing graduates of older Ivy League schools in the North.

In May 1905 lackluster student support for Johns Hopkins athletics led the campus paper to call for the sale of $5 student passes to boost attendance. Not only did many faculty and students support the paper's plan, but Canadian-born student athlete turned professor Charles R. McInnes complained about poor attendance. As president of the Athletic Association in 1903 and 1904, H. W. Plaggemeyer concurred: "The absence of rooting at games this year has been a disgrace. When I was an undergrad, almost the entire undergraduate body used to turn out to every game, and when the contest was over march to the cage in long parade, following the bus containing the players." These calls for increased attendance complemented game accounts characterizing spectators as primarily classmates, parents, and girlfriends—not the general public. The student press also pointed to close player-spectator ties at a match between Johns Hopkins and Mount Washington: "Among the onlookers were many ladies, both relatives and friends of the players, and many a mother was there to witness the prowess of her Willie or Freddie or whatever the name might be." Although the *News-Letter* surmised that "the presence of so many ladies was a detriment to more systematic rooting," the student editors supported the presence of women: "Bring all the ladies you wish to the games; the more the merrier. We are always glad to welcome them; and besides it means greater gate receipts."[85] For a group of sportsmen who claimed to champion amateurism, they seemed particularly concerned about spectators and their entrance fees.

The periodic assault by athletics personnel and the student press on the undergraduate student body did not go unchecked. Some annoyed students hated the sanctimony and hypocrisy of the self-appointed apostles of lacrosse. In April 1907 Johns Hopkins senior Stanley M. Reynolds attacked student leaders who chastised undergraduates, yet failed to show up for contests themselves. For instance, Reynolds suggested that a lack of enthusiasm by student leaders at a Johns Hopkins–Harvard game equaled their obnoxious behavior. Apparently when everyone's attention was focused on the contest and its athletes, these leaders offered no vocal support. However, their demeanor changed at intermission: "Between the halves, to be sure, these pleaders for more spirit became very active,—promenading in a conspicuous manner about the stands, or dashing about the field with lacrosse sticks in a manner calculated to place them in prominence," Reynolds asserted. "Just as soon, however, as the referee's whistle consigned them to obscurity amid the 'undergraduate body,' they became at once inactive, setting effective example to a few freshmen whom they had gathered under their wings."[86] Troubled by pompous, fashionable leaders and indifferent undergraduates, lacrosse pioneers faced a tough struggle to make their game popular on campus. The student editors at Hobart College espoused similar attitudes toward student officials. Because the editors of the *Hobart Herald* believed that undergraduates were well suited to handle both schoolwork and athletics, they blamed not the students, but their so-called leaders: "In how many cases does a man think that when he has finally secured some office or other of leadership that his troubles are over, his position is secured."[87]

Meanwhile, alumni perpetuated traditions and established ties among themselves, students, and their alma mater. Emphasizing a need for amateur athletic social networks akin to campus fraternities, those who embraced lacrosse at Johns Hopkins called for a more socially oriented program that did not feature commercialism. These men attended athletic contests, offered funds for new facilities and resources, sponsored intraclass lacrosse contests, and made direct appeals to current students to live and play according to the code of amateurism. In May 1906, for instance, when the Johns Hopkins varsity traveled to Stevens, alumni living in New York City entertained the team at the New York A.C. Perceiving a great contrast between spirited alumni and apathetic undergraduates, one anonymous member of the varsity, calling himself "ONE-TWELFTH," appreciated the support of the New York alumni: "Certainly the Hopkins spirit is not extinct among the older men. That was shown at the dinner, when old and new Hopkins songs were sung, and toasts to the team drank."[88] Apparently alumni prized socio-occupational fraternities more than did undergraduates. As alumni, the Johns Hopkins lacrosse team of 1902 praised subsequent squads and emphasized the importance of maintaining championship-caliber play. At Johns Hopkins or elsewhere, such alumni efforts showed how concerned they were with the image of their university. Long after graduation, alumni wanted to be able to brag about their alma mater's athletic exploits.

Aside from making efforts to goad students to attend matches, advocates at Johns Hopkins exploited undergraduate feelings of guilt over failure to live up to the responsibility to uphold university tradition. They depicted the lacrosse team as a tangible expression of the distinct excellence of the university. One of the most important defenders of gentlemanly amateurism and university tradition at Johns Hopkins was attorney William C. Schmeisser. Born in 1880, he had graduated from Baltimore City College in 1899 and from the Johns Hopkins University in 1902. After leaving Johns Hopkins, he had clerked with a bank and then with a law firm. Schmeisser's playing career had lasted from 1900 through 1902, and he had played again in 1905 when he had attended Johns Hopkins as a graduate student in political economy. Upon graduation from Maryland Law School in 1907, Schmeisser had begun work as an attorney with Willis and Homer. Known to players affectionately as "Father Bill," he served without pay either as nominal head coach (1902–3, 1905–9, and 1923–25) or as coach emeritus for the next three decades, until his death in 1940.[89] Relying on yearbooks, daily newspapers, and oral testimony, Schmeisser published a history of lacrosse at Johns Hopkins in the student newspaper in the spring of 1909. Championship dinners in private homes led to the installation of annual lacrosse banquets and team meetings. To socialize players into the university's athletic brotherhood, Schmeisser taught newcomers the folklore, history, and philosophy of the team. At the annual banquet in May 1916, he spoke on the history of lacrosse at the university and on the origins of the school Hullabaloo yell, and he showed players his collection of souvenirs, player photographs, and newspaper clippings. During preseason meetings he stressed the importance of team play, "the Hopkins system," and learning the play-ing styles of teammates. From the scant attendance at matches, it is readily apparent that lacrosse advocates at campuses such as Johns Hopkins had a difficult time selling the game to students. However, the repetition and re-inforcement of traditions invented by Schmeisser and others spawned a loyal group of alumni who vehemently supported the team in subsequent decades.

Lacrosse partisans at Johns Hopkins did not ignore the potential of their game to bolster the image of their university. After all, by the time Schmeisser published his history of the game, the university was little more than three decades old. Athletics, however, could possibly lessen the gap be-tween Johns Hopkins and older, more prestigious institutions such as Har-vard and Yale. "The game advertises the University and gives it a certain form of prestige," the *News-Letter* proclaimed in June 1914, "just as a major league baseball team does a city."[90] The student editors applauded a new se-ries of posters depicting universities excelling in particular sports. Along with Harvard football, Yale baseball, Columbia rowing, and Princeton track, a novelty firm chose to highlight Johns Hopkins lacrosse. As a result, university officials were able to use the success of the lacrosse team as an advertising vehicle for the institution. Unlike professional baseball teams, the Johns Hopkins lacrosse team would not attract tens of thousands of ticket-purchasing middle-class and working-class spectators, but it would attract something more valuable: a well-to-do, homogenous cadre of college-bound young men who might otherwise have attended other pres-tigious universities out of state.

Part of the appeal of lacrosse was the potential for violence stemming from the use of the wooden lacrosse stick. One careless swing of the stick might result in broken teeth, a bloody gash, or a concussion. Lacrosse oc-casionally drew derision from coaches of other sports. Yale football coach Walter Camp recalled in 1899 that injuries sustained by lacrosse players had led him to refer to the lacrosse team as "the refuge for invalid athletes."[91] All of these injuries, however, could be seen as badges of masculine honor. Most players accepted the possibility of injury, but believed rough play did not necessitate poor sportsmanship. As the self-appointed champions of wholesome sport, the lacrosse community in Baltimore frequently voiced displeasure with the misbehavior of opponents. Under the sarcastic head-line "NICE, GENTLEMANLY GAME," in May 1900 the *Baltimore Sun* reported the outrage of Johns Hopkins students at spectators from the Stevens Institute: "Rough play has to be met at times, but such things as hissing at injured and bleeding men, as was done by the Stevens contingent last Saturday, together with bad language flung at the Hopkins players from the stands, [were] an unwelcome novelty."[92] In October 1914 at the tenth annual USILL convention in New York, the frequency of such accounts led league administrators to increase referees' authority to "keep the game free from unnecessary roughness."[93] Given the persistence of violent play in subsequent years, the new policy did not curb injuries. Regardless, lacrosse advocates idealized their sport's ability to develop character. After all, they presumed, only true gentlemen—at Johns Hopkins or anywhere else in the collegian world—could play a team sport with seemingly fatal weapons in hand. As long as they did not experience the conditions seen in Canada— having professional athletes who deliberately delivered violent blows— rough play was considered acceptable.

The rhetoric of fair play played a public role in the conduct of most every sport patronized by affluent enthusiasts, but on-the-field violence made the practice especially problematic. Most athletes from private clubs and colleges accepted rough play, but disagreed with the general public that lacrosse was a savage game. To observers outside the lacrosse community, player violence seemed deliberate. As in Canada, American advocates often associated the crudest and most brutal dimensions of their game with the Irish. These attitudes stemmed both from general Anglo attitudes toward Irish immigrants and from the reputation for rowdiness of the champion Shamrock L.C. of Montreal. In May 1901 the student press at Johns Hopkins published a fictitious dialogue between two Irishmen, "Mr. Dooley" and "Hennessy," the often-copied characters of Chicago political humorist and journalist Finley Peter Dunne. This native-born Irish American utilized his barkeep Dooley as an unrefined but wise spokesman of Chicago's Irish Sixth Ward who mocked affluent people and criticized politicians and businessmen. His thick brogue and simple speech gave away his indigent social origins, but he was an American patriot and sympathetic to the views of the native born.[94]

The Johns Hopkins student newspaper's version of Mr. Dooley gives the impression that Baltimore's lower-class Irish community was ignorant of lacrosse and the values associated with it. The dialogue between Hennessy and Dooley demonstrated that Johns Hopkins lacrosse men were primarily interested in cultivating the game among other college men and those prep-school students who were heading for university life—not among the white lower classes:

> "Well," said Mr. Dooley, "Oi've been radin about th' Lacrosse game."
>
> "The Lacrosse game, pwhat's thet?" interrupted Hennessy.
>
> "Thet's just pwhat Oi asked Hogan's bye th' ither day whin he came in with his face all br-ruised up, an he sed 'it's lacr-rosse Oi've bin playin,' ses he 'an wan iv th' la-ads str-ruck me over th' head with a stick.' Oi hope ye lathered wan with your shillalah me bye, ses Oi. 'Ye don't understand' ses he, "twas in the game an it didn't mather f'r Oi kep th' ball an' our team wan. Would ye loike t' see the game Mr. Dooley?' Thet Oi would ses Oi. So Hagan's bye br-rought me a thicket an' Oi win t'see th' game."[95]

This fictional conversation suggests that collegians at Johns Hopkins regarded the rough play and violence inherent in lacrosse as incidental. To the working class of Baltimore, represented by poorly educated and thus poorly assimilated Irish Americans who still spoke the brogue, violence was paramount to any interest in the game. This cultural gap would sufficiently guarantee the elite's desire for social division. Conversely, perhaps the dissenters on the editorial staff at Johns Hopkins wished to attack the perceived barbarism of lacrosse by utilizing well-known, respected, but non-Anglo voices.

While the game was still in its infancy, lacrosse partisans at the Johns Hopkins University helped to construct a body of cultural values for their springtime game of choice that contrasted significantly with the values of the national pastime, baseball. By fighting student apathy, inventing traditions, cultivating alumni-undergraduate ties, and promoting character development through rough amateur sport, these enthusiasts provided a cohesive ideology for the American lacrosse community that served as the basis for future growth. While baseball supporters across the nation targeted the larger urban community in their own campaigns for a grandiose "search for order," the apostles of lacrosse focused on refining an elite class of young men. Baseball was not immune to the effects of nativism, Jim Crow legislation, or Sunday blue laws, but the most vociferous defenders of the national pastime called for a socially integrated and democratic society. Although baseball did not always practice what it preached, lacrosse men made no apologies for their own hypocrisies. Despite numerous pleas for greater popularization, lacrosse was essentially a game for the affluent. In future decades the Johns Hopkins approach to lacrosse would serve as an ideal for the rest of the intercollegiate world.

"The Most Romantic of Pagans": American Gentlemen and the Noble Savage

Although the ethos of football was similar to that of lacrosse in that it possessed both rough and socially exclusive qualities, lacrosse men differed from football fans in their historical conception of their game. While football proponents occasionally portrayed their game as a modern version of an ancient Roman blood spectacle, their sport lacked a coherent American past that allowed them to link it with the present. In other words, football was very much viewed as a product of the modern capitalist world. Despite the many cultural values lacrosse and football advocates shared, the sense of historical longevity that lacrosse men attached to their game was more similar to that of baseball. Somewhat akin to baseball's emphasis on its mythological origins in an idyllic agrarian republic, the rhetoric of lacrosse included images of a remote, noble, Indian past. Many baseball proponents believed the pastoral connotations of their game enriched American life by encouraging the country to identify with its rural Jeffersonian roots. With lingering anxieties over the closing of the frontier, the aftermath of the Populist revolt, the migrant adjustment to urban life, and the great inflow of new immigrants from Europe, many older-stock Americans brought order to cities through the imposition of agrarian values analogous to those professed by the City Beautiful Movement. In 1907 a blue-ribbon panel of prominent Americans proclaimed that baseball was an indigenous game, the creation of West Point cadet Abner Doubleday at Cooperstown, New York, in 1839. Politicians attached patriotic overtones to baseball, and President William Howard Taft even inaugurated the tradition of throwing out the first pitch on Opening Day of the season.

Unfortunately for baseball proponents, some assumptions about the game's origins were inaccurate. Baseball was not an indigenous game; it had actually been derived from an English game for girls called rounders. Baseball had not been invented by Doubleday in rural Cooperstown; it had been modernized by Alexander Cartwright's aristocratic New York Knickerbocker club. Baseball was not a game that had originally been played and dominated by American farm boys; rather, it was a city game that had been played by urban gentlemen. Regardless, this agrarian myth played a large role in shaping the baseball ethos. By constructing playing facilities with names that had pastoral connotations, such as Ebbets Field, Shibe Park, and the Polo Grounds, many Americans were induced to believe that these "green oases" allowed spectators from the urban deserts of America to escape temporarily from the modern world back to the nation's agrarian past. In contrast to the proponents of baseball, who saw it as a game rooted in the cultural values of agrarian Jeffersonianism, elite lacrosse advocates openly acknowledged what they perceived to be the nobility of the Native American origins of their sport.

In contrast to the largely inaccurate understanding of baseball's origins, some lacrosse enthusiasts possessed remarkably authentic knowledge of traditional Indian ball games. However, while they celebrated and romanticized the "noble savage," they usually did not glorify the game as played by Indians before the era of George Beers. In April 1894 *Harper's* sportswriter and patron of gentlemanly football Caspar Whitney not only implored American amateur athletes to adopt lacrosse, but recounted for readers the Indian origins of the game. Relying on the writings of missionaries, anthropologists, and Canadian nationalists, Whitney apologetically pointed to the early history of native contact with whites and its impact upon lacrosse: "We are obliged to accept the very little actually known of the game's early history, bearing in mind that the relations of Indians and the early white settlers were rather of a bellicose than a sporting nature, and our forefathers more likely to be familiar with the weapons of the Indians than with their instruments of recreation."[96]

Taking into account cultural distortions, we can see that much of Whitney's portrait of the traditional Indian ball game, including various tribal names for the game, team and field sizes, scoring rules, contest occasions, prematch rituals, player dress and behavior, and stick and ball characteristics, is fairly accurate when assessed against late twentieth-century scholarship by anthropologists. It appears especially accurate when laid next to the history of baseball. Passionate followers of lacrosse employed racist and romantic imagery, but still possessed a more accurate body of knowledge about the origins of their sport than did their baseball counterparts. However, by reading Victorian amateurism into the Indian past, Whitney overemphasized the physical features of native men at the expense of the spiritual dimension of ball play: "Differing from the games of the ancients, lacrosse of the Indians was not of a religious nature, nor had it any con-

With his 1837 "Indian Gallery," George Catlin
provided white patrons of the arts with several paintings of traditional Native American
ball games from the southeastern "Five Civilized Tribes." These games survived the effects
of European colonization and American westward expansion, though in altered form. By
the mid-nineteenth century the games were
still serving as a rite of passage to manhood.
(Smithsonian Institution.)

By the 1880s members of white "gentlemen's" clubs were playing lacrosse in many eastern cities of Canada and the United States. The largest lacrosse communities were in Montreal, Toronto, and New York. Idealistic organizers worried that athletes were taking each contest too seriously and playing too roughly. Crowds grew from a few hundred to a few thousand. (*Harper's Weekly*, May 10, 1884. Courtesy Henry H. Stansbury and U.S. Lacrosse.)

Sportsmen on both sides of the Canadian-
American border witnessed the transformation of lacrosse from a "gentleman's game" to
a commercial sport. Clubs routinely resorted
to making covert payments to their players.
(*Harper's Weekly*, August 21, 1886. Courtesy
Henry H. Stansbury and U.S. Lacrosse.)

The young men of Baltimore who played as
the Druid Lacrosse Club in 1890 lost a championship match against the Staten Island Athletic Club. The Druids' relaxed poses in this
photo, typical of those seen in team portraits
for other sports in the late nineteenth century,
eventually gave way to more rigid stances because of the perceived need to appear more
masculine and a desire to project a more
structured image. (U.S. Lacrosse.)

The "noble savage" loomed large in the minds of lacrosse enthusiasts. In this 1892 illustration from the Johns Hopkins University yearbook, a noble female Indian passes a wreath to a young white athlete as a symbol of cultural authority. Collegians were expected to play the rough, manly sport and accept injuries as badges of honor. (Johns Hopkins University *Hullabaloo*, 1892.)

By the early twentieth century, many affluent sportsmen in Baltimore had begun to view lacrosse as a vital part of the spring calendar. Victories by the Johns Hopkins lacrosse team filled alumni with particular pride, as this yearbook poem illustrates. (Johns Hopkins University *Hullabaloo*, 1903.)

BALTIMORE

On stirring football days,
    You give the Princeton cheer;
While rowing is the craze,
    A Yale girl you appear;
And for lacrosse you find it pays
    To hold the Hopkins dear.

Still, your inconstancy
    Leaves us no whit depressed;
For, in our victory,
    When we're approved the best
By smiling eyes like those—then we
    But pity all the rest.

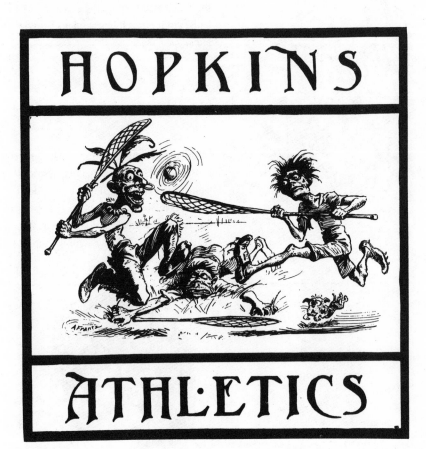

Sometimes enthusiasts emphasized the savage nature of the game rather than its noble qualities. In order to excel on the field, athletes at Johns Hopkins and Ivy League campuses learned the spirit of lacrosse from their encounters with Indian reservation teams from Onondaga, Saint Regis, and Caughnawaga. (Johns Hopkins University *Hullabaloo*, 1904.)

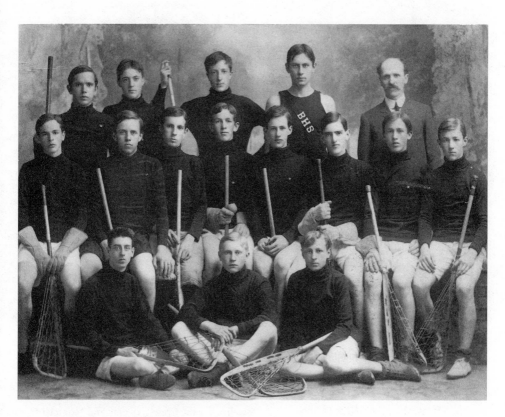

American universities and private clubs created a system to feed talent to themselves by
promoting lacrosse in nearby secondary
schools. Like Boys' High School in Brooklyn,
whose 1905 team is pictured here, many
schools in greater New York City were encouraged by the Crescent Athletic Club. (U.S.
Lacrosse.)

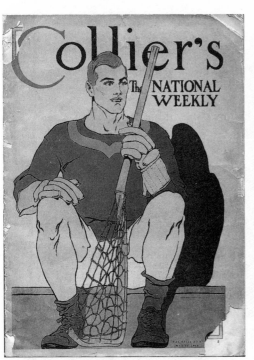

National magazines were not oblivious to the increasing popularity of lacrosse on university campuses. *Collier's* produced this cover portrait for its May 15, 1909, issue. (U.S. Lacrosse.)

Many collegiate players continued their athletic careers well after graduation. Norris Barnard played for Swarthmore College, as well as for the Crescent, Penn, and Montclair Athletic Clubs. This photograph, taken in 1919, shows the typical equipment of a goal tender. (U.S. Lacrosse.)

During the 1920s and 1930s the Mount Washington Lacrosse Club of Baltimore usually dominated collegiate and club competition. This 1926 club included mostly alumni from Johns Hopkins and other nearby universities. (U.S. Lacrosse.)

Oxford and Cambridge Universities maintained close ties with organized lacrosse in the United States during the Roaring Twenties and the early years of the Great Depression. While the Britons reinforced the value of sport for sport's sake during their U.S. visits, many North American Rhodes scholars actually played on teams for these prestigious institutions. Pictured above is the 1922 Oxford and Cambridge tour team, along with Syracuse University coach Laurie Cox (*insert, number 10*). (*Official Lacrosse Guide 1922–1923.*)

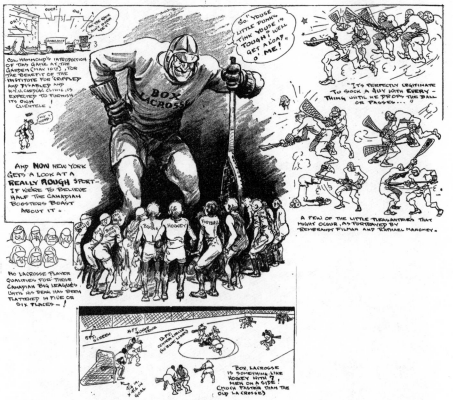

Lacrosse traditionalists in Baltimore and Syracuse feared the introduction of "box" lacrosse by professional hockey promoters during the summer of 1932. This new Canadian game was played either in enclosed fields on baseball diamonds or in indoor arenas during the summer. Professor Laurie Cox of Syracuse University encouraged other coaches to remain loyal to the outdoor field game. Meanwhile, organizations in Quebec, Ontario, and British Columbia all voted to endorse "boxla." As this cartoon indicates, spectators would soon learn that "it's perfectly legitimate to sock a guy with everything until he drops the ball or passes." (U.S. Lacrosse.)

TOP: The Squamish Indians of British Columbia presented the U.S. lacrosse team with a miniature totem pole during their visit to Vancouver for the Lally Cup series of 1935. The Squamish lacrosse club usually played as the North Shore Indians. (U.S. Lacrosse.)

BOTTOM: American women's lacrosse resulted from the efforts of physical education instructors trained in England. During the 1930s the United States Women's Lacrosse Association exchanged tour teams with the British ladies' community. The American tour of Great Britain in 1935 emphasized genteel play and friendly social relations. (Helen Wheeler scrapbook, U.S. Lacrosse.)

During the Great Depression some Native Americans escaped austere conditions on reservations by playing semiprofessionally for box lacrosse clubs in Canada, New York, and California. This 1935 Rochester Iroquois squad featured Harry Smith (*top row, third from right*). His speed in white sneakers led him to take the name Jay Silverheels. After comedian Joe E. Brown convinced him to turn to acting during a trip to California, he landed the part of Tonto on TV's *The Lone Ranger*. (U.S. Lacrosse.)

During the 1940s and 1950s box lacrosse clubs
such as the Hamilton Tigers of the Ontario
Lacrosse Association featured both native and
white players. The winner played against the
Inter-City Lacrosse League champion from
British Columbia in the Mann Cup competi-
tion for the national championship of
Canada. (Ontario Lacrosse Association Hall
of Fame, Saint Catharines Museum, Saint
Catharines, Ontario.)

nection with superstitious rites in worship of the Great Spirit. It was decidedly a sport from first to last, and one in which the impetuosity and vigor of a wild nature were let loose. It developed nature's athletes in the highest degree, and gave young warriors a hardy lesson in close and vigorous combat."[97]

Elite celebration of the noble qualities of the game was consistent with more general attitudes toward Indians by affluent Americans living in the urban East. During the late nineteenth century, many well-to-do older-stock American families called for humanitarian and paternalistic treatment of the American Indian population. Concerned with the "vanishing" tribes of the Great Plains and the Southwest, they established organizations such as the Indian Rights Association and gathered at conferences such as the one at Lake Mohonk in New York's Catskill Mountains. With the founding of off-reservation schools like the one at Carlisle in 1879 and the passage of the Dawes General Allotment Act of 1887, these East Coast paternalists believed they secured the future health of Indians and their assimilation into American society. While the entertainment industry pandered to lower-class hatred of Indians and other Americans living in the West called for extermination, the eastern elite expressed what it believed to be a legitimate concern for native peoples. Conceptualizing "the Indian" and his game of lacrosse within the context of progressivism and social evolutionism, these aristocratic Americans viewed him as a creature in need of civilization. Even though lacrosse enthusiasts convinced themselves of their own social and racial superiority, they celebrated the noble qualities of an early American Indian past.

For many thoughtful supporters, elite adoption of a native ball game was justified by affluent white men's successful transformation of the old Indian game into a modern sport by refining the rough play inherent in the game. To complete the link between tribal ball games and modern lacrosse, sportswriters felt obligated to explain this transformation to readers. Connecting contemporary white athletes with the positive qualities of the "noble savage," in May 1905 H. V. Blaxter declared lacrosse "a real American game, indigenous to the home of the copper colored homo americanus" in *Outing* magazine. Blaxter saw a close relationship between the traditional and modern versions of lacrosse: "It is shorn of the glamour of its former settings of savagery, paint and the wilderness; but, however tamed, it still gives opportunity for the skill, trickery and agility that made the redman the most romantic of pagans."[98] Some sportswriters claimed that earlier generations of Native Americans had even shared their game with white men. In a magazine serial on the origins of modern sports that appeared in May 1910, Arthur B. Reeve alleged that when "the Indians became civilized and came to town they brought the game with them and the whites were not slow to take it up."[99]

Commentators offered many views on the utility of lacrosse. Gentleman advocates of the "old Indian game" frequently commended the high degree of "scientific individual play" they perceived to be part of their game and credited Indians as its founding fathers. According to one City College of New York alumnus, writing in 1901, the Indians had cleverly invented a game that developed "muscular prowess, speed, agility, dexterity," and "quick mental perception."[100] Like so many lacrosse devotees, William Harvey Maddren of Johns Hopkins emphasized the transition from tradition to modernity within the context of social evolutionism. Pointing to the eclipse of the Indian in Canadian lacrosse, Maddren wrote in 1904 that "before many years had elapsed, his place as a player became less secure, and he was destined to see his pupils not only equal but far exceed his own ability."[101] According to Harvard coach Paul Gustafson, writing in 1914, "Lacrosse is a game for which we are indebted to the Indians, primarily, and to the Canadians, who have revised the play and formed a code of playing rules."[102] In an account of the history of the game at Syracuse University that was published in April 1918, the local student press declared that "the ancient game of the aboriginal American Indians" was "more entitled to the name of the national American game than baseball."[103] Essentially, all of these men thanked Native Americans for providing white men of affluence with a rough game that reinvigorated them at a time when many men were suffering from a crisis of masculinity. It was the white men's game now, and they had no intention of giving it back.

While most enthusiasts believed lacrosse possessed inherent practical values, a few believed this element of native culture could help bring about Anglo-Saxon unity for the ruling classes in North America. Cyrus Miller, a member of the Crescent A.C. and president of the Inter-University Lacrosse League from 1900 to 1902, looked back on the continent's remote native past and viewed the future of the game with optimism: "When the United States and Canada are united, Lacrosse may well claim to be the national game of the Union; for long before the earliest white pioneers and voyageurs in

North America, the game of baggataway, which afterwards became lacrosse, was played by the Indian tribes in widely scattered parts of the northern continent of America." Espousing views consistent with scientific management and progressivism, Miller stressed the importance of modernity: "With the elimination of old methods of play, the white man has introduced team play and science into the game, so that now it is recognized that no team of individual players, no matter how skilful [*sic*], can beat a team of merely good players who have fine team organization."[104] The use of lacrosse to symbolize a future potentially united republic in North America seems fanciful, but plausible from the perspective of the social elite. Moreover, unlike baseball fans, lacrosse advocates made little pretense of trying to recruit new adherents from all rungs of the American urban social order. While baseball supporters assumed that the national pastime promoted community pride and acculturated newcomers to national values, lacrosse enthusiasts believed their sport unified the sons of affluent families in their university settings by teaching them an elite value system that cut across national boundaries among anglophone countries. In 1910, for example, league president Charles E. Marsters praised lacrosse: "Many a good game has come over the Anglo-American borders for which we are debtors to the affection for clean, manly sport manifested by our English cousins at home and abroad."[105]

Elite promotion of lacrosse as the game of the "noble savage" probably guaranteed that the lacrosse community that would remain restricted to the eastern elite for the foreseeable future. But such a consequence easily suited those who supported collegian and club lacrosse. With the perceived close of the frontier in 1890, mainstream white society still regarded native people and their culture as both archaic and irrelevant to the future of their imperial republic. Some well-to-do sportsmen may have found no problem with adopting the game of the so-called primitive red man, but the general public perceived Indians as living far away on federal reservations or as sources of entertainment in pulp fiction and Wild West shows. Because during the years surrounding the turn of the century most white people regarded Indian culture as obsolete and native peoples as on the verge of extinction, it made little sense to them for the country's youth to play an Indian game when baseball offered patriotic nationalism, social mobility, and urban pride.

The lacrosse community's knowledge and appreciation of the Native American origins of the game was confined to the eastern elite, but such views also reflected paternalistic white dominance both on and off the field. Confident of their social superiority and unthreatened by "the Indian," white lacrosse advocates accepted him as a fellow human being, so long as he knew his place. Some supporters even reified their conception of the "noble savage." For example, Colonel Robert M. Thompson, president of the New York A.C., supported the Public Schools Athletic League in New York City by donating a thirty-inch-tall silver and bronze trophy topped by "an American Indian, seated on a rock, shielding his eyes with his left hand and holding a lacrosse stick across his lap." The figure rested on a silver base covered with arrow heads, "raised bludgeons," and "scalp braids."[106] Thanks to Thompson, New York teams could contend against one another for possession of a physical representation of the stoic noble savage. Gentleman sportsmen believed they could learn from fictional Indians, but the lessons should be made to conform to the ideology of modern progressivism. They essentially turned to the distant past of their adopted game to validate their invented tradition, continuity between the graduating classes, and the permanency of their institutions. By fusing gentlemanly amateurism with the indigenous game of the Indian, these elite athletes from New England to Maryland provided themselves with a useful yardstick for measuring their manhood and respectability. They would certainly need it, as they would be tested briefly by the fires of the Great War raging in Europe.

Reservations and Boarding Schools: Indian Lacrosse during the Age of Progressivism

With romantic conceptions of ancient Indians dancing in their minds, collegian and club sportsmen engaged in lacrosse competition not only among themselves, but with real flesh-and-blood Native American athletes. By the turn of the century, most native peoples were coping with the immediate consequences of the reservation system and the long-term influence of the European conquest of North America. Fighting poverty, disease, federal assimilation policies, and land encroachment in the United States and Canada, native peoples faced great difficulties in sustaining life, let alone their traditions. Meanwhile, the outside white man's world was experiencing industrialization, urbanization, overseas immigration, and internal migration to cities from rural areas. In their "search for order," corporations and middle-class interest groups introduced a "progressive" reform movement to instill some semblance of a rationalized society. Even though white men had organized and subsequently controlled modern lacrosse, native peoples played a variety of ball games during this so-called Progressive Era. These included both traditional ball games and modern lacrosse. Indians from many different tribes—but especially those living on Iroquois reservations in New York, Ontario, and Quebec—participated with and against clubs in Canada and occasionally competed against intercollegiate teams in the United States during the early decades of the century. Ironically, another impetus for play came from the creation of a modern lacrosse program at the Carlisle Indian Industrial School, which reenergized lacrosse throughout Iroquoia.

The interplay of white "scientific" lacrosse with the traditional ball game reflected many of the political anxieties, economic pressures, and cultural and social relations between Native Americans and the surrounding white society. The state of native lacrosse during the first two decades of the twentieth century illustrates many of the tensions between "modernity" and "tradition" as understood by all enthusiasts, native and non-native alike. Attempting to extend the line of their cultural continuity with Native Americans of centuries past, many Indian tribes played recreational forms of their traditional ball game. These modern versions of the ancient game lacked the religious, economic, and military purposes the game had served prior to dominance by European colonizers. However, they expressed a cultural value system that preserved a confrontational, manly form of individualism and the maintenance of symbolic ties with a native past untainted by outsiders. Though circumscribed by European languages, Christian religious beliefs, a market-oriented laissez faire economy, private property ownership, and a republican political system, many tribes persevered with their ball games, using playing styles that reflected a native sporting ethos that was distinct from the socially elite principles of scientific play and amateur sport. With the exception of Native Americans working at construction sites, serving in the military, acting in Wild West shows, or living in urban ghettos, white-Indian relations remained limited. During the Progressive Era the modern lacrosse field provided a setting for contact between reservation Indians and the socially elite sportsmen of eastern universities and athletic clubs. Many reservation communities continued to play traditional ball games, but wished to field teams against white opponents. By scheduling matches against universities and private clubs, they were simply making an effort to play the best competition. However irregular white-Indian matches may have been, they served as a cultural arena in which more than a game was at stake. Mirroring white-Indian political conflicts over tracts of land, these encounters gave natives a chance to assert their authority over the spiritual property of their ancestors. They also gave white athletes an opportunity to play against real-life "noble savages." For the white man the contested ground of the lacrosse field may have been the site of gentlemanly sport, but for the Indian it furnished an opportunity to prevent total racial subordination.

Following in the footsteps of the Caughnawaga and Saint Regis teams that had toured New York City and Boston during the 1870s and 1880s, several Iroquois nations competed in modern lacrosse matches against colleges and clubs. For example, a team from the Six Nations Reserve traveled to Staten Island in late May 1900. Despite losing to the Stevens Institute at the Saint George Cricket Grounds, these Native Americans recognized and capitalized on white fascination with Indians by accentuating showmanship. According to the Brooklyn press, the Indians, dressed in "yellow knickerbockers and jackets, trimmed with fringe, made a very picturesque appearance. All were girted with broad blue belts. Their chief, John A. Gibson, who is an old man and nearly blind, wore a handsome headdress of feathers."[107] At the Pan-American Exposition held in Buffalo in 1901, two native teams—the Senecas of the Cattaraugus Reservation and the Seneca Pagans of the Akron Reservation—joined with the Toronto L.C., the Capitols of Ottawa, the Crescent A.C., and the Rochester Rangers for an international and cross-cultural tournament.[108] Three years later, at the 1904 Olympics in Saint Louis, the Mohawk Indians from the Six Nations Reserve won the bronze medal as a team representing Canada. The other Canadian entrant, the Shamrock L.C. of Winnipeg, won the gold, and the Saint Louis Amateur Athletic Association took the silver for the United States. A club of Seneca Indians also visited the grounds of the Crescent A.C. in Brooklyn in May of 1905. Although the Brooklyn Daily Eagle commended the ability of the Seneca team, it politely emphasized the supremacy of the local gentlemen in the Crescents' 9–2 victory: "'Lo the poor Indian' journeyed to Bay Ridge yesterday to meet the paleface champions in the picturesque game of his ancestors. He came, he saw, but he did not conquer, for the Crescent lacrosse players were his superiors in every department of the game."[109]

Blending the language of noble savagery with that of Social Darwinism and an ancient Roman saying, the press offered both praise and pity to the native sportsmen.

Just as it seems plausible to suggest that white teams desired to play Indian teams in the 1870s and 1880s because of the perceived alien qualities of the latter, native teams made a conscious effort to participate in the white lacrosse community for their own reasons. These reasons included pride, money, competition, and the opportunity to travel beyond the confines of the reservations. In April 1900 the student manager of the Johns Hopkins team received correspondence from the manager of a team of "genuine" Indians from the West who wished to include Baltimore in a proposed eastern tour. According to the student press, the Indian representative "also quoted the gate receipts taken in at former games where the Indians had played against Eastern college men. Such a game would be quite novel, and should create great interest."[110] The Johns Hopkins manager expressed skepticism, but the *Baltimore Sun* was more receptive: "If they are bona fide Indians no doubt it would be a lucrative scheme to meet them on the lacrosse field, but there is also a stern possibility that Hopkins would get all that was 'coming to it' and something more if it crossed sticks with a crowd of real Comanches or Sioux fresh from plain or reservation."[111] The manager of the Indians said his team could demonstrate a Ghost Dance after the game. The latter offer was ironic, considering that the U.S. Army's fears of the Ghost Dance had resulted in their killing of Sioux Indians at Wounded Knee in 1893. By offering glimpses of a recently "closed" frontier, this Indian lacrosse team might reinforce elite images of the noble savage. Regardless, the match apparently did not take place.

In Geneva, Hobart College played no fewer than ten contests against reservation teams between 1900 and 1912 and sometimes played against a Syracuse L.C. featuring Indian athletes. After Hobart had dropped two matches to the Six Nations team from Ontario in 1900, the student press reported that the Indians had "put up a good article of ball and in spite of their war clothes were very good natured." Aside from depicting cross-cultural contests as pitting the Indian body against the white mind, many press reports tapped into white notions of both noble and ignoble savagery. Commenting on a match between Hobart and the Seneca Indians in 1903, student editors said, "It was the strength and the speed of the forest against the brain of the white man." Suggesting that the Hobart athletes had been consumed with racial fears, the *Hobart Herald* reported that the hard-fought game had resulted in a tie:

> It was nip and tuck all the way through. Frierson scored the first goal for the pale faces, followed in quick succession by the arrow-like drive of an Indian. At times the strife waxed warm. The quick blood of the red skins would resent fiercely an accidental encounter with a Hobart crosse. It was a pretty exhibition to behold. Doup again drove the rubber by the corpulent body of Chief Cornplanter the Indian goal keeper, whose activity, considering his size, was marvelous. Soon another dark skinned warrior got one by Ellis. The score was tie. Now it was a battle royal. Each side was determined to win. Maddigan after a neat pass from Doup whirled the ball under the bar making the last score of the game for Hobart. The Indians seemed to get new life as Capt. Jamison gave the war cry. Again Hobart's goal was invaded. The Indians seemed continually to do better but failed to secure another before time was called.

In commenting on Hobart's tie match with the Tonawanda band of Seneca from the Akron reservation in late April 1911, the *Herald* referred to the Indians as "lusty" and as "the descendants of Hiawatha and Minnehaha." About a year later, when Hobart trounced Akron, 7–0, the student press declared, "A tribe of Red Skins, armed with war-whoops, lacrosse sticks, and an abundance of nerve and skill, sallied forth in full war paint to take by storm the camp of Mr. Hobart's paleface warriors."[112]

Hobart players apparently highly valued their matches with Indians. They sometimes guaranteed larger payments to the Indians than to intercollegiate teams traveling similar distances. This policy made little economic sense, because the Indian contests were fairly expensive when compared to matches with Ivy League squads that drew bigger crowds. For three of Hobart's four home matches in 1903—against Cornell, Toronto, and the Seneca Indians—gate receipts totaled roughly $30 each. However, Hobart guaranteed a payment of $50 to the Seneca Indians, but only $30 to Toronto and $20 to Cornell. For the popular Harvard match, Hobart guaranteed a payment of $60, but raked in $133.25 in receipts. The following season, Hobart made adjustments for its five home games and took no financial loss on any contest. For the least profitable match of the spring, Hobart paid the Onondaga Indians $44.41, but gate receipts totaled $44.70. The 1906 campaign produced much the same financial rewards. Playing eight of its eleven matches at home, Hobart attracted its largest crowds for contests against the Buffalo L.C., Cornell, and Toronto. Aside from the Rochester L.C., the Seneca and Onondaga Indians drew the smallest gatherings, but the Hobart men still agreed to guarantee payments exceeding gate receipts. Spectators at Geneva essentially preferred to watch Hobart play Ivy Leaguers than Indians. Assuming that many Hobart fans were consistent game-to-game supporters, anywhere from half to three quarters of the spectators who witnessed matches against Harvard and Cornell did not bother to attend games featuring reservation teams.[113] Despite this lukewarm interest in Indians of Hobart spectators, the college's players valued competition with natives. The team's willingness to guarantee payments to opponents who would not even draw a large enough crowd to allow the school to break even indicates the Hobart men's attraction for the Indians. No doubt fascinated with what they regarded as the physical prowess of Iroquois athletes, the Geneva collegians placed a premium on direct contact with Indian players. Undergraduates marveled at Indians' stick-handling skills, and they believed they might learn something from the noble "vanishing Indians." Regardless of whether they won or lost, perhaps the students' sense of the racial otherness they encountered helped reinforce their notions of social and racial superiority.

College lacrosse teams certainly valued Indian competition, but Indians were often the ones who initiated contest negotiations. For example, a Seneca team from Cattaraugus unsuccessfully attempted to schedule a match with Johns Hopkins in 1915. The student press printed a letter from Chief Edward Cornplanter.[114] Cornplanter made three important points. First, he said, "We play clean fair" seeking with these words to put the Johns Hopkins student manager at ease by dispelling any myth of Indian savagery. The university men should not fear the Indians, he suggested, but should expect them to play as would any team of collegians. By 1915 the experience of playing matches against white teams had led many natives to grasp white racial fears. In other words, Cornplanter was consciously answering any questions arising from his potential host's preconceptions. Second, the chief acknowledged that his squad would not or could not make the journey south without Johns Hopkins funds. He differentiated "garrantee money [sic]" from "exspenses return transpation [sic]," which probably demonstrates that the Seneca were seeking to benefit financially from the excursion, because the gate receipt guarantee would supplement traveling expenses. Moreover, Cornplanter indicated that the Indians wished to make "only once trip," perhaps playing other matches in Maryland and Pennsylvania. By doing this the Seneca would profit from several encounters in one region. Third, he said, "I like to meet every team in this city & others," possibly expressing a sincere effort to introduce his Seneca squad and white teams to one another. Elite white collegians and reservation Indians lived in different worlds, but shared a common love for lacrosse. Besides, not only were many natives curious about the world beyond the reservation, but a victory over a white team might serve as an important cultural triumph, a way to preserve something uniquely native. Although a Hopkins-Seneca match never took place that particular season, Cornplanter's letter helps illuminate Indian motives.

The willingness of native teams to travel sometimes hundreds of miles to play matches against collegians and club sportsmen indicates the seriousness with which they approached the sport. However, because the host universities or clubs agreed to pay the Indians' expenses, we know that the relationship was reciprocal. Although there was a potential for tumult resulting from clashing wooden sticks, Indian-white contests did not result in excessive violence. As a setting for infrequent contact between the sons of the eastern elite and reservation-bound Indians, the modern lacrosse field was the only place a Native American could deliver a jarring body check or swing a wooden stick near a white man's head without fear of a general melee. After all, native and non-native players alike accepted physical contact as part of the game, injuries as badges of honor. For the brief time allotted during a game, Iroquois Indians asserted their authority over the sport derived from their ancestors. In the end, however, white teams' guarantee payments and the infrequency of play indicated that although the organized lacrosse community accepted Native Americans as fellow sportsmen, it relegated them to the periphery. After all, native teams did not and could not compete for national championships in the United States. The rank and file of white society may have demonized the American Indian, but lacrosse men tolerated him so long as the he knew his inferior status.

Besides continuing to engage in contests with white lacrosse teams during the Progressive Era, many Indian reservation communities perpetuated their traditional stick-and-ball games. Although it is impossible to know the degree to which these games resembled those played before contact with European colonizers, they nonetheless survived. Fortunately, aside from the tribal oral tradition, contemporary advocates of organized modern lacrosse provided commentary on older forms of the native ball game. According to one contributor to the lacrosse guide issued annually as part of Spalding's Athletic Library, in 1913 "the more civilized tribes" of New York state and the Northeast played a version of lacrosse similar to the intercollegiate game. Meanwhile, a more traditional form of ball game survived in the Midwest. "Among the Menominee Indians of Wisconsin, for instance, the game played to-day is practically the same as the game played by the early aborigines," the guide asserted.[115] This descendent of the Great Lakes ball game was played on an unmarked field approximately 250 yards long, with a single ten-foot pole serving as the goal for each of two evenly matched teams of up to one hundred players who were playing with three- to four-foot-long sticks.[116] Obviously, though, the old ball game was surely affected by all the important economic, political, cultural, and religious challenges posed by the non-native world.

Besides the Great Lakes game, early twentieth-century forms of the old two-stick southeastern game survived on reservations of the former Five Civilized Tribes in North Carolina, Mississippi, and Oklahoma. Anthropologists such as Raymond Fogelson and Kendall Blanchard have documented the persistence of modern forms of the traditional ball games among the Cherokee and Choctaw, respectively. For example, the Mississippi Choctaw played their stickball game, *toli*, until baseball supplanted it during the 1930s.[117] The southeastern game also survived among displaced tribes in Oklahoma. At a 1935 intercollegiate lacrosse meeting, former Carlisle lacrosse and football player Gus Welch said he had witnessed "old style lacrosse" and showed coaches the sticks used by these western natives. According to the official lacrosse guide, this traditional ball game featured hundreds of participants. The young and the quick played attack, and the elder and the heavier played defense on a field stretching miles. At each end were two goal markers painted yellow, red, and black. Obviously the Spanish introduction of the horse to the Americas affected this traditional game, but these natives did not use a clock: "A dozen or more of the older Indians ranged over the field on horseback, acting as officials and to prevent the excitement of the contestants reaching a pitch where bloodshed might result. No timekeepers were necessary. Everyone could see the sun, and as it set the game was concluded."[118] Along with a traditional Iroquoian reservation stick game that was distinct from that played against collegians, the Great Lakes and southeastern ball games signified various native attempts to maintain a sense of cultural continuity with the past in the face of modernity.

All three major forms of traditional ball games—northeastern, Great Lakes, and southeastern—persisted in the face of modernization. Although "traditional" by name, these recreational, secularized games were hardly untainted by modernity. Despite the continuation of these older, largely undocumented patterns of culture, many Native Americans also directly and indirectly confronted modern versions of lacrosse. Even though this cultural exchange occurred mainly in New York state between reservations and universities, another compelling cultural drama unfolded during the second decade of the century at the Indian boarding school in Carlisle, Pennsylvania. Founded in 1879, the federally supported Carlisle Indian Industrial School attempted to acculturate young Native American men and women into white society by teaching them the middle-class values of Protestant America. However, the students advocated the adoption of white culture not to lose their native identity, but rather to become competitive individuals.[119] In their "History of the Class of 1911," students Emma LaVatta (Shoshone) and William Owl (Cherokee) argued that American Indians attended Carlisle to adjust to civilization: "The aim of the institution is the betterment of the Indian by taking him from his camp life and surroundings, where the influences are often degrading, and bringing him into close touch with other students who have had the advantage of a longer civilization and with teachers and friends who represent the highest types of manhood and womanhood." Carlisle's curriculum produced men suited for skilled blue-collar jobs and women for domestic work. The school experience was no doubt culturally disorienting, if not destructive for many natives, but some students felt that their Victorian lessons in self-reliance, industry, loyalty, and personal independence allowed them to endure as a distinct people. They could also disprove a common white proverb: "Your only good Indian is a dead one."[120]

Although they focused on providing trade-related training, school administrators presumed that athletics fulfilled the school's mission of acculturation. Carlisle's football, baseball, and track teams had national reputations, producing world-class athletes such as Jim Thorpe and Louis Tewanima.[121] The football program developed a sense of disciplined teamwork among the athletes and served as a public relations vehicle for the school, painting for white society a positive image of Indians as respectable people whose accomplishments could be measured favorably according to white standards. Athletics officials at Carlisle presumed the middle-class conception of baseball aided their efforts to acculturate students. However, these administrators encountered difficulties in policing the behavior of student athletes. Although baseball players publicly paid homage to the amateur creed of the national pastime, the distinction between amateur and professional was not always clear; many nominally amateur college baseball players covertly performed professionally during the summer. Realizing that their varsity athletes yielded to the pressures of commercial sport by accepting pay from fast-talking pro scouts, Carlisle officials understood the harm of professional baseball to their summer apprentice plan. After all, the $15 to $20 per month a student could earn doing farmwork in the school's Outing Program paled in comparison to the money he could make playing baseball.

With students violating school policy by playing summer baseball, Carlisle officials faced a crisis. These men believed baseball possessed an ideal value system, yet ignored the national pastime's position in the commercial marketplace. After weighing the pros and cons of continuing a varsity baseball program, officials replaced the intercollegiate baseball team with both intramural baseball and varsity lacrosse in early 1910. They despised professionalism and its accompanying evils, but tolerated intramural baseball because they did not wish to entirely purge Carlisle of the national pastime. Officials wanted to combine the amateur ethos of gentlemanly lacrosse with baseball's values of social democracy and agrarianism. Ironically, school officials concluded that the modernized version of lacrosse could teach Native Americans to become respectable citizens. Administrators assumed that by eliminating varsity baseball they could protect students from the worst elements of white society—vice, greed, and ungentlemanly conduct—but, oddly enough, also from free enterprise. In mid-January the student-run *Carlisle Arrow* cast doubt on the integrity of fellow classmates: "It is thought, because of the evils of summer or professional base ball and the fact that many students have been lured away from school and into temptations and bad company by professional offers before they had finished school, it would be best not to develop, by encouraging base ball, an ambition in the students to become professional players, since so few have the strength of character or the ability to engage in such a calling successfully." By terminating varsity baseball, Carlisle effectively deemphasized the development of baseball talent so students would not "be subjected to the tempting offers of the 'Bush league' managers."[122]

From the birth of the varsity lacrosse program, football coach and athletic director Glenn "Pop" Warner constantly had to explain and defend the superintendent's decision to replace the democratic national pastime with the seemingly elite sport of lacrosse. At the end of the 1910 season, Warner reminded the Indian students that very few sportsmen became professional athletes: "Two Carlisle students are playing on professional baseball teams—the only two to make good out of a half dozen or more who have been lured away by managers with promises of thorough tryouts and an idea of the value of an Indian player as an advertisement. Since the school is on trial, it must not give the public a chance to say that its chief business is turning out professional athletes." Furthermore, Warner defended amateur sport and the school's mission of acculturation: "Athletics at Carlisle . . . are here for the students, not the students here for the athletics."[123]

Warner's proclamation that summer baseball had transformed Carlisle athletes into "bums" drew flack from baseball advocates. At the annual National Collegiate Athletic Association convention of 1913, Warner exonerated himself of charges that he had attacked the sacred national pastime. The problem was not with baseball, he argued, but rather with how professional summer baseball affected Indian students. "I realized," he told an interviewer, "that the problem we had to solve at Carlisle was more troublesome than among colleges, and, therefore, it was necessary to adopt more drastic measures and abolish the game and substitute lacrosse."[124] Warner thought the students were at fault, not baseball; the problem was not with the game, but with the college athletes who played it for pay. By eliminating varsity baseball, the school had supposedly eliminated the temptation to become a professional baseball player. Most universities and colleges with players who covertly played summer ball for pay maintained their programs, but Carlisle's rigid mission of acculturation largely shaped its decision to eliminate varsity baseball. Oddly enough, Warner and other Carlisle officials judged Indian athletes by the standards of collegian sport, despite the fact that the Indian students received only a trade school education.

The spirit of Warner's comments to intercollegiate officials contradicted earlier justifications given to students of the decision to replace varsity baseball with lacrosse. To the Indians at Carlisle Warner and other administrators claimed that the problem of student athletes playing summer ball lay within the management ranks of organized professional baseball. To the intercollegiate athletics community Warner implied that weak-willed Indians succumbed to the malignant pressures of the commercial world. The inconsistency of the explanations given for Carlisle's shift from baseball to lacrosse mirrored the inherent contradiction between the institution's view of its mission and its view of the purpose of the baseball team. In the view of administrators, the Carlisle school existed to "Americanize" and acculturate Indian students. They believed that baseball would help bring about this assimilation by teaching the students scientific teamwork and the Protestant work ethic. Emphasizing culture at the expense of economics, Carlisle officialdom dismissed the possibility that a skilled, hardworking Indian could succeed in white society by playing professional baseball. The Carlisle coaching staff and administration thought sport built character and developed decent citizens, but did not provide a livelihood. School officials apparently did not recognize the hypocrisy and irony of their institution's purpose. After all, Carlisle was training Indians to be skilled, hardworking manual laborers.

In 1914 Warner continued to defend the change in spring sports by penning an article entitled "Lacrosse vs. Baseball: One Solution of the Summer Ball Problem" for the annual national lacrosse guide. As athletic director of Carlisle, he declared that modern lacrosse was a worthwhile antidote to the general problem of summer professionalism in college baseball. The substitution "would seem to be about the only feasible way to settle the ever-present and much discussed evil of the so-called 'summer base ball problem,'" he wrote. Because the "temptation of publicity and enormous salaries for doing something which is all play and no work" was "too alluring," Warner believed school officials had to intervene and save students from ruining their lives. Contrasting Carlisle's mission of civilization with student aspirations to fame and fortune, Warner believed Indians should aspire to respectable blue-collar work. "The students here, unlike at colleges, did not go home for their summer vacations, but were placed out in the country upon a farm or at some trade under the school's outing system," Warner said, "and it was impossible to convince the base ball boys that it would be better for them to spend their summers in this way for a small monthly wage when they could earn many times more by playing base ball." In the belief that the lessons learned at Carlisle could be applied elsewhere, he claimed that lacrosse "would provide an excellent substitute for base ball if it should be eventually decided that the evils of college ball can only be corrected by eliminating it as a representative college sport."[125]

Despite attacks on the commercial and professional elements of the national pastime, the continuation of intramural baseball signified that the two springtime sports could coexist at Carlisle. During the spring of 1914, a school league featured eight squads using nicknames taken from American and National League franchises, indicating the influence of professional baseball on campus. "The boys and girls have taken much interest in the games and large crowds turn out every evening to root for their favorite team," according to the *Carlisle Arrow*. "There have developed some good players in spite of the fact that they have had no coaching."[126] Apparently, despite the efforts of officials, the allure of baseball among students reflected some adherence to the professed belief system of the national pastime and its position within the larger commercial world. Moreover, Carlisle's decision to abolish varsity baseball and use lacrosse to foster amateur sporting values was consistent with the attacks of the American Indian Association (AIA) on the commercial entertainment industry's employment of Indians. According to the campus press, both the AIA and Carlisle sought to eliminate what each saw as the "viciousness and vice" imposed by whites upon Indians. Whereas Carlisle targeted intercollegiate baseball, the AIA focused on Wild West shows. "The influence of these shows is antagonistic to that of the schools. The schools elevate, the shows degrade," a former Indian commissioner said. "The schools teach industry and thrift, the shows encourage idleness and waste. The schools inculcate morality, the shows lead almost inevitably to vice."[127] Carlisle administrators were hopeful that the socially elite value system of modern lacrosse would do a better job of teaching Indians to become worthy citizens.

School athletic policy aside, the Carlisle lacrosse team possessed a superior win-loss record during its brief existence, often defeating collegian opponents. Knowing the identity and tribal origins of the men who played for Carlisle is crucial to understanding whether the school's assimilationist policy was successful. In other words, if the school could take disparate groups of Native Americans from the several sections of the country, teach them the modernized version of an old Iroquoian ball game, and make them compete successfully against affluent athletes from the Ivy League, the school's policy could be deemed a true success. Not only would they gain prestige for Indian boarding schools, but they would reassure white audiences that the twentieth-century progeny of the "noble savage" could be considered civilized men. According to Pop Warner, writing in 1914, most of the varsity had never seen, much less played, the modern game: "Most of the students at Carlisle come from the West and Southwest and only a very few boys here had ever played the game when the sport was introduced at the school."[128] Responding to criticism that Carlisle players possessed some innate advantage over white opponents, in 1922 Warner recalled that the lacrosse team's success had resulted primarily from the coaching of William T. O'Neill of Cornwall, Ontario, and from the persistence and hard work of student athletes: "The students at Carlisle took to the game quickly. Although generally considered as originated by the Indians, none of the Indian boys at Carlisle had ever played it; while the Indians in New York State, and naturally in Canada, were playing Lacrosse, most of our boys came from the western part of the country."[129] Essentially, Warner argued that the school had taken athletes from various tribes across the country with no tradition of playing ball games and had turned them into a winning team.

However, there are problems with Warner's claims. Even though he acknowledged that modern lacrosse was a derivative of an Iroquoian game, Warner neglected the fact that some of his student athletes had come from tribes originally located in the Southeast and around the Great Lakes. Some of these so-called western tribes, especially those of the "Five Civilized Tribes," lived in Oklahoma and still played traditional ball games. The four seniors on the 1917 squad illustrate the tribal diversity of Carlisle's lacrosse program as well as the ties of its students to traditional ball games. Two men whose course work focused on mechanical arts were Peter Tarbell, a Mohawk from New York, and Jesse Wofford, a Cherokee from Oklahoma. In addition, Mike Gurno, a Chippewa from Minnesota, studied plumbing. All of these men came from tribes whose ancestors had played one of the three major forms of the traditional ball game: Tarbell's forebears had played the northeastern game, Wofford's the southeastern, and Gurno's the Great Lakes. Furthermore, the captain of the team was Edwin Miller, a Miami from Oklahoma who served as student body president, played John Hancock in the student production of *Continental Congress*, and dreamed of becoming the president of the United States.[130] Miller's ancestors had played a game that was similar to that played by Gurno's.

Warner's deemphasis of these traditions is only one problem. An examination of player rosters reveals that Warner's claims that the program was dominated by "western" Indians were completely false. In 1911 half the team were Seneca Indians from western New York, while most of the rest were from other Iroquois reservations. Of the sixteen players listed on the 1914 roster, at least half had come from Iroquois communities. The other athletes included men from formerly eastern tribes with a tradition of playing ball games, such as the Chippewa and the Cherokee. Only a few players had come from authentically western tribes without a tradition of playing ball games. Regardless of the year in question, Warner's assertions that the school had a program with natives who had had to learn lacrosse were simply erroneous. In reality, most Carlisle players had probably been playing some form of lacrosse since they were very young. Carlisle's on-field success should have been no surprise. These Indians had had years of experience and enjoyed the coaching expertise of a professional Canadian.

Regardless of the composition of the team from year to year, the Carlisle team was indeed a diverse, multitribal group of Native Americans who were coached by an Irish Canadian and playing a modernized version of an old Mohawk ball game to learn respectable Victorian values at a school established by the U.S. federal government. However, since the cultural baggage they brought with them included their own particular tribal ball games, it made their ability to perform well under O'Neill exceptional. These native athletes learned an element of Iroquoian culture as repackaged and reconceptualized by a white coach. Clues to how the Carlisle Indians coped with the cultural struggle between the traditions of the past and the assimilation policies of the time they attended the school can be found in game summaries published in city and campus newspapers. The Indians may have been a well-coached team using a scientific, team-centered style of play similar to that of their white opponents, but many of Carlisle's players obviously had brought with them from reservation life their individualistic, running-oriented style of ball play. In May 1910, for example, the *Baltimore Sun* warned that the Mount Washington L.C.'s upcoming match with Carlisle would feature "traditional" tactics: "From all reports the Indians have one of the fastest teams in the country, when it comes to legwork, and have a tendency to play the game in true Indian style, where dependence is placed rather on the ability of a man to run the entire length of the field, dodging and shooting all by himself, rather than on a man's ability to work with his mates."[131] About two weeks after Carlisle had defeated Mount Washington, an Annapolis newspaper documented the Indians' peculiar playing style in their victory over the U.S. Naval Academy: "They played the ball on the ground largely and this proved confusing to the middies, who do most of their work above the heads of their opponents. On the whole, it was a splendid contest, with two types of players and playing opposed."[132]

Other city and campus newspapers pointed to traces of traditional ball play and their imprint on gentlemanly lacrosse. Following Carlisle's 8–4 victory over Johns Hopkins in April 1912, the *Baltimore American* referred to Indian "tactics and tricks" as "cunning and beautiful to watch." It said that the Carlisle victory could be attributed to "wily body-checking and accurate wary passing," frequent player dodging that had caused confusion among the Johns Hopkins players, and the Indians' "playing in bunches" of six men following the ball.[133] In June 1915 the student press at Carlisle accented technical skills the team had possibly inherited from reservation play, as well as an amateur ethos learned from their coach: "Throughout the season the boys have gained a reputation not only for their skill in the contests but also by their gentlemanly behavior on the field and on the trips."[134] Such testimony alluding to the Indians' emulation of white standards, combined with evidence of the infusion of traditional tactics, indicates the complex interplay of modernity and tradition at Carlisle.

For many students the lacrosse team served complementary functions, enhancing the Indians' desire both to preserve their cultural heritage in some form and to confront the new conditions of the modern world. For some the team served as a reminder of the sacred ancient game. For example, Tuscarora student Edison Mount Pleasant informed his classmates that his tribe had long ago won a contest from the Mohawk because of the work of their medicine man. He wrote: "The modern Tuscarora Indian athletes are considered dauntless by their white brothers. A few are classed with the best athletes in this country, while one is classed with the world's best athletes." Mount Pleasant continued: "The athletic teams tour the white communities, but they no longer rely on the medicine man with his magic bone, but upon strength, brain and courage." Because students turned out en masse to witness matches, the varsity team functioned as a vehicle for Native American pride. In April 1911 "a large crowd of students and commencement guests" saw the home team defeat the boys from Baltimore City

College.[135] Carlisle's purpose may have been to anglicize the native students, but one unintended consequence was the fostering of an ill-defined pan-Indian identity.

Opponents on the playing field usually applauded the Indians, often pointing to their gentlemanly conduct. White commentators accepted these Indians because of their exceptional athleticism as well as their acculturation to the value of "fair play." Although it was never a member of the United States Intercollegiate Lacrosse League, the Carlisle team drew praise from most non-native observers. The student press at Johns Hopkins was gracious after Carlisle beat their university in 1913: "The game itself was interesting to watch and was not marred by the slightest dirty playing. The Indians deserved their victory, for the tirelessness of their mid-field was remarkable, and their intercepts before their goal were beautiful."[136] In 1914 lacrosse pioneer John Flannery rejoiced at Carlisle's success: "It is indeed eminently fitting that lacrosse, the creature of the American Indians, should again come into its own in this manner."[137] Praise for Carlisle's students from white enthusiasts was always forthcoming, but accompanied by subtle condescension. After all, regardless of whether they won or lost, intercollegiate sportsmen were secure in knowing that they would soon enter the world of the managerial class armed with Ivy League educations, while their Indian opponents would have to settle for remaining somewhere near the bottom of the American social order. Losing a game to a group of real-life "noble savages" was certainly nothing to make collegians feel any shame.

Aside from the superior quality of the Carlisle lacrosse team, their status as flesh-and-blood Indians appealed to many white audiences on the East Coast. During the team's second season, the Indians defeated Stevens Institute before an alumni-day crowd of ten thousand.[138] A few years later the New York press used frontier imagery to describe another Carlisle match. As if reporting an Indian attack on a wagon train in the "wild west," the *New York Times* reported in 1917 that the Carlisle Indians had once again "descended" upon the Engineers of Stevens Institute and "scalped" them in a game with a score of 9–3.[139] Although city newspapers made such references to ignoble savagery, most white coaches and athletes regarded the Indians with awe. Taking after Carlisle's more famous football team, the school's lacrosse squad was always on its best behavior in order to paint for the socially elite crowds an image of the American Indian as respectable and civilized.

The Carlisle lacrosse program served as a very peculiar cultural exper-iment, but a brief one, lasting from its first season in 1910 until 1918, when the federal government converted the school into a military hospital. Coach O'Neill and his Indian athletes maneuvered through a complex set of cul-tural and social circumstances to forge a model of a civilized Indian that was a source of pride for the school's students. The elite ethos of gentle-manly lacrosse surely confused the student athletes who attended this school that was preparing men and women to be industrious blue-collar workers. Possibly the greatest significance of the Carlisle team, however, was its role in contributing to an increased interest in the game among many reservation communities. Ultimately the Carlisle program reenergized sev-eral Iroquois nations in New York state to provide support for the twentieth-century version of their sacred game. Largely because of the successful lacrosse program at Carlisle, many teams from Iroquois reservations played private clubs and universities on a more frequent basis during the 1920s. Natives now had a way to demonstrate their cultural vitality to themselves, but also to the non-native world surrounding them. For most of the rest of the century, while white players in Canada and the United States were de-veloping their own versions of lacrosse, Iroquois Indians were finding in the modern version of their ancient sport the seeds of opportunity.

Chapter 3　**"What Are a Few Cuts . . . ?"**
Defining and Defending Lacrosse,
1920–1945

THE PERIOD AFTER the First World War saw a dramatic series of new developments in the history of lacrosse. In the United States and Canada, the game went in two very different directions. Canadian enthusiasts witnessed the decline and fall of their once mighty "national game," but the Americans' game expanded throughout the northeastern part of their country. In many ways, the period between the world wars saw the United States become the symbolic center of the sport. Specifically, sportsmen in Baltimore began to view their community as the game's mecca. Despite the great economic collapse after 1929, the leadership of the American game still defined their game in aristocratic terms. Rejecting the growing trend toward professionalism and commercialism in American sport, U.S. proponents of lacrosse frequently made contact with the British lacrosse community through a series of exchange tours. The games encouraged Americans to continue defining their sport in amateur, gentlemanly terms. Many American coaches and officials hoped to learn much from the lacrosse teams from Oxford and Cambridge Universities. It was also within this context that a women's lacrosse community developed in the United States.

In Canada, on the other hand, an openly commercial form of lacrosse emerged in the early years of the Great Depression. The owners of ice hockey arenas engineered the development of the new game of "box" lacrosse in the hope of attracting hockey fans who were looking for a summer version of their winter love. Many vocal coaches in the United States openly condemned box lacrosse as a crass version of the old Indian game that encouraged especially violent play. Though professional box lacrosse failed on both sides of the Canadian-American border, an amateur version of the game caught on in southern Ontario and southwestern British

Columbia. Meanwhile, Indians from reservation communities in New York, Ontario, and Quebec continued to participate within the larger lacrosse community. However, losses to top-flight collegiate competition led many natives to explore other options. Ironically, Indians found the new version of lacrosse that had been invented by professional hockey promoters a more culturally satisfying game. These Indians and all of the other non-native enthusiasts who called lacrosse their sport sought to define and defend their game in the face of a number of adversities during the 1920s and 1930s. Cultural struggles ensued, and the winners controlled the terms under which the game recovered from the ordeals posed by the Great Depression and the Second World War.

"Athletics for All" Who Can Afford Them: American Lacrosse during the Roaring Twenties

The Great War did not significantly damage the American lacrosse community. However, to remind the campus community of wartime sacrifices, in 1919 the Johns Hopkins lacrosse team affixed a flag with three stars honoring slain players to one of the lacrosse field's goal nets. According to a team resolution, the pennant was used to honor "the memory of a great national service ably, heroically, and cheerfully performed and for the further purpose of inspiring the present and future teams of this University to noble, manly, and efficient action."[1] As much a tribute to Progressive-era principles of martial sacrifice, Anglo-Saxonism, virile masculinity, and scientific management as to the dead athletes, this action led to the performance of an annual flag ritual at Johns Hopkins. As did the rest of middle- and upper-class America, the world of lacrosse experienced tremendous prosperity during the first postwar decade. As affluent citizens trumpeted newfound personal wealth, liberating social mores, and a booming stock market, lacrosse organizers spoke optimistically about their favorite pastime. In January 1919, delegates to the annual convention of the United States Intercollegiate Lacrosse League (USILL) recommitted themselves to a full revival of play. Two years later, these men voted for a more "progressive" style of play by adopting an "off-sides" rule. By mandating that at any time each team have no fewer than three of its twelve players (excluding the goal tender) on its own half of the field and no fewer than three players on its opponent's half of the field, lacrosse organizers further elevated the principle of scientific positional play.[2]

Through the 1920s organized lacrosse grew rapidly, primarily in the states ranging from New England to Maryland. Ten colleges held memberships in the USILL in 1922, and another eight operated as independents. By 1929, both figures had doubled. The growth of schoolboy lacrosse was slower; the number of preparatory and secondary programs increased only from sixteen to twenty-one. Since 1906 the USILL had crowned separate champions for the northern and the southern sections of the lacrosse community. This system precluded the possibility of a national championship game or poll and prevented nonleague schools from becoming champions. Debate at a 1925 meeting led to the reorganization of the USILL into the United States Intercollegiate Lacrosse Association (USILA). The association continued to distinguish member schools from nonmembers, but provided greater flexibility in terms of entrance requirements, which gave members leverage in scheduling tougher competition. The new governing body allowed its Championship Award Committee to crown any college or university, regardless of membership status. Dropping regional championships, the association bestowed gold, silver, and bronze medals upon the three top-ranked institutions, based on win-loss percentages.[3] The smaller club community hovered between eight and twelve teams in any given year, but club athletes still provided important organizational leadership and support. In December 1926, the first USILA convention included delegates from the Mount Washington and Crescent clubs, and even from the Canadian Lacrosse Association. Unfortunately, the informality of club play resulted in less complete records, but the club game ranged from New England to Maryland, played in roughly the same regions as intercollegiate lacrosse. Besides several athletic clubs in New York and Baltimore, there were clubs in Syracuse, Buffalo, Montclair (New Jersey), Philadelphia, Washington, and even Chicago. The Crescent A.C. remained popular in Brooklyn, attracting crowds of several thousand to its matches with leading American intercollegiate teams and Canadian clubs. Although the "Half Moons" maintained an exclusionary attendance policy, officials sometimes opened the club grounds at Bay Ridge to the public when popular opponents such as Syracuse University appeared. The Crescent men also organized a short-lived Metropolitan Lacrosse League, which featured players with club or intercollegiate experience, white and Iroquois imports from Canada, and local schoolboys.

Club athletes and collegian alumni convinced undergraduate students of the authenticity of their invented traditions, and as a result some intercollegiate programs started gaining acceptance on their respective campuses. At Syracuse University, in 1921 the *Daily Orange* claimed that lacrosse would benefit off-season football players, bolster the image of the university, and allow more athletes to win the coveted varsity "S" award. When students and organization leaders demonstrated overwhelming support for making it a "major sport" at Syracuse, the university's Athletic Governing Board officially added lacrosse to a group of sports that already included football, baseball, basketball, crew, and track.[4] Although support for football always exceeded that for lacrosse at Syracuse and other universities, lacrosse often outdrew baseball. Given the rising popularity of intercollegiate lacrosse in 1927, the *New York Times* reported: "Some sportsmen predict that the red Indian's game will one day supplant baseball as the Spring major college sport."[5]

College coaches and organizers continued to promote lacrosse in nearby preparatory and high schools. At the USILL convention in 1920, the league targeted New York, Boston, and Baltimore as areas in which to cultivate the game and offered to help fund intercity contests. A Brooklyn schoolboy lacrosse revival, under way since 1916, accelerated during the 1920s.[6] The war killed interscholastic lacrosse at most New York City area schools, but the Crescent A.C. established a new Metropolitan Interscholastic Lacrosse League in 1922 that included Boys' High, Erasmus Hall, Manual Training, Stevens Prep, Commercial High, Polytechnic Prep, and the Country and Day School.[7] Other New York City area schools with lacrosse teams included Jamaica High School; Curtis High School of Staten Island, Peekskill Military Academy, and the New York Military Academy in Cornwall-on-Hudson. Ironically, the Crescent club's missionary work established a system for feeding players to area universities and colleges, not for the club's own benefit.

Coaches created similar systems in and around Baltimore and Syracuse. In Maryland, interscholastic participants included Baltimore City College and Baltimore Polytechnic Institute, but others followed. In March 1925, when students at the Friends and Park schools debated the feasibility of fielding baseball and lacrosse squads, both groups voted to stick solely with lacrosse. Commenting on Friends' focus on lacrosse, the *Baltimore Sun* reported, "The old Indian game has finally taken a tight grip on the Little Quakers and has replaced the national pastime—baseball."[8] By the end of the decade, Calvert Hall and the Donaldson, McDonogh and Severn schools had also adopted lacrosse. In upstate New York, enthusiasts from Syracuse University promoted the game at Central High School and the Christian Brothers Academy. Meanwhile, advocates from Hobart College kindled interest at nearby Geneva High School. These schools eventually joined with Vocational and East Syracuse High Schools to form a Central New York Interscholastic Association. Besides two other Syracuse high schools—Nottingham and Valley—schools in the towns of Skaneateles, Weedsport, and Cortland also experimented with the game. Regardless of region, these programs grew from the tireless efforts of collegian and club enthusiasts, who believed that without their proselytism there would be no gentlemen to continue the old Indian game into the future.

Growing interest among collegians and schoolboys did not lead to any significant change in the cultural milieu surrounding the game during the 1920s. As before the Great War, enthusiasts at Johns Hopkins best articulated the cultural ideals of American lacrosse, celebrating amateurism and the mental and physical skills derived from play. They also still chastised apathetic undergraduates, cultivated local traditions, and recognized the native origins of the game. More fiercely than before, however, supporters defended their game by attacking commercialism. In 1922 the Johns Hopkins school paper criticized the *Baltimore Sun*'s extensive coverage of professional baseball's Class AA International League Orioles, declaring the team less an advertising vehicle for the city than a private enterprise. "In pushing non-professional sports," the *Johns Hopkins News-Letter* contended, "the press would not only succeed just as well in advertising the city, but would give a great boost to a system that is serving, in a large measure, to make America's manhood physically better off." City newspapers should not feed more fan dollars to "the already overpaid professional," but rather should use the money to fuel "a machine designed to produce strong, clean American citizens."[9] Contrasting baseball's entrepreneurs and paid athletes with the sons of affluence who supported lacrosse, the student press tied urban boosterism to an elite cultural agenda. Lacrosse served the interests of the city by developing the character of Baltimore's future leaders in law, education, and medicine. Despite the affluence of many Johns Hopkins athletes, student supporters of lacrosse challenged what lower-class Baltimoreans thought of as snobbish athleticism. Lacrosse was simply a tough sport. "Blood spilt on the Lacrosse Field is of the red variety, and never composed of blue corpuscles," the 1923 Johns Hopkins yearbook declared. "A good lacrosse player must be the embodiment of perpetual motion, possess the speed of Mercury, the physique of Jack Dempsey, and the temperament of a Devil Dog. He must delight in trotting through the snow and wallowing in the mud-clay only in the most abbreviated of costumes and armed with a glorified butterfly-net."[10]

Besides attacking professionalism and defending the public image of lacrosse players, university leaders also focused on student involvement and support on campus. In the spring of 1926, the fraternities and sports teams at Johns Hopkins had to sell twelve hundred tickets (worth $6,000) to eliminate most of the fall athletics debt of $8,000. The ticket campaign also sought to counter the "very low ebb" in interest in Johns Hopkins athletics among Baltimore residents. Concerned with city-campus relations, the *News-Letter* implored students to fight the debased image of the university. "In addition to pure distinterestedness, there exists in this city a certain amount of actual antagonism to anything connected with Hopkins," the paper observed. Disregarding allegations of snobbery, the *News-Letter* argued: "There is no justifiable basis for this, and the athletic authorities believe that if these persons can be persuaded to attend the lacrosse games, this feeling can be largely eliminated."[11] Despite these efforts, Baltimoreans continued to support professional sports and a cultural gap remained between city and campus. In the future, support for lacrosse would have to come from the expanding ranks of alumni.

Lacrosse advocates at Johns Hopkins also promoted amateurism and other Victorian values among students. Many at the school revered the "Hopkins Ideal," which stressed honesty, character, and gentlemanly behavior, but that hardly ended book theft, the handing in of false assignments, and cheating. Lacrosse players were characterized as ideal athletes, self-sacrificing noble warriors who were fighting for the honor of the university. In May 1926, the student editors praised the physical education policy whose motto was "Athletics for All," under which the university sponsored interfraternity baseball and interclass contests in sports such as lacrosse. The policy called for adherence to the elite sporting ethos reflected by the Johns Hopkins lacrosse team. In October the *News-Letter* charged each freshman class with a responsibility to uphold an honor system con-

sistent with amateur sport, stating: "Life at Hopkins is based on the fundamental assumption that every student is a gentleman." The prized but fragile honor system survived because of the enormous pressure on freshmen
to keep and maintain the tradition.[12]

Lacrosse supporters continued to attack undergraduates who did not
attend matches. In May 1920, the *Johns Hopkins News-Letter* admonished
students who had ignored the baseball and lacrosse teams' recent contests
with Saint John's and Stevens, respectively: "Two games, both of them
championship games, and only 130 students in the stands; no not even that;
the 130 included some of the men who were on the two teams and who had
to show their tickets at the gate!" For the upcoming match with the University of Toronto, the paper offered this challenge: "What are the students,
who can sit back in the stands and suffer no discomforts or the chance of
getting a broken head, going to give? How about getting out and backing
up the team?" With freshmen still disinterested in spring sports, student editors offered more reprimands in 1922: "If the members of the Class of '25
have not as yet imbibed the spirit and traditions of Johns Hopkins it is
probable that they never will. . . . It is perfectly true that a number of the
first year men have fallen down in their obligations to the University activities since the lifting of regulations. These same duty-dodgers will find
little trouble in uncovering excuses for missing our Saturday games." As the
number of alumni grew, attendance increased substantially during the
1920s, but the student press inflated crowd expectations. Whereas mere attendance had been emphasized in the Progressive Era, the press now called
for systematized applause: "Unorganized cheering is of no avail."[13] Clearly,
"gentlemen" must be taught how to be gentlemen. Just as American consumers remained overconfident about the national economy, so were
lacrosse enthusiasts unrealistic about the support their game deserved.

Johns Hopkins enthusiasts felt great harm would result from the dis-
ruption of any university "tradition" that was passed from one class to the
next. The newspaper editors and student leaders developed headaches trying to cultivate the support of the whole campus population, but the
lacrosse team officials had a different task. At the start of each season former coach William Schmeisser spoke to the lacrosse squad. At a March 1928
team meeting he discussed the "early history of lacrosse in Baltimore, the
importance of team spirit, and the need for candidates to 'stick to it.'"[14]
Schmeisser was never paid for his coaching duties, but he gladly propagated

"tradition" at Johns Hopkins. Likewise, landscape engineering professor Laurie Cox accepted no wages for coaching at Syracuse. Cox also respected the authority of tradition and used modern technology to instill it. In February 1925 he showed "several reels of film depicting the Orange championship lacrosse teams of the last two years in action" to coaches, athletics officials, and prospective players.[15] As did undergraduates in general, lacrosse players at Syracuse and Johns Hopkins had to learn their institutions' invented traditions.

These efforts to promote gentlemanly amateur lacrosse paralleled practices at the armed forces academies. To prevent the much-feared professionalization of sport at West Point, as early as December 1909 the United States Military Academy informed the Intercollegiate Athletic Association that Army athletics instructors would no longer be professional coaches, but rather alumni or administrators. After Brigadier General Douglas MacArthur became superintendent of the academy in August 1919, he implemented a universal athletics program that began in the summer of 1920. During his tenure from 1919 through 1922, MacArthur added ten new intercollegiate sports, including a revived lacrosse program in 1921.[16] Under this new system, from early July through mid-August all plebes devoted one week each to lacrosse, football, basketball, soccer, track, and baseball. At summer's end, these cadets joined either intramural or intercollegiate squads. During the fall, winter, and spring seasons the members of the varsity "Corps" played one to two dozen sports. Each sport had first, reserve, and plebe teams. Cadets without varsity membership played on intramural teams representing the academy's twelve companies. To develop talent for the spring varsity campaign, intramural lacrosse was included in the fall season.

Aimed at developing well-conditioned, thinking men, the West Point athletics program shared many of the values of amateur sport as practiced at Johns Hopkins and on Ivy League campuses. Unlike elite universities, however, the service academies adhered to the principle of social egalitarianism. The academy lived up to its slogan, "Every cadet an athlete," and homogenized every cadet into a gentleman scholar-soldier-athlete, "regardless of his previous experience or occupation, the financial or social standing of his family, or his ability or lack of ability in any respect," according to one source. The diversity of the student body at West Point, drawn from every state, guaranteed that few cadets had had any lacrosse experience as youth.

With only the intramural program to feed players to the varsity, the Army lacrosse team was essentially homegrown. Sporting a 60–15–2 lacrosse team record in the 1920s, West Point proved that socioeconomically diverse men could excel at what was regarded as an elite sport if given the rigid discipline for which the academy was noted.[17]

On-field roughness remained part of lacrosse during the Roaring Twenties, but partisans rebutted allegations of excessive violence by asserting that the game developed manly character. According to a Johns Hopkins supporter who called himself "Stick Wielder," the most common injuries included slashed fingers, blackened eyes, broken noses, cut lips, and smashed teeth.[18] Far more serious head injuries occurred as well. In June 1920 a Crescent player struck Johns Hopkins third attackman F. Paul Nicklas in the head with the ball. "Nick stopped a swiftly thrown ball from a scrimmage with his eye and was knocked cold," the Johns Hopkins paper reported. "When he courageously arose and started once more he was soon knocked out for the count."[19] Even with such violent episodes, collegians and club men esteemed rough play. Referring to a "dying lacrosse player," one Rutgers athlete reveled in an athlete's pain:

> I long for scenes that I once saw:
> The gory field—the sweet "Rah-Rah!"
> The soft-toned "Sock!" as stick meets jaw,
>   And victims 'round me reel
> Ah just to hear that cheerful groan
> That follows sound of crunching bone—
> No sweeter sound was ever known—
>   Ah, one more blow to deal![20]

Social discourse was cordial between the Crescents and their guests, but the lacrosse remained ferocious. In 1920, for example, the Crescents knocked four university athletes from Toronto unconscious.[21] Despite such injuries and rough play, dozens and sometimes hundreds of undergraduates tried out for varsity squads.

Many coaches and sportswriters believed that the rough character of lacrosse invigorated young men and aided football teams. "A man who sticks out a lacrosse game to the end will be likely to last out a football contest," the *New York Evening Post* declared in 1919. "The element of body checking appeals to the football man, and certainly his moral nature is toughened through the necessity of frequent acts of self-sacrifice, as, for example, when he so maneuvres as to allow the blow from an opponent's stick to fall upon his body instead of upon the racquet in which he is holding the ball."[22] In December 1922, Laurie Cox argued that lacrosse had "the same elements which have elevated football to its present intercollegiate standing. It is a sport in which fight, brawn and skill combine to make victory a reality."[23] Cox's reference to football marked a clear trend that was emerging in the 1920s. Many lacrosse coaches believed future success depended upon their sport's compatibility with the rough fall sport, and they recruited football players to play defense for them in the spring.

Praising rough sport, many enthusiasts saw the Native American origins of lacrosse as an antidote to the overcivilized lifestyle of affluent young men. Reflecting on the old Indian game of antiquity, newspaper and magazine writers usually emphasized the relationship between lacrosse and warfare rather than the game's social, spiritual, and economic functions.[24] The *New York Evening Post* equated the game's savagery with its appeal to modern civilized sportsmen. Even though the paper proclaimed, "Lacrosse is most enjoyed by the man who has a fair dash of Irish or Indian blood in his veins," it went on to say that "the man of whatever race or blood" can have fun with it.[25] In 1924, the *Washington Daily Star* asserted, "A relic of early American times is lacrosse, and it comes to satisfy the twentieth century demand for speed, skill and constantly recurring thrills."[26] In a radio broadcast from Philadelphia, Clarence Goldsmith recounted the old Fort Michilimackinac story: "So interested were the British, they were surprised when the Indians, hundreds of them, suddenly stopped playing, snatching tomahawks from the blankets of the waiting squaws and fell upon the unsuspecting garrison."[27] Goldsmith thought the modern game combined the best elements of other sports, such as the "open-field running," dodging, and "personal contact of man against man" of football and "a constant succession of separate contests as in polo." The personal confrontations in lacrosse especially made for a test of manhood: "It is not a mollycoddle game; it tests the mettle of men for mental alertness, agility and sportsmanship."[28]

At a time when baseball's Babe Ruth loomed larger than life, supporters of intercollegiate, club, and interscholastic lacrosse established their game as an elite amateur alternative to baseball. In four decades American lacrosse grew from a game played by Canadian immigrants and scattered athletes at a handful of private clubs and universities to a sport with dozens of teams at the intercollegiate and club ranks throughout the northeastern and mid-Atlantic states. In a collegian sport world that was becoming more receptive to professionalism and commercialism, lacrosse coaches fought to keep their game amateur. Feeder systems established among preparatory and secondary schools all but guaranteed future expansion, but that growth had to take place within the context of the Great Depression. Even though the ideal of sport for sport's sake that had been professed decades earlier by George Beers was culturally obsolete by the 1920s, lacrosse players remained committed to their rough sport as a friendly, competitive activity for affluent young men. Seeing themselves as the symbolic descendants of the "noble savage," lacrosse enthusiasts alienated the general public from their sport. The image of lacrosse as the sport of rich men and savage Indians ensured the loyalty of the affluent and the disinterest of just about everyone else.

Surviving Hard Times: Gentlemanly Ideals, Economic Realities, and Wartime Necessities

Institutionally stable at the end of the 1920s, American lacrosse faced numerous dilemmas over the next fifteen years. The economic reality of the Great Depression and the military demands of World War II provided significant challenges. Many universities and colleges maintained their programs, but growth and expansion were severely curtailed, forcing financially strapped schools to cut resources or cease play. Professionalism and commercialism increased within college sport, threatening the lacrosse community's commitment to the amateur ideal. Coaches less committed to amateur sport tried to implement spectator-friendly rule changes and introduce a more competitive ethos akin to that of football. These challenges allowed for a general referendum on the direction of American lacrosse. However, the unique conditions of depression and war produced an unlevel playing field in this cultural struggle over the meaning of the game. The shortage of leisure dollars gave proponents of gentlemanly lacrosse an advantage that undermined alternative conceptions that were more friendly to commercial promoters and mass audiences. Although lacrosse officials introduced innovations intended to attract more spectators, traditionalists at universities such as Johns Hopkins provided a model of amateurism that would endure for decades.

The Great Depression arrested the growth of American intercollegiate, club, and interscholastic lacrosse and sometimes reversed it. Some teams disbanded for one campaign only, returning the following year; others ceased play for several years or indefinitely. According to official guides published by the USILA and the National Collegiate Athletic Association, American lacrosse suffered a decline of over 40 percent during the Depression and the war years. Despite the destabilizing effects of both the Depression and the war, most full members of the USILA maintained regular playing schedules. Although in the early 1930s twenty-nine other schools were playing lacrosse as nonassociation members in states ranging from Massachusetts to Georgia and westward to Ohio and Michigan, the USILA schools were the backbone of organized lacrosse. Some institutions slashed funding for all or some of their sports, as did Brown in 1937, but athletes at Cornell, Colgate, Hobart, and Syracuse financed play when university money was lacking.[29] Typical crowds for collegian or club lacrosse ranged from a few dozen to several thousand people during the 1930s, but top-flight teams typically attracted between one and three thousand people. Late-season showdowns attracted crowds of eight to ten thousand. Even with increased play in New England prep schools; the birth of the Dixie League in North Carolina, Virginia, and Washington, D.C.; and new youth organizations, the Second World War eventually squelched any late Depression rejuvenation.[30]

Aside from the service academies and the public City College of New York and Penn State, most USILA institutions were private, including most of the Ivy League schools. Others included the Massachusetts Institute of Technology, Syracuse, Union, Stevens, Swarthmore, Johns Hopkins, Loyola, the University of Maryland, and Saint John's of Annapolis. Meanwhile, clubs like Mount Washington also participated in regular season competition, even taking championship honors and providing administrative leadership within the USILA. In Baltimore and New York City, local college alumni established clubs to compete among themselves and against collegian squads. Club leagues included the Maryland Sunday Lacrosse League, drawing from Baltimore's affluent neighborhoods and suburbs, and the Metropolitan and Long Island Lacrosse Association, stocked with former collegians from New York City. Annual USILA conventions included delegates from clubs, universities, colleges, and high schools. Most club athletes were college graduates with white-collar professional careers. Their leadership made the values of amateurism real for their undergraduate counterparts.

The shortage of funds led officials to develop schemes to stimulate interest or at least maintain the status quo. At the fiftieth annual USILA meeting in 1932, officials reduced a match from two forty-five-minute halves without time-outs or player replacements to fifteen-minute quarters with time-outs and unlimited substitutions. They also tinkered with the amount of playing space behind each goal, allegedly to increase scoring, so the between-goal distance fluctuated between eighty and ninety yards. Furthermore, the on-field squad was reduced from twelve to ten players to decrease traveling expenses. Financially strapped athletic departments applauded the latter modification, and coaches believed two fewer players would accent passing and hence increase public interest.[31] "Under the new rules . . . the game will be faster and more open, and consequently will be more interesting to watch," Princeton's Albert Nies said in 1932. "The view of the goal play, the most interesting feature of lacrosse, will be improved by shortening the field."[32] The student press at Syracuse believed the USILA was "making a strong bid for popularity thru the medium of sensationalism" with its "attempt to speed up the game and give the crowd more thrills."[33] Coaches hoped the changes would increase much-needed gate revenues, but not betray the game's historical spirit.

The alterations reflected a new way of thinking about lacrosse, emphasizing spectator appeal. Besides making changes in the playing of the game, the USILA also reformed its system of determining championships. They wanted the most legitimate, cost-effective, and "fair" method of selecting a national champion. USILA coaches recognized that the pursuit of championship titles satisfied the public as well as athletes and coaches who sought some tangible reward of their success. As did professional athletes, the sons of affluent families believed in the competitive ethos found in commercial sports. When officials realized during the late 1920s that some schools were padding their schedules to ensure that they would win one of the annual championship medals, they abandoned championships. Saint John's of Annapolis earned the unofficial championship in 1931, and Johns Hopkins won a three-round Olympic trial tournament in 1932, but the association awarded no titles from then until 1935. Still, most coaches recognized undefeated or prominent teams as de facto champions. Beginning in 1936, polled association members honored the top-ranked team with a memorial trophy named for Baltimore sportswriter Wilson Wingate.[34] These changes in the system for crowning champions reflected the tension between not taking sport too seriously and a more competitive spirit.

The USILA and individual universities introduced other innovations to increase interest in lacrosse. Syracuse University staged and won the first "nocturnal lacrosse game ever staged in this country" against Penn State on May 10, 1930. Purists and sportswriters noted how artificial light altered standard play. "The huge flood lights enabled the spectators to watch the game without any difficulty," the *Daily Orange* observed, "but the players were unable to follow the ball on long passes, consequently both teams were forced to adopt a slow and deliberate passing attack."[35] Following baseball's lead, the USILA sponsored a first-ever intercollegiate all-star game between players from the North and those from the South on June 14, 1940, before thirty-five hundred spectators at Municipal Stadium in Baltimore. Other events at the floodlight affair included a match between two women's teams representing Philadelphia and Maryland and individual stick contests for schoolboys and collegians. According to *Baltimore Sun* sportswriter Craig Taylor, local lacrosse fans emphasized the glorification of lacrosse rather than the North team's victory.[36] The next year, the South team got revenge, as Johns Hopkins alumnus and All South Coaches Committee chairman Gardner Mollonee "waved a Confederate battle flag in the brisk night air" in front of twenty-five hundred people.[37]

Commercial influences were a new development, but the old Mason-Dixon line also intruded into American lacrosse. Some southern institutions' adherence to racial segregation created controversy. In most sports, southern universities banned the use of "Negro athletes" by visiting northern teams. In 1941 the Harvard lacrosse team's trip to the Naval Academy sparked debate. When Navy's athletic director, Rear Admiral Russell Wilson, found out about Harvard's black student athlete, Lucien Alexis, Jr., he informed Harvard athletic director William J. Bingham that Navy did not play against racially integrated teams. Confronted with benching its black player or accepting a forfeit from the academy, Harvard sent Alexis home. Bingham justified his decision by saying, "We were guests of the Naval Academy and had no choice in the matter. Had the game been played at Cambridge . . . I would have insisted that he be allowed to participate."[38] The student-run *Harvard Crimson* criticized the university for "kowtowing to the intolerable jim crowism of Navy Bigwigs."[39] Sportswriters chastised northern schools that used the argument that as "guests" they could not impose northern racial attitudes on southern institutions, and Harvard student leaders questioned university athletic policy regarding African American athletes. Linking an aristocratic conception of sport with modern political philosophy, the Harvard Council for Democracy in Education expressed its outrage to President Franklin Roosevelt: "We feel you will be shocked at this violation of American fair play and democracy." The Harvard Corporation ordered Bingham to inform all future opponents that Harvard's teams would not tolerate racial discrimination against its students. One writer of a letter to the *New York Times* applauded Harvard's new policy: "Many schools have taken Navy's undemocratic attitude toward Negro athletes. When schools with Negroes on their teams have met these intolerant institutions they have acted with an appeasing spirit reminiscent of Munich." The critic called for a new spirit in athletics: "Let's make it all-out for democracy and sportsmanship in theory and in practice, in the classroom and on the athletic field."[40] Ironically, this support of racial equality and social democracy originated in one of the most exclusive educational institutions in the world.

The Alexis incident symbolized a cultural tug-of-war that was beginning to emerge by the Second World War. It pitted the proponents of sport for sport's sake against those calling for popularization. The reference to Neville Chamberlain's capitulation to Adolf Hitler served as a rallying cry for reform within intercollegiate sport in general and within lacrosse in particular. Removed by a few generations from the gentlemanly ethos propagated by men such as George Beers and William Schmeisser, an increasing number of intercollegiate lacrosse enthusiasts could imagine greater popularization without abandoning the values of amateurism. However, to overemphasize the Alexis incident or the efforts to make the game more commercial would be wrong. American lacrosse remained an amateur sport for affluent athletes in eastern universities. Regardless of the lure of mass sport and the pursuit of social democracy, poor economic conditions and later military exigencies had a greater impact. Spectator-friendly innovations seemed part of a movement toward mass sport, but lacrosse enthusiasts still operated within a socially elite world.

The U.S. entry into the Second World War disrupted sporting activities as it did almost every aspect of life in America. Major league baseball continued play with aging veterans and 4-F athletes, but many minor league franchises, colleges, high schools, and semipro and amateur clubs simply shut down for some or all of the war years. Even though the war caused some programs to cease operation altogether, the lacrosse community in Baltimore rallied to keep the game going. For the 1944 campaign, for example, Johns Hopkins combined with the Mount Washington L.C. and athletes from nearby universities and schools to form a Johns Hopkins L.C. Among the lacrosse players and coaches who joined baseball stars Bob Feller and Joe DiMaggio in the march to war were Syracuse University coach Roy Simmons and Mount Washington attackman Jack Turnbull. Simmons had lettered in lacrosse, baseball, and boxing and served as class president and quarterback of the football team. Graduating in 1926, he had joined the Athletic Department as an assistant coach for several sports. When Laurie Cox retired in 1932, Simmons became head coach of lacrosse and remained in that position until April 1942, when he entered the navy. For the remainder of the war, Simmons served as an athletic instructor in the navy's Division of Physical Education, where he prepared naval aviators by teaching boxing at a preflight school in Athens, Georgia.[41]

Coaches and administrators argued that lacrosse prepared their players well for military service. In their view, warrior skills honed on the athletic field were easily transferred to the battlefront. The USILA dedicated its official guide for 1943 to the "real MEN OF LACROSSE" who had answered America's call to arms. "With a deep feeling of humility," editor Albert Brisotti of New York University applauded the nation's lacrosse players, whom he termed a "superior breed." In Brisotti's view, the athletes turned soldiers were "translating the gameness of the playfield to the courage of the battlefield."[42] The next year he drew parallels between the modern lacrosse player and the ancient Indian warrior. The ancient native stick, ball, field, and equipment had changed, Brisotti wrote, but "the heart of the game" was still preparing the modern athlete for the crises in Europe and the Pacific: "So, with the call of war, almost en masse, he 'joins up.' Teamwork, sacrifice! Certainly that's his game!"[43] Navy coach William "Dinty" Moore bragged about lacrosse players from the naval and army academies who were serving in the war. Retelling an anecdote from the Guadalcanal campaign, Moore alleged that one high-ranking naval officer and former lacrosse player had said, "A lacrosse team midfield winging its way downfield to the attack approximates nothing so closely as a fleet formation."[44]

The game of lacrosse might have been seen as preparing men for war, but many officials also wanted to use the war to promote their sport. At the 1942 meeting of the USILA, delegates voted to promote lacrosse as a form of war training. In a letter to the *New York Times* a Philadelphian praised lacrosse as a "more effective body-builder" than baseball: "As a conditioner of men, the Indian game, which demands stamina, quick thinking, speed and pluck, has few peers." Seeing the military benefits of lacrosse, the editors concurred: "Because lacrosse is such a rough-and-tumble sport, timid folk were for giving it back to the Indians long ago. But it's good to know that it's still afoot and a move is on to spread it around the armed camps, where rough-and-tumble sports are in high favor."[45] According to Harvard graduate and Boston L.C. president Charles E. Marsters, lacrosse players outperformed their baseball and track counterparts as athletes. An "improvement in work index" study published in the *Yale Journal of Biology and Medicine* concluded that its continuous running gave lacrosse a superior fitness rating. "Seldom . . . has superior ammunition been put into the hands of lacrosse organizers for the reduction of antagonism toward installation or continuance of the Indian game," Baltimore sportswriter Craig Taylor wrote. "It is shown to be most beneficial in the very direction in which most programs of athletics are being pointed."[46] At last, Taylor concluded, lacrosse would have a chance to expand.

High school lacrosse experienced many of same problems as the intercollegiate game during the Depression and World War II. Unavailable or expensive equipment, a lack of trained coaches, and an image of the game as excessively violent all stunted the growth of schoolboy lacrosse.[47] The interscholastic game declined from about forty programs to thirty-two, but regional and local conditions differed. For instance, the Depression and the war especially devastated lacrosse in high schools in Brooklyn and upstate New York. Short on funds for athletics, about two-thirds of these predominantly public institutions abandoned the game. However, in New England and Maryland, where many of the participating institutions were prep schools, financial and moral support was more forthcoming. At the beginning of the 1930s, the New England and Maryland schools had accounted for 45 percent of all schools playing lacrosse; by the end of the war, the figure had grown to 78 percent. During this same period, the number of schools in Maryland playing lacrosse fell from seventeen to fifteen. These patterns highlight the close ties between the Ivy League and schools such as the Phillips and Exeter Academies in New England.

Universities and colleges in Maryland and southern Pennsylvania also possessed very close relationships with surrounding secondary schools.

Prep and elite public schools in Baltimore often hired former college players to coach their programs. In 1930 former Johns Hopkins, Swarthmore, and Saint John's players coached at many local schools. In 1934 the Gilman Country School secured the coaching services of former Johns Hopkins and current Mount Washington players Jack and Doug Turnbull. Many of the schoolboys they coached found their way onto varsity college rosters. According to Baltimore native Caleb Kelly, the affluent neighborhoods around Johns Hopkins, northern Baltimore, and surrounding suburbs such as Catonsville typically sent their sons to Johns Hopkins. During the late 1920s Kelly had attended the Quaker-run Friends School in Bolton Hill, about a mile and a half southwest of the Johns Hopkins campus. Kelly characterized Bolton Hill as decidedly affluent, home of the "shabby elite." Most residents of this "old Baltimore" were physicians, dentists, attorneys, bankers, and stockbrokers. "They didn't work with their hands. Most of them worked with their minds," he said. These families stressed the importance of the social customs of the affluent: "Within two blocks of where I lived, there must have been in some years a half dozen debutantes. Even if they had no money, they came out. Different life entirely. You had the idea that some were blue bloods and some weren't."[48] Although many college-bound men from such neighborhoods came from the professional class, they often lacked the means to attend an Ivy League school, especially during the Depression. Recalling the mostly local composition of the Johns Hopkins teams for which he had played from 1930 through 1933, Kelly said, "A lot of the guys who came to play for us would have gone to other colleges except their parents couldn't afford it. Hopkins was cheap so they sent them to Hopkins."[49] In 1941, twenty-five of the twenty-six men on the Johns Hopkins varsity were native Marylanders, including eight from the public Baltimore City College and six from Friends School.[50]

The affluent composition of schoolboy lacrosse in Baltimore allowed the local interscholastic association to prosper during the Second World War. Although there had been 683 schoolboys representing nine schools in 1941, there were 943 boys from eleven schools by 1945.[51] Five thousand fans turned out to see six-time champion Saint Paul's School defeat the Maryland Scholastic Association all-star team at Johns Hopkins in 1945. Such support for lacrosse in Baltimore caused younger schoolboys to emulate undergraduates by taking up the game at an even earlier age. Seeing youth playing on the city's back lots, Boys' Latin School coach Claxton W.

O'Connor observed that young children had succumbed to "Maryland Madness."[52] Sportswriter Craig Taylor referred to a group of boys who lived near Johns Hopkins and called themselves the Hopkins Bulldogs as "a guerilla band of lacrosse players" with "no clubhouse, no coach" who "represent nothing except a liking for lacrosse."[53] These scrappy youngsters made Johns Hopkins their home long before enrolling, even playing on the varsity field between halves of university contests. Never mind its medical school; it was Johns Hopkins' championship-caliber lacrosse program that strengthened ties with local schoolboys.

Prep school lacrosse in New England also survived the ordeals of the period. Schools with teams in the 1930s had included the Deerfield (Massachusetts), Governor Dummer (South Byfield, Massachusetts), Kimball Union (Meriden, New Hampshire), Lawrence (Groton, Massachusetts), Phillips (Andover, Massachusetts), Thornton (Saco, Maine), and Worcester (Massachusetts) Academies. Due to the great distances between them, their squads scheduled contests with frosh and varsity teams from area colleges, creating occasions for frequent social contact between prep schools and centers of elite higher education.[54] Phillips Academy had periodically fielded teams as early as the 1870s, later abandoning but reviving the game again in 1930. The new interest resulted from the efforts of recently hired Dartmouth graduate Hernon Hagenbuckle, a French teacher known for throwing chalk at drowsy students. An eccentric who played the violin while dancing nude in his apartment, Hagenbuckle enrolled about forty students to play lacrosse. Throughout the 1930s, Phillips played against the Boston L.C. and freshmen teams from Harvard, MIT, Springfield, and Tufts. The Andover boys also began a rivalry with the Exeter Academy in 1935.[55] Lacrosse at these elite academies solidified social ties with Ivy League universities, with many prep school graduates later attending Harvard and Yale, among others.

Club and intercollegiate coaches also fostered schoolboy play in greater New York City and upstate New York. The Crescent Athletic–Hamilton Club sponsored a Brooklyn high school league, while coaches and players from Syracuse, Cornell, Colgate, and Hobart nurtured the game in central New York. Walter Smith, president of the Syracuse Interscholastic Football League, noted that Syracuse University promoted schoolboy lacrosse around the city, especially among youth less affluent than their Maryland counterparts. "It is almost as common to see youngsters playing lacrosse upon the vacant lots of Syracuse as to see them engaged in base ball," Smith asserted. "Each spring finds numerous informal groups of small boys of grammar school age forming themselves into so-called lacrosse teams, often outfitted entirely with homemade equipment, even including the sticks."[56] Under local attorney and former Syracuse University player Frank Fiori, Central High School played its own alumni, Geneva High School, and college freshman teams. While Syracuse University had to develop talent on campus to a greater extent than did universities in Maryland, the varsity included experienced athletes from Brooklyn and central New York.

Although public school lacrosse in New York City and Brooklyn had seemed vibrant during the 1920s, the Depression brought ruin. Manual Training and Boys High had had programs for more than two decades, but the league of public and private schools slowly disintegrated during the 1930s. Brooklyn's intercity high school championship series with Baltimore was abandoned, and the local Public School Athletic League dropped its high school championship tournament in January 1939 because of declining interest and insufficient playing space. Although the western division schools of the Metropolitan and Long Island Interscholastic Lacrosse League folded in 1940 due to lack of funding, playing space, and teacher supervision at Alexander Hamilton, Manual Training, Erasmus Hall, and Boys High, the eastern division continued play with Poly Prep, Manhasset, Garden City, and Sewanhaka. What had long been a hotbed of youth lacrosse was decimated.

The Great Depression and the Second World War strained the efforts of collegiate and club officials to foster scholastic lacrosse. By 1945, however, it became clear that the conception of lacrosse as an elite game had survived. After all, while play had been severely curtailed among public schools in New York, prep school lacrosse in New England and Maryland had remained stable. Unlike their public school counterparts elsewhere, those who attended private schools in Baltimore or academies in New England had remained active members of the American lacrosse community. The Depression and the war had stifled any immediate potential for social diversification. After the war, however, schoolboys who had attended these private institutions headed for elite universities throughout the Northeast, and some later coached the next generation of lacrosse players. After the war the less affluent enthusiasts in New York City and central New York faced difficulty in reestablishing interscholastic play and in maintaining their position within a sport dominated by more affluent sportsmen. In the end, the apostles of American lacrosse battled economic and wartime disruptions and came to focus attention on the importance of amateur sport.

Searching for an American Identity: British Ideals and Olympic Glory

Organized American lacrosse was relatively young and fragile in the years following the First World War. Seeking to keep the game amateur, advocates built ties with the organized lacrosse community of Great Britain. This led to a series of exchange tours between America and Britain. Even as tour commentators contrasted British sportsmanship with an American tendency to take games too seriously, American coaches and organizers learned valuable cultural lessons. They did not emulate the British approach to sport completely, but they followed the contours of an elite British model of sport rather than one accepting professionalism and commercialism. The Anglo-American link justified the preexisting exclusive aura of American lacrosse. Meanwhile, other international competitions punctuated by two Olympics also helped to define the American game. Because of these developments, a growing number of Americans believed the cultural center of George Beers's game had moved south into their country. The expansion of collegiate and scholastic play during the 1920s created alternatives to the gentlemanly conception of the game, but lessons learned during foreign competition, combined with the crises of the Great Depression and World War II, effectively purged organized lacrosse of any significant dissent.

Oxbridge and America

Syracuse coach Laurie Cox led efforts to organize a series of transatlantic tours between 1922 and 1937. In December 1921 Cox negotiated an agreement: a combined squad from Oxford and Cambridge would journey to the United States in 1922, and his Syracuse varsity would go to England the following year. According to one English official, "We will have established an international alliance to be likened to that which prevails between the two British universities and Harvard, Princeton, Yale and Cornell."[57] The month-long excursion of 1922 reflected several themes, including American celebration of British amateurism, cordial Anglo-American social relations, and heightened support for lacrosse on many campuses. Ironically, half the British team was Canadian-born. The roster also included Frank

Morley of Haverford, Pennsylvania, a Rhodes scholar from Johns Hopkins and a U.S. Army veteran. The team also featured an English nobleman and eight former British Army officers. According to the American press, the Oxbridge squad played an important role in the cultivation of lacrosse in the United States: "They are fast, keen exponents of the game once played by whole villages of Indians, and their swing around the circuit . . . should do much to extend the popularity of the sport."[58] The British compiled an 8–7 record against American opposition, but then lost the finale to the University of Montreal. Most American opponents were collegian squads, except for the Mount Washington L.C., the Crescent A.C., and a team of college graduates and Seneca Indians who called themselves the Scalp and Blade A.C. of Buffalo.[59]

The extensive press coverage of the tour revolved around the differences between the American and Oxbridge athletes. While the British athletes paid the initial costs out of their own pockets or through bank loans and played for their health and for sport's sake, journalists wrote, the Americans were excessively aggressive, too serious about winning, and over-trained. The Oxbridge athletes accepted easier training methods and a healthy approach to sport, but the Americans seemed hell-bent on winning, body checking when necessary and occasionally incurring injuries. Against this backdrop, the commentators felt, the Americans might learn from the British. For instance, Syracuse head coach Laurie Cox explained to readers an incident during Syracuse's 4–3 victory before five thousand spectators that had shown the meaning of elite sportsmanship. In an article entitled "BRITONS SHOW SPORTSMANSHIP IN LOCAL GAME" for the *Syracuse Herald,* Cox said the Oxbridge athletes had been true gentlemen: "On the first goal scored, the ball coming with great speed struck the Syracuse goal tender in the forehead and knocked him down and out, the ball rolling slowly into the net. Captain Hopkins of the British team at once refused the goal, but the goal had been legitimately scored and the Syracuse captain insisted it be allowed." Since spectators could not have heard the on-field discussion, Cox went out of his way to show how the British valued sportsmanship over victory. He also urged students to support lacrosse on campus: "If in the future, we do not get crowds to see good lacrosse games in Syracuse then Syracusans are not connoisseurs of thrilling sport."[60]

Alumni, fraternities and sororities, athletic clubs, and various Anglo-American social clubs entertained the Englishmen during the tour. Most pregame ceremonies emphasized harmony between England and America, displaying crossed flags of the two countries and playing patriotic songs such as "God Save the King" and "The Star Spangled Banner." Prior to the match with the Crescent A.C. in Brooklyn, four thousand spectators saw a local Scottish Highlanders marching band escort first the Oxbridge team onto the field playing "The Campbells Are Coming" and then the local Crescents to the tune of "Yankee Doodle."[61] These symbols of transatlantic Anglo-Saxonism and class solidarity accentuated American praise for elite British sportsmanship. Syracuse University's athletics department even published a guide on how to treat the British visitors: the campus community should have friendly conversations with them, cheer for them, and serve them graciously.[62] Tour and game organizers portrayed games as civic events, but lacrosse enthusiasts in Baltimore thought otherwise. Instead of using the label "tourists" to describe the Oxbridge athletes, the student press at Johns Hopkins called them "invaders" and "foreign forces" and depicted the contests as "engagements" and "hostilities." When Johns Hopkins beat Oxbridge, the paper employed historical rhetoric: "It was at Baltimore that the English sustained a serious defeat in the War of 1812; it was in that same city that another invading force from the British Isles was repelled on April 8, 1922."[63]

To American lacrosse officials, the English tour of 1922 was a major public relations coup. Lacrosse became more popular on many campuses, and the display of British amateurism reinforced an existing principle of the Americans. "No team of sportsmen that has visited this country has made a more favorable impression or contributed more to the establishment of a permanent Anglo-American accord," the Crescent A.C.'s magazine observed, "no team ever exemplified to a higher degree the qualities which go to make up a sportsman and a gentleman."[64] American enchantment with English amateurism illustrates a willingness by lacrosse enthusiasts across the United States to be real gentlemen. The tour's close win-loss record surely made this cultural pill easy to swallow. Sufficient gate receipts and athletic department funds forestalled any significant controversy. Ironically, the tour's commercial success allowed lacrosse officials to celebrate the lessons of sport for sport's sake. Although confident of the quality of their play, the Americans realized that their community was still relatively small. However, they knew they had strong institutional support.

Shortly after the English visit, Syracuse University proposed to retake the informal international championship in 1923. Although many coaches acknowledged Laurie Cox as a major leader in American lacrosse, the selection of the Orangemen elicited criticism, especially from the school with the most adversarial stance against the British the year before. In May 1922, the *Johns Hopkins News-Letter* questioned Syracuse's belligerent play. Commenting on Syracuse's victory over Hopkins, they accused the Orangemen of holding, tripping and slugging their players, and admonished one penalized Syracuse defense man who "sneaked back upon the playing field, openly defying the authorities." The paper strongly questioned the USILL's choice of Syracuse as the American representative to tour England. "If the New Yorkers do decide to take the big trip," the editors observed, "we sincerely hope that the cleansing properties of the great Atlantic will first wash off the nasty black spot upon the Orange."[65] Although this indictment may have been sour grapes, it reflected a belief in Baltimore that more authentic gentlemen were found at Johns Hopkins.

With funds raised by student athletes and sorority sisters, the Syracuse team toured England in 1923 after playing its domestic schedule of fifteen matches. Much as during the Oxbridge trip the year before, private clubs, universities, and even city officials played host to the visitors, treating them to parties, car rides, and concerts.[66] Even though Syracuse won six of the nine contests, taking the international title, the English press complimented the team for "taking their successes with becoming modesty and their defeats without excuses."[67] Apparently any alleged unsportsmanlike behavior by Syracuse exhibited in Baltimore, or anywhere else for that matter, had been suppressed. Financially, the tour resulted in a $5,000 deficit for Syracuse, but coach Cox and other officials deemed it a success.[68] Compared to the Oxford-Cambridge tour of 1922, the Syracuse tour of England likely had less of an impact on American lacrosse. Aside from possibly stirring the dreams of collegians back in the United States, the tour probably made Cox more conscious of his own role as a national figure in the sport. Even after he retired from coaching in 1932, he remained active as an intercollegiate administrator.

Oxford and Cambridge athletes returned to the United States in the spring of 1926. In the opening match the University of Maryland trounced the British before a Washington, D.C., crowd of four thousand spectators, including British Ambassador Sir Esme Howard and Lady Ward. Howard told both teams that friendly sporting rivalries would cement good relations between the two anglophone powers. Injuries forced the English to cancel their Yale match, but the Crescents loaned them one of their first-string players after the English goal tender suffered a knee injury. This gentlemanly act demonstrated how well the Americans understood the British notion of sport for sport's sake. Despite the dismal 1–12 record of the visitors, the American press once again praised English sportsmanship. Examining "English Ideas of Sport," the *New York Times* noted that on-field losses by the English had had nothing to do with their off-field social status: "The young Englishman undoubtedly likes to win quite as much as does the young American, but he seldom yearns to die for dear old Alma Mater." The Oxbridge athletes had probably enjoyed themselves more because they had not just been pursuing victory. "Striving hard to win in any game is always right, but perhaps our players might enjoy sports really more if they took them just a trifle less seriously," the New York press commented. "After all, second or third or last place in an intercollegiate athletic contest does not necessarily forecast total failure in life." An athletic defeat did not mean that the sons of affluent families would not enjoy careers as businessmen. Chastising the Americans for their tendency to be overly competitive, one of the newspaper's columnists endorsed British amateurism: "Who can say their policy is not the wisest?"[69]

At every tour stop students and alumni showered the English team with parties and concerts. "Regardless of what we Americans say about America First, about the superior vestments of the red-blooded American, about the enjoyment of being a resident and child of these United States," the *Syracuse Daily Orange* observed, "there is always a distinct feeling of satisfaction in encountering a son or daughter of England. . . . It will be a long time before we reach the point of refinement topped today by the English."[70] The Syracuse press also noted that the Englishmen had "showed as much ability on the dance floor and in the gentler arts as they had on the lacrosse field."[71] Except for the poor on-field performance by this group of Englishmen, the lacrosse tours of 1922 and 1926 had much in common; relations on and off the field augmented the valuable cultural lessons learned. Unfortunately for the American organizers, however, the second English visit was less successful financially and competitively than that of 1922. As a result, the USILA insisted that the English would be invited again only if they could field a stronger team.

The English did not return until 1930, when thirteen men from Oxford and four from Cambridge came to New York to retake the International Cup. Since athletic directors around the country doubted the marketability of the visitors, many schools submitted meager gate guarantees to the USILA. Apparently the lessons of amateurism were not enough; commercial concerns had become paramount. Offered fewer dollars, the executive committee tried to collect half the guarantees in advance to allow the visitors to purchase round-trip steamship tickets, but many schools made payments slowly, forcing the committee to fund the balance. The on-field victories and national origins of the British team bothered some American officials. Eight Oxford men were Rhodes scholars from North America, including team captain and 1928 Olympic veteran A. E. Grauer of British Columbia and captain-elect Larken H. Farinholt, a veteran of the Johns Hopkins Olympic team. This edition of the Oxbridge team dominated American collegians, with a 12–2–1 record before crowds smaller than in 1926, possibly due to poor weather. Following accusations that some of the visiting players were "ringers," the American feeling of goodwill toward the British lessened. Because some of the athletes were enrolled in correspondence courses instead of in Oxford or Cambridge, the Americans had a point.[72]

The 1930 tour demonstrated that the English had learned something from the Americans, namely taking winning seriously. Even though the tour included the usual campus parties and a visit to the British embassy, the Americans were less forthcoming in their praise for British amateurism. Perhaps Americans were sore over the on-field superiority of the English. After all, American praise for English standards was most plentiful when the former equaled or bettered the latter. Noticeably absent from the tour was a match against Johns Hopkins. The university's student press admonished Syracuse coach Laurie Cox for scheduling the Naval Academy instead of Johns Hopkins, and also criticized the Johns Hopkins faculty for not permitting the varsity to play in a last-minute midweek match with Oxbridge: "So Hopkins has lost a game that would have been very attractive both from a competitive and a social standpoint due to the arbitrary and dictatorial tactics of one man and faculty opposition."[73] At the tour's end, Cox knew it would be a while before the Americans made a return trip to the British Isles, because they would have to pay their own way due to the lack of gate fees in England.

The Depression-era reduction in athletics budgets explains the short-age of tours in the 1930s. Many American teams were lucky to receive funding for their own abbreviated playing schedules. English organizers invited the USILA to send a team several times, but a lack of money precluded any tour. Even the International Olympic Committee had to back down from including lacrosse at the 1936 Berlin Games.[74] When the English made cash guarantees to the Americans to help offset a touring team's expenses, the USILA agreed to send a team in 1937. To preclude one school's paying the remaining expenses, the USILA sent an all-star team, with institutions paying for their own members.[75] Despite congressional allegations of a conspiracy between Britain and American arms manufacturers before American entry into the Great War, passage in the United States of neutrality legislation, and the American public's dismay over the British government's handling of King Edward's VIII's abdication in 1936, the English and American lacrosse communities ignored strained diplomatic relations for the sake of gentlemanly sport. Aside from displaying the American flag, the English accommodated their American guests by consenting to American rules, which included playing on a smaller field with ten instead of twelve players. They also abandoned their prohibition on substitution by allowing three player replacements during a match.[76]

The American all-stars outperformed previous tour teams by winning all seven matches against club, county, district, and national teams, attracting crowds of up to five thousand spectators. As before, the hosts emphasized the social features of the sporting venture, overwhelming the Americans with free bus transportation, July Fourth entertainment, dinner parties, and trips to "estates, factories, libraries, museums," and a cricket match. Describing the Americans as "fine fellows and sportsmen," one English paper suggested that the Americans had learned to be gentlemen: "On the field they play a clean, sporting game; off the field they are a good lot of fellows to meet socially and they are certainly having a good time and appreciate the spirit in which they have been met."[77] Unfortunately for fans in both countries, there would be no further tours anytime soon, largely due to the outbreak of the Second World War. Although gate receipts and tour guarantees concerned the British and Americans alike, the transatlantic tours reaffirmed the importance of gentlemanly sportsmanship for American lacrosse enthusiasts.

The Origins of American Women's Lacrosse

Oxford, Cambridge, and clubs throughout the United Kingdom served as athletics tutors for American sportsmen during the interwar period, but the phenomenon was not confined to the realm of male sport. The push for women's and girls' lacrosse in the United States came not from American men, but from female physical educators trained in Britain. English women had adopted lacrosse after Indian and Canadian gentlemen's lacrosse clubs toured England in 1876, and eventually formed their own English Lacrosse Union by 1892. Women's lacrosse started at Saint Leonard's School for Girls in Saint Andrews, Scotland, in 1890. The version of lacrosse formalized under headmistress Frances Jane Dove was quite different from the men's game, prohibiting bodily contact and emphasizing feminine etiquette. After the game had spread to other schools, alumni formed a Southern Ladies' Lacrosse Club in 1905 in London, and then several club representatives created the Ladies' Lacrosse Association in 1912.[78] Returning home from school in England during the early 1930s, American women introduced lacrosse into physical education curricula when they became instructors. After early experiments at Wellesley and Sargent Colleges, the first successful effort was made in 1912 at a women's field hockey camp in Mount Pocono. Over the next few years, physical educators in New England, Baltimore, and Philadelphia introduced lacrosse to their students.[79] During 1931 and 1932, these pioneers formed the United States Women's Lacrosse Association (USWLA), and they held their first national tournament in 1933 at the Greenwich Academy in Connecticut. The USWLA was a national alliance of local associations of mostly adult athletes, along with affiliated universities, colleges, and private and public secondary schools. In 1932 there were associations in Baltimore, Boston, New York, and Philadelphia, which included five collegian and eleven secondary programs. A fifth Association in Westchester County, New York, was added in 1932. The number of universities, colleges, and secondary schools grew to forty-one by 1935.[80]

Proponents of women's lacrosse constantly distinguished their version of the sport from the rougher male game. The women's game lacked boundaries, and the prohibition of bodily contact made most forms of protective gear unnecessary, except for the goal tender. Pioneers of the ladies' game feared that casual spectators and potential players would assume that the men's and women's games were synonymous. In 1935 Olney High School instructor Martha Gable of Philadelphia urged parents and school officials not to be skeptical of the advisability of allowing their girls to play lacrosse based on perceptions of the male game. By adapting the sport to "the capacities of girls," rules makers had altered it to provide "little chance for roughness and undesirable physical contact." After initial skepticism, brothers and other relatives endorsed women's lacrosse at the national women's tournament in Philadelphia in 1935. "They were surprised and delighted by the skill and speed of both school and association players, and by the absence of the expected roughness," Gable wrote. "In every case, the response of the men was enthusiastic approval."[81]

The guiding ethos of American women's lacrosse was in line with that of the Women's Division of the National Amateur Athletic Federation during the interwar period. These educators viewed extreme competition as injurious to the cultivation of respectable womanhood. In response to the growing commercial influence in female athletics, they took a stand against "mannish" sport. By excluding overcompetitive women and those who did not come from affluent families, they hoped to develop a genteel identity for the game that did not threaten gender roles. By championing healthy and virtuous sport and deemphasizing rigorous activity, these women battled advocates of popular women's sport who called for vigorous and sensual athletics emphasizing competition.[82] Many believed field hockey expressed this conception of elite women's sport, and lacrosse was often regarded as compatible. At a convention of the American Physical Education Association in 1929, Joyce Cran of Wellesley College said women's lacrosse was an "ideal game for girls" because it provided for healthy, graceful, and unselfish fair play. In contrast to the awkward crouching in field hockey, Cran noted that lacrosse players ran in the upright position and thus achieved proper posture.[83] At a New York Women's Lacrosse Association meeting in February 1934, some leaders predicted that lacrosse would rival and eventually even replace field hockey.

Because many early enthusiasts of the women's game were either English-trained Americans or transplanted Britons, English and American organizations exchanged tours from 1934 to 1936. As in men's lacrosse during this period, English lady athletes provided a model for Americans to follow. Unlike their male counterparts in 1930, however, the fifteen English women who arrived in New York City in April 1934 came to teach lacrosse at American colleges and private schools. Greeted by officials from the USWLA, the U.S. Field Hockey Association, and the International Federation of Women's Hockey Associations, the English ladies' "goodwill tour" had stops in New York, Philadelphia, Baltimore, Virginia, Boston, and Greenwich, Connecticut. The English women rarely competed as a unit, but instead played on mixed squads with rather than against local aggregations. This allowed the far more skilled English women to achieve equilibrium in play, deemphasize national rivalry, and teach skills and tactics during play. Dubbing these women "English missionary maids,"[84] the press highlighted the differences between the male and female versions of the game. Commenting on the match at Saint Mary's Cathedral School for Girls in Garden City, the *New York Times* referred to women's lacrosse as "a far milder form of competition than is the game of assault and battery perpetrated by the men." To reinforce the lessons learned during the English visit, the USWLA sent a team to Britain in 1935 for additional instruction. After one week of lessons from the All England Ladies Lacrosse Association at Brighton, the Americans played matches in London, Oxford, Dublin, and Liverpool. "They helped us tremendously and were such good sports that often they would stop during a game, after scoring," noted team manager Amanda Norris of Baltimore, "and show our defense how we should have played to prevent a goal."[85] An All-England team returned to the United States in 1936 for a six-week expedition, which included exhibitions in Chicago and Philadelphia and participation in the fourth annual USWLA tournament at the Riverdale School in New York.

As did male advocates of lacrosse, supporters of the women's game emphasized character development through sport. After the 1936 national tournament, the *Literary Digest* noted a dilemma: "Despite the fact that it is less dangerous than men's lacrosse, the women's game still involves fast-moving and swinging wood." Apparently women blended their sense of femininity with a toughness to cope with injuries. One sportswriter said women played with great "vim, vigor, and verve and never call for stretchers, broken-bone splints or arnica until the last whistle blows and nothing further need be done for Alma Mater."[86] Women's lacrosse proponents carefully distinguished their genteel version of the game from the rougher male form, but also stressed common benefits. According to 1934 All-American reserve Virginia Bourquardez, lacrosse instilled judgment and confidence. In her mind, the "feeling of initiating the attack, and urging it forward, is one of the big thrills of defense play and cannot be experienced in any other game to the same degree."[87] The spirit professed by Bourquardez called for a tamer version of the male game that did not threaten contemporary gender roles. By developing an athletic ethos consistent with that of other elite sports and engaging English lady athletes as teachers, advocates of American women's lacrosse made their game a permanent part of the landscape.

From the mid-1930s through the Second World War, schools in New York, Poughkeepsie, Baltimore, Garden City, and Greenwich took turns hosting the national tournament. The USWLA crowned no official champions, but the women from Philadelphia almost always dominated. The desire of the USWLA to deemphasize rivalry between institutions or cities can be seen in its decision to combine players from different cities regularly. For these enthusiasts, participation and health took precedence over competition and exuberance. The USWLA even created a generic team called the "Et Ceteras," a conglomeration of reserves plus a handful of girls from cities like Chicago that did not have full rosters. Originated by Iroquois Indians, modernized by Canadian gentlemen, adopted by English sportsmen, and feminized for British schoolgirls, women's lacrosse in Britain and then America was as much a product of Victorian sporting culture as it was of Native Americans. The All England Ladies Lacrosse Association cultivated interest among American women, representing the further shaping of American sport according to strict amateur standards. Abhorring the emphasis on competition seen in popular women's sports, U.S. advocates of lacrosse called for a form of healthy athletics learned from England. However, just as it did men's lacrosse, World War II curtailed women's play considerably. Collegian and schoolgirl programs fared much worse than the club game. In 1940 there were only twenty allied institutions. Although this figure grew to twenty-seven in 1942, it fell to twenty-two by the end of the war.[88]

Lacrosse as an International Sport

While the English were providing useful cultural ideals throughout the interwar period for lacrosse enthusiasts in the United States, other international contests were also creating cultural forums for the definition of the men's game. Competition at the 1928 and 1932 summer Olympics, as well as a Canadian-American series from 1930 to 1936, provided American advocates with another way to understand their sport in nationalistic terms.

After lacrosse was sanctioned as a demonstration sport for the 1928 Olympics in Amsterdam, American Olympic Committee president Major General Douglas MacArthur created a special lacrosse committee.[89] Instead of selecting an all-star team to represent the United States, it sent an existing team that was determined by a play-off involving the University of Maryland, Rutgers, Johns Hopkins, Army, Navy, and the Mount Washington L.C.[90] The $19,000 raised from gate receipts and the fifteen thousand people who witnessed Johns Hopkins triumph over Maryland in the finale seemed a good omen.[91] In Holland forty thousand spectators witnessed the first day of lacrosse competition at the Olympic Stadium, even though the end of the marathon and the women's high jump had delayed the match by two hours. Despite praising lacrosse as a "highly entertaining and stimulating game," the Amsterdam press characterized the Americans' victory over Canada as particularly violent: "There can be no doubt that the opinion which most prevailed among our uninitiated was that the players were just there to beat each other up with the sticks."[92]

Meanwhile, officials from the United States, Canada, England, and Australia used the Olympic setting to establish an International Federation of Amateur Lacrosse. For readers back home, coach Ray Van Orman emphasized the gentlemanly behavior of his players: "MacArthur and others unknown to me said that the Johns Hopkins team was the most mannerly and the most attractive group of fellows on board the boat. Even in Paris . . . the boys were easily controlled. There was no boozing and when the boys were told to go to bed they went to bed."[93] Orman surely exaggerated the restrained behavior of his players, but his statement was meant to uphold a positive public image of the program. Despite a three-way tie resulting from each team's winning one game in a round-robin tournament, fans at Johns Hopkins claimed a "world" championship on the basis of goal differential. Ironically, the Johns Hopkins men undermined the prevailing notion of gentlemanly sport by emphasizing victory in this unofficial competition.

Olympic play inspired other international matches. For a two-game international championship slated for 1930, the Canadian Lacrosse Association chose the Oshawa General Motors L.C. to represent their country, with the USILA opting for a college all-star team. After the Americans won the first match in Toronto, sour Canadians contended that Yankee conditioning had triumphed over Canuck skill. The *Toronto Telegram* commemorated the loss with a poem:

Since the days when Hiawatha made Lacrosse the daily dozen,
Of his Tribe of Noble Red Hides made lacrosse clubs fiercely rattle,
So that when they went to battle with some other copper nation
War would seem a quiet vacation,
Since them days this here Dominion always felt it had a corner
On lacrosse and how to play it,
Til last night it dawned upon us as the haughty Oshawanas
Broke their ranks in wild disorder that old John J. Hiawatha
Did his stuff across the border.

—Moaner McGruffey

Oshawa won the second match and the overall goal count, thereby securing the new cup donated by CLA president Joseph Lally. Even though the
Toronto press labeled the Americans "first class athletes and real sportsmen," it also said the narrow victory served as a national warning. "Canadians were taught a lesson that they will have to take their national game
more seriously," the *Toronto Mail and Empire* observed, "for with the American players improving all the time and picking up many pointers in the international series it will be doubly difficult to keep the lacrosse laurels here
in future championships."[94] Canadians who still praised lacrosse as their
national game saw the series as a foreboding sign. Excessive violence and
the rise of baseball had already contributed to the decline of lacrosse in
Canada. Losing a contest to Americans simply worsened matters.

A Canadian-American rematch came one year later in Baltimore. Saint
John's College of Annapolis captured the Lally Cup by achieving more goals
in two matches with a Canadian all-star team before crowds of six thousand and eight thousand at Johns Hopkins. During the second match a fistfight cleared the two teams' benches, with about two hundred spectators
pouring onto the field until policemen intervened. Asking his countrymen
"What's Wrong with Our Lacrosse?," Fred Lorenson argued that Canadians
had allowed their national game to fall into obscurity. "They lacked nothing in the finesse of the game," Lorenson commented, "and used none of
this heavy arm-clouting which has come to be regarded as part of the Canadian sport and which, as much as anything else, soured the sport-minded
public of Canada on lacrosse." Praising the men from the tiny Annapolis
college, Lorenson believed the younger American collegians possessed advantages over Canadian club men based on age and time available for practice. Citing the quality of play at all levels of American lacrosse, Lorenson

argued that Canada's neighbors had achieved supremacy. Lorenson's fears were well founded; Canadian participation in lacrosse had declined by one-third since 1923, and three-quarters of all Indian-made lacrosse sticks were sold in the United States.[95]

Lorenson contended that "needless clouting" and unenforced rules accounted for much of the sport's decline in Canada. However, he and others believed that cultivating the game at high schools might halt the trend. Toronto teacher Donald Graham introduced lacrosse in 1928 at his Runnymede High School, and some 250 of 278 male students played with and owned sticks by 1931. Espousing views George Beers would have agreed with, Lorenson praised Graham's efforts: "These lads are compelled to play without pads and the game is regarded as its originators intended it to be, and as our American friends play it—one of speed, science and endurance." With most students abandoning the game upon graduation, Lorenson believed that Canadians would have to relearn the game from the Americans, who played roughly, to be sure, but shunned excessive violence. "There's nothing wrong with lacrosse itself," Lorenson concluded. "But there's something wrong with lacrosse in Canada. What are we going to do about it?"[96] Actually, the president and executive secretary of the CLA claimed that amateur lacrosse in Canada was experiencing a partial revival by 1932. Ontario, Quebec, Manitoba, Alberta, and British Columbia all had district associations, administering about 300 clubs, including 125 teams and 2,120 players in Ontario alone.[97]

Lacrosse advocates worked hard to include their game at the Los Angeles Olympics of 1932, settling for demonstration rather than medal status.[98] Efforts to include Australia and England failed due to traveling costs and the fact that most of their players were "young businessmen" who were unable to take time off from work. The Olympic organizers wrestled with the idea of having a Native American team representing Iroquois peoples as competition for the United States and Canada.[99] After all, an Indian team had won the bronze medal in 1904, but those Mohawks had represented Canada, not a sovereign tribe. Cognizant of the financial success of the six-team 1928 Olympic tryout tournament, the American Olympic Lacrosse Committee (AOLC) hoped an eight-team elimination tournament would generate funds for the new Olympic team. By late spring, however, problems surfaced. Teams bailed out before taking the field, and some officials criticized the possible presence of an Indian team and the entire scheme for selecting the national Olympic representative. In February, international officials still intended to have an Indian team selected from the several Iroquois reservations and coached by Onondaga chief and former Carlisle star Jesse Lyons. However, they eventually decided against the idea.

The AOLC automatically gave tournament berths to Army, Navy, Johns Hopkins, Saint John's, Maryland, and Mount Washington. The committee bypassed three Ivy League schools to give Rutgers and an all-star team of Six Nations Indians the other two spots. The shift in thinking from automatically giving the Indians an Olympic spot to requiring them to compete in the American tryout tournament had resulted from several considerations. Automatically granting the Indians a berth might have raised troublesome national sovereignty and organizational jurisdiction questions that sports authorities in Canada and the United States wished to avoid. Besides, the Olympics were a forum for nation-states; most of the world saw indigenous peoples as wards of national governments. But many lacrosse officials understood the Indian origins of the game and felt obligated to include an Iroquois team. Because the strongest teams in the country resided in Maryland, AOLC and USILA officials probably felt the Iroquois were no serious threat to the other teams that wished to represent the United States anyway. Declaring "Choice of Redskins for Play-Off Lacks Logical Explanation," the *Baltimore Sun* echoed Johns Hopkins coach Ray Van Orman's contention that the Indians did not merit Olympic consideration because of their dismal performance against top-flight collegiate teams.[100] Criticizing the athletic quality of the Iroquois was one issue, but that this strong opposition came from a Baltimore coach was very significant. After all, Baltimore enthusiasts believed lacrosse was *their* game. Meanwhile, the withdrawal of the two service academies forced the AOLC to scurry for replacements. To fill in for Army, the committee picked the Crescent A.C., but the club's two star Canadians would not be allowed to play. After Navy pulled out because twelve varsity athletes had to report for ship duty, the committee substituted Syracuse for the midshipmen.

Unfortunately for the tournament organizers, gate receipts did not meet expectations. Only 1,200 people watched the Crescents defeat the Six Nations team and Rutgers clobber Syracuse on the Columbia University campus in New York. A more respectable crowd of six thousand spectators gathered at Baltimore Stadium to see Maryland defeat Mount Washington and Johns Hopkins edge Saint John's. But a sparse, rain-tormented crowd of five hundred saw Maryland and Johns Hopkins defeat Rutgers and the Crescents, respectively, in the semifinals in Baltimore. The poor gate receipts put the committee in a precarious situation. Even the crowd of five thousand spectators who turned out to see Johns Hopkins subdue Maryland in the final on June 25 disappointed officials. The small crowds led the AOLC to kill plans for the tournament winner to tour the country raising money.[101] Even with the cancellation, amateur sport purists denounced the upcoming Olympics and the recently completed tournament for their signs of commercialism and professionalism. According to the *Baltimore Sun,* the Olympic motto "Swifter, Higher, Stronger" had given way to "Riches, Professionalism, Racket." Johns Hopkins' regular season performance, the paper argued, should have kept it from "being forced to keep in training and play through an elimination tournament." Johns Hopkins Dean E. W. Berry called the Olympic tryouts "nothing but a gate receipts racket" and said the university would not participate in a similar tryout if lacrosse was included in the 1936 Olympics.[102]

At Los Angeles, between seventy-five and eighty thousand spectators saw Johns Hopkins defeat Canada in the opening game at the Olympic Coliseum on August 7, but most of them had come to see the track and field competition. Officials even interrupted the match in the second half to allow for the finish of the marathon. Canada won the second match, but Johns Hopkins won the third contest to capture the unofficial Olympic title and the 1932 Lally Cup. Incidentally, Cherokee descendent and cowboy philosopher Will Rogers provided play-by-play commentary for the first half.[103] Johns Hopkins' victory meant little to the rest of the American lacrosse community, but it reinforced a belief in Maryland that the heart and soul of lacrosse was in Baltimore. Now that their lacrosse team was in possession of two mythical Olympic championships, coaches, athletes, and alumni of Johns Hopkins developed a greater sense of their own self-importance. Neither Iroquois Indians nor Canadians could tell them otherwise.

International lacrosse fizzled after 1932. USILA authorities scheduled a Canadian-American series at the Chicago World's Fair in 1933, but poor gate receipts for soccer and track competition led fair officials to cancel lacrosse. Efforts to resurrect the series at the Toronto Centennial Celebration for 1934 also met with failure.[104] After a local British Columbia team defeated an American team in Vancouver in 1935, Canadian officials changed the Lally Cup format for the 1936 series in Vancouver from field to box lacrosse, ensuring victory for Canada in three straight matches but marginalizing their efforts within the larger international community. The USILA sent a team to England in 1937, but international competition among the Americans, British, and Canadians ceased until after World War II. Canada won the last two Lally Cups in 1935 and 1936, but lacrosse players in the Great White North were segregating themselves by abandoning the field version of what had once been the national game. With this Canadian withdrawal from the field game and renewed claims by enthusiasts in Baltimore of their supremacy, the cultural balance of power in North American lacrosse was shifting.

During this era the consequences of international competition revolved around two themes: the inconsistency between amateur values and spectatorism and the growing cultural authority of Baltimore lacrosse. Veteran lacrosse supporters in the United States saw lacrosse as an old Indian game that elite British sportsmen and women had taught Americans how to play for the game's sake. At a time when the British government often ceded to the diplomatic interests of the United States, Oxford and Cambridge still demonstrated proper amateur behavior and thought. The United States might eclipse Britain in international power, but the English could still teach the neophytes how to be good gentleman athletes. Despite this preoccupation with cultural lessons, the various tour and game promoters were always concerned with the commercial presentation of lacrosse. After all, staging contests and tours cost money. Moreover, international competition during the 1920s and 1930s confirmed the emergence of Maryland—and, more specifically, of Baltimore—as the cultural center of North American lacrosse. Not only had Johns Hopkins represented the United States at two Olympics, but the top teams, in athletic and socioeconomic terms, were found in and around Baltimore and Annapolis. Enthusiasts in Baltimore convinced themselves of this notion, and no doubt supporters of the game elsewhere grumbled about the power of Maryland lacrosse. Olympic lacrosse provided publicity for the sport in general, but it also reinforced the perception of people in Baltimore of the importance of their city to organized lacrosse. The Canadian abandonment of the outdoor field game in favor of box lacrosse reinforced these thoughts.

American apostles of lacrosse had conquered many of the challenges facing their sport during the Great Depression and World War II. They hoped the post-war era would bring prosperity. Such dreams were shared by the entire country, whether sports fans or not. The British lessons in amateur athleticism had had a dramatic impact on the spirit of American lacrosse. Even though commercial issues always concerned these men and women, sport for sport's sake remained paramount. Americans had learned the modernized version of an Iroquoian ball game from their white Canadian neighbors, but had borrowed an elite English value system that had refined the meaning of their game. Supporters of baseball, football, and other mass sports had openly embraced the consumer-oriented values of modern capitalism, but lacrosse enthusiasts in the United States had defended and upheld the lessons taught them by British amateur sportsmen and -women. The lack of international support for lacrosse had inevitably doomed the Olympic status of the sport, but American victories and the eventual Canadian abandonment of the field game in favor of box lacrosse would help to relocate the cultural hub of lacrosse from Canada to America.

The Rise of Box Lacrosse:
Reconfiguring the Canadian Game

While college coaches and organizers in the United States were refining what they regarded as a game for gentleman athletes during the 1920s, entrepreneurs were creating another version of the game in Canada. Led by the owners of the National Hockey League's Montreal Canadiens, Joe Cattaranich and Leo Dandurand, ice hockey arena and club operators introduced an indoor version of lacrosse to utilize their empty facilities during hockey's off-season. This new version of lacrosse was called box lacrosse— "boxla" for short. Because it was played on the smaller cement floors of hockey rinks, teams could use only seven men at a time instead of the twelve men traditionally used on an outdoor field. With the rink walls making any notion of imaginary field boundary lines irrelevant, the ball almost always stayed in play. The possibility that one player might push another into the wall greatly increased the likelihood of injuries during play. The introduction of box lacrosse had far-reaching consequences within a few years. Not only did professional lacrosse teams struggle for summertime consumer dollars during the Depression, but the new game affected amateur field lacrosse communities on both sides of the Canadian-American border. The Canadian abandonment of field lacrosse in favor of the box version of the game was quick and complete. If clubs in Ontario and British Columbia did not have access to idle hockey arenas, they constructed outdoor facilities with enclosed playing spaces. But American coaches and organizers fought off what they viewed as a dangerous contaminant. Lacrosse played "in the box" was very different from the outdoor field game, but indoor lacrosse was hardly new. Amateur sportsmen in the U.S. had dabbled with indoor lacrosse since at least the 1890s, but the experiments had been very temporary. In December 1929, for instance, Colonel James R. Howlett of the New York National Guard had established a team representing the Brooklyn men in Squadron C of the 101st Cavalry regiment, and this team had played against the Crescent A.C. and local universities in the regimental armory's dirt riding ring, but was short-lived.[105]

When the hockey men launched their enterprise in the summer of 1931, gate revenue was their foremost goal. Cast as the International Lacrosse League, the circuit included the Montreal Canadiens, Montreal Maroons, Toronto Maple Leafs, and Cornwall Colts. According to lacrosse veteran Ted Reeve, "Among those with the second sight and the first payments who gambled their money and sporting judgment on the success of this new form of muscular frolic were men whose vision had helped build up professional hockey into big league status."[106] Cramming thousands of men into "sweltering" arenas during the summer might seem odd to a lacrosse fan, but the promoters were catering to hockey fans longing for their winter game. "The incongruity vanished when the players crashed into the boards and the crowd cheered wildly at mad hockey melees in front of the goals," Robert Reade explained to *Cornwall Freeholder* readers in August 1931. "When the rubber projectile was passed swiftly from end to end of the rink and bulged the nets behind padded goalkeepers and the lights flashed dramatically and instantaneously on the electric scoreboard, I felt that by some meteorological miracle I had been transported back from July to January." Many of the elements of winter ice hockey were incorporated into this new "summer hockey": a smaller number of players (seven instead of twelve), liberal substitution during play, three twenty-minute periods, rough play, and occasional fistfights.[107] Whether spectators would support summer boxla in hot indoor arenas was another matter. After all, northern winters made Canadians appreciate the summer months, when they could spend more time outdoors.

Some lacrosse fans believed the new version of the game was an improvement. "They see in it not an artificial product, a freak hybrid," Reade wrote, "but the authentic thing geared higher, the old machine accelerated."

The best elements of the old game—fancy stick work, body contact, frantic and close attacks on the goal, and plenty of scoring—had been preserved and made more common. Many field lacrosse players also liked the pace of box lacrosse. "They would rather 'step on it' for a few swift minutes of glorious lacrosse life," said Reade, "than loaf on it for a whole afternoon on a big field, where they would never have to give way to substitutes." Other fans viewed the indoor game as too frantic. "You might imagine that players accustomed to galloping the wide open spaces like wild mustangs might not relish running around like mice in a psychologists cage," Reade observed.[108] Owners recruited former professionals who had played prior to the Great War, younger field lacrosse players who were willing to abandon their amateur status, and professional hockey players seeking summer pay. The Maple Leafs finished in first place during the inaugural twenty-four-game campaign, but the Canadiens won the three-game title series. The following year the Toronto Tecumsehs replaced the Colts, but the league's owners pulled the plug on the experiment. Their willingness to pump money into the league disappeared when attendance declined.[109]

Before the owners killed the league, however, they tried to expand beyond Ontario and Quebec by staging a match between the Montreal Canadiens and the Toronto Maple Leafs at Madison Square Garden on May 10, 1932. After a U.S. Military Academy band played "God Save the King" and "The Star Spangled Banner," about eight thousand New Yorkers saw Montreal defeat the Maple Leafs, with proceeds going to local medical charities. "The phase of the game which appealed most to the spectators last night was the body checking, which invariably resulted in at least one player falling to the heavily padded floor after every collision," the *New York Times* remarked. "The players, swinging their short sticks, or crosses, with considerable vigor and apparently reckless abandon, often hit one another heavy blows, causing the crowd to gasp and cheer alternately."[110] Shocked and titillated, the New York audience surely included both hockey fans and curious supporters of field lacrosse. Baltimore sportswriters disdained what they regarded as an excessively violent game. According to the *Baltimore Sun,* boxla was "a throwback to action marking the stone age when one of the most popular sports was the bouncing of bludgeons and large boulders off the oblong skulls of your opponent." The paper said the new game combined "Dempsey-Firpo boxing, hockey, mayhem, homicide and intent to kill."[111] Nine days before the New York exhibition, promoters committed to the formation of a new American Box Lacrosse League (ABLL). It featured six franchises—including the New York Giants, New York Yankees, Brooklyn Dodgers, Toronto Maple Leafs, Boston Shamrocks, and Baltimore Rough Riders—playing a fifty-game season that lasted from June to September. "Among the thrilling features of the new game," the New York press noted, "are the mass plays, unknown in the old field game. They are run off with football interference, giving protection to the ball carrier clutching ball and stick to his body as he spins over the crease line toward the goal-keeper."[112]

For decades supporters of field lacrosse had perpetuated violent representations of the origins of their sport in newspapers and magazines. The new hockey-inspired Canadian game reinforced those images. Now the proponents of the gentlemanly concept of the game were confronted by their worst fear: a commercial form of lacrosse supported by entrepreneurs and fans who were committed to victory over character and roughness over athleticism. For a long time the American general public had viewed field lacrosse as nothing more than organized mayhem. Canadian box lacrosse confirmed the stereotype. If fans supported the new sport, American field lacrosse might change significantly, perhaps by becoming more multiclass in composition as well as openly commercial and professional. If they rejected box lacrosse, however, the socially exclusive worldview of athletes and coaches from places such as Johns Hopkins and the Ivy League would be reinforced. Regardless, collegian coaches could only wait and watch to see if the new ABLL succeeded or failed.

The ABLL's franchises played in baseball parks such as Yankee Stadium and Fenway Park, attracting crowds of one to five thousand people. Rosters included imported Canadians and former American collegians. "The violence and swift pace with which the game is played naturally evokes considerable hand-to-hand conflict, and this condition was emphasized several times during the battle," the *New York Times* reported on a game between Toronto and the Yankees. Besides "fistic flare-ups" and belligerent player behavior that excited the crowd, "scintillating passing and clever blocking" impressed spectators.[113] Tough play characterized a contest between Baltimore and the Shamrocks at Fenway Park: "Both teams slashed, held, tripped, cross-checked and board-checked to make it one of the roughest games at Fenway this season." In the heartland of amateur lacrosse, the Baltimore franchise tried to bridge the cultural gap between affluent patrons of field lacrosse and boosters of mass sport by showing a compassionate side of boxla. When the local Rough Riders trounced an undermanned Toronto team featuring three Indians in front of twenty-five hundred fans at Oriole Park, the *Sun* noted that "the Baltimore boys seemed loathe [*sic*] to add undue physical violence to the lacrosse beating they were giving the enemy." Fearing a similar result, the Yankees signed several local men working as coaches in Maryland prior to their match with the Rough Riders, including Western Maryland assistant football coach Neil Stanley. The hometown team won 19–2, but the local press said fans loved the brutal play of Stanley: "So much did the spectators relish his style of play that when he was sent to the penalty bench for a minute for body checking his opponent into the steel post of the fence it was Referee Fenny Baker to whom the boos were directed, and Stanley was cheered as he reentered the game."[114]

The spectators who cheered on the Rough Riders may not have been the ones who supported lacrosse at Johns Hopkins or Mount Washington. Regardless of who attended the games, there were too few in Baltimore and elsewhere to make the league commercially viable. Financial woes caused the Yankees and Maple Leafs to bail out of the league by the end of June, and the league soon folded. Commercial sport producers on both sides of the border were tired of losing money. Whether U.S. followers of the outdoor amateur game were turned off by the excessive violence or baseball held the loyalty of most sports fans during the summer, the message was clear: American lacrosse was still an outdoor, affluent "player's game." Amateur versions of box lacrosse surfaced from time to time during the Depression, but the teams did not last for long. After Syracuse University decided to drop financial support for spring sports in 1933, coach Roy Simmons raised money to fund his team by staging commercial indoor matches in Rochester. Three thousand spectators saw Cornell defeat Syracuse in the first intercollegiate box lacrosse game. Subsequent experiments in the United Stated included efforts by Johns Hopkins and Yale to keep players active during the off-season. The Greater New York Lacrosse League, later renamed the Eastern Amateur Box Lacrosse Association, fielded clubs in Washington Heights, Manhattan, Westchester, the Bronx, and Brooklyn and played before crowds of as many as five thousand people.

Traditionalists such as Laurie Cox viewed box lacrosse with disgust. Because other coaches respected Cox, his opinions carried weight. "What Walter Camp was to football," the Syracuse student press noted, "Laurie Cox is to lacrosse."[115] This comparison ignored the fact that although Camp was a founding father of modern college football, he also played a lead role in commercializing and even professionalizing college sports. Cox abhorred those traits in lacrosse. Before retiring in 1932, having won one international and seven American championships, Cox attended a boxla championship in Canada that attracted seven thousand spectators.[116] Citing exploitation by commercial promoters, in 1934 he penned a critique of the enclosed version of the game entitled "The Future of American Lacrosse—What?" and posed questions about the fate of the outdoor amateur field game.[117] Dubbing box lacrosse "a peculiar hybrid between ice hockey and basketball," Cox believed it reflected the intersection of several developments: "degenerating" professionalism, the rise of ice hockey, and the eclipse of Canadian field lacrosse. "Given the lack of leaders with the right lacrosse background," Cox wrote, "it has been natural for Canada to try and change their game to meet the competition of hockey and the line of least resistance is to imitate hockey, although such a plan is of course fatal in the end." Dismayed by newer coaches who wanted to replace field lacrosse with the new enclosed game, Cox issued a stern warning against making commercial concerns a priority. In his eyes, few coaches knew the sacrifices made by pioneers of the American game: "They have no true sense of the peculiar and vital elements which make lacrosse distinctive and enduring and too easily become pessimistic because college lacrosse does not attract the public interest which they claim 'other college sports' do."[118]

Instead of recognizing the socially exclusive nature of their sport, Cox and others believed sportswriters who lacked any knowledge of lacrosse limited the game's potential appeal to a broader audience. In 1931 Manual Training High School coach Joseph F. Harrigan argued that too many writers had "decided that the game must be nothing less than legalized assault and battery."[119] Rather than learning and explaining lacrosse, sportswriters devoted most of their summer reporting efforts to baseball. Since few lacrosse players had become sportswriters, the dilemma remained. The lack of sympathetic coverage ensured the survival of the public perception of lacrosse as a "rough and brutal" game "with few or no rules."[120] Any exposure to box lacrosse merely validated this view. Although lacrosse players sustained their share of lacerations, bruises and broken bones, Cox's commentary on the sport's reputation was valid. A 1929 Carnegie Foundation study on intercollegiate sport showed that only 4.8 percent of lacrosse players suffered injuries, far fewer than in football (17.6 percent), wrestling (7.5), and even baseball and basketball (7.2).[121] Besides the public display of players swinging dangerous wooden sticks, Cox blamed lacrosse's reputation on "the many published accounts of the brutality of early Indian games," including nineteenth-century illustrations by men such as George Catlin, as well as "the disgraceful examples of dirty and brutal tactics indulged in over many years by the professional lacrosse teams of Canada."[122]

The expansion of lacrosse was also curtailed by the time and effort required for stick skill development, by equipment cost, and by competition from other spring sports. Cox believed too many teams took the field unprepared, with inadequate coaches and impatient players, guaranteeing an image of "a weird game to watch and a foolish game to play."[123] Lacrosse entailed expenses similar to those of football for a helmet and shoulder pads and those of baseball for handwear, but in addition a lacrosse team required two Indian-made sticks per man, a uniform, and two pairs of shoes, one for wet and one for dry fields. Most colleges and high schools supported baseball and track teams during the spring, and Cox accused graduate managers and athletic boards of favoritism. But athletics officials could easily justify these choices. After all, the U.S. track team demonstrated American athletic prowess every four years at the Olympics, and baseball was the national pastime.

Admitting that some features of box lacrosse might boost field lacrosse attendance, Cox asked supporters to stick with the field game. Having seen lacrosse crowds grow in his lifetime from two hundred to as many as ten thousand, he pleaded with organizers to steer away from "the cheapened hippodromed roughhouse of athletic hybridization" found in box lacrosse. He applauded the "unselfish" guardians of American lacrosse, including Harvard graduate and New York physician Morgan Vance, who, Cox said, "gave up his annual vacation and at his own expense organized and coached the first Yale lacrosse team." Cox pleaded with coaches, athletes, sportswriters, and anyone else who might read his article to reject commercialism and embrace elite sport for sport's sake. He reserved his final praise for the gentlemen of the Crescent A.C. who had encouraged the game among collegians, "teaching them the game as they defeated them by deliberately close scores, then giving them royal entertainment afterward, and when finally their proteges had grown strong enough to win an occasional game, showing the same sportsmanship and good comradeship in defeat as in victory."[124]

Cox's treatise was a rebuttal to the intrusion of commercial entrepreneurs into his game. Following Cox's lead, proponents of field lacrosse defended their game by deemphasizing rough play. A coach at Erasmus High School and an assistant at City College of New York, former Syracuse All-American Lou Robbins compared the game of 1938 with the version he had played as a youth: "It is much more humane today than previously, and there is less chance of getting butchered. Brains have been substituted for brawn, giving the smaller men more of a chance at the game."[125] Aware of the game's reputation for violence, officials focused on derived physical and mental skills. In 1939, Swarthmore coach Avery Blake challenged the public's conception of lacrosse as "murder on the lawn" by declaring that while it might be "a game of bodily contact . . . it isn't murder by any means."[126] The challenge of boxla and Cox's defense of the field game highlighted tensions within American lacrosse, between rigid adherence to elite amateurism and a desire to expand the game and also between affirming rough play to bolster masculinity and disclaiming it to show gentlemanly refinement. Although professional box lacrosse failed in the United States, it prompted many American field lacrosse coaches to ponder the future of their game. Their growing concern with public opinion foreshadowed efforts after World War II to promote amateur lacrosse beyond the social boundaries of elite institutions. Given the hardships of the Great Depression, that expansion would have to wait.

Meanwhile, professional box lacrosse inspired a revolution within Canadian lacrosse. Almost overnight, nominally amateur field lacrosse enthusiasts in Ontario and Quebec converted to the new game. Clubs in the western provinces adopted boxla after the 1932 national championship Mann Cup competition, when the Hamilton Tigers defeated the Winnipeg Argos under a new box lacrosse format. Clubs in British Columbia saw the writing on the wall and switched to the new game. Box lacrosse completely replaced the field game across Canada. By the end of the Great Depression, however, the only communities with substantial numbers of players were in southwestern British Columbia, southern Ontario, and around Montreal. Boxla began to fade by the Second World War in Manitoba, Alberta, and Saskatchewan, reviving only in the 1960s. The strongest clubs formed leagues in Ontario and British Columbia. League champions alternated traveling to each other's province to play for the Mann Cup. Along the railway route, the visiting provincial champion from Ontario or British Columbia was required to play other champions in sudden death matches to legitimize the idea that the team was worthy of a national title. Clubs typically challenging the Ontario or British Columbia champions included those found in Cornwall and Montreal in the East and those in Calgary, Winnipeg, and Medicine Hat in the West. Regardless of who actually made it to the Mann Cup final, Ontario clubs usually dominated. The Orillia Terriers won three straight titles from 1934 through 1936, and the Saint Catharines Athletics won four cups between 1938 and 1944. Clubs from New Westminster—either the Salmonbellies or the Adanacs—often represented British Columbia.

Though box lacrosse was nominally amateur in nature, gate revenue determined whether a boxla club survived. Gate fees allowed clubs to pay for all expenses. Though not outright professionals, boxla athletes fully understood the economic reality of their sport. During the 1933 playoffs in British Columbia, for example, controversy marred the ending of a two-game series between the New Westminster Adanacs and Abbotsford Hotel. Gordie McEvoy of Abbotsford apparently scored a game-ending goal, but the local league president ordered the referee to disallow it. When McEvoy's team refused to play on, the president awarded the game to New Westminster. Then a league commission returned the victory to Abbotsford and the Adanacs cried foul. With both clubs claiming the status of victor, the Adanacs asked a judge to stop the next round of the play-offs until another hearing could take place. The judge's decision to dismiss the case demonstrated the commercial motives of the Adanacs: "The whole thing is a question of money and gate receipts. It all comes down to dollars and cents. By the way, who gets the money?" the judge asked. "The players, of course. Why should I stop this (final) game? Where does it help you? It doesn't. A lot of people are waiting to witness an ordinary, clean, lawful game and, if I stopped it, it would disappoint them. Don't ask me to beat the team for you. I think you came to me because you thought I was an old lacrosse player. Why, I don't even know the difference between a lacrosse stick and a chop stick."[127]

The harsh economic conditions of the Depression made many players more adamant that they needed compensation. Seeking to make money from professionalized box lacrosse in southern California, American promoter Frank Sweeney recruited four groups of players to his Pacific Coast Lacrosse Association (PCLA) beginning in January 1939. The association included a predominantly Native American team called the Warriors. The other three clubs included the Los Angeles Yanks, composed of players from the New Westminster Salmonbellies along with a few Americans from New York; the Los Angeles Canucks, a recast version of the New Westminster Adanacs; and the Hollywood Terriers, a transplanted group of Ontario men from Orillia. Even though the British Columbia Lacrosse Association gave permission to its athletes to play for PCLA teams, the Canadian Lacrosse Association (CLA) scorned open professionalism. Insisting "I can't live on air," Jack Hughes of New Westminster felt offended by the CLA's claim of jurisdiction at a time when every dollar counted more than ever. Unable to afford playing without a full-time job, Hughes could not turn down a Los Angeles offer. "Don't you realize, gentlemen," he explained to CLA officials, "I'll be out of work for a period of six or seven months and no money coming in. It's swell for you fellows to have nice cushy jobs; you can afford to sit back and say don't go away [to the United States for the winter] or you'll be suspended. It's just like dealing with a cop; you always come off second best." Though the new league attracted over four thousand spectators for many contests, strained relations between Sweeney and Olympic Stadium officials caused it to fold. When the Canadians returned home to begin the amateur season in May, suspensions greeted them. CLA president Jim Mc-Conaghey eventually lifted the bans in mid-June.[128] With the Adanacs-Abbotsford controversy, the Los Angeles experiment demonstrated that even though conditions were not ripe for fully professional boxla, many players—especially working-class athletes—wanted compensation to continue their summertime sport passion.

Iroquois Indians quickly took to the new version of lacrosse, as did some of the western native peoples of Canada. In the early 1930s a team of Squamish Indians in British Columbia competed with clubs from nearby Vancouver, New Westminster, and rural Richmond. Calling themselves the North Shore Indians, this club of fishermen and seasonal laborers attracted crowds as large as ten thousand to matches at the Vancouver Arena during the mid-1930s. However, unlike reservation teams in the United States, these Canadian Indians competed for national honors. In the United States an Indian club from an Onondaga, Mohawk, or Seneca reservation could not capture any such postseason title. In 1936, when the Squamish traveled to Toronto and lost the national championship to the Orillia Terriers, the four-game Mann Cup series attracted 30,782 patrons. During the war the team shut down temporarily, because many Squamish players worked at Vancouver shipyards and dry docks. In 1945 the club was revived, but because many natives still worked at the shipyards, the club had to rely on natives' playing while on break or recruit non-native players. The club eventually disbanded after 1955 and was not revived until the 1990s.[129]

Early in the club's history, supporters of a non-native club hatched a devious plan to defeat the Squamish. In 1932 the underdog Winnipeg Argos defeated the favored North Shore Indians club for the western championship one round before Mann Cup play. According to British Columbia lacrosse historian David Savelieff, "The North Shore Indians were talked into drinking a number of glasses of 'milk,' which of course as all lacrosse players will tell their wives is all that they drink on a road trip. The Indians thought that they were drinking with the players from the Winnipeg team, which meant that both clubs would be in the same condition after spending half the night debating the world's problems." However, the next day they realized that the men they had drunk with the night before had actually been fans of the rival club posing as their club's players.[130] Controversy seemed to follow Indian squads. Before traveling out West to play against the British Columbia champion Richmond Farmers in the Mann Cup final of 1941, the Saint Catharines Athletics were required to play a combined team of Caughnawa and Saint Regis Indians. Police arrested Indian team captain Angus Thomas after he struck a referee.[131]

"Clever" Indians between the World Wars: Real and Imagined Indian Lacrosse

As Laurie Cox and others wrestled with the specter of box lacrosse, another image of the game revolved around its noble American Indian origins. Many supporters declared its indigenous status made it deserving of public support. Former Cornell and Crescent A.C. player Roy Taylor stated, "Lacrosse is probably the only real American game we have today."[132] Others invoked stereotypes of Native Americans as part of a receding frontier to rally support. When Manual Training coach Joseph F. Harrigan gave his Brooklyn schoolboys an overview of the history of the game one month before the first practice, he made "special reference to its importance in Indian life," according to one source, "for lacrosse is as American as the American birch bark canoe and the wild variety of American turkey."[133] Most fans admitted the ancient native origins of the sport, but they also believed that it had been transformed into a civilized, character-building sport for white men. In February 1940, in response to a Brooklyn fan who had praised the game for its ability to cultivate "initiative and quick thinking," the *New York Times* agreed, then proclaimed, "Nobody around here ever suggested that lacrosse be given back to the Indians."[134]

As the "founding fathers" of lacrosse got older, sportswriters' conceptions of the sport's origins became more fictitious and embellished. To amateur historians of the game—sportswriters and coaches who had read the words of nineteenth-century commentators—lacrosse was a form of intertribal warfare. They combined an aristocratic celebration of the "noble savage" with commercial images of natives that were familiar to audiences of Hollywood westerns. Citing the works of Captain Basil Hall, Charles Lanman, George Catlin, and Francis Parkman, Baltimore journalist W. Wilson Wingate portrayed the bygone Native Americans as violent. "Only war seems to have been more absorbingly interesting than lacrosse to some Indians," he wrote in 1930.[135] Writing in 1935, Kyle Crichton recounted the infamous lacrosse match that had preceded the massacre of the British garrison at Fort Michilimackinac during Pontiac's Rebellion. As a former player, he questioned the natives' choice of weapon: "I have never been able to understand why the Indians bothered with the tomahawks when they had those lacrosse sticks already at hand."[136] According to one farcical 1938 composition from the student press at Syracuse, "Our red-skinned forefathers used to take time off between buffalo hunts to participate in this spring massacre. Tom-tom reports also say that each brave pinned a tomahawk under his g-string to penalize rule offenders." *Daily Orange* references to "redskins," "stick brawls" that turned into "scalping parties," or colorful participants "decorated with paint and feathers"[137] fleshed out the "savage" image. By emphasizing the imagery of frontier warfare, Wingate and Crichton characterized the Indian lacrosse player of yesteryear as one of Hollywood's "bad Indians" who had tortured and killed white settlers.

Publicity for women's lacrosse also emphasized the violence of ancient Indian ball games. According to a *Literary Digest* selection from 1936, traditional native lacrosse had been a very bloody affair. The article fused historical record with exaggerated folklore, fanciful conceptions of the "noble savage," and outright fiction. Offering another version of the 1763 massacre at Fort Michilimackinac, it said that the stick skill of the "2,000 free-swinging, rough-and-tumble warriors . . . was not nearly so vital as the ability to carry on despite terrific punishment from enemy stick-wielders." The Indians had wanted "to cripple as many opponents as possible before settling down to the business of scoring a goal." Not only had deaths been common, the story continued, but injuries had been taken as jokes. As for the attack at Fort Michilimackinac, the *Digest* said, "The British cheering section was intrigued with the fascinating game until suddenly every warrior on the field dropped his lacrosse stick, rushed into the fort and proceeded to tomahawk the English spectators."[138] Ironically, just as American coaches were fighting against the influence of Canadian boxla, all of the historical images were reinforcing a conception of lacrosse as nothing more than organized mayhem. Regardless of these inaccurate portrayals of traditional lacrosse, enthusiasts praised what they perceived as ideal, noble, and even mystical qualities of the sport. According to an editorial at Johns Hopkins written in 1941, the spectator could "sense the beauty that is lacrosse" by watching the player's straining leg muscles, rhythmic arms, sensitive eyes, and tense nerves. It concluded: "If then we associate the beauty of delicately controlled motion with an unknown primitive origin, with the wildness of the rushing rivers of the Americas before Samoset met Standish, with the demoniac rigour of savage training, and the wild abandon of pre-game nocturnal rituals, we feel the mystery that is lacrosse."[139] Socially elite proponents of amateur lacrosse celebrated the intellectual and historical function of the "noble savage," but the fictionalization of the traditional game by sportswriters produced a view of lacrosse that was consistent with mass consumer interests. Anyone who watched Hollywood westerns understood these icons. The entry of these views into public discussion reflected a fissure of attitudes toward lacrosse according to class and culture. The gentlemanly conception of lacrosse remained dominant, reinforced by the upper-middle-class composition of the lacrosse community during the Great Depression. But the new consumer-oriented, roughhouse view of the game symbolically demonstrated multiclass, commercial approaches to the sport.

Violent images from Canadian boxla or mythical ideas about the sport's antiquity redefined field lacrosse in a way that was increasingly hostile to real violence, but tolerant of a distorted past. At the same time, many college coaches maintained ties with native teams. Several reservation teams played universities and colleges throughout the period between the world wars. The closest relationship was between Syracuse University and the nearby Onondaga Reservation. As had many Iroquois communities, the

Onondagas received a boost of renewed enthusiasm for the game when students returned from the Carlisle Indian School. The Onondaga began a four-decades-long rivalry with Syracuse in 1916, when Laurie Cox arranged an encounter between his College of Forestry students and the local Indians. Although the Onondaga won the first four meetings from 1916 through 1918, the results usually favored Cox's teams. From 1919 until 1954, Syracuse won eighteen matches, tied three times, and lost only once. Likewise, in Geneva, New York, Hobart College compiled a 9–1–1 record against the Onondaga, Akron, and Cattaraugus reservations from 1923 to 1952. Although Indian squads defeated other schools, the duration and unbalanced results of their contests with powerhouses Syracuse and Hobart provide valuable insights into collegians' relations with the descendants of the game's originators.

Even though sportswriters in Syracuse, Geneva, Baltimore, and elsewhere invoked the mythical frontier by making frequent references to "cowboys and Indians" and "scalping" in their stories, they also noted the dissimilar playing styles of white and Native American players. They usually depicted the native approach as one emphasizing running rather than passing, "bunching" offensive tactics, and a strong sense of individualism. Showing off a "natural" sophistication of stick handling, native players outmuscled collegians with their physical play. Meanwhile, college men played a "scientific"-style game, emphasizing passing and integrated team play rather than personal effort. White athletes allegedly showed a greater mental discipline and thought of their team over themselves. Journalists used the word "clever" to describe the play of both Indians and whites, but usually employed it when referring to the stick skills of the former and the passing schemes of the latter. Whereas their accounts of collegian lacrosse reflected principles of gentlemanly amateurism and scientific management, their descriptions of Indian play could be mistaken as merely racist clichés.

Applying phrases such as "aggressive onslaught" and "swift offense" to the Indians and "iron defense" and "clever" to the collegians, the *Syracuse Daily Orange* described the university's first contest with the Onondaga reservation in 1916 as one matching Indian malevolence, physical prowess, and instinctual abilities against white determination, mental superiority, and trained expertise. According to the paper, the Indians had employed centuries-old tactics against the "scientific" methods of the university men in their 3–2 victory: "The second half started with the braves massing their entire team on a strong offensive play. The ball was kept near the Syracuse goal for about five minutes, repeated shots being made, but always being halted by the strong defense of the Foresters." During Syracuse's 10–1 triumph over the Onondaga in 1922, the well-drilled university squad had accentuated team play and a strategic pass-oriented offense, while the Onondaga had operated using traditional tactics and had emphasized individualism. "Syracuse presented a scientific attack while the Indian attack was simply run and shoot," the campus press reported. "The stick work of the Indians was probably as good as Syracuse will face this year, but their team work was far from perfection." The only authority Indians respected was the unwritten code of fairness. When told to comply with a referee's decision though they knew he was wrong, they had balked. Unwilling to quarrel over the codified "white man's" law of modern lacrosse as interpreted by the on-field white judge, the Indians had avoided confrontation: "Near the middle of the second half the Indians began to walk off the field as the referee allowed a goal of the varsity to count which the Indians did not believe was correctly scored. The Indians proved to be right and the game was resumed."[140]

The *Hobart Herald* also depicted that school's contests with native teams as pitting white science and teamwork against Indian skill and passion. In 1924 the paper complimented the campus men for keeping calm against the Onondaga in the face of escalating on-field violence: "The slashing of the Indians became very bad and it looked for several minutes as if the game were going to degenerate into a fight." In describing other matches, the Hobart press employed a variety of images. "Wielding their sticks in an expert manner and whooping war cries to echo about the campus," the paper reported in 1926, "the redskins seemed certain of securing many scalps." However, because the match had ended with a 5–4 Hobart victory, the student editors declared, "The clever stick-work of the Indians was by far the outstanding feature of the game but on account of the lack of consistent teamwork they lost a hard fought game."[141]

Following the lead of Syracuse and Hobart, the Johns Hopkins team also crossed sticks with the Onondaga. On the Indians' trip south in 1925, the campus press observed, "The Onondagas play their ancient native game in a truly aboriginal manner," frequently using "long passes, running attacks," and the "mass formation."[142] The *Baltimore Sun* invoked racist myths, describing the ensuing contest as an "old game of cowboys and Indians," but it also unwittingly illuminated native tactics and traditions, such as the emission of loud "whoops" before and during play. After the reservation's Irving Powless had scored the first goal, Johns Hopkins had shut down the Indian offense. The Indians had employed "all tricks of dodging," but had grown tired during the second half. "The aborigines have been expected to play a rough game," reported the *Sun*, "but the spectators were agreeably surprised at the sportsmanship they displayed. Hard play was introduced by the Hopkins team in a seeming effort to beat the Indians to the punch. The latter never exceeded the bounds of clean play, although they fought harder when the locals had gained the lead."[143] The Johns Hopkins spectators had applauded the stick work of the Indians, but the campus paper said its team had "scalped" the Onondaga 4–1, supposedly because the Indians had lacked stamina.[144]

Before a contest between Syracuse and the Onondaga in 1930, university and city newspapers reinforced dominant images. Referring to the Indians as "a fighting band of Redskins" who were "out to scalp the Hillmen," the campus press characterized the contest as pitting "a team of clever stick-wielders" against "a well coached outfit that has been trained to the minute."[145] Citing the varsity's strengths as "aggressiveness, stamina and power," city editors also emphasized the physical relentlessness of the Indians. Despite game accounts sprinkled with stereotypes, sportswriters provided evidence of cultural borrowing. Given the pregame hype, one thousand spectators were surely surprised when a better-conditioned Indian team edged out the university men. The *Syracuse Post-Standard* suggested that the Onondaga had adopted collegian methods, demonstrating "superior stick-work and passing" and exploiting an advantage in physical conditioning.[146] In fact, it was the Indians' lack of physical conditioning that often guaranteed Syracuse victories. This predicament reflected not only the different values the Onondaga attached to lacrosse, but the substandard health conditions of reservation life. Hot weather tainted the 1934 match; "scientific" lacrosse triumphed, with the better-trained varsity squad outpacing the Indians by eight goals. Noting the industrial precision of Syracuse goals, the student press reported: "The attack of the orange-jerseyed men was at times remindful of a machine gun in action." Even though the "Orange stickmen rated slightly better than their opponents by virtue of their better conditioning," the *Daily Orange* stated in 1935, the Onondaga "will take plenty of punishment." During the following season, the paper acknowledged the Indians' lack of conditioning in a 7–1 loss to Syracuse: "The Redmen weren't in any sort of playing condition, but made the contest interesting by their willingness and fight."[147] These images of Indian players unable to compete with collegian athletes challenged the popular stereotype of the Indian as a long-distance runner with a superior natural endurance.

The legal, spatial, and temporal structures of modern lacrosse presented a quandary for the Onondaga and other Indians during the period between the wars. Although collegians acknowledged that the Iroquois were expert stick handlers, most Indians placed a greater emphasis on running with the ball than did their white counterparts. In an open field without boundaries, Iroquois men had always assumed it was better to run than to pass. After all, ball games had been played that way as far back as they could remember. But on the modern field, with circumscribed playing space, it had become more efficient to pass than to run. Oddly enough, a running-oriented game worked to the whites' advantage, too, since the physical fitness programs of college teams produced better-conditioned athletes than those from the reservation. Even though some Native American players worked at physically laborious jobs at construction sites, collegian defenders could match Indian attackers step for step. Moreover, the positional play of the modern game negated the Iroquois emphasis on the individual. The offside rule neutralized the Indian maneuver of bunching attackers against an opponent's goal. The survival of older native principles of traditional ball play—virile individualism and mass attacks on the goal—along with the lack of a "scientific" physical regimen program, ensured the Indians' defeat. Regardless of attempts by Iroquois teams to adjust to modern conditions, the depressed social, cultural, and health conditions of reservation life often shaped the outcomes of matches between Indians and collegians.

Laurie Cox and other coaches often measured their teams against the yardstick of Indian abilities. With several former Carlisle players on the Onondaga reservation squad, the *Syracuse Daily Orange* declared, "The Indians are practically invincible." Syracuse players certainly admired native stick skills. Players and coaches hoped that competition against the Indians would improve students' stick skills as well. Describing the Onondaga as "an exceptionally clever outfit" in 1931, the *Daily Orange* reported that coach Cox believed much could be learned from the Indian approach to lacrosse.[148] While Syracuse and Hobart had firm relationships with reservation teams, other collegiate officials believed white-Indian competition benefited organized lacrosse. In 1924 the USILL encouraged colleges and clubs to schedule games with the Onondaga or Seneca teams: "They play excellent Lacrosse and put on a picturesque game. Properly featured, they should add much to the publicity of the game, and more of the college and club teams should meet them."[149] Throughout the 1920s and 1930s, native teams from Onondaga and Saint Regis traveled to West Point, Syracuse, Penn State, Yale, and Dartmouth, and they even went to the New York World's Fair in 1940.[150] Laurie Cox also recruited Native Americans to coach and play for his team. For example, he hired Ike Lyons from the Onondaga reservation as an assistant coach in 1919.[151] When Cox named Victor Ross to the 1923 All-America team, he said Ross was "without much doubt the cleverest attack player yet seen in college circles, and it is doubtful if any of the club players surpass him."[152] After losing to the Onondaga in 1930, Cox recruited Clint Pierce away from the reservation to play for Syracuse.[153] The tiny minority of Indian undergraduates faced a dilemma whenever a reservation team came to campus. In 1924 one native student found his loyalty divided for an upcoming match: "Don't ask me whom I favor in tomorrow's game. I am a Mohawk and also a senior in Syracuse University. I win and lose, any way you look at it."[154] This sentiment reflected prevailing internal tensions of Indians living in a white man's world.

Despite the efforts of coaches like Cox to establish friendly ties with reservations, spectators were not always cordial. In 1932 the student press at Hobart condemned the behavior of local fans during the college's 8–1 victory over the Seneca Indians from the Akron reservation. The poor sportsmanship of Hobart spectators "literally 'burned us up,'" the campus paper remonstrated, "and left us wondering if there wasn't some vestige of the true conception of a gentleman left in some people." Attacking the idea of lacrosse as savage entertainment for effete students, the newspaper chastised "certain individuals in the Hobart cheering section, certain notorious, lily-white handed, tea-hounds who get most of their exercise on plush-lined sofas, yelling at the top of their weak lungs advice to rugged varsity players to 'cut down that Indian—don't be such a sissy' or moaning with extreme disgust when some player doing his level best for his team happened to drop the ball." Perhaps if these snobby spectators bothered to play, the paper declared, their attitudes might change. It concluded: "We admit lacrosse is a rough game, but we do not admit the main purpose of the game to be the mutilation of the opposite team at the behest of squittering weaklings or the destruction of all inter-team good will to appease the abnormal desires of cheap thrill-seekers."[155] These editors thought amateur sport and Indian bashing did not go together.

These reports indicate much about whites' attitudes toward the Indians, but discernment of Indians' views is more problematic. Despite numerous losses to Hobart and Syracuse, the Onondaga and other Indian teams regarded the matches more than mere athletic events. Given the lack of job opportunities for Indians—especially during the Depression—reservation teams played for a portion of gate receipts. Since most Indian contests with white teams took place at campuses or country clubs, anticipated gate revenues were attractive to native athletes. Sometimes things did not work out. The inability to agree on a gate receipt guarantee led Syracuse to cancel a scheduled match with the tough-bargaining Onondaga Indians in April 1932.[156] Besides universities, private clubs also staged matches with Indian teams. In 1926, for instance, a doubleheader in Philadelphia featured victories by the Onondaga and Caughnawaga Indians over the Quaker City Club and New York L.C., respectively.[157]

Indian teams also played games to raise money to help the needy. Just as their ancestors had done centuries earlier, when medicine men had called for contests to be played to cure the sick, twentieth-century Iroquois did the very same, but now for money. In 1951 Syracuse coach Roy Simmons recalled a match for charity between the Onondaga and a hastily assembled university team during the Depression. One spring a Native American player had broken his arm during a game against Syracuse. When the arm healed improperly, he eventually sought professional medical care. During the university's August football training camp, several Onondaga chiefs asked Simmons if he could put together a university lacrosse team and play against the reservation to raise money for the injured man. "They said they'd give us half the gate, so I got together a team, mostly football players, and went over to the reservation. We didn't know exactly what would happen. But nothing did, and after it was all over, an Indian named Angus Lozare came over with the money and split it nickel for nickel, dime for dime," Simmons recalled. "All that just to show nobody was getting cheated. I think we made something like 44 dollars."[158] Simmons's comment about "what would happen" reflected the common fear of whites, who approached Indians with unease.

The desire to make money from lacrosse sometimes conflicted with Native American views of the game as an extension of the community. Economics and culture did not always mix. The economic context of native lacrosse is illustrated by one episode from the 1924 season that highlighted social divisions within an Indian community. In May the Syracuse press reported that Onondaga reservation coach George Jordan either had been "fired" or had "resigned" from his duties. Apparently Jordan's decision to lease a lacrosse field with a grandstand on the northern edge of the reservation near a trolley line had increased ticket revenues from white patrons, but the reservation chiefs contended that the site was inconvenient for reservation residents. Moreover, tribal animosity led to prejudice against Jordan, who was a Mohawk from Saint Regis. Indians loyal to their traditional chiefs felt Jordan espoused a version of lacrosse too closely resembling the collegian game, a claim based on his having already coached and played in California. Jordan eventually formed his own renegade Syracuse Indians club composed of Mohawk and Onondaga Indians who were personally loyal to him.[159]

Clearly Indians attached great cultural significance to the game. First and foremost, participation on and support for the team helped maintain cultural continuity with the past, despite the many changes in the game over the previous two centuries. Many Indians still conceptualized the game according to its traditional purposes. By donning feathers at matches, Onondaga players reminded spectators of the team's native origins. They probably wore such paraphernalia for white audiences expecting "savage" Indian play, as well as for loyal reservation fans who had journeyed from their homes to project an image of Indian unity on campus. Indian teams usually began matches and celebrated goals with what journalists called a loud "war-whoop." These vocal exhibitions entertained white spectators, instilled fear into young collegian athletes, and demonstrated for Indian spectators adherence to rituals associated with traditional ball play.[160]

Despite the numerous losses they incurred after 1920, the Onondaga kept playing against Syracuse University for their own reasons. Most obviously, these Indians sought competition with any team, regardless of victory or defeat. The Indians probably played in part for the same reason as their well-to-do white amateur counterparts, who enjoyed sport for its own sake, regardless of outcome. Also, the political and military defeat of the Iroquois during the late eighteenth century had significantly altered the meaning of lacrosse. Since many Indians had become Christians, native ball play had become a largely secular activity. For most Iroquois, lacrosse was primarily a form of recreation and an important, tangible link with the past. Despite a significant degree of acculturation to the ways of the colonizers, these natives believed they possessed cultural authority over the modern version of their ancient sport. So any victory on the lacrosse field against a white team signified a temporary success against the dominant culture. The various motives for participating in the wider field lacrosse community show that twentieth-century Indians were caught between upholding the traditions of the past and coping with the problems of the contemporary world.

Cross-cultural contact also occurred at the schoolboy level. Unlike their prep school counterparts in Maryland, most central New York schoolboys who adopted lacrosse came from middle- and working-class families. One was Ken Drum, the son of a university music instructor who lived on the city's multiethnic South Side. Disinterested in baseball, Drum and his neighborhood friends learned lacrosse at a high school attended by children from white- and blue-collar urban families, farmers and apple growers from adjacent rural communities, and the Onondaga Reservation. "We saw the Indians doing it out on a field near Onondaga Valley Academy," Drum recalled. "That's where we saw it first and then we went out onto the reservation which wasn't far from the city line. It was easy to get to and you could go out on Sunday afternoon to see the game. Their ability to handle the stick that adeptly was the most interesting thing."[161] Sunday afternoon matches pitted the Onondaga against other reservation teams. Crowds ranged from a few dozen to a few hundred, about a third being white. Local Indians usually sold arts, crafts, and lacrosse sticks.

During the 1930s white-Indian relations in youth lacrosse paralleled relations among adults. Drum attributed his school's undefeated record against the Indians to the different playing styles of white and Indian teams: "They liked to play and either be the hero or the victim. It didn't matter if they ran through a defense and got a big cut or lost some teeth. They held that as a badge of honor." Drum believed the Indians' run-and-gun style of individualistic play doomed them: "Their defenses were too casual. They didn't play any organized defenses, no shifting. They didn't go at it in a scientific way as in the colleges." According to Drum's friend Albert Paige, weekly Onondaga Valley Academy matches with the reservation were very useful: "We'd start maybe at three o'clock in the afternoon. By four o'clock their pa's would come home from work and they would step in, so we'd have to play against their fathers also. They were mostly masons and steel-workers. . . . It gave us a chance to improve our skills." Reservation Indians resented white schoolboys' domination of contests. Daring white players to adopt individualistic Indian tactics, teenage Onondaga girls yelled to the academy boys, "Why don't you go down alone and see if you can make it?" Academy victories resulted in awkward postgame moments. "Because they started the game around this area they figured they should be better," Paige remembered. "Of course when we beat them, it didn't sit too good with them. They'd razz us a little bit as you walked off the field, but you had to accept it. 'Oh you think you're good! You think you're good!'"[162] Both Drum and Paige—and all of organized lacrosse for that matter—theorized that the individualistic, traditional style of play ensured Indian defeats.

The fundamental differences between Native American and white lacrosse were apparent when Drum refereed an Iroquois championship at the Onondaga reservation during the late 1930s. Drum's high school coach recommended him to promoter Louis Bruce, who was the son of a Mohawk father who was a Methodist missionary and an Oglala Sioux mother. Bruce had graduated from Syracuse in 1930, served as a National Youth Administration project director during the Depression, and later advised presidents Franklin Roosevelt, Harry Truman, and Dwight Eisenhower on Indian matters before serving as commissioner of Indian Affairs under Richard Nixon.[163] Shortly before the beginning of the contest he had been asked to referee, which would pit the Onondaga against Saint Regis, Drum asked Bruce, "Are we going to play white man's rules or your rules?" Bruce reassured Drum by agreeing to "white man's rules," but Drum delayed starting the contest when he discovered that many players were wearing spiked track shoes and carrying sticks with bands of copper wound around the stick heads. Drum told Bruce he would not permit the game to begin until everyone took off their shoes and tossed away the "illegal"sticks.[164] The willingness of the teams to abide by Drum's decisions was likely due to the presence of Bruce.

Relations between Indian reservations and the intercollegiate lacrosse community were carried out in the 1930s against the backdrop of new national legislation on Indians. The Indian Reorganization Act (IRA) of 1934, largely rejected by New York's Native American communities, affected citizenship and game and fish laws. The Roosevelt administration's "Indian New Deal" included many benefits for native peoples—new freedoms of elective self-government, economic opportunities, a pluralistic education system emphasizing Indian culture, and an end to the land allotment policy that had been stated in the Dawes Act. However, Iroquois chiefs contended that the new legislation challenged Iroquois sovereignty. In referenda held on the Allegany, Cattaraugus, Onondaga, Saint Regis, Tonawanda, and Tuscarora reservations in June 1935, about 80 percent of participating Indians rejected the IRA.[165] Given this political background, it is no surprise that white-Indian lacrosse matches occurred more infrequently during the late 1930s. Perhaps losses in lacrosse matches played according to the white man's rules became harder to accept during the era of the IRA. The Onondaga discontinued their annual Syracuse excursion after 1935 and did not revive the rivalry until after World War II. Moreover, the war brought other challenges to Iroquoia. For instance, the Selective Service Act of 1940 made Indians subject to a federal military draft. Rather than face the draft, many Iroquois enlisted. To symbolize Iroquois autonomy, a faction of Iroquois chiefs, including 1932 Olympic tryout lacrosse coach Jesse Lyons, issued an unofficial declaration of war against the Axis Powers in Washington, D.C., on June 11, 1942, proclaiming: "A state of war exists between our Confederacy of Six Nations on the one part and Germany, Italy, Japan and their allies against whom the United States has declared war, on the other part."[166] Whether playing lacrosse matches against universities or declaring war against foreign governments, Iroquois Indians told each other and the rest of the world that they were participants in the modern world, a culture that would not be silenced.

Baltimore Lacrosse: The Triumph of Amateur Athleticism

Throughout the period between the wars, organized lacrosse in the United States confronted not only a series of serious economic and wartime challenges, but also several different cultural models of the sport. Frequent contact with the British reinforced the importance of amateur sport for American coaches and players. Participation in two Olympics allowed them to conceptualize their game in nationalistic terms never really explored before. Contact with Canadian field and box lacrosse revealed American domination in one and scorn for the other. Contests with reservation Indians provided collegian and club athletes with chances to evaluate their own on-field skills. While those on the other side of those contacts—British sportsmen, Canadian field lacrosse players, commercial hockey promoters, and Iroquois Indians—had their own motives, Americans generally sought to reinforce the meaning of the game for the gentleman amateur athlete. This was most important in Baltimore and especially on the campus of the Johns Hopkins University. As part of the general collegian sport reform movement that was afoot during the Depression, Johns Hopkins elevated its clout within the lacrosse community. With commercial sports promoters profiting from middle- and working-class anxieties during the 1930s, schools like Johns Hopkins reevaluated the role of athletics on campus. Advocates of amateur sport argued that the growing commercial and professional elements of college sport contradicted the intellectual mission of the American university. Institutions such as the University of Chicago rebelled against the obsession with victory and gate receipts. In this context the administration at Johns Hopkins decided to adopt a new athletics philosophy that was intolerant of both commercialism and professionalism.

University administrators supervised Johns Hopkins athletics until 1919, when a group of alumni athletes called the Varsity Club convinced president Frank J. Goodnow to hand them fiscal and administrative control. Although the athletics program benefited from the financial resources mustered by the alumni through gate receipts and donations, some students resented graduate control of undergraduate sport.[167] Soon both the Varsity Club and the university trustees deemed the new system a failure and in 1922 replaced it with an athletic council led by physical education professor Ronald Abercrombie. With gate receipts a determinant of a sport's fate, less successful programs such as basketball and swimming suffered. The varsity baseball team even disappeared for a decade, beginning in 1925. To remedy this dilemma, in 1933 president Joseph S. Ames appointed a faculty committee to study both commercialism in sport and apathy toward undergraduate recreation. According to G. Wilson Shaffer, a psychology professor who played a major role in reforming Johns Hopkins athletics during the 1930s, Ames was influenced by Howard Savage's 1929 Carnegie Foundation for the Advancement of Teaching report warning of growing professionalism and commercialism on American campuses.[168]

Savage had objected to the relationship between traditional scholarship in the spirit of German university life and the commercial demands of American sport. "The question is whether an institution in the social order whose primary purpose is the development of the intellectual life can at the same time serve as an agency to promote business, industry, journalism, salesmanship and organized athletics on an extensive commercial basis," the report stated. "The question is not so much whether athletics in its present form should be fostered by the university, but how fully can a university that fosters professional athletics discharge its primary function."[169] Reflecting the views of amateur sport proponents, the report depicted commercial sport and intellectual advancement as inconsistent.

According to the Carnegie study, the professional and commercial elements of intercollegiate sport produced negative consequences: the infusion of an overly competitive ethos into secondary schools, undergraduate athletes who emphasized physical training at the expense of mental advancement, star sportsmen who received a rude awakening when cast aside at the end of their athletic careers, professional coaches who were interested in the development of athletes only for the sake of the team's performance, the subsidization of high school recruits through "pecuniary and other inducements," "unsportsmanlike" and "immoral" alumni who recruited new athletes without the approval of officials, the stratification of undergraduates into participants and spectators, and a form of athleticism whose primary function was to publicize the sponsoring schools.[170] The presence of these elements on campuses suggested that college sport had wrongly and destructively turned from pastime to profession. A growing emphasis on dollars, overtraining, long train rides, and unethical favors given to the "weak scholar" all revealed a need for reform.[171] Many faculty agreed with the Carnegie report's conclusions. In their eyes, too many universities had violated their commitment to pristine amateurism.

In the spring of 1934 a Johns Hopkins committee chaired by psychology professor Knight Dunlap recommended faculty control over the athletics program, termination of the football team, and commitment to a universal intramural plan. To accommodate the new program, Ames allocated $30,000 for a new gymnasium, which opened in November.[172] Critics of commercial sport also charged that undergraduate apathy was a fundamental problem. Although such complaints had stretched back decades, some argued that student disinterest had become acute in recent years. In

1930 the campus press claimed that undergraduates took championship lacrosse at Johns Hopkins for granted: "They go to a lacrosse game in the same spirit that they go to a movie; for an afternoon's enjoyment and nothing else." The only thing worse than an excessive expression of "college rah-rah spirit" was the lack of it. Student leaders believed intramurals would help bring an end to impassivity, misbehavior, and general laziness. In 1934 the *News-Letter* declared, "We cannot avoid a feeling of downright disgust upon beholding youths, ranging in age from sixteen to twenty-three, indolently sit back in their chairs around a card table and waste hour after hour and day after day in such passive and desultory forms of recreation."[173]

In addition to—and, some felt, related to—the general apathy toward intercollegiate sport, the faculty became increasingly aware of students' discontent with their professors. Many undergraduates felt the emphasis professors placed upon research and graduate student development was at their expense. "There is prevalent among the undergraduates a feeling of indifference which, in the case of the keener minds, mounts to indignation and resentment, and which springs from the attitude of patronage practised by most of the faculty," one student calling himself "Scribo" said in 1934. "With a few notable exceptions, these latter gentlemen consider that their undergraduate courses are bread and butter affairs which are necessary as a means of commanding a salary, but are to be escaped from as soon as possible so that attention can be paid to the graduate students." Scribo pleaded that the faculty make a more concerted effort to provide for more professor-undergraduate contact: "At present Hopkins is top heavy with snobbish emphasis on research. Cooperation is needed by everyone to hasten the growth of the New Spirit."[174] Essentially this critic asked why students should engage in community building when the faculty expressed disinterest. If faculty ignored the students, perhaps the students should ignore intercollegiate sports.

Hoping to counter undergraduate apathy and the influence of commercialism on campus, the faculty embraced reform. With Dunlap on sabbatical, Shaffer supervised a revised athletics program in the guise of the newly created Department of Physical Education and Athletics. Besides teaching psychology, Shaffer administered the Playground Athletic League of Baltimore and served as chief psychologist at the Sheppard Pratt Hospital. For the first year under the new system, Shaffer's new department had a budget of $21,000, with a coaching staff composed of graduate students, faculty, two full-time holdovers from the old system, and local alumni volunteers. For instance, Johns Hopkins graduate and assistant professor of mathematics Kelso Morrill joined the lacrosse staff. The faculty expanded the intercollegiate program—which had already included football, lacrosse, basketball, track, cross country, handball, and tennis—by adding soccer, wrestling, fencing, handball, golf, and baseball. Shaffer also managed the mandatory athletics program for freshmen that was intended to socialize students into university life, teach everyone a lifetime or "carry over sport" such as tennis, and introduce newcomers to team sports in the hope that they would join intercollegiate and intramural teams.[175]

By shifting control of athletics from the alumni to the faculty and eliminating professional full-time coaches committed to intercollegiate victories, Johns Hopkins essentially deprofessionalized its athletics. Prior to establishment of the new program, 15 percent of Johns Hopkins students had participated in some form of intercollegiate or intramural athletics; within three years, the rate had jumped to 90 percent.[176] With the prodding of some students, the university even retained the football team. Making a direct link between the two rough-and-tumble sports, the *News-Letter* boldly claimed, "If football is to die, lacrosse will not be long in following it to the grave."[177] Despite fears that athletic performance would plummet, Johns Hopkins' thirteen varsity teams sported a combined 56–46 record in 1934–35. Shaffer emphasized the explicit amateurism of the new system: "We would like to win, of course, and we probably shall win our share of games, but honestly are not primarily concerned about winning. The important thing to us is to put as many teams as possible in competition and to keep them playing."[178] More important was strengthening the university's social system during a time of economic crisis; this was critical. In hindsight, the new system merely reinforced Johns Hopkins' relationship with local private schools that provided the university with numerous middle-class young men. Indeed, the commitment to deprofessionalized sport did not alter many boys' decisions to attend the university. It may even have enhanced them.

With the new program a success, the university's board of trustees decided in late February 1937 to decommercialize Johns Hopkins sports to complete a restoration of amateurism. As of October, the trustees proclaimed, the university would no longer charge fees for entrance to intercollegiate athletic contests. Instead the university would issue admission cards for all events and grant season tickets to alumni. Furthermore, Johns Hopkins would no longer pay or receive guarantees from opponents. All traveling expenses, the trustees declared, would be paid by the visiting institution. Although the university eliminated gate receipts, as well as the student athletic fee, the policy mandated university payment for all intercollegiate and intramural sports.[179] With faculty in control of the Department of Physical Education and Athletics, the university treated sports as it did academic departments. With the connection between athletic performance and financial support completely severed,[180] the student press declared, "The importance of this move will be appreciated by all those who deplore the present semi-professionalism of college athletics, and launches Hopkins into a field which has not yet been explored." The new policy drew positive responses from area institutions and the Baltimore press. In Annapolis the *Saint John's Collegian* praised the university's decision to eliminate gate receipts: "Johns Hopkins becomes the first major institution of learning in the United States to break away completely and unequivocally from the professional athletic system. . . . To 'operate' teams for the single purpose of collecting gate receipts destroys the entire purpose of athletics."[181] According to the *Baltimore Sun*'s Craig Taylor, Johns Hopkins had made a bold move: "At Homewood there is a belief, idealistic to many, and crack-brained to others, that the best way to abolish commercial hypocrisy in sports is not to stop with abolishing the hypocrisy, but to eliminate the commerce."[182]

After eliminating its professional coaching staff, Johns Hopkins' fourteen-sport budget totaled only $5,350 by 1940. The lacrosse team accounted for $1,300, second only to football's $1,500.[183] Even those outside Baltimore recognized the importance of the change. The *New York Times* praised the plan: "The experiment at Johns Hopkins shows that an intramural and intercollegiate program in athletics can be carried on without gate receipts and, to this innocent bystander, it still seems to be a fine idea."[184] According to the *Baltimore Sun*, the new program was a true wonder: "How is it done? Not with mirrors or country bookkeeping. Simply by using some horse sense in administration and direction. Hopkins teams take no long jaunts over the country; they play teams that have undergraduate bodies somewhat close to Hopkins in size and scholastic requirements; their equipment is adequate, but not of the silk and satin variety, and it is cared for, so that it lasts out several seasons."[185]

Although cynics argued that the university had implemented the program to save money, Shaffer noted in 1937 that the payment of coaches as athletics instructors actually cost $2,000 more than had the old system. However, the university did not raise tuition to offset greater athletic expenses. By standing against prevailing trends, Johns Hopkins administrators defended amateur sport to a greater extent than did the Ivy League. Even when Johns Hopkins participated in a commercial lacrosse match against Mount Washington in 1941, the gate receipts benefited a British War Relief fund. In 1942 the university named Shaffer dean of the College of Arts and Sciences, but he retained his psychology and physical education responsibilities. Looking back, Schaffer later judged Johns Hopkins sport in 1945 positively on the grounds that it associated amateur sport with the social elite and commercial sport with the masses: "It appeared evident that Hopkins had provided an example of the distinction between pure college athletics and the public amusement industry."[186]

Although some institutions within organized lacrosse copied this renewed commitment to noncommercial, amateur sport, the Baltimore university had scored an important symbolic victory. Johns Hopkins took the moral high ground, and its lacrosse team remained a national power. However, this triumph of amateur athleticism was partially by default. Because the university's commitment to deprofessionalized sport had little effect on the path of affluent schoolboys who would have enrolled at Johns Hopkins in any case, the new program cannot be considered terribly radical. Moreover, adherence to amateur sport was attractive to well-to-do athletes during the Great Depression. At a time when Americans expected one another to tighten their belts and make sacrifices, playing sport not for pay but for sport's sake seemed morally praiseworthy, but hardly demanding.

The exaltation of amateurism at Johns Hopkins validated the efforts of many older officials and coaches within American lacrosse. The Johns Hopkins administration had given the sports world in general, and lacrosse in particular, a model of pristine amateurism by which to govern campus life. In a feature that appears in *Collier's* in 1935, former lacrosse player Kyle Crichton invoked familiar stereotypes as well as praise for amateur play in a discussion of lacrosse: "It has everything an American crowd is supposed to like, being a combination of football, basketball, cross-country, hockey, second-degree murder and sleight of hand. The game is fast, rough and clever." He also pointed to its significance in Maryland: "Down around Bal-

timore, it is a religion, a mark of social standing and a form of dementia."
Crichton also alluded to an aristocratic quality of Baltimore lacrosse, likening players' leather gloves to "the paraphernalia of the armored warriors of
King Arthur's day." Apparently Baltimoreans had no problem with rugged
sport: "'What do you mean—rough?' they demand in Baltimore. 'There has
never been a casualty in lacrosse, and few serious injuries. What are a few
cuts among gentlemen?'"[187] Even though many lacrosse fans in Maryland
knew the game's native origins, they took pride in dominating their
adopted game and claiming it as their own. In 1940 the *Baltimore Sun* declared, "It is time now, if it has not already been done, to put lacrosse among
the distinctly Maryland things of wide reputation along, say, with the literary works of Poe and Mencken, certain superior cookery styles, and liberal
tolerance."[188] With lacrosse enmeshed in Baltimore's elite social fabric,
sportsmen at Johns Hopkins believed their favorite game and renewed
commitment to amateurism counted as high culture. According to a 1941
game program, the athletic policy at the university "demands the avoidance
of intolerance, vindictiveness, selfishness, and other vicious habits." Instead
Johns Hopkins officials sought "the development of fairness, respect for
ones [*sic*] opponents, self sacrifice, and obedience to laws."[189]

Although lacrosse successfully provided a cultural setting for greater
unity among the social elite in Baltimore, the formation of a new Baltimore
A.C. lacrosse team in 1935 provided for dissent. Because Mount Washington could not accommodate the growing number of lacrosse-playing graduates of local schools as well as those returning home from the Ivy League,
Johns Hopkins alumni Caleb and Donaldson Kelly helped to establish the
new club. During its first spring of competition, in 1935, Baltimore A.C. officials asked for a contest with the Mount Washington club. The latter declined, citing a full practice and game schedule running from March 1 to
May 30. According to a Mount Washington statement, "Our schedules have
always been considered one of the longest and most difficult in the country, and since our players are business men, the requirements of practice
and training necessitate the sacrifice of free time for personal pleasure in
order to stay in condition to complete our schedule." Mount Washington
club officers also sought to uphold the "unquestionable amateur status" of
its own players by avoiding competition against professionals. By hinting at
the experience that former Saint John's and current Baltimore A.C. player
Phil Lotz had gained in Canada, Mount Washington tacitly accused him of

professionalism. "We felt that such a game would make an interesting contest this year," the statement read, "but gave us no assurance that it might not affect our relations with certain undergraduate bodies in future years."[190] American clubs and collegian squads had crossed sticks with paid Canadian teams for decades, but the conditions of the Great Depression made amateur sportsmen less tolerant of their professional counterparts. The failure of Canadian box lacrosse confirmed the intolerance.

Bowing to pressure from local sportswriters, the two clubs privately negotiated an end-of-the-season contest. In his personal history of the Baltimore A.C., Caleb Kelly, by now a Baltimore attorney, wrote of Mount Washington, "It was obvious from their attitude that they did not want the new B.A.C. to profit financially from the tilt and thus be encouraged to continue competition."[191] Mount Washington officials eventually offered to play Kelly's club, but only to benefit the Johns Hopkins Hospital general campaign fund. Banning professionals and imported players who did not play during the regular season, they also agreed that expenses would include only the Homewood Field rental fee, payment for referees, and travel reimbursements for players who had already left town.[192] Local journalist Paul Menton pleaded with the men of both teams to set aside partisanship. He characterized Mount Washington's terms for the contest as "dictatorial" and the source of the Baltimore A.C.'s resentment: "It reminds me of the rich boy in the gang who owns the balls and the gloves, and says he is the pitcher or he'll take his things and go home."[193] Mount Washington eventually won the contest, which attracted two thousand spectators. The Baltimore A.C. fielded squads until 1941, and even won the national "open" club title in 1937, but World War II halted its activities and restored Mount Washington to a position of supremacy.

Both Johns Hopkins and Mount Washington achieved on-field victories while abiding by the amateur code, but the lacrosse communities in New York City and upstate New York did not fare as well. Instead of celebrating a healthy sixty-seventh birthday, the New York L.C. was forced by "a serious shortage of players" to seek new recruits through a newspaper plea in 1938. In a letter to the editor, Eliot M. Stark of Brooklyn outlined the expectations of the club toward any potential player: "Our club is an amateur outfit in the strictest sense. Each player pays for his own equipment and travelling expenses."[194] Similarly, the Crescent A.C. team—an overpowering mainstay of American lacrosse for four decades—disappeared from competition during the late Depression. By the end of the Second World War, the lacrosse community in Baltimore was clearly the cultural center of the sport. Not only was its secondary school feeder system intact, but the area had a strong core of university and college programs, especially at Johns Hopkins. With several thousand affluent alumni and other patrons of the game, it wielded much organizational clout on the national stage. Moreover, the two mythical Olympic championships, memories of contests against Oxbridge, satisfaction with the failure of box lacrosse in the United States, and even occasional games against Iroquois Indians all reinforced the self-importance many Baltimore lacrosse fans attached to their game. In their minds, lacrosse was their game.

Chapter 4 **"Mayhem on the Lawn"**

Lacrosse in the United States and Canada,
1945–1970

THE GREAT DEPRESSION and World War II curtailed play and stunted the
growth of lacrosse at many universities, colleges, and secondary schools in
the United States, but the two crises also renewed the commitment to the
ideals of amateur athletics. Economic malaise and the demands of the war
neutralized any serious change in the guiding ethos of the American
lacrosse community. Despite the silencing of a conception of lacrosse that
had been more sympathetic to commercialism, devotees emerged from the
war with their sporting community intact. Throughout the quarter century
after 1945, numerous officials, coaches, players, and supportive journalists
tried to maintain some connection with the values of the prewar decades.
Many sportsmen and -women still conceived of their game as a healthy and
socially exclusive sport that was tied indirectly to a romanticized Native
American past. However, while the men celebrated tough, manly play, the
women condemned such conceptualizations of their game. The postwar
decades may have had much in common with the years before Pearl Har-
bor, but new trends unfolded in the years between 1945 and 1970. Not only
did lacrosse spread from upper- and upper-middle-class sporting communities to suburban, middle-class athletes, but enthusiasts helped to colonize
the game in regions beyond the Northeast and the mid-Atlantic. Moreover,
the general sports and leisure boom during the years of postwar affluence
led field lacrosse partisans to advance their game by employing commercial mechanisms.

While the sport's leading advocates adopted modern promotional tech-
niques, they remained devoted to elite, amateur sport and their conception
of themselves as the symbolic descendants of the "noble savage." The apparent inconsistency between geographic growth, social expansion, and insti-

tutional reform, on the one hand, and cultural continuity, on the other, created tensions that would not be fully realized until later decades. By the end of the 1960s, despite the absence of overt conflict, these tensions made rigid adherence to pristine amateurism problematic. Most notably, supporters of men's lacrosse in the United States often frowned upon popular conceptions of their game as nothing more than "organized mayhem," but many Canadians and Iroquois Indians thrived on them. As they had prior to the war, the latter pursued their own indoor summer version of lacrosse—boxla—away from the world of the outdoor field game. These Canadian and Indian enthusiasts extolled a game wherein the club was an extension of the community. Native lacrosse players were especially attracted to boxla's replication of the basic conditions of traditional ball play.

The American Field Lacrosse Community in an Age of Affluence

Lacrosse proponents in the United States greeted the postwar era with optimism and planned a renewal of play. As did the rest of America, they wanted to remember personal wartime sacrifices, look forward to peace, and escape from Cold War fears. Prior to Johns Hopkins' first postwar match with Army, director of athletics C. Gardner Mallonee rededicated the university's Great War service flag, adding a new banner honoring six players killed and one missing in action during the war. Among the dead was Lieutenant Colonel Jack Turnbull, who had been shot down during a B-17 bombing mission over Germany in 1944. Lacrosse organizers honored this former Johns Hopkins All-American by dedicating a statue trophy in his name that was to be awarded annually to the best collegian attackman.[1] As chairman of the United States Intercollegiate Lacrosse Association lacrosse guide committee, Albert Brisotti of New York University believed the peace would bring prosperity to lacrosse in 1947.[2] He expressed anxiety over the deterioration of international relations, but reaffirmed the gentlemanly qualities of lacrosse. Citing a hostile world abroad, he declared, "It is a rather pleasant thought to know that there are people who can rise above this and devote a good part of their time to the promotion of a sport which in the main can bring no profit to them but does bring health and recreation to many others."[3] By the late 1940s the major lacrosse powers—Army, Navy, Johns Hopkins, Maryland, Rensselaer Polytechnic Institute, and the

Mount Washington L.C.—attracted crowds of eight to ten thousand for big contests.[4]

Many lacrosse coaches and college alumni aggressively cultivated their sport during the quarter century after World War II, and intercollegiate lacrosse experienced significant growth. The number of college teams expanded roughly 400 percent during these years, with New York state outpacing all regions. Only the City College of New York, Cornell, Hobart, Rensselaer, Syracuse, Union, and the U.S. Military Academy had teams at the end of the war, but the number had swelled to three dozen by the end of the 1960s. The other three traditional hotbeds of intercollegiate play— New England, Maryland, and the mid-Atlantic states of Pennsylvania and New Jersey—also experienced dramatic growth. With the spread of the game to the South, the Midwest, and the Far West, the proportion of programs in the Northeast fell from nine-tenths to less than three-quarters of the intercollegiate community. In every region the game germinated primarily at private institutions, but also took root at some public schools. Prior to 1945 the only publicly funded schools with lacrosse programs had been Penn State, City College of New York, and the two armed forces academies. However, by 1970 the college ranks included a dozen public schools, such as Cortland State and Towson State, and nine community colleges in New York and Maryland.

Looking at growth over time, the immediate postwar years saw the largest boom; the size of the community had doubled, to 58 institutions, by the end of the 1940s. Growth slowed during the 1950s, but accelerated again in the 1960s, when the community doubled again. Rising interest in intercollegiate competition resulted mainly from experienced high school graduates who wanted to keep playing in college. School by school, these athletes formed clubs, then achieved varsity status. The expansion of organized lacrosse does not suggest that the sport had begun to rival the intercollegiate giants, football and basketball. At lacrosse-rich Syracuse University, for example, the 1950–51 athletics budget totaled $242,863. With 150 men on the varsity and freshman rosters, the football team accounted for two-thirds of all funding. Even though the 80-man lacrosse program's budget of $4,260 exceeded the baseball team's, it still trailed the budgets for football, basketball, crew, boxing, and track. Hardly a revenue-generating sport, lacrosse remained on the periphery of mass sport. Compared to the

Syracuse football team's $242,000 income, the lacrosse program earned a mere $350.[5]

With more lacrosse-playing institutions there emerged tensions over determining a national champion. In 1953 the USILA began using a system of divisional alignment based on an evaluation of the relative strengths of teams, which were rated according to five-year cumulative records. Initially the USILA used the ratings to assign each school to one of three divisions named for leading officials from the first half of the century. The team with the most points in its division at season's end won the division cups, while the university or college with the most total points earned the championship Wingate Memorial Trophy.[6] As USILA membership grew, the divisions multiplied, more cups were awarded, and the point-determination scheme became more complex. Beginning in 1960, the USILA created an elite National Division and adopted division names based on regions. Throughout the decade, the USILA modified this system to match its growth; the number of divisions by 1968 was eleven.[7] Changes in the means of determining champions and the expansion of divisional alignments highlighted the relationship between institutional growth and organizational reform. Two institutions dominated the championship during this era. Navy won eight titles outright and shared four others, holding the title for a continuous stretch from 1960 to 1967. Johns Hopkins won six titles alone and shared another four, including straight titles from 1947 to 1950.

The postcollegian club lacrosse community also revived after 1945 in Boston, New York, Philadelphia, Baltimore, and Annapolis. Organizers established a United States Club Lacrosse Association (USCLA) in 1960 to provide order. The largest and most vibrant clubs resided in Maryland, where squads played summer schedules and occasionally played to benefit charities.[8] In Colorado and California, graduates of eastern colleges founded teams such as the Denver L.C. and promoted the game on nearby campuses during the late 1950s.[9] Although the social composition of postwar club lacrosse was probably more heterogeneous than in previous decades, the athletes still came primarily from affluent neighborhoods. The *New York Times* described the 1968 edition of the New York L.C. as well-to-do: "They are businessmen, bankers, brokers, dentists, doctors, teachers and students. Most are in their late twenties. Several are married, have growing families and enjoy backyard barbecues in suburbia. But they all share a driving dedication to the violent sport."[10] Unfortunately, the informality and irregularity of club lacrosse make it difficult to assess the growth and geographic distribution of clubs, because they formed and disbanded with great frequency. By the late 1960s, the USCLA was sponsoring summer leagues in Philadelphia, Baltimore, and Rochester, while about two dozen clubs fielded teams from New England to Maryland. The association split into two divisions; the northern section included club teams from Boston, the Connecticut valley, Long Island, New York, New Jersey, and Philadelphia, while the southern division, in the Chesapeake Bay area, had the Maryland, Mount Washington, Severna Park, and Carling clubs. Teams in other regions represented Pittsburgh, Cleveland, Columbus, Chicago, and Denver.[11]

The American field lacrosse community continued its ties with England and Australia after 1945. However, the postwar trips lacked the cultural significance of the Anglo-American tours of the interwar period; American men looked to the future with confidence and hence did not require English leadership. The people of England were still suffering from austerity and the loss of their empire overseas, while the United States was becoming the leader of the "free world." This new reality was not lost on sportsmen. The Rensselaer Polytechnic Institute lacrosse team toured the British Isles during the London Olympics of 1948, followed by teams from Yale (1950), Virginia (1954), Washington and Lee (1956), and Johns Hopkins (1958). In contrast to the practice on the tours of the 1920s and 1930s, visiting American teams played according to English rules. Comfortable with their athletic superiority, the Americans were not threatened by this accommodation to British clubs. In 1959 Washington and Lee and the University of Virginia toured Australia, the first such encounter between the two countries. Like the interwar exchange tours, most of these international contests included formal receptions, dinner parties, and award ceremonies. Australian and English teams also traveled to North America. After an Oxford-Cambridge squad toured the United States in 1961, an Australian team arrived the following season.[12]

Interscholastic schoolboy lacrosse grew by more than 800 percent during the quarter century after 1945, primarily in areas already supporting the sport. After steady growth during the 1950s, the interscholastic community more than doubled during the following decade. Most growth took place in Maryland, New England, greater metropolitan New York City, and upstate New York—all regions with traditions of schoolboy play predating the

Second World War. In the greater Baltimore area, officials segregated schools into public and private school divisions, with teams from the latter usually winning the city title. At Saint Paul's School, winner of fourteen titles from 1940 through 1962, social pressures to excel in lacrosse led many a boy to make his stick an appendage. "As soon as the basketball season was over, lacrosse sticks appeared. These were carried around to classes and placed in the back of the room during the period, so that during recess they would be available," coach Howard "Howdy" Myers observed. "Boys walking down to the drug store to get a soda, would walk on opposite sides of the street, passing back and forth across the street as they walked. Boys going on a date, always carried their sticks with them to get in a little stickwork. At a game, all the younger players would swarm the field at half-time to pass the ball around."[13] The 1960s brought expansion in and around Baltimore, Annapolis, and Chestertown; other parts of the state; and even Delaware and Washington, D.C. Meanwhile, private academies and prep schools dominated interscholastic play in New England. With only seven schools participating in the first postwar campaign—academies in Exeter, New Hampshire, and in Andover, Deerfield, Mount Hermon, South Byfield (Governor Dummer), Lawrence, and Worcester, Massachusetts—schoolboy lacrosse included contests against Ivy League freshman squads. This brotherhood doubled in size during the decade after 1945, a growth that intensified during the 1960s.

In downstate New York, lacrosse enthusiasts cultivated their game swiftly on suburban Long Island and along the lower Hudson valley. In 1945, only Garden City, Manhasset, and Sewanhaka High Schools on Long Island and the Peekskill Military Academy and Polytechnic Prep in Brooklyn possessed teams. Within a few years, however, Freeport, Mineola, Huntington, and Massapequa had started programs. After 1957 other suburban Long Island communities—Hempstead, Uniondale, New Hyde Park, Floral Park, and Levittown—adopted lacrosse in batches. The rapidity of growth on Long Island led to the replacement of the old Metropolitan–Long Island Lacrosse Association with separate leagues for Nassau and Suffolk Counties.[14] By 1970 seventy-five schools possessed programs, the greatest concentration of schoolboy play in the country. Lured away from Johns Hopkins to start a program at Hofstra University in 1949, Howdy Myers played a leading role in the expansion of Long Island lacrosse. To cultivate a local feeder system, Myers went from school to school encouraging principals to adopt the game. "Like a modern-day Johnny Appleseed, Myers put lacrosse sticks in the hands of thousands of Yankees," the *New York Times* reported in 1975. "The sport used to be popular only among Maryland schoolboys, New England preppies and American Indians. Today, many suburban youngsters carry sticks and pads to lacrosse leagues on Saturday morning— just the way it was in Howdy Myers's native 'Ballamer' (Baltimore)."[15]

Aside from these traditional enclaves in Maryland, New England, and New York City, interscholastic lacrosse developed in other areas. One such area was a region of upstate New York stretching from Syracuse to Rochester in the west, Watertown to the north, and Rome to the east. The outburst of lacrosse among central New York public schools signaled the revival of schoolboy play. In 1940 New York state's new physical education and athletic regulations banned coaches who did not teach classes at the schools where they coached, ending the coaching careers of part-time high school lacrosse mentors who worked other full-time jobs. However, former high school and college players of the Syracuse L.C. helped renew interest in the game.[16] According to former club member Charles Perkins, they targeted area schools: "We designated certain guys that would go to the high schools and get a teacher there that would want to become a coach."[17] Besides schools in upstate New York, small handfuls of schools in New Jersey and eastern Pennsylvania developed programs during the 1950s, with the total reaching thirty-five by the end of the next decade. Inspired by area club men and collegians, pockets of schoolboy lacrosse also developed in Colorado and California.[18]

The price and lack of availability of lacrosse equipment often slowed the expansion of the game at the college level and especially the schoolboy level, but administrators tried to lessen the sport's potential cost. For example, the athletic director at Phillips Exeter Academy in New Hampshire, Martin W. Souders, argued that most other team sports exceeded lacrosse in cost. During the 1949–50 school year the Exeter athletics budget totaled $7,750 for seven sports. In terms of average cost per student, lacrosse ($4.15) ranked behind baseball ($12.87), football ($10.00), hockey ($7.79), basketball ($6.70), and swimming ($6.25), but ahead of soccer ($4.03). However, because a team's use of uniforms and equipment from other sports lowered the potential cost of a lacrosse program, these figures are deceiving. According to Norman B. Grant, athletic director at Lawrence Academy, "We use cotton football shirts, hockey arm pads and gloves, soccer shorts and old football helmets which have been converted to lacrosse use by the addition of a face mask and visor."[19] Instead of spending $620.50 to outfit a new thirty-man program in 1951, Penn State coach Glenn Thiel believed portions of uniforms could be taken from football (jerseys and shoes) and from basketball and soccer (shorts). A well-managed team might require a budget of only $300.[20] The program at Ohio State University relied upon old gear from eastern schools and upon borrowed shoes and jerseys from the football team.[21] Assistance from other colleges or universities essentially permitted the early survival of many new programs. Head coaches at City College of New York, Army, and Cornell all donated equipment to a new C. W. Post team in the late 1950s.[22]

A direct comparison of the costs for lacrosse and baseball gear shows why, at least financially, some schools might not have accepted the "new" Indian game. In the mid-1960s lacrosse sticks could be purchased for between $14.24 and $20.00, while a baseball bat cost between $2.25 and $4.90. A pair of lacrosse gloves went for $11.95 to $30.00, and a baseball mitt ranged from $5.95 to as much as $46.00. Moreover, a baseball player in the 1960s did not have to wear a helmet ($16.50–$21.00), face mask ($4.00–$4.95), arm pads ($8.50–$13.75), or shoulder pads ($9.95–$11.50). Other equipment aside—such as the special equipment of goal tenders and catchers, as well as goals and bases—totaling the bare essentials of lacrosse and baseball revealed a lower price tag for the latter. Any school with a lacrosse team that appeared to require fewer dollars than baseball was hiding the real cost. So in addition to lacking skilled coaches and experienced players, many intercollegiate lacrosse coaches felt hampered by the poor quantity and quality of equipment, especially the Indian-made wooden sticks. To make matters worse, an equipment distribution monopoly gave an advantage to established programs such as Johns Hopkins.[23]

The growth of interscholastic play depended on the ability of coaches to convince schoolboys of the cultural values and the health and educational benefits of the springtime game. Faced with a public perception of lacrosse as savage, coaches had to portray lacrosse as no more dangerous than other sports. Yet they also rationalized to school officials the need to adopt the game's rough qualities. Alluding to the emphasis on height in basketball and on size in football, in 1950 Glenn Thiel reminded high school coaches that "courage, stamina, brains, speed, teamwork, and stick work" took precedence over the lacrosse player's physique.[24] Comparing a bygone

Indian past with the world of the twentieth century, Thiel emphasized "self-control" as the primary cultural value of lacrosse: "To the Indian warrior, from whom we inherit the game, a lacrosse stick was as much a weapon as it was an implement of skill. When his opponent hit unnecessarily hard he probably returned it with interest. That old instinct is not entirely submerged by the veneer of civilization. It some times takes considerable self-control for a red blooded youth of today not to make a similar response in a similar situation. It might also be stated that in a little different situation the fact that every player is armed with a stick induces the bully to refrain from 'laying it on' a less rugged opponent who may have the ball. He knows that soon the situation will be reversed and he will probably receive as good as he gave."[25] By referring to perceived instinctual qualities of native players, Thiel accentuated the alleged character-building ability of the rough and potentially dangerous game. Lacrosse might teach young men useful social skills that would allow them to gain an edge in a bureaucratic, conformist world.

Many lacrosse coaches and athletic directors in New York and New England argued that high schools should adopt their game because of its ability to cultivate "character." According to Albert W. Twitchell, an associate professor of physical education at Rutgers, lacrosse "strengthens the body, the mind, and the character to a high degree through the very nature of the games which require great skill, courage, speed and a sense of team play." Kimball Union Academy headmaster William R. Brewster thought lacrosse served as a critical part of a "well-rounded education," because the sport developed "many skills, endurance, team work and 'guts.'" Pointing in a different direction, Phillips Exeter's Martin Souders wrote: "The game is just rough enough to meet the needs of the animal instincts of these youngsters and still is not the dangerous game that the average layman thinks it is." Coaches praised the controlled roughness of lacrosse, while physicians and athletic trainers dispelled popular misconceptions. One doctor at the Children's Medical Center in Boston demonstrated that the injury rates for soccer, basketball, hockey, wrestling, baseball, and lacrosse players were roughly the same: "To slash at your opponent's stick may seem dangerous to a spectator, but it only rarely injures the player."

While most coaches saw virtues in the roughness of lacrosse, school officials noted that the sport provided social mobility opportunities for less affluent athletes. Sewanhaka High School vice principal Howard Nordahl

said, "We feel grateful to the game because many of our graduates have returned to tell us how much the sport has meant to their development and
adjustment while in college."[26] In Baltimore, for example, many Saint Paul's
players advanced to prestigious universities. Between 1943 and 1964, the
school produced twenty-three first-team intercollegiate All-Americans, including seven each at Johns Hopkins and Virginia. The Saint Paul's program epitomized the perception that lacrosse could develop exceptional intellectual skills and gentlemanly cultural values. According to athletic
director Martin "Mitch" Tullai, "A high degree of school spirit has been generated, academic pride has been fostered, school citizenship had been promoted, and a fine winning attitude—winning according to the rules and
within the bounds of fair play—has been developed."[27] Public and private
school officials reached a consensus: lacrosse was rough enough to promote
masculine character, but not so violent as to encourage savagery.

As the ranks of administrators, coaches, and athletes endorsing college
and schoolboy lacrosse increased, the game remained especially popular in
Baltimore. According to an article printed in *Time* magazine in June 1947,
"When American kids everywhere else are reaching for baseball bats each
spring, Baltimore's small fry fondle lacrosse sticks."[28] Though many proponents of lacrosse conceived of Baltimore as the game's cultural capital,
many city residents did not embrace the game. As *Time* continued, "There
is no middle ground among Baltimoreans: they either love the game or de-
spise it."[29] Lacrosse may have been popular at prep schools, but baseball
dominated working-class neighborhoods. In 1962 a *Sports Illustrated* feature captured the place of lacrosse in Maryland: "Now the first signs of a
Baltimore spring are the dents in auto fenders where youngsters have
missed passes while playing catch en route to school, and fans find themselves having trouble thinking about that more typical springtime sport,
baseball." The support many affluent Baltimore families offered to lacrosse
helped college lacrosse outdraw minor league baseball. One day during the
first postwar spring, for instance, a Navy-Maryland game attracted 11,500
fans, but the Baltimore Orioles played before only 3,800.[30] Eventually, when
the American League's Saint Louis Browns moved to Baltimore and became
the major league version of the Orioles, professional baseball overtook collegian lacrosse. An elite aura and a close relationship between schools and
intercollegiate programs remained part of the cultural fabric of lacrosse in
Baltimore and other cities, but many coaches and supporters realized that

they needed to portray their game in terms familiar to a mass audience if it was going to have a future.

Unlike the men's game, women's lacrosse continued to operate in a world nearly devoid of varsity female athletics. The United States Women's Lacrosse Association (USWLA) governed a national network of local organizations that had survived the hardships of the Great Depression and the Second World War. Local associations existed in Baltimore, Philadelphia, New York, Westchester, and Boston. Similar clubs in Pittsburgh and the Adirondack Mountains region flopped, but one in New Jersey reemerged in 1952. In addition to these local associations composed of adults, the USWLA also had relationships with universities, colleges, and secondary schools, which spurred significant growth. The USWLA's allied membership grew from 20 schools in 1940 to 33 in 1949 and reached 104 institutions by 1957. Secondary schools usually outnumbered the universities and colleges by a margin of three to two. Many of these institutions had formal ties with a nearby USWLA local association. During the 1950s roughly 32 percent of allied institutions were affiliated with the association in Philadelphia, 20 percent with Boston, nine percent with Westchester, eight percent with Baltimore, and seven percent with New Jersey. Much smaller pockets of interest could be found in New York, Long Island, and Virginia.[31] Confined to only a half dozen locales, women's lacrosse clearly trailed the men's game in size and scope.

The women's seasonal format also differed greatly from that of the men. Instead of an eight- to twelve-game schedule with a complicated championship point system, women's teams with association memberships mainly engaged in intrasquad and exhibition play. Athletes viewed the "regular season" as preparation for an annual national tournament. The clubs were "largely made up of teachers of physical education and ex-schoolgirl players,"[32] according to a physical education journal. In May 1958 the *Baltimore Evening Sun* reported that the twenty-five members of the local women's club consisted mainly of "teachers, housewives and students," ranging in age from eighteen to thirty-five.[33] With most lacrosse programs at private institutions such as Bryn Mawr, Radcliffe, and Smith Colleges, women's lacrosse enthusiasts came from roughly the same social category as their male counterparts. Considering that men outnumbered women in higher education during the 1940s and 1950s, most lacrosse players were probably affluent.

Women's coaches, officials, and sportswriters constantly fought against not only public perceptions of their game as too rough, but also comparisons with men's lacrosse. In December 1944 USWLA president Lesley C. Wead of Wells College complained to *Journal of Health and Physical Education* readers that the men's game provided a negative frame of reference for women's lacrosse. "One of the major problems confronting us is the existing but erroneous belief that lacrosse is a dangerous and brutal form of mayhem," she argued. "What the non-player does not realize is that lacrosse for women is *not* comparable to men's lacrosse. Our emphasis is placed on superior stickwork and body control as *bodily contact is prohibited,* thus eliminating the element of roughness."[34] Describing their game as the antithesis of male sport, however, women's lacrosse supporters stressed that their game did not threaten femininity. Sympathetic journalists portrayed women's lacrosse as "extremely graceful,"[35] as if twenty-four women were racing "through a ballet without music."[36] By outfitting players in skirts, women's officials underscored ladylike decorum and modesty.[37] After retiring from the Bryn Mawr School of Baltimore in 1950, pioneer Rosabelle Sinclair continued to mentor the Baltimore Women's Lacrosse Association team for years. Dubbed the American "Grand Dame of Lacrosse," this transplanted Scotswoman frowned on the view of her players as "muscular Katrinkas with the fortitude of lady wrestlers." Sinclair believed women's lacrosse should be played according to "a British idea toward games," emphasizing physical proficiency and feminine refinement. "Lacrosse, as the girls play it, is an orderly pastime that has little in common with the men's tribal-warfare version except the long-handled racket or crosse that gives the sport its name," she argued. "It's true that the object in both men's and women's lacrosse is to send a ball through a goal by means of the racket, but whereas the men resort to brute strength the women depend solely on skill."[38]

Although schools did not always fund men's and boys' lacrosse, the scarcity of secondary schoolgirl lacrosse resulted from the paltry funding for all female athletics. As a result, many women's lacrosse programs in colleges and universities featured not competition with other schools, but only intramurals or physical education classes. By the mid-1950s only 39 percent of private colleges and 13 percent of public colleges with lacrosse programs engaged in intercollegiate play. About 67 percent of private secondary schools and 52 percent of public schools did the same. Many of these programs stayed afloat because of a few hands that were doing much work. In roughly three-fifths of these programs a single physical education instructor managed the team. Three quarters of these instructors had learned the game as undergraduates, and most had refined their play in summer camps and lacrosse camps. About a third played with a local association. Compared to men's lacrosse, the women's game had little contact with Iroquois Indians. In the mid-1950s women's lacrosse hardly represented a grassroots movement among secondary or college students; about 80 percent of all programs grew out of a physical education teacher's interest. In only one quarter of schools did schoolgirls or undergraduates ask for lacrosse, though in private schools this was far more common. Most equipment was purchased directly from a retail sporting goods company, but about 20 percent of public institutions and 10 percent of private schools received equipment loans from the USWLA.[39]

Many directors of physical education programs for women and girls believed lacrosse complemented their other offerings,[40] but lacrosse competed for athletes with other spring and summer sports. According to Gretchen Schuyler of Sargent College in Cambridge, Massachusetts, in 1947 lacrosse possessed several advantages over other team sports, including the high rate of participation derived from a call for twelve participants, the sport's compatibility with the playing surface of field hockey, and its tactical similarity with basketball. Citing benefits noticed when the game had first been introduced to America, she noted that girls played lacrosse in the "upright position," with far less crouching than in field hockey. "Breathing is easier," Schuyler contended, "and it would also seem that this game has more posture values than most other team sports which are popular today."[41] Lesley Wead saw lacrosse combining "the freedom and grace of dancing with the fast-cutting tactics of basketball." References to posture and grace illustrate that lacrosse did not violate contemporary notions of femininity.[42] Despite widespread criticism of alleged similarities between men's and women's lacrosse, Wead felt confident enough about her sport to propose that women's exhibitions be staged as preliminaries to men's contests to boost interest in the ladies' game.

The women's lacrosse community expanded much more slowly than the men's, but nonetheless carved out its own distinct athletic niche. Like other supporters of women's athletics, lacrosse enthusiasts emphasized the feminine qualities of the game, especially the prohibition of bodily contact, the demonstration of graceful motion, and the deemphasis on rough, intense competition. Looking to the anticipated postwar sports boom, Lesley Wead called for peer action: "Now is the time for schools and colleges to make preparations for including lacrosse in their curricula. This is one game that we do not want to "'give back to the Indians!'"[43] With this bold statement, she labeled lacrosse a viable, proper sport for young women that had been tamed from a "savage" Indian activity. Although Wead's views testified to a small but vibrant women's lacrosse community, the women's male counterparts were simply better organized and better funded, and they capitalized on traditional male dominance of sport. Regardless of gender, lacrosse proponents grew in numbers during the quarter century after the Second World War. But just as female advocates of lacrosse were resigned to their slower progress, several proselytizing coaches and officials of the men's game were aggressively building up their infrastructure.

Promoting Lacrosse: Confronting Limitations, Enshrining Ideals

During the 1950s and 1960s an emerging consensus among men's lacrosse coaches, officials, and players in the United States called for a concerted effort to publicize lacrosse and advance the ideals of amateur sport. No effort on such a large scale existed among Iroquois Indians, Canadians, or women. Since the turn of the century, intercollegiate and club representatives to USILA meetings had annually announced efforts to colonize the game at neighboring institutions, but those ventures had amounted to little more than a few men's acting as part-time missionaries. Their work had often entailed unpaid coaching duties, with private clubs providing playing space for local schoolboys. Colonization had been piecemeal, local, and individualized, because proselytizers had focused on the technical aspects of the sport. Coaches had focused on getting prospective athletes to pick up sticks and give the game a chance. After the Second World War, however, they actively promoted their sport at colleges and high schools. The problem these men faced was how to overcome cultural, social, institutional, and material limitations on the growth of lacrosse in the age of the "baby boom." Regardless of who they recruited, conversions had to take place amid enormous conformist pressures that gave the national pastime, baseball, a seemingly insurmountable advantage.

Two problems confronted many college and high school coaches: the lack of access to the Indian-made lacrosse sticks and the difficulty of finding athletes willing to abandon other springtime sports such as baseball and track.[44] In 1947 Union College head coach Frederic Wyatt advised coaches to avoid sporting goods retailers by purchasing sticks directly from Indians on the Onondaga and Saint Regis Reservations and to target varsity football, basketball, and hockey players for their own teams.[45] Wyatt's plan made sense to many enthusiasts. In Onondaga County, Syracuse L.C. member Charles Perkins drove to the Saint Regis Reservation and purchased sixty Mohawk sticks at $5 each for use by five local high schools. Adults like Perkins did everything they could to convince youth to play by hiding or paying equipment expenses. Though money was saved by purchasing sticks directly from Iroquois craftsmen, driving to Indian reservations in New York, Ontario, and Quebec was an option unimagined by coaches in other sports. Moreover, the stick supply depended entirely upon the production capacity of reservation craftsmen. As long as they produced all lacrosse sticks, production of potentially smaller batches or poorer-quality sticks could restrict the number of athletes adopting lacrosse. Furthermore, a coach might be able to convince some student athletes who played fall and winter sports to join the lacrosse team, but it would be difficult to attract baseball players. Athletes on the football team might find the roughness and teamwork of lacrosse comparable with those of their own sport, but baseball remained the national pastime, a sport with icons such as Joe DiMaggio and Ted Williams. With the sports world increasingly receptive to commercialism after World War II, in 1949 NCAA lacrosse editor Albert Brisotti told readers to embrace reform and defend masculine amateur sport: "The virile game of lacrosse, the high standards of leadership in its coaching brotherhood, the sportsmanship and good fellowship of its adherents, warrants a more vociferous reception and acknowledgment by the general public."[46] Convincing the public would be tough.

Although individual efforts increased interest in the late 1940s, coordinated endeavors spread the gospel of lacrosse for the next two decades. Collegiate, club, and scholastic leaders from the United States Lacrosse Coaches Association (USLCA) led these efforts. These men utilized existing networks created by club-college competition, regional promotion chairmen, print materials and motion pictures, a used equipment pool, staged publicity events, and old-timer reunions. Pragmatic social ties arose from competition between collegian and club athletes, as young men formed cordial relationships with their more mature career-oriented counterparts. By the

1950s coaches were openly acknowledging the value of these ties. Although college coaches had already been promoting the game off the field, University of Delaware coach Milton Roberts emphasized the importance of club guidance for readers of *The Mentor* in January 1956. "The club rosters are composed of former high school, prep school and college players who wish to continue their lacrosse playing careers after graduation," Roberts noted. "This feature, undergraduate-graduate competition, affords a wholesome opportunity for friends and associates of school days to continue their friendly rivalries after scholastic and collegiate eligibility has ended."[47] Although postgame conversations revolved around who had won and lost, specific plays, goals scored, and past and future contests, this socialization implicitly linked men at various stages of their careers in business, law, and medicine.

Regional promotion and informal national communication contributed to expansion efforts. By tapping into stable communities of coaches, athletes, and alumni, the USLCA regionalized plans to encourage play. In 1957 Boys' Latin School (Baltimore) athletic director Claxton "Okie" O'Connor outlined such a scheme: William M. Ritch of Sewanhaka High School in Floral Park, New York, as chairman of the USLCA committee on the promotion of lacrosse, would supervise fourteen separate areas. These would include five in New York state (Onondaga, Suffolk, Nassau, and Westchester Counties and metropolitan New York); one each in New Jersey, New England, Philadelphia, Washington, D.C., Annapolis, Baltimore, and Ohio; and two others in Pennsylvania.[48] The focus of promotion would be primarily regions where lacrosse already existed, not new areas. These advocates also realized the need for a body of literature: rule books, instructional guides, historical resources. Besides circulating copies of books by American coaches such as William Schmeisser, enthusiasts relied on a book published by Johns Hopkins coach Kelso Morrill in 1952 and on one published by two Governor Dummer Academy coaches in 1966.[49] Other sources included Jack Kelly's *Lacrosse Newsletter,* articles in coaching journals, the NCAA's annual *Official Lacrosse Guide,* and occasional features in national magazines. To assist journalists the USLCA established a primitive archive in 1956 to give them easier access to materials for stories about lacrosse.[50] USLCA officials also made available to coaches and players two silent instructional movies and a sound film of a college all-star game. To preserve the game's history, the twenty-minute movie *What Is Lacrosse?* emphasized the Native American origins of the game.[51] Together, print materials and films reinforced the efforts of coaches.

Some lacrosse enthusiasts believed that sharing equipment was a noble deed. The USLCA formalized this old practice by creating a system whereby veteran institutions could deposit equipment into a pool for newer programs. Men such as Claxton O'Connor of Boys' Latin believed the program made it easier for schools to embrace a potentially expensive sport: "We remember a young man who was interested in starting Lacrosse at his school. At the time he discovered that twenty-two used helmets could be secured from the pool. Armed with this promise of helmets, he was able to get his school to buy enough other equipment to field a team."[52] Young programs at midwestern colleges and universities especially benefited from the transfer of used equipment. By donating old but paid-for gear to the USLCA program, older enthusiasts were able to help novices.[53]

Lacrosse organizers had to surmount other problems during the 1950s and 1960s: the perception of the game as an elite eastern sport and the feeling of geographic isolationism among coaches. Some coaches not only tried to dismantle the elite image of the game by exporting it to public high schools, but emphasized how a north-versus-south college all-star contest might continue to wear down the eastern stereotype. With university and college campuses playing host to most contests from 1946 to 1970, all-star game sites highlighted important local lacrosse communities north and south of the Mason-Dixon line. The state of Maryland hosted the game eleven times, nine times in Baltimore. Greater metropolitan New York hosted five games, with others at upstate communities Troy (twice), Geneva, Lake Placid, and Syracuse. Beginning in 1950, the USLCA also sponsored a short-lived series of coaching forums, clinics, and all-star games in Palm Beach, Florida, during the Christmas season.[54] In 1954 officials established an All-American reunion to complement the regular All-American banquet for active players.[55]

Besides connecting disparate communities and indirectly attacking the eastern stereotype, many events celebrated the feats of *individual* athletes, a practice usually associated with commercial sport. To publicize the game, officials depicted matches as pitting northern "Yankees" against southern "Rebels." In promoting the 1955 contest at Johns Hopkins the *Baltimore American* highlighted two young women dubbed Miss South and Miss North in a feature on "Lacrosse Week." The preview displayed two contrasting photographs. One depicted the two women sitting on the ground wearing gowns and title sashes. In the other the two women, wearing men's lacrosse gear except for helmets, were about to face off the ball.[56] Using beauty queens to advance a rough-and-tumble men's game, as had surely been agreed to by promoters and the press, provided a somewhat confusing commentary on gender within the lacrosse world. After all, advocates of women's lacrosse had been passionately working to dissociate themselves from the rougher men's game. Regardless, promoters employed a combination of sectionalism, elegant femininity, and sex appeal to sell the male all-star contest.

Aside from these efforts to promote lacrosse, creation of a lacrosse hall of fame and a not-for-profit foundation were the most significant developments. Inspired by the baseball shrine at Cooperstown, New York, advocates of lacrosse memorialized heroic figures by deifying coaches and athletes. In earlier decades lacrosse had been seen as a virile, affluent, amateur alternative to the pastoral, democratic, and professionally oriented game of baseball. Although the USILA had awarded national championships and All-America honors, the game had lacked the cult of personality of mass sport. Lacrosse players had not made good cultural icons; indeed, Jack Turnbull was no Babe Ruth. But by the 1950s lacrosse men had begun to bow to the larger cultural forces shaping postwar America, especially social pluralism, cultural conformism, masculinity anxieties, and consumerism.

Encouraged by Penn State coach Glenn Thiel, in 1954 Army coach Morris Touchstone began to plan for a lacrosse hall of fame by gathering materials from other sports' halls of fame. The West Point coach believed the lacrosse hall should honor individual men and centralize records and other materials.[57] With an eye toward making the game more acceptable to the public, some organizers criticized the status quo mentality of coaches and alumni. To accommodate television, Thiel believed lacrosse should borrow from other sports: "I am becoming more and more of the opinion that we are being too conservative on changing the rules of the game. We are not keeping up with the demands of the public. The game is too long." He suggested replacing the face-off with basketball's system of giving the ball to the team scored upon. "Also," he said, "as I watch sports on T.V., I can see how a shorter field with fewer players would place the game in great demand as a sport for T.V. broadcast." Coming close to blasphemy, Thiel even proposed moving the structure of the American game toward that of box lacrosse.[58] But Thiel warned that complacency among coaches would result in the marginalization of lacrosse, possibly even in Baltimore, where the major league Orioles had begun play in 1954. In Thiel's view, "If we don't look out major league baseball will push us right out of the Baltimore papers in a few years."[59] Perhaps because of these fears, in February 1957 lacrosse officials settled on a modest budget for display cabinets, picture frames, and storage materials for a hall of fame, with the USILA and USLCA contributing 75 and 25 percent of the funds, respectively. Acknowledging Baltimore's importance to the American lacrosse community, they chose Johns Hopkins as the permanent location of a future facility.[60]

Just as a system was being created to honor lacrosse men, taking cues from the world of professional and commercial sport, a blueprint for financial support was also being established. Along with "Okie" O'Connor, Baltimore attorney Caleb Kelly, Jr., supplied much of the zeal for this effort. After the war, this graduate of the Friends School and Johns Hopkins had coached at the University of Baltimore, revised the intercollegiate rule book, and directed the Lacrosse Forum in Florida.[61] Kelly told Thiel that a tax-exempt Lacrosse Foundation could be established only if it served an "educational" purpose. "There are many rich men who have played lacrosse, and who, I am sure, would be willing to leave money to a Foundation, if that bequest were tax exempt," Kelly wrote.[62] The hall of fame and the foundation became real on May 28, 1959, when Kelly obtained a charter for the organization.[63] According to its articles of incorporation, the Lacrosse Hall of Fame Foundation had five basic purposes: (1) to act as a holding center for historical documents and materials; (2) to educate the public about the "the spirit of true sportsmanship, honor and fair play"; (3) to develop interest in the sport; (4) to generate and collect funds; and (5) to honor players and coaches who "personify the great contribution of the game of lacrosse to our way of life."[64] In other words, although an aura of elite sport pervaded lacrosse, a hall of fame and a tax-exempt foundation should help popularize the amateur game.

The new organization served as a headquarters for the spread of field lacrosse in the United States. Even with this new base of operations in Baltimore, lacrosse organizers recognized a slew of familiar problems: insufficient coaches, an unpredictable and limited supply of wood sticks, competition from entrenched spring and summer sports like baseball, and public views of lacrosse as both snobbish and too violent. Advocates simply wanted to promote what they regarded as a superior athletic activity, but they did not always recognize that they were also seeking adherents to their brand of gentlemanly, masculine, amateur sport. They agreed that lacrosse was best kept amateur, but whether newer enthusiasts would agree remained to be seen. Regardless, the multiplication of lacrosse supporters created potential for cultural change. As for the new foundation, its tax-exempt status permitted intercollegiate and club officials to disseminate information, support infant programs, and do publicity work. As first president (1959–66) of the Lacrosse Foundation, former Saint John's and Navy coach Dr. William "Dinty" Moore argued that the post-collegian clubs should play a leading role, "taking the game into virgin territory."[65]

As for the hall of fame, honorees were celebrated for on-field accomplishments, but selectors were also aware of the inductees' successes as businessmen, physicians, attorneys, stockbrokers, and educators. Although the vast majority of inductees through the first decade were white, American-born, upper-middle-class college graduates, the hall did honor one Cherokee Indian, Carlisle School graduate and former City College of New York head coach Leon Miller, in December 1960. Apart from his career as a professor of health and physical education, the New York Times reported that Miller's working life had included service as "a banker, an engineer, a Government adviser on Indian affairs, a professional football and lacrosse player, a member of the Cherokee Indian Council of Chiefs and a member of the American Stock Exchange."[66] Noticeably absent from the Hall of Fame were Iroquois Indians who had worked at construction sites throughout the Northeast, men well known for their stick-handling skills in box lacrosse and their lack of college degrees.

The Hall of Fame and Foundation provided lacrosse advocates with a new sense of optimism, but highlighted an unspoken fissure among organizers and coaches. All of the enthusiasts loved lacrosse, but they did not agree on its relationship to the rest of the sports world. After Caleb Kelly completed the incorporation of the new organization, he expressed his frustration with the greater popularity of baseball and football: "Those of us who have been bitten by the 'lacrosse bug' invariably gather together at social functions to talk lacrosse, and, if you are not one of us, you soon realize that our sport must be something out of the ordinary for us to conduct such prolonged [sic] and spirited bull sessions on one subject," Kelly wrote. "In spite of our passionate love of the game and our undying devotion to 'the greatest of all sports,' most of us are somewhat taken aback when an outsider propounds to us the question: 'Why has not your game spread throughout the United States?'" In response to such queries, Kelly blamed the "horse and buggy" mentality of lacrosse organizers and coaches "who take the attitude that 'since lacrosse is perfect, why try to beat perfection?'"[67] Although his solutions focused on the play of the game, he also characterized lacrosse officialdom as archaic. In Kelly's view, too many administrators, organizers, and coaches liked the status quo. Answers to Kelly's criticisms would not come until after 1970.

The lacrosse community unveiled its shrine at Johns Hopkins in 1966. Officials dedicated the new $15,000 "sanctuary" prior to the twenty-fifth annual North-South contest.[68] University president Milton Eisenhower presented the key to the new Lacrosse Hall of Fame, which was located in a wing of the new Newton H. White Jr. Athletic Center. The center was a monument to amateur sport; the widow of Colonel White had funded a building for a universal intramural program committed to sport for sport's sake.[69] Noting that this was the first amateur hall of fame in the country, the NCAA's annual lacrosse guide reminded fans that the new foundation "must depend upon the largess of our wealthier alumni to continue the inspiration which the Shrine has become."[70] The financial success of the shrine depended on private donors, not on the commercial marketplace.

The facility represented the convergence of older romantic conceptions of the game's past and a newer proselytizing ethos. Aware of the competitive nature of the postwar consumer economy, lacrosse enthusiasts had adopted practices from commercial organizations. Yet the hall reflected the lacrosse community's traditional belief in the value of the "noble savage." In 1979 former Delaware coach Milton Roberts recalled the shrine's "huge fireplace, above which an eight foot figure of an Iroquois lacrosse player, outlined in bronze and mounted on a great slab of Travertine marble, dominated the room. It would have been impossible to have sculpted another Indian figure which would have given visitors . . . the same feeling for lacrosse—that of standing on some hallowed ball ground of antiquity. Truly, the bronze sculpture . . . is an inspiring reminder of lacrosse's aboriginal heritage."[71] The inclusion of the bronze Indian certainly acknowledged the native origins of the sport, but it also signified that the hall welcomed, consciously or subconsciously, only two types of Native Americans: artificial, reified images of the "noble savage" and real-life Indians who had succeeded in white middle-class America. The hall ignored working-class reservation Indians who had played box lacrosse. Regardless, by the late 1960s the leadership of American lacrosse had begun to adapt to the larger marketplace. A new generation of coaches and organizers implemented a more practical and focused program of colonization. Although no overt schism among the sport's leaders occurred, the trend toward popularization through education posed a challenge to the elite traditions of amateur lacrosse.

The "Button-Down Sport" to 1970: Popularizing Amateur Lacrosse in the United States

The growth of field lacrosse within traditional enclaves, the game's geographic expansion to areas outside the Northeast and mid-Atlantic, and its diffusion from affluent families to the suburban middle class in the postwar era provided potential for disagreement over guiding values. If the world of lacrosse continued to accept many novices to the game, it might be impossible for the older generation of coaches and officials to maintain cultural authority. The athletic code of lacrosse espoused by old hands was remarkably similar to the one that had existed before the war, despite the emergence of more egalitarian and commercial elements. Specifically, the old hands continued to support the character-building qualities of gentlemanly athletics and a romanticized understanding of the game's Native American origins. These veterans applied the older approach to the puzzle of the postwar world, a world full of anxieties and opportunities. Some argued that sport for sport's sake memorialized wartime sacrifices and provided guidance for the future. "The winning of games will be our proximate, not ultimate goal. Sportsmanship, teamwork, self-sacrifice, enthusiasm; will they be merely words? Not if we revere the memory of those who are gone," Albert Brisotti wrote in his first postwar lacrosse guide editorial. "Rather let us feel that we have a duty to instill in the growing youth the fine quality of our heroes. They would want us to do this. Having done this, we may expect a sort of sacred 'Well done.'"[72]

The two most obvious havens of the amateur spirit included universities and postcollegian clubs. In 1958 one author's study of "the right people" reported that Ivy League undergraduates had abandoned college football once the game had become too commercialized and professionalized. Declaring that elite university sport had not "gone all effete and namby-pamby," however, he observed that the "fairly rough and tumble sports" of lacrosse and hockey had "been rapidly moving up the social ladder to fill the gap left by college football."[73] More to the point, "the right people" had grown tired of losing football games to colleges that drew athletes from less affluent social classes. While most lacrosse proponents lauded the expansion of their game after the war, others believed accelerated growth would detrimentally affect the sport's ethos. For lacrosse to be reserved for "the right people," all growth would have to be closely monitored. In 1950 the annual lacrosse guide affirmed the "club-like camaraderie" of early twentieth-century intercollegiate and club play, but asked readers if expansion would damage this amateur atmosphere: "Will any of the evils generally accompanying bigness creep in? We sincerely hope not. We trust that the old idealism—which made lacrosse the game we all love—prevails in the future development of our grand old sport."[74]

To distinguish their game from other more commercialized sports, lacrosse advocates emphasized the occupations of prominent coaches. Viewing lacrosse as an "intellectual game," in May 1963 the *Baltimore Sun* celebrated "the scholarly attainments of the coaches who pioneered the game in Maryland." Athletes from other team sports saw championships as proof of the greatness of coaches, but lacrosse partisans pointed to their mentors' accomplishments as professors of zoology, mathematics, bacteriology, veterinary surgery, chemistry, and history. "These men were to lacrosse what Stagg, Warner and Rockne were to football—innovators and masters of technique and strategy," the *Sun* reported. These men of scholarship had demonstrated their well-roundedness by being "men of action and agony" who had led their squads to victory. "When these Nestors of the game were not studying such trifles as elliptic functions and differential equations, the life cycle of ostrea virginica, Supreme Court decisions, pathogenic microorganisms, and the like," the *Sun* observed, "they were inventing and refining the screen shot, extra man play, the shifting defense, the fast break from center, behind the goal play, and ball control combined with frequent shooting."[75]

Defense of sport for sport's sake remained basic to the cultural fabric of postcollegian lacrosse. Faced with ascendant commercial sports, the Mount Washington L.C. of Baltimore epitomized the spirit of amateur athleticism. Led by part-time coach and full-time attorney Ben Goertemiller, the Wolfpack included former All-American college graduates living in the area. Describing his team as "the antithesis of professional sport" in 1969, Goertemiller reflected the club attitude that their game was more whole- some than one dominated by athletes who played for pay: "Around here the only thing provided is a chance to play. The only compensation is the spirit of competing and the satisfaction of winning."[76] Enjoying a comfortable lifestyle, these athletes scrimmaged on Sunday mornings, as well as Tues- day and Thursday evenings. According to *Sports Illustrated*, "These were among the few hours in the week that the doctors, lawyers, stockbrokers, bankers and advertising men . . . could all get together for practice."[77] The team's on-field leader was Baltimore City College and Johns Hopkins grad- uate Emil "Buzzy" Budnitz. Besides directing the team's offense, he worked as an insurance salesman. A defender of the amateur ethos, Budnitz be- lieved in sport for sport's sake: "I'm delighted there's no professional lacrosse. If there were, the sport would attract people who might not be out for the love of the game; it would change the complexion of the sport."[78] Without profit-driven franchise owners and working-class athletes who might not appreciate the old Indian game's virtues, these amateur sports- men possessed authority over their sport. Having compiled a record of 358–31–3 and numerous national "open" championships since 1925, the Wolfpack's players paid for their own sticks and shoes. Gate receipts paid for the club's other equipment, game jerseys, and traveling expenses.[79]

Players also participated in this postcollegiate system for reasons of mental health and social status. According to one who played for the brewery-sponsored Carling L.C. in Maryland, the much-needed physical outlet from his job as an engineer justified the long commutes. "It's a test of whether you can accomplish something physically after working with your mind all day—you go out and use your body and make it perform," he declared. "And there's a release in the tensions that build up when you can go out and knock heads a little."[80] For many athletes, playing lacrosse alleviated the pressures of white-collar work. Moreover, the social dynam- ics of club lacrosse resembled the dynamic of other societies of high status that fostered group solidarity and cohesiveness.[81] Club lacrosse gave young men from the business, legal, and medical communities the opportunity to unite as a social class and establish important and useful professional ties. This aspect of the sport was hardly confined to the club ranks; some un- dergraduate students exploited the perceived social advantages of playing lacrosse. In a 1961 cartoon, the student press at Hobart College ridiculed trendy lacrosse players on campus. Referring to his lacrosse stick, one cartoon character says to another, "Be serious! Of course I can't play, but you're forgetting that this things a status symbol!"[82] Given the elite aura of lacrosse, many collegians and schoolboys understood the social benefits of play. This elite stereotype may very well have been the game's greatest selling point, especially to young men looking up the social ladder.

Nowhere was the commitment to amateurism as intense as in Baltimore. In April 1967, *Evening Sun* sportswriter Bill Tanton provided three scenarios reflecting the place of lacrosse in Baltimore:

—A Roland Park woman will drive her Mercedes-Benz out [on] Falls Road to St. Paul's School, where she will stand atop the hill over looking the lacrosse field and watch her son play. At one point in the action she is guaranteed to shriek, in very un-Roland-Park-like tones, "Ride him, Skippy, ride him!" (When it comes to athletes with names like Skippy or Booty or Buzzy or even Myrt, lacrosse people are in a class by themselves.)

—A club lacrosse player who sells insurance for a living will scratch late afternoon appointments for a week so that he can make all the practices prior to the Mount Washington game. After his team has lost, probably by 11 goals, he will shower wearily in the clubhouse at Norris Field. Then dressed in Bermudas and Weejuns, he will walk down the driveway toward the parking lot. Beside him will be his pretty, young wife, pushing a baby carriage. The defeated warrior will carry his lacrosse stick and his equipment bag in his right hand. In his left will be a throwaway bottle of National beer.

—In the Valley Inn on a Monday evening, a group of lacrosse officials will debate over some liquid refreshment after their weekly meeting. "I tell you," one will say emphatically, "Jim Brown was the greatest player who ever picked up a lacrosse stick."

"The greatest athlete, maybe," his companion will answer, "but strictly as a lacrosse player he couldn't carry Billy Hooper's jock." It is the same argument they had last spring, and the spring before that.[83]

Whether concerned mothers, white-collar club athletes, or boastful veterans, lacrosse enthusiasts in Baltimore all loved a sport beyond the control of the entrepreneur.

By the 1960s the rapid adoption of lacrosse by collegians and schoolboys challenged these ideals. The increase in players and coaches strained the ability of older leaders to preserve their notion of sport for sport's sake. Although the coach at Loyola College in 1950 felt lacrosse would never become a truly national game because it was "strictly a button-down sport," reporter

Tanton observed seventeen years later that there had been a great change. "That—the button-down aspect of it—was precisely the quality that endeared it to its greatest admirers, and yet since that time the game has undergone a transition," Tanton continued. "It has, in a manner of speaking, been losing its buttons—and growing." The game might have been losing its socially elite buttons, but the amateur shirt had remained. Eventually most area high schools in Baltimore had adopted the game: "Lacrosse in Baltimore, like everything else, changes, but some of its traditions hang on. It is still, to some extent, a button-down sport, but at its heart it is such an action game, so much in tune with 1967 and the current public taste, that it had to outgrow the boundaries of Roland Park and Mount Washington."[84]

With the adoption of lacrosse by a generation of novice supporters, the emergence of a new relaxed approach to the "button-down sport" signified the most pronounced feature of the social history of lacrosse in the postwar decades. Many of the new enthusiasts were born at the start of the "baby boom" and were the sons of blue-collar families. The postwar population surge led to the construction of new schools whose students might be recruited to lacrosse, with greater financial resources channeled toward athletics and lacrosse gear. A similar expansion in higher education brought with it a more permissive campus culture and more iconoclastic behavior. When alcohol consumption mixed with spectator rowdyism, the resulting conduct challenged the sport's ethos. In 1946 the dean and athletic director at Hobart condemned the "public misbehavior" of undergraduates at a game against Cornell. According to an official college statement, "The evidence is that Hobart men were drinking openly and to excess at the game, that they were using foul and abusive language towards the players, and that they involved themselves in fights on the field where they had no right to be.... Such behavior is contrary to all traditions and regulations at the college. It is unsportsmanlike and ungentlemanly."[85] Returning war veterans attending Maryland and Johns Hopkins used their upcoming match in 1947 to engage in pranksterism. From graffiti to kidnapping a mascot statue, they exchanged covert strikes against each other's campuses. About two hundred policemen raced to the Johns Hopkins campus to squelch an "out-and-out brawl" between students,[86] which illustrated that even an elite sport could provide a context for fraternal misbehavior usually associated with more commercial sports such as football. The editors of *International Lacrosse Magazine* criticized an incident involving a liquor bottle tossed onto a field and obscene language screamed at players in 1967: "It is precisely because the incident was so rare that it commands mention. The sportsmanship of lacrosse players and fans is a tradition we can be proud of. Let's keep it that way."[87]

This more boisterous aspect of lacrosse signaled the surfacing of new social elements. Oddly enough, a "girlie" magazine provided insight into the emerging blue-collar dimension of lacrosse in 1969. Frustration with twentieth-century technocracy and repetitive factory work compelled modern man to test fate by seeking thrills. "The game has quite a bit to offer the man tired of punching buttons for his livelihood, his home entertainment and even his lunch break at the Automat," *Climax* magazine commented. "There's nothing automatic about lacrosse and the only punching a guy does is with his fist or his stick, knowing of course that whoever he punches also punches back." Lacrosse players did not suffer from serious injuries, but cuts and bruises were routine. "But what the hell, it sure beats punching buttons down at the factory,"[88] opined *Climax*. Unlike the exclusive "buttons" of Baltimore lacrosse, these buttons inspired working-class and lower-middle-class athletes to use rough sport as an antidote to mind-numbing technology.

Just as veteran supporters reaffirmed the place of amateurism in the face of new coaches and athletes, they also emphasized their own interpretation of the Native American origins of the game. Modern advocates of lacrosse still saw themselves as the symbolic descendants of the "noble savage," but the intensity of this sentiment had lessened. This belief no doubt provided evidence that lacrosse could be characterized as excessively savage. For most sports fans, lacrosse still stood as the rough, elitist, regional opposite of the pastoral, democratic, national pastime, baseball. At many lacrosse-playing institutions the "savage" qualities of the game gave modern enthusiasts a persona to adopt temporarily. A Hobart College newspaper cartoon from 1951 depicts three members of the Hobart lacrosse team outfitted as "savage" Indians, complete with war paint, feathers, and breech cloths. One of these players has an opponent pinned down and is about to scalp him with a tomahawk, while a second, armed with a lacrosse stick and a knife, chases another adversary. An onlooking coed says to her male companion: "It looks like Hobart is really out to win this year!"[89]

During this period newspapers and magazines provided readers with small vignettes on the Native American origins of lacrosse. In 1946 the student press at Syracuse University referred to lacrosse as "the Indian form of mayhem," which allowed Indian tribes to prove their "military prowess."[90] Journalists sometimes allegorized modern contests by romanticizing ancient Indian play and demonstrating the sport's progressive evolution to collegian sport. In his preview of the 1947 North-South all-star game *Baltimore Sun* sportswriter Craig Taylor made direct connections between traditional and modern lacrosse. Because most match attendees were loyal "hunkers," these connections substantiated the views of people who supported lacrosse and undoubtedly embraced amateurism. Taylor described a fictitious traditional lacrosse match pitting 450 "Cherokee braves" from the "Southland" against 500 Iroquois from the north, meeting on a "plain north of the Patapsco River for their warlike game of baggataway." His description included authentic elements of traditional ball play, such as single-stake goal markers, a half-mile irregular playing surface, "tribal dances," and "squaws" on undefined sidelines who were "ready to ply their switches on the laggards."[91]

Like most white enthusiasts, Taylor distorted the ancient game: "The two sides go into their tribal dances, with medicine men exhorting their youths to their most strenuous efforts in the game which, next to war, is first in the hearts of the red men." True, Taylor's game was a journalist's concoction, but he asked readers to consider parallels between the two versions of lacrosse. What was important to Taylor was getting lacrosse fans to conceive of their own athletes in idyllic terms: "Substitute the young athletes from Johns Hopkins, University of Maryland and Naval Academy for the Cherokees, and Princeton, Cornell, Dartmouth and Army for the Iroquois, trim down the squads to teams of ten, with an alternate for each man, and the parallel continues. There is even the interest in war—so far as Army and Navy are concerned." He even drew connections between female supporters of the two eras. "True, the squaws will not whip the faltering athletes into renewed action, but the luckless youth who makes a bad error will get a tongue lashing from some of the girls in the stands." Finally, Taylor suggested links between "medicine men" and modern coaches. To complete the allegory, the *Sun* published photos of a modern collegiate game and crowd along with photos of contemporary Cherokees playing traditional stickball on their western North Carolina reservation.[92] By linking modern lacrosse with southeastern traditional Native American ball play, from which the modern game had not originated, Taylor characterized affluent athletes as noble, masculine heroes.

Most references to the original Native American game alleged the superiority of the modern sport. In a 1947 feature on the evolution of lacrosse and a recent Mount Washington victory over Johns Hopkins, *Time* described the current "Mayhem in Maryland" as particularly rough. While an ancient "game wasn't considered very spirited if there weren't a few broken skulls and fractured arms," the magazine noted, "civilization and 300 years had changed the game, but it still could not be called sissy."[93] Nearly a decade later, citing an incident in which University of Maryland students had burned an "M" on the Navy field the night before a May 1955 match, *Time* elaborated on the ritual element of "Mayhem on the Lawn": "Rules, referees and two centuries of civilization have failed to temper the spirited spring sport that white men learned from the American Indian."[94] In other words, enough of the savage qualities of ancient lacrosse remained to benefit modern white athletes. Journalists made references to the infamous Chippewa and Sauk massacre of the British garrison at Fort Michilimackinac in 1763.[95] The legendary Indian ruse inspired comments as to how the Indians had "grabbed tomahawks . . . and proceeded to wipe out the fort." According to a 1962 article in *Boy's Life,* "What a lot of historians have never been able to figure out is why the Indians bothered with the tomahawks when they had those lacrosse sticks on hand."[96] The white lacrosse community had already embedded the Fort Michilimackinac incident into the myth-history of their sport, but clubs commemorated the romanticized event. In 1963 two white clubs played three contests as part of a lightly attended four-day celebration of a "Lacrosse–Fort Michilimackinac Massacre" bicentennial.[97] It is unlikely that native people would consider having Indian baseball teams play games to honor the Spanish conquest of the Aztec Empire, the Trail of Tears, or the Wounded Knee Massacre.

The emphasis on violence and mayhem underscored contradictory messages about modern lacrosse. Partisans celebrated the rough nature of the game as a way to develop character, but also were dismayed with popular assessments of the game as excessively violent. In 1948 *Popular Mechanics Magazine* reported that many high school officials saw lacrosse as excessively rough: "Unofficially, the game has been tagged 'organized mayhem,' and anyone who has watched a runner caught in the 'crosse fire' of two clubbing defense men might agree."[98] Proponents praised the noble qualities of ancient ball play, but contrasted them with those of the "civilized" modern game. Lacking any first-hand testimony or scholarly method, the student press at Syracuse characterized ancient Indian matches as violent: "When the smoke cleared away, the body-strewn ground looked like a battlefield. That was lacrosse when the Indians played it, but it has come a long way since then, despite what the critics of the sport may say."[99] Examining collegian play in 1962, *Sports Illustrated* reported that thousands shared the misconception "that dirty fellows naturally gravitate to it because in it they can slake their devilish thirsts." Other writers noted that lacrosse appeared to be a "riotous sport," complete with flying bodies, but that "refinement has come steadily since the bloody days of its origin when Indians played to kill. Nobody gets killed playing lacrosse anymore. It only seems like it."[100]

Such journalistic assessments highlight the tension between praise of lacrosse as a rough sport and defense of the game against allegations of excessive violence. Sportswriters were not the only ones with a romanticized and condescending attitude toward traditional ball play. Faced with an ever-changing world, some enthusiasts believed an ordered presentation of the past might bring meaningful structure to understanding the present. The new hall of fame, foundation, and archives allowed them to develop a more sophisticated sense of the history of their sport. By the 1950s most of the individuals who had participated in the early years of field lacrosse were either very old or dead. Preserving the history of the sport became urgent. Former Army All-American football player Colonel Alexander Weyand and former University of Delaware lacrosse coach Milton Roberts accepted the challenge. After nine years of research and writing, they published the first book-length history of lacrosse in 1965. Neither Weyand nor Roberts had been trained as a historian, so the book simply chronicles anecdotes and important on-the-field information for fanatic "hunkers." *The Lacrosse Story* invokes and preserves old myths. One such fiction surrounded the origins of the game allegedly made perfect by affluent sportsmen: "How came the Indians to fashion a racket?" the co-authors asked. "No one will ever know," they surmised. "They were not very inventive."[101] Casting ancient Indians as unsophisticated yet noble savages secured a place for modern collegians atop the evolutionary ladder of lacrosse development.

Unfortunately for these authors, the lacrosse world apparently greeted their book with apathy. In contrast to baseball enthusiasts, who routinely devoured scores of new books on their game, the lacrosse community demonstrated their lack of seriousness about sport off the field by not buying the book. Publishing and retail expenses exceeded sales receipts through 1971, with a local Baltimore book publisher losing about $3,365 on the venture.[102] The initial commercial failure of *The Lacrosse Story* suggests that most lacrosse men focused on playing the sport for sport's sake. Neither the old guard of traditionalists nor the growing mass of new adherents took much interest in the Weyand and Roberts book. Older members of the community had lived through much of the book's history, but younger folk simply wished to play the game and exploit its social advantages. References to teams that no longer existed and star athletes long retired meant little to fans.

The numerous defenses of the game show that men's field lacrosse enthusiasts were at the crossroads of great social change and cultural continuity. The potential for change during the 1960s was similar to that of the two decades after the Great War, without an economic depression to silence less affluent components of the community. The unique conditions of the 1960s—a great expansion of higher and secondary education due to the baby boom, a permissive youth culture, a spirit of egalitarianism, and the aging of veteran lacrosse advocates—all pointed to a potential for transformation of the sport's guiding ethos. The massive growth and expansion of lacrosse threatened to decentralize and fragment the sport and possibly dethrone the values of amateur athletics. Few coaches, journalists, or alumni realized the potential for chaos they were creating by encouraging the game to become more democratic and popular. In spite of the great social change within their community, many of these proponents rigidly defended amateurism and continued to perceive white lacrosse players as continuing the athletic legacy of the "noble savage." The question for future generations would be whether to continue to embrace the elite traditions of the old-timers or to institutionalize a more inclusive view of sport that was more receptive to commercialism. By 1970, for instance, some three decades after it had replaced gate fees with free admission to athletic contests, Johns Hopkins finally overturned its experiment with decommercialized sport by charging admission.[103] Even the strongest haven of sport for sport's sake could not resist the force of the consumer-driven marketplace.

Finding Manliness in a Box: The Iroquois
Movement Away from Organized Field Lacrosse

Almost every aspect of the newer Canadian sport of box lacrosse contrasted greatly with men's and women's field lacrosse in the United States after World War II. The Canadian and Iroquois men who played the "box" game were far removed from the field game. During the 1950s and 1960s, box lacrosse was played mainly in Iroquois communities in New York, Ontario, and Quebec and in small cities and suburbs of Ontario and British Columbia, during a summer season in which most sports fans preferred outdoor games over sitting in a hot arena watching lacrosse. Supporters of the box and field versions both believed that manliness derived from lacrosse, but disagreed on the appropriate levels of roughness. American advocates of field lacrosse expressed dismay over their sport's being labeled "organized mayhem," but Canadians and Iroquois Indians thrived on the thrill-seeking, roughneck qualities of their game. That white Canadians had quickly abandoned field lacrosse in favor of the indoor game during the 1930s can be attributed to the cultural hegemony of ice hockey, but the choice of Native Americans to do the same requires further exploration. After all, Iroquois Indians played both versions of lacrosse before and after World War II.

As did everyone else, native and non-native lacrosse enthusiasts sought a more normal routine after the war. For instance, with the end of the war Syracuse University resumed its long-standing rivalry with the nearby Onondaga Reservation. The results were even more lopsided after 1945 than had been the results of matches played during the interwar period. The university's string of victories over the Indians caused the student press at Syracuse to adopt a more condescending view toward natives. Prior to a match in May 1950, for example, the *Syracuse Daily Orange* invoked racist stereotypes when it reported that Onondaga chief Percy Smoke would lead an Iroquois team to Hendricks Field in possession of much "enthusiasm and little know-how." Not only did the paper irreverently refer to Smoke by his first name; it said that the contest would not be terribly competitive. "Chief Percy promises that the usual number of squaws and papooses will be on the sidelines to whoop things up," the *Daily Orange* noted. "Whatever happens, the general tenor of the festivities should be in a somewhat lighter vein than the accustomed intercollegiate matches." About seven hundred spectators witnessed the 14–3 university victory, which was described as "a show a bit rougher than the collegiate version." The paper continued: "The Indians seemed very intent on winning and combined a little more stick dexterity than usual with their perennial amount of vitality."[104]

Even with the lopsided relationship between university and reservation and the racist coverage by the campus press, personal relationships between the varsity and the Indian communities survived. One long-time native friend of the Syracuse lacrosse team was Eli Cornelius. Because he played well into his fifties, the *Daily Orange* often described him as "ageless," "ancient," or "legendary" and as "the Satchel Paige of lacrosse." Though he usually played on campus with Onondaga Reservation teams, he also made a guest appearance in an annual varsity-alumni game in April 1947. Christened "Chief Eli Tomahawk" and described as the "best stickman on the reservation," Cornelius played for the alumni. Portraying him as an amusing addition to the game, the press suggested that Cornelius might have been drunk: "The contest's comic relief, Eli Tomahawk was sent in for the alums in the third period and dazzled the crowd with his fancy footwork and he fell four times in less than a minute. As soon as he was taken out of the game for a rest, Eli yelled to coach Roy Simmons, 'Roy, give me another chance and the aloomni can't lose.'" "Simmie" and the alumni laughed at Eli's antics. Natives such as Cornelius knew they could not hold their own against Syracuse, but they valued maintaining a relationship with the university. Prior to a contest in 1951, for instance, the Onondaga leadership planned a pregame ceremony making Roy Simmons an honorary chief for his role in promoting lacrosse around central New York. However, they canceled the ritual due to inclement weather. According to one Onondaga, "We can't bring our head dresses out in the rain because of the damage to the feathers which are just about irreplaceable. Since we couldn't do justice to the occasion without them, we would rather not have continued with the ceremony." The rain was not the only reason for the cancellation: Simmons backed out when the chiefs asked him for $25 for the honor. Calling the fee "the price of Manhattan Island, plus interest," the Syracuse student press stated, "It also brought a sudden end to Roy Simmons' career as an Indian chief."[105]

By the early 1950s, the university regarded the Onondaga Indians' team an easy, "amusing" opponent, but recognized it had not always been that way. Simmons recollected in 1951 how active and competitive Onondaga teams had been during the 1920s, just after the closing of the Carlisle School: "Back in the old days, the games were quite colorful affairs. The whole tribe would come over, dance, sing and every time an Indian scored a goal, they'd all run out on the field and congratulate him. It always took at least five minutes to get the game started again." The Onondagas had also been very competitive with other colleges and universities. After World War II, however, Syracuse typically crushed the Indians, leading to the end of the annual official tilt after their match in May 1954. Subsequent matches were informal and often held on the reservation. The student press sensationalized the Indians' final appearance at Hendricks Field, likening them to a Wild West troupe: "Many of the Indians do without the usual body paddings and are a hustling band. Their play is reminiscent of an old time Indian attack upon a western town." Syracuse University's dominance over the Onondaga after World War II was concrete evidence of a postwar boom in intercollegiate athletics and showed a growing seriousness among white lacrosse players. Compared to college rosters of earlier decades, these rosters were now increasingly stocked with student athletes who had played in high school. Experience and skill, when combined with practice, resulted in better play. As the general quality of intercollegiate lacrosse improved, coaches saw contests with Indians as less significant than in previous decades. Even worse, white-Indian contests no longer attracted large crowds. Syracuse University even stopped charging admission to contests with the Onondaga.[106]

Another reason for the decline of Onondaga performances against top-level collegians was the general Iroquois movement away from the world of the organized field lacrosse community and toward the newer Canadian game of box lacrosse. Reservation communities may have kept playing the field game among themselves, but boxla proved more culturally satisfying. Early in the 1930s, Mohawks in the Saint Lawrence River valley had adopted box lacrosse as their own. Played on smaller, enclosed fields with fewer players, box lacrosse emphasized the run-and-gun style of play the Indians favored. In fast break situations, even the goal tender became an attacker. This feature contrasted significantly with the division of labor seen in field lacrosse, which was manifested by an offside restraining line separating a team's offensive players from its defensive players. According to the oral tradition of Akwesasne Mohawk elders at the Saint Regis reservation, box lacrosse was closer to the spirit of traditional ball play. Ironically, the game created by commercial ice hockey promoters seemed more culturally gratifying to the Indians than the field game under the organizational jurisdiction of American colleges. According to the official Mohawk history of lacrosse that was published by the North American Indian Travelling College in 1978, "The Indian players particularly enjoyed the increased body contact afforded by the reduction in space and more lenient rules regarding the use of the stick for purpose of checking than field lacrosse afforded."[107] Non-natives also noticed that box lacrosse encouraged the degree of individualism that Indian lacrosse players valued highly. In 1951 Roy Simmons hypothesized that the Onondaga's shift toward box lacrosse in the 1930s and their creation of the short-lived semiprofessional Syracuse Red Devils team had put them at a disadvantage when they had played field lacrosse against collegians: "That's one of the reasons . . . that they're not so good today. They still play it out on the reservation, and every man has to be a shooter. Watch them, they'll shoot from any place on the field, and very fast, too. . . . One of the weaknesses of the Indians is that they just love to dodge. . . . Why, hell, they'd rather run down the field, fake around one man and, rather than shoot, dash across the field so they can dodge around someone else. . . . Another thing the Indians don't like is defense. Offense they enjoy, but when an opponent comes down with the ball, they'd rather just let him go by and figure somebody else can bring it back. I've seen a goalie run the length of the field, just so he can dodge some guys and get in a shot."[108] Iroquois Indians found another version of lacrosse more in the character of the ancient game, which had allowed for the individual expression of manliness. Syracuse's victories over the Onondaga Reservation simply confirmed for many natives that they were better off playing box lacrosse.

The ties between Saint Regis, Onondaga, Six Nations, and other Iroquois communities allowed for the quick diffusion of box lacrosse during the 1930s.[109] Over the years a network of Indian lacrosse clubs emerged, with a home playing facility on the reservation or in a nearby town. These clubs included Tuscarora, near Niagara Falls; Pinewood and Newtown, drawn from the Seneca reservations at Cattaraugas and Allegany in southwestern New York; Onondaga, just south of Syracuse; Saint Regis, Cornwall, and Caughnawaga, all in the Saint Lawrence River valley near Montreal; and four teams in and near the Six Nations Reserve in Ontario, including Hagersville, Caledonia, Oshweken, and Brantford. Aside from temperance leagues and powwows, only lacrosse linked the various Iroquois reservations socially. According to Wes Patterson of Tuscarora, matches were played within the context of intertribal social occasions. "When we played the Senecas, we always had a big picnic or party after the games. We'd talk and got to know each other and be friends," Patterson recalled. "And then we'd go to the Onondagas and do the same thing. I think it was a very cultural and social game among the native people. That's how you got along so well. And it seemed to knit us as a group of our own. We play the game and then had a feast after."[110] Besides reservation communities, urban Indians in cities such as Rochester, Buffalo, and Montreal played as well, especially during the Great Depression.[111] A player from one such club was Harry Smith, a Mohawk from the Six Nations Reserve in Ontario, who had moved to Buffalo during the Depression and had played for professional barnstorming Indian box lacrosse teams. Eventually moving to California, he became Jay Silverheels, began appearing in films in 1938, and played the character Tonto in the TV series *The Lone Ranger* during the 1950s.[112] Allegedly his new surname had come from a pair of shiny new white lacrosse shoes he had once had. Another lacrosse-playing Mohawk, Ross Powless, recalled how Harry Smith had given up his native life on the reserve for a fictional one on the silver screen: "One time a writer asked me, 'How was Jay Silverheels seen on the Six Nations Reserve?' 'Hardly ever,' I told her. I wasn't lying. After Joe E. Brown, the comedian, met Harry out in Hollywood, he didn't come too often. No jets in them days. If Harry hadn't gone to Hollywood to play lacrosse, Joe E. Brown would have never met him and convinced him to go into the movies."[113] Smith had traded his birth name and box lacrosse to become a Hollywood actor, but most Iroquois loyally played the game while pursuing construction work.

By choosing box lacrosse, native athletes all but walked off the contested ground of the outdoor field sport and left it to their socially affluent collegian adversaries. They concentrated their energies on a game more suited to Native American sporting culture. Not only did the new game provide Indians with greater opportunities to engage in a modernized form of an element of their traditional culture; it permitted them to escape from the American colleges' administrative, legislative, and athletic stranglehold on the game. Natives had grown tired of the constrictive rules-making and jurisdictional authority of affluent men from Baltimore, New York, and New England. Given the general relations between Iroquoia and the United States after World War II, this sentiment should not be surprising. The Indian policies of presidents Harry Truman and Dwight Eisenhower, which called for the "termination" of the federal government's relationships with distinct tribes, and disputes over the Kinzua Dam, the Saint Lawrence Seaway, and the Tuscarora Reservoir had aggravated Indian-white relations. Moreover, the U.S. Congress had transferred criminal and civil jurisdiction over New York state reservations from Washington to Albany, thereby impairing Iroquois assertions of their political sovereignty and their status as nations within a nation.[114] Although many chiefs refused to accept this transfer—arguing that because the Iroquois Confederacy enjoyed a government-to-government relationship with the United States, it had to remain under federal jurisdiction—most natives begrudgingly acknowledged the new order.

Beginning in 1954, efforts to appropriate Indian land compounded these political problems. For example, Senecas of the Allegany Reservation unsuccessfully fought against Congress, Pittsburgh industrialists and politicians, the Army Corps of Engineers, and the Eisenhower administration in an attempt to block the $125 million Kinzua Dam project, which was completed in 1966. Mohawks and Tuscaroras fought the industrialization of the Saint Lawrence and Niagara frontiers, respectively, by various public- and private-sector development commissions and corporations in Canada and the United States. Saint Lawrence Seaway construction began in 1954, and controversy surrounded the entire affair through the 1960s. In December 1968 and February 1969, Mohawks of the Saint Regis reservation staged sit-down protests on the Cornwall-Massena International Bridge, which caused the condemnation of Mohawk land and challenged Indians' right of free passage across the Canadian-American border, which had been guaranteed by Jay's Treaty of 1794. On the Niagara frontier, the New York State Power Authority took Tuscarora land in 1958 to foster a joint Canadian-American hydroelectric power project. The losses were staggering to the Seneca, Tuscarora, and Mohawk nations, which lost 9,000, 1,380, and 130 acres of land, respectively.[115]

Those Indian losses severely damaged Native Americans' sovereignty. The destruction of fishing and dairy industries in these areas by industrial pollution severely diminished the economic self-sufficiency of Indians.[116] The conflicts also fostered support for a "Red Power" nationalism movement. As Edmund Wilson observed in 1959 in his *Apologies to the Iroquois*, these feuds awakened political consciousness on the reservations: "What has set off the Iroquois resurgence and caused it to gather power is the glut-tonous inroads on tribal property . . . by state and federal projects."[117] The several contests over land drew the Iroquois together, but other social forces reinforced factionalism. The Canadian-American border effectively made the Iroquois Confederacy a two-headed organization, with separate tradi-tional capitals at Six Nations and Onondaga. The different Indian policies of Canada and the United States and competing elective and hereditary chief systems made for complex and contentious politics in many Iroquois communities. Moreover, two cultural worldviews existed throughout Iro-quoia. A "progressive" camp included Catholics and Protestants, religious agnostics, businessmen committed to legal or illegal entrepreneurship, and racial integrationists. The "traditional" camp included practitioners of the conservative Longhouse faith who used the early nineteenth-century code of Handsome Lake to reassert natives' cultural sovereignty and traditional-ism, as well as others who desired to remain racially and culturally distinct from non-native society.

With all of their external and domestic problems, not to mention poor education and high rates of alcoholism and unemployment, people living on these reservations lacked traditional ways to solve intranation disputes. Prior to the military defeat of the Iroquois during the American Revolu-tion, a dissenting band had simply separated from the nation and estab-lished a new town. Under the reservation system, this was not an option. It seems plausible that the rough-and-tumble game of box lacrosse func-tioned as a surrogate for the traditional system for resolving disputes. While sociologists could endlessly debate whether player fistfights and spectator fanfare had a cathartic effect on the community, the historian can declare with certainty that lacrosse united native people from different factions for common public events. More important, it gave individual native men the chance to express their hardened manliness. Giving or taking hits, playing a game with a hangover, or driving furiously for hundreds of miles to get to a game, many Iroquois men believed box lacrosse was the one cultural arena where they could demonstrate their manliness, regardless of the out-come of the game.

Ironically, the strong American industrial economy provided box lacrosse enthusiasts with another challenge. Since the late nineteenth cen-tury construction companies had employed Indians to do high-elevation steelwork.[118] The building boom after 1945 drew many Indian men away from the reservations in pursuit of construction work. Whether these men returned to the reservation or were assimilated into mainstream American culture and took up residence near their jobs, the construction industry strongly affected Iroquois society. The steady income strengthened a blue-collar Native American middle class and challenged the willingness or ability of families to remain on the reservations. Even those who preferred reservation life found that the prolonged time spent away challenged their Indian identities. Despite the distance between reservations and construction sites, many Indians returned to their reservations to play box lacrosse and maintain other social and cultural ties. For example, besides playing for clubs in Niagara Falls and Saint Catharines in southern Ontario, Frank Benedict drove home to Saint Regis for weekend games. His wife, Lilly Benedict, remembered the intensity of Mohawk men who desired to maintain a cultural link with the reservation: "He was always an ironworker, so I followed him around and wherever he worked he played lacrosse. . . . My husband loved lacrosse so much. . . . This one day they had a game on Friday night in Drummondville. It's way on the other side of Quebec City. We left Buffalo at two o'clock in the afternoon, got in Drummondville for the second period and he played only one period. This is how much he loved to play lacrosse. He drove like ninety miles an hour all the way up there, without getting caught, to play lacrosse. And no pay."[119] The playing career of Angus George also typified the experiences of many Iroquois men. Born in 1910, this Mohawk son of a mason and homebuilder played with the Cornwall Island Indians against Canadian clubs during the 1930s. He also worked on construction jobs in Quebec, Ontario, and New York, including the St. Lawrence Seaway project.[120]

For most Iroquois Indians, the rough play and Native American origins of the game provided much of the appeal of lacrosse. Although Indians took great interest in modern football and baseball, they made box lacrosse part of their sport calendar precisely because it was *their* ancestors' game. Living in a world where they spoke English, prayed in Christian churches, received paychecks from white employers, and lived on land prescribed by non-native governments, Iroquois Indians saw box lacrosse as something from the past over which they possessed authority. That ice hockey entrepreneurs had invented box lacrosse mattered little. Canadians certainly recognized the function of box lacrosse among the Iroquois, especially in light of the controversies over the Saint Lawrence and Niagara

frontiers. In a discussion of "how the Indians are leading one more comeback for our first national sport," in 1964 *Maclean's Magazine* reported on a
new Quebec league that included the Caughnawaga Reserve: "The renewed
Indian interest in lacrosse is part of a new national identity many Indian reserves are discovering for themselves these days, but it is also a part of a
small, slow but steady revival of the sport in several parts of Canada." Highlighting native nationalism, the article continued: "Quite a lot of the present fans in Montreal are Indians, whose interest in the Forum evenings may
be as much social or even nationalistic as they are sporting, but quite a lot
of French Canadians too."[121] Cross-generational diffusion preserved the
centrality of lacrosse among the Iroquois. For instance, Peter Burns had
been born in 1930 on the Saint Regis Reservation and he had lived part of
his childhood in a Syracuse orphanage with white children. However, when
he returned to Saint Regis as a young man, a local Mohawk stick maker re-
introduced him to lacrosse. According to Burns: "In 1948, I went up to his
lacrosse factory to pick up my stick. He hands me this stick—it's a nice
beautiful stick—he says to me 'you plant potatoes, you get potatoes; you
plant lacrosse players, you get lacrosse players.' I've been saying it for forty
years and everybody thinks it's my saying. It wasn't mine; it was Frank
Roundpoint who said it. . . . He had a lacrosse factory and he gave a lot of
sticks to kids. He gave me this stick. I didn't buy it; he gave it to me. That's
when he said it—you plant potatoes, you get potatoes. Through life, I've
used the phrase. Little did I know that I was one of his potatoes. So I went
out and played the best I could be."[122] For Burns, the preservation of Iroquois lacrosse depended on transmitting the game from one generation to
the next. Almost five decades after receiving his first stick, Burns built an
outdoor box lacrosse facility named for the deceased stick maker.

Besides box lacrosse, some Iroquois continued to practice traditional
medicine games. At the Onondaga Longhouse on the Six Nations Reserve,
for example, one Yale anthropologist reported in 1961 that Indians included
a lacrosse game as part of the summertime Thunder Ceremony to water
fields and heal the sick:

> In this game any number of men could participate, and the teams were
> arranged according to moiety affiliation. The players brought their own
> lacrosse sticks, and a ball was borrowed from a member who owned one as
> a result of having had the game performed previously as a "pass dance." The
> rules followed were those of the old field lacrosse (as opposed to the mod-

ern box lacrosse), and the players were told before they started the number of goals required to complete the game. Usually, either three or seven goals for a team ended the game. The speaker explained the occasion and purpose of the game to the players and finally, before tossing up the ball, admonished them to play fairly and without malice. (Indeed such an admonition was apropos, for lacrosse traditionally was, and is, an emotionally charged game, in which high feelings and witchcraft play a prominent role.) Naturally, malicious sentiments are out of place when performing the game as the supernaturals' "pass dance." No emetics were taken for the medicinal, or devotional, lacrosse games, nor did competition run as high as in the sport. Medicinally it was completely unimportant which side won the game.

After the game, the players engaged in a symbolic war dance. Before the military collapse of the Iroquois Confederacy in the late eighteenth century, the dance allowed combatants to boast about battlefield accomplishments.[123] Whether they played lacrosse as a medicine game or a competitive game, the Iroquois regarded both versions of the sport as central to their cultural lives.

Sticking with the Home Team: Canadian Box Lacrosse after World War II

Box lacrosse allowed Iroquois Indians to explore a more culturally satisfying version of lacrosse, but they also traded the jurisdictional authority of American field lacrosse for that of Canadian box lacrosse. Anglo-Canadian and Native American proponents of box lacrosse created a model significantly different from that of field lacrosse in the United States. By the 1950s the social and cultural elements of Canadian box lacrosse differed from those of American field lacrosse in several ways. Whereas American field lacrosse was played throughout the Northeast, Canadian boxla was confined primarily, but not exclusively, to two geographically isolated areas: southwestern British Columbia and southern Ontario. Separated by some two thousand miles, this sport's enthusiasts could hardly support their claim that lacrosse was the national game of Canada. In reality, ice hockey dominated the country's collective sporting consciousness. Second, support for box lacrosse was strongest in small cities such as Brantford, Ontario, and Victoria, British Columbia; in the suburbs of Vancouver and Toronto, which were less affluent than the suburbs of the United States; and on native reserves in Quebec, Ontario, British Columbia, and New York.

Compared to the generally affluent field lacrosse communities of New England, Long Island, and Baltimore, the Canadian boxla communities were decidedly more working class. Whereas an affluent class gave American field lacrosse its identity, locale defined the social world of box lacrosse. Because Canadian enthusiasts included everyone in a city, from businessmen to firemen, community mattered more than class. Unlike the outdoor field game, which was played in the late spring and early summer, box lacrosse was played indoors during the second half of the summer, at a time when most Canadians were outdoors enjoying warmer weather and looking forward to the coming hockey season.

If enthusiasts of field lacrosse and boxla shared anything, it was the pursuit of manliness and rough sport. The main difference had to do with how much roughness they wanted. After all, a fight in an American field game resulted in expulsion, but the same offense in a Canadian box contest earned a five-minute trip to the penalty box. Moreover, whereas field lacrosse fans in the United States often saw baseball as an opposing summertime game, box lacrosse enthusiasts embraced ice hockey as a positive cultural role model. American field lacrosse was essentially elite, amateur, and largely noncommercial; it was rough but intolerant of outright violence; it was rooted in university and college campus life and utilized the Indian as a mythical cultural symbol. In other words, it was similar to the original game of George Beers. On the other hand, Canadian box lacrosse had a more working-class character; it was tolerant of fisticuffs and roughneck play and was both receptive to and dependent upon limited forms of professionalism and commercialism; it was oriented around local clubs; and it included native peoples as both participants and spectators.

Provincial associations provided stable leadership for Canadian box lacrosse, but clubs formed, dissolved, and changed classifications with regularity. Not every club fielded teams year after year at the same level of play, under the same name, in the same locale, with the same sponsor in the same arena, but the basic structure of the sport changed little. As it had for field lacrosse, the Canadian Lacrosse Association supervised all box lacrosse competitions and awarded several championships. The highest tiers, the senior (no age limit) and junior (age twenty-one and younger) ranks, included clubs throughout Canada and Iroquoia. In 1964 organizers subdivided these age brackets into "A" (elite talent) and "B" (open) sections, and awarded four separate trophies. Because lacrosse lagged significantly

behind in the prairie and maritime provinces, national championships essentially pitted the winners of Ontario and British Columbia against one
another. A series of short-lived dynasties dominated the Senior A Mann
Cup. For instance, Peterborough won four straight cups from 1951 to 1954.
Beginning in 1955, at the height of the so-called golden age of box lacrosse,
the momentum shifted westward, and British Columbia clubs won twelve
of the next sixteen cups. The winners included New Westminster, Vancouver, and Victoria. Senior B clubs competed for the President's Cup. Junior-
level competition followed the structure of the seniors. A championship series between the Junior A provincial champions of Ontario and those of
British Columbia determined the winner of the Minto Cup. Given the age
restrictions on junior clubs, most dynasties lasted only two or three seasons.
The exception was the Oshawa Green Gaels, which won seven straight cups
from 1963–1969. The dominance of Minto Cup play by Ontario clubs from
cities and towns such as Saint Catharines and Brampton suggests a more
extensive level of youth development in Ontario than in British Columbia.
The Junior B championships—known as the Castrol Cup from 1964 to 1971
and then as the Founders Trophy beginning in 1972—also drew from
provincial leagues throughout Canada. Besides national coordination at
the highest levels, provincial and local governing bodies provided guide-
lines and organized age groupings covering everyone from younger teens
to little boys.

Socially, culturally, and economically, box lacrosse changed little
throughout the twentieth century. The game attracted men from a cross
section of social classes. Despite the presence of white-collar professionals,
club rosters typically included large numbers of firefighters, police officers,
teachers, construction workers, public works groundskeepers, and long-
shoremen. The profession of firefighting and the pastime of box lacrosse
were especially intertwined. Many fire departments encouraged their men
to play, and their flexible schedules made it easy for those who were boxla
athletes to go to practice or a game. Culturally, the two activities reinforced
many common traits. The typical box lacrosse player and the typical fire-
man both had to know how to work closely with other men in confined,
hectic environments in short bursts of time. Unlike field lacrosse, box
lacrosse players played in shifts lasting only a few minutes of real time. Likewise, seconds and minutes were critical to both. Another skill the two activities had in common was knowing how to use equipment properly and

precisely—whether it was a lacrosse stick or an axe—under the pressures of time and heat. A sweltering arena and a burning house taught these men that one's work site was itself part of the challenge. Upper body strength and endurance in short-distance running also mattered a great deal to both firemen and box lacrosse players. For some athletes, getting a job with a fire department might guarantee a spot on a local lacrosse club roster. During the 1960s, Kerry Gallagher had played junior- and senior-level box lacrosse in Coquitlam. However, after he was hired by the New Westminster Fire Department in 1971, he became a member of the local Salmonbellies.[124]

Whenever a box lacrosse club recruited a player to move to the club's town, it was obligated to provide a job. Much as in the world of amateur hockey in the winter, a boxla club could not expect someone to relocate without an economic security blanket, such as work at a paper mill, retail store, or construction site. Clubs also found lodging for these transplants. A local club's supporters often gave a temporary residence to an adventurous young man who was visiting their part of the country for lacrosse season. Players moved from club to club and from province to province for many reasons: for promised jobs, to escape old girlfriends, to have a chance to win a cup. Born and raised in Peterborough, Paul Parnell had become a lacrosse star as a teenager. In 1959 Parnell and the senior Peterborough club journeyed west to confront New Westminster for the Mann Cup. Even though Parnell's team lost, he met a woman and within a few days asked her to marry him. The following year he moved to British Columbia and began to play with the Victoria club. Two firemen from New Westminster orchestrated Parnell's trade to the Salmonbellies. "With much bafflegab and an undisclosed amount of cash," retired sportswriter Stan Shillington observed, "the pair wrestled Paul's transfer to New Westminster, a transaction described as the biggest heist since the sale of Manhattan." Parnell wracked up trophies and records as a Salmonbelly, and eventually he rose to the rank of chief in the fire department.[125] Some box lacrosse players were content with seasonal, temporary work, but others realized they could parlay their athletic prowess into upwardly mobile careers. During his tenure with the Saint Catharines Athletics, for example, Mohawk player Ross Powless learned the carpenter's trade, was employed by several construction companies in southern Ontario, and eventually worked on the Burlington Skyway Bridge. He recalls: "I'd been playing in St. Catharines . . . because some of the kids were in school at Six Nations and I had a growing family to support. I decided I wasn't gonna spend my life doing seasonal work, picking berries here, working in tobacco fields there. Through lacrosse I got into the carpenter's union, Hamilton Local 18. From there I never looked back. . . . I don't know, maybe having all those kids at home, I figured I could eventually handle two dozen carpenters on the job. It wasn't long before I became a foreman."[126]

Everyone said publicly that box lacrosse was an amateur sport, but players, coaches, and sponsors knew otherwise. Talented lacrosse players, like players in other team sports, could be valuable drawing cards. The more talented the player, the more likely was his club to attract steady crowds from game to game. Throughout communities supporting clubs, local citizens took great pride in their hometowns. Inhabitants coined nicknames for their cities referring to the communities' unique characteristics. For instance, residents referred to Hamilton as the "Steel City." In Oshawa, the local automobile industry gave rise to the name "Motor City," while a canal inspired the name "Lift Lock City" for Peterborough. Club names such as the Victoria Shamrocks, Oshawa Green Gaels, Fergus Thistles, and Orillia Terriers reminded fans of the importance of Irish and Scottish culture in local communities. People from these tight-knit locales came in crowds of two to five thousand for lacrosse matches. Although no one openly signed a pay-for-play contract akin to the contracts in professional baseball, lacrosse players earned compensation in other ways. Using revenue from gate fees and sponsorships, clubs offered players cash under the table. City hall bureaucrats, factory managers, school administrators, and store owners offered athletes temporary or permanent jobs, off hours, flexible work schedules, and free merchandise. These civic-minded men were very proud of their communities, but also knew that support for a club was a useful public relations move. In one case at the end of World War II, several men asked the city government of Peterborough for financial support to build a playing facility to replace a demolished site. Offered only a land lease, the enthusiasts earned the support of a local bank manager, who engineered a loan to purchase lumber. By the start of the 1947 season, the Peterborough senior team had a new home.[127]

Many clubs relied on sponsors to stay afloat financially. Sometimes a club adopted a sponsor-inspired nickname. The Peterborough club, for instance, had a variety of local sponsors over the years and hence the nicknames Lumberjacks, Timbermen, and Trailermen. During the 1960s, breweries funded clubs in British Columbia. The Vancouver Burrards became the Carlings, the New Westminster Salmonbellies played as the O'Keefes, and the Nanaimo club took the name Labatts. Clubs also paid their bills by hosting annual dinners and golf tournaments, selling advertisements in team programs, and selling advertising space on their jerseys. In 1966 *International Lacrosse Magazine* provided a vignette of the social and economic world of box lacrosse. According to the magazine, the Vancouver Carlings had a telephone installer for coach, a printer for captain, and a roster including several firemen, high school teachers, and a ship unloader. Even though the brewery sponsored the club, box lacrosse lacked free-spending venture capitalists. "Canadians won't take a chance on something unless they're sure of doubling their money," one player complained. Although clubs were nominally amateur, the magazine editors observed, they possessed many professional qualities: "Vigorous recruiting procedures may include good job offers in towns sponsoring teams, expense arrangements and compensated time off from jobs to compete in tournaments."[128]

When a club recruited an athlete for its team, the player weighed the merits of a current or future job against the chance of winning a cup. For instance, a player might turn down a chance to play with a better team if his current team kept him in a city with an employer offering a pension. Any player who did move from one club to another had to secure permission from his current team. That club would insist on compensation, usually cash or another player in exchange. These practices commonly associated with professional sport became confusing when two clubs operated in different provinces. In 1956 scoring star and Peterborough native Bob Allan decided to play for the Nanaimo Timbermen. Peterborough's Harry Whipper went to Nanaimo as well. Ironically, Nanaimo defeated Allan's hometown Trailermen in the Mann Cup competition. Controversy raged when Allan returned to Ontario, despite having agreed to play with Nanaimo again. Allan not only won the Ontario Lacrosse Association (OLA) scoring title, but also led Peterborough to victory in the Mann Cup competition against Victoria. Meanwhile, the OLA declared that Allan's original transfer to Nanaimo in 1956 had been illegal, because Nanaimo had violated a rule prohibiting clubs from acquiring more than one player from the same club. But the CLA and the Inter-City Lacrosse League in British Columbia both argued that Nanaimo still held the playing rights to Allan. As the postseason unfolded, Peterborough won the eastern championship and the right to compete for the cup against Victoria. OLA commissioner Ed Blair eventually sided with the other organizations, but the Peterborough men refused to play without Allan. After forfeiting game one of the cup competition, the CLA forced the OLA champions out of their hotel, told them to fly home at their own expense, and handed out five-year suspensions. The replacement Long Branch Pontiacs lost to Victoria in four straight matches.[129]

With typical senior box lacrosse contests attracting anywhere from a few hundred fans to a few thousand, the resulting gate revenues varied. Crowd sizes depended on who was playing, the clubs' promotion efforts, the disposable income of spectators, and what leisure alternatives might have been available. Local clubs relied upon former players and other community-minded individuals to volunteer as club president, vice president, and secretary or treasurer or to sit on the club's board of directors. Offering their time and work, these individuals scheduled events, provided organizational leadership, and kept the clubs financially viable. These conditions fostered an intimate relationship between spectators and players. According to veteran Vancouver broadcaster Jim Cox, contests in the 1950s were community affairs. Reflecting back from the end of the century, Cox said the eventual mandatory adoption of helmets and construction of modern playing facilities diminished some of the charm of the old game: "You heard the sound of feet running down the floorboards, ten men running and sounding like a cattle stampede. And the wire may have looked ugly around the boards, but that allowed you to hear the grunts, groans and swearing, or whatever, that went on. You heard every check . . . every time a stick hit a shoulder you almost felt it yourself. Now with the cement floors and the plexiglass around the boards, there's nothing but deadly silence at a lacrosse game. And plus, with no helmets in those days, there was instant identity with the players. They were people with real faces and real smiles and real scowls and real groans to the fans. With helmets came that loss of identity and I don't think lacrosse has ever been the same since. You need a program now. You just needed your eyes then." Perhaps the most intimate of relationships was between the fans who packed Queens Park Arena and the men who played as the New Westminster Salmonbellies. Supporters regarded this club as *the* dynasty, much like the New York Yankees of baseball. The team had a long history, dating back to the late nineteenth century when Vancouver lacrosse players had given nearby New Westminster fishermen who doubled as lacrosse players a derogatory nickname: "fishbellies." The accumulation of championships led Salmonbellies fans to regard their community as both the Mecca and the Vatican of box lacrosse.[130]

The world of Canadian box lacrosse—rooted in locale, semiprofessional in nature, and confined to a remote corner of Canadian national life—differed from that of American field lacrosse in another way. Enthusiasts on both sides of the Canadian-American border made different assumptions about the social relationship between Native Americans and non-natives and about the presence of alcohol in the sport's cultural milieu. For most of the twentieth century, organized field lacrosse in the United States used the Indian as a noble historical figure to define the game in mythical terms and tolerated a limited real-life native presence on the field. Alcohol consumption was certainly part of the culture of undergraduate life in the United States, but any acknowledgment of it undermined the gentlemanly image of lacrosse. Stereotypes of all natives as "drunken injuns" kept loose the ties a university might have with a reservation. In Canadian box lacrosse, on the other hand, not only did native teams compete with non-native teams, but many clubs throughout Ontario and British Columbia recruited native athletes. Moreover, an athlete's ability to consume significant amounts of beer and buy rounds for friends after games indicated his social status in the game. Postgame beer drinking reinforced friendships forged through frantic competition in hot arenas.

Alcohol consumption by fans and players often took place in the same setting. During the 1950s, whenever the Victoria Shamrocks and Nanaimo Timbermen played one another, the visiting team's fans poured into railway cars and made the trip to watch their team. En route to the game, coaches kept players isolated in the train's last car, away from fans drinking themselves toward intoxication. But between periods and after the game, visiting Victoria fans in Nanaimo went to the nearby Newcastle Pub. When a game ended, Shamrock players accompanied their supporters and sometimes found themselves close to hometown Nanaimo fans who had yelled against them all game. "These huge Nanaimo loggers would be throwing beer caps at us and taunting us in the pub," recalled former Victoria Shamrock Whitey Severson. "Then the next thing you know, they were sending us beers."[131] The consequence of this cultural practice to an athlete, however, might be the loss of a younger man's physique. For instance, Jack Northup played for clubs in New Westminster and Victoria in the 1950s. His ability to consume postgame brews matched his prolific scoring records. "As his goal totals increased, so did his waistline," recalled long-time box lacrosse enthusiast and *Vancouver Sun* journalist Stan Shillington. "One story, often related around a certain Esquimalt tavern, had Jack winning rounds of beer for his firemen buddies by betting he could run a certain distance in a specific short period of time. No way, not with that belly; but, indeed, he invariably won his bet."[132]

Social alliances between native and non-native athletes might also be cemented over a few beers. Mohawk player Ross Powless recalled how his non-native teammates from the Peterborough Timbermen had stood up for him at a tavern prior to the 1951 season: "One night during the tryouts some of the Timbermen and me went over to the Montreal House in Peterborough for some ale. We'd had a hard practice and we wanted to restore some of them lost body fluids. That's what we used to say in them days anyway. Pretty soon the tap man starts talking to the waiter and the waiter walks over and asks me if I've got my blue card. The blue card showed enfranchisement and only people who'd given up their Indian status and become enfranchised could drink legally. I told the waiter I didn't have one and he said he couldn't serve me. Right away the Timbermen stood up and said "If he's not good enough, we're not good enough neither." When they walked out of the Montreal House for me, it made my season. Shortly after that, I made the team and it wasn't long till I was drinking ale with my teammates in the Montreal House."[133] White and Indian lacrosse players acknowledged racial differences, but the rough-and-tumble culture of box lacrosse promoted group cohesion. What mattered most was not whether the racial "other" spoke with a forked tongue or acted like a savage, but whether he would feed the ball properly to his buddy, stick up for someone if a melee broke out, or buy beers for friends.

The playing career of Ross Powless's son Gaylord illustrated many of the important themes in box lacrosse. Playing through the 1960s and 1970s, he chose lacrosse over a possibly more lucrative career in hockey. Gaylord's love for the sport, not any rejection of professionalism, had governed his choice: "Anybody who can attract crowds and bring in X number of dollars to the entertainment industry deserves everything he can get. I just wish it had happened to me." As did many others, Powless played for several different amateur and professional clubs in British Columbia, Ontario, and New York, often following job offers. As had his father, Gaylord became a carpenter. Powless played for four seasons with the Junior A Oshawa Green Gaels during the mid-1960s. To combat player partying, Oshawa coach Jim Bishop placed disciplinary restrictions on Powless and his teammates. Powless later recalled that Bishop's strictness had saved young men from getting into trouble. The Green Gaels often held two practices in the same day, with a game that night. "All you're doing is showering all the time," Powless recalled. "Bishop kept them off the street, kept them playing lacrosse."[134]

As did all lacrosse players, Powless witnessed and participated in his share of rough play. His father, Ross, remembered an incident during a Minto Cup game against New Westminster's junior team: "Gaylord tangled with three of them Salmonbellies. One guy cut him for ten stitches in the mouth. Cross-checked him but good. It was deliberate, the guy was trying to put him out of the game. Blood's pouring from Gaylord's mouth when two more Salmonbellies attack him from behind. Gaylord turned around and spit blood in their faces. Then the fight was really on! Them Salmonbellies were gone for the game and Gaylord got a total of seven minutes."[135] The Green Gaels went on to win the game and the cup. As a star native athlete with Oshawa, Gaylord endured verbal and physical attacks both on and off the court. According to Jim Bishop, "He took a lot of abuse because he was a native—nobody else had to take that abuse." By hurling racial insults, crowds in places such as Hastings, Ontario, thought they could distract Powless. "They used to have chicken fence along the boards, and some of the old-timers would get boozed up. I didn't know what kind of drink I'd get thrown in my face when I got close to the screen," Gaylord recalled. "I just ignored it. They paid money to get in—they could call me what they wanted."[136]

Natives overlooked the potential problems caused by playing a rough sport with white athletes. From 1946 to 1974 Peter Burns of Saint Regis played for several reservation and Canadian city clubs. "Back when I played, they used to call us wagon burners," he remembered. "We'd show up, and they'd say, 'Oh, the wagon burners are here.' It was more of a joke. It never bothered me."[137] In tolerating the verbal abuse, men like Powless and Burns demonstrated their commitment to the game. Their general disinterest in spectator racism reflected their conceptualization of the game as a vehicle to demonstrate masculinity. Friendships with non-native athletes mattered far more to native players than the drunken, racist shouts of spectators. Conceiving box lacrosse as a game in which men might prove their manliness to others, they focused on athletic activity and the respect of their peers rather than on the limitations and demands imposed on them in the outside world. A box lacrosse player could prove his mettle in no better way than by standing up for himself during a fistfight. Although many critics blamed poor officiating for fights, individual athletes controlled the extent of violent play. To men like Gaylord Powless, keeping track of licks over a career mattered: "There are a couple of guys I still owe—they retired before I got even—but, with most of them, I got revenge."[138]

Canada, America, and Lacrosse

A variety of factors limited the appeal of box lacrosse in Canada. Perhaps most obvious, many Canadians did not find ovenlike summertime arenas appealing. After cold winters in Ontario and even mild ones in British Columbia, many Canadians simply preferred to be outdoors in the fresh summer air. During the early years of box lacrosse, air conditioning was not available in sports arenas during the summer. However, even in the latter decades of the twentieth century, the installation of expensive air conditioning made fiscal sense only if large gate revenues were guaranteed. With many potential spectators not wishing to sit in hot arenas and clubs financially unable to fund the installation of cooling equipment, boxla operators were caught in a Catch-22 situation. Adding to the dilemma was the lack of entrepreneurs to provide important infrastructure investment.

The lack of mass support for the game across the provinces demonstrated how deceiving and hollow was the notion that lacrosse was Canada's national game. Lacrosse enthusiasts received a rude awakening in the 1960s, when two separate developments underscored the peripheral status of box lacrosse both in Canada and in the international lacrosse community. Canadian lacrosse partisans established their own hall of fame in New Westminster's Centennial Community Centre in May 1967, about a year after the Americans had built theirs in Baltimore. Losing the race to create a hall did not bother Canadian box lacrosse fans, but the destruction of a century-old myth did. From 1964 to 1965 Durham Member of Parliament (MP) Jack Roxborough had researched the issue and proved that George Beers had never received an endorsement of lacrosse as a national game of Canada from the Canadian government. Whereas Beers had claimed that Parliament had given its stamp of approval on Canada's birthday, July 1, 1867, Roxborough showed that the first Parliament had not convened until that November. Meanwhile, this former president of the Canadian Amateur Hockey Association tried to get his favorite sport endorsed. Burnaby-Richmond MP Robert Prittie countered with a bill favoring lacrosse. Despite the posturing, the national government adopted neither sport officially until 1994. The final bill named hockey the country's official winter game, and an amendment endorsed lacrosse as the official summer game. According to one MP, "This is in itself a great symbol of the way we do politics in the country because this is the quintessential Canadian compromise."[139]

That box lacrosse took root only in southwestern British Columbia and southern Ontario can perhaps be explained by the fact that the early development of the game had taken place when the region's cities were small and the cultural activities were few. In 1990 radio announcer Jim Cox recalled the easy time boxla had had commanding the attention of people on Vancouver Island during the 1930s: "Not even inter-city baseball was here yet. There were no golf courses and not as many distractions or attractions as there are today in the summer. Lacrosse essentially had everybody's undivided attention. I remember the radio station used to be flooded with calls if they thought I was favouring or pulling for one team over the other." Former Victoria Shamrock player Whitey Severson recalled that the same had been true in the 1950s: "There were few bars, few pubs, not much theatre ... simply nothing else doing."[140] With little competition from other cultural venues, box lacrosse had developed a loyal clientele in these small cities and suburbs.

When the big booms in television viewership, big-league professional sports, and American mass culture—often one and the same—began to sweep across Canada in the 1950s, box lacrosse became one of many consumer choices. Besides the rise of the Canadian Football League, which began its season during the second half of the summer, the most direct competition facing box lacrosse came from professional baseball. Several Canadian cities with pockets of box lacrosse support acquired professional minor league baseball franchises, sometimes at the top level of play. For example, both the Toronto Maple Leafs and the Montreal Royals played in the AAA-level International League after the Second World War. Beginning in 1951, the transplanted Jersey City Little Giants began competing in Ottawa. The former Oakland Acorns moved to British Columbia in 1956 and became the Vancouver Mounties in the AAA Pacific Coast League. During the late 1940s and early 1950s other cities such as Victoria, Hamilton, and

Ottawa also hosted franchises in lower-level minor leagues. By the end of the 1950s and the early 1960s, however, most of these franchises had folded for the same reason many minor league teams had ceased operations in the United States: television programming in general and televised major league baseball in particular had stolen their audiences. Many Americans and Canadians wondered why they should support local spectator sports of any variety when the world of hyped celebrity sport made its way into living rooms across the continent. Canadian box lacrosse organizers were not oblivious to the interests of spectators. Prior to the 1953 season, the Inter-City Lacrosse League and then all of Canadian lacrosse reduced the on-field squad of players from seven men to six to make the game more exciting. Regardless, the combination of television and other professional sports did not necessarily steal away box lacrosse fans, although that likely happened as well. Instead, television and baseball lured *potential* supporters away from box lacrosse. This trend underscored many Canadians' Januslike feelings of attraction to and repulsion from the mass culture of the United States.

One way to combat this threat was to unite the two main lacrosse communities. In July 1966 the twin cities of Detroit, Michigan, and Windsor, Ontario, celebrated an International Freedom Festival with a Canadian-American lacrosse game. Because the two clubs playing—the Birmingham L.C. of Detroit and the Ontario L.C.—practiced different versions of the sport, they had to compromise on the playing rules beforehand. After the Canadian victory, organizers in both countries believed international lacrosse should be revived. To commemorate the centennial of modern lacrosse, the several national governing bodies in the United States, Canada, England, and Australia all sent teams to the first World Lacrosse Tournament in Toronto in 1967. The occasion consummated the efforts of various national organizers to unify their communities of amateur sportsmen. While the Peterborough Pepsi Petes represented Canada, English and Australian all-star teams toured the United States to prepare for the tournament. The American representative, the Mount Washington L.C., defeated the other national teams before crowds of between one and four thousand to win the title.[141] Although the four anglophone nations did not reunite until 1974, the American, Canadian, English, and Australian athletes had achieved a symbolic cultural unification. Collectively, they were now able to insulate themselves—consciously or subconsciously—from many of the developments elsewhere in the world of sport, such as the politicization of the Olympics, the increasing prominence of African American athletes, and the commercial interests of professional sports promoters. After that, national teams from the four countries reunited every four years to celebrate their amateur game. That the world cup adopted an outdoor field format reinforced the international marginalization of box lacrosse. Victories by the United States simply confirmed the commanding position of the American game within the larger international lacrosse community.

By 1952, when this match between Navy and Maryland took place, collegiate lacrosse had experienced growth and achieved a greater competitive balance. Seven different schools claimed the national United States Intercollegiate Lacrosse Association championship during the 1950s. (U.S. Lacrosse.)

During the years following World War II, many Indian athletes came to prefer box lacrosse over the field game. This 1953 Onondaga Athletic Club photo features Oren Lyons, Jr. (*center*), who was eventually recruited by Syracuse University to play goal tender. (U.S. Lacrosse.)

By the 1950s college lacrosse programs featured intense conditioning and elaborate offensive and defensive schemes. During this
1955 match between Army and Rutgers, three
players converged to stop an attacker's shot.
(U.S. Lacrosse.)

Under the tutelage of talented coaches, Bob
Scott (*right*) prominently among them, Johns
Hopkins University fielded reliably strong
teams and won its full share of men's collegiate lacrosse championships in the second
half of the twentieth century—ten USILA and
seven NCAA crowns between 1947 and 1987.
(U.S. Lacrosse.)

Originally from Long Island, future Cleveland Browns running back Jim Brown played his "favorite sport" at Syracuse University as a senior in 1957. Besides playing lacrosse, Brown also ran track that spring. As a black athlete, Brown especially stood out in a sport dominated by affluent whites and Iroquois Indians. (U.S. Lacrosse.)

The U.S. national women's lacrosse team's tour of Great Britain in 1964 featured games against local and regional all-star teams as well as social functions hosted by organizations such as the East Anglian Ladies' Lacrosse Association, the English-Speaking Union, and the All Wales Ladies' Lacrosse Association. The Americans were greeted by mayors and visited numerous churches, castles, and campuses. (1964 scrapbook, U.S. Lacrosse.)

The United States Naval Academy won or shared eight consecutive national championships from 1960 to 1967. In 1962, during his senior season, Midshipman Jimmy Lewis, number 22, helped revolutionize collegiate play with his stick-handling skills. (*Lucky Bag* yearbook, 1966, U.S. Naval Academy archives.)

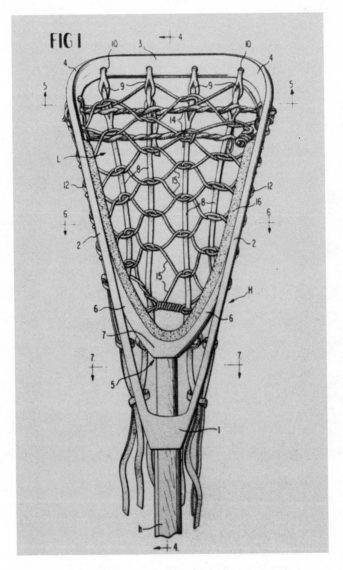

The plastic molded lacrosse stick head revolutionized the game during the 1970s. Mass-produced synthetic sticks contributed greatly to increasing the numbers of participants in the sport. However, their introduction, by companies such as STX of Baltimore, pushed Indian wood craftsmen to the margins of the sport's economic world. Shown here is a diagram accompanying an application approved by the U.S. Patent Office in 1970. (U.S. Lacrosse.)

Three generations of the Simmons family (from the left, Roy III, Roy Jr., and Roy Sr.) played and coached at Syracuse University from the 1920s through the 1990s. Roy Jr. succeeded his father as head coach in 1971. (U.S. Lacrosse.)

The Indian nationalism movement of the 1970s inspired Mohawk Indians to add their voices to the public discourse on Native American history. In 1978 the North American Travelling College at Akwesasne produced a book recounting a Mohawk interpretation of the history of lacrosse. The book's title, *Tewaarathon*, is the Mohawk name for the game. As indicated by this illustration, the volume emphasized the importance of the oral tradition in transmitting historical knowledge from one generation to the next. (North American Travelling College, Akwesasne Reservation, *Tewaarathon* [*Lacrosse*], 1978.)

Created in 1983, the Iroquois Nationals
lacrosse program used sport to generate intertribal pride, create scholarship opportunities,
and promote a national sovereignty agenda.
In 1990 Onondaga faith keeper Oren Lyons
(*center*) led a team to the World Games to
compete against the United States, Canada,
England, and host Australia. (U.S. Lacrosse.)

Twin brothers Gary and Paul Gait of British
Columbia led Syracuse University to three
consecutive NCAA championships from 1988
through 1990. During a NCAA tournament
game against the University of Pennsylvania,
Gary performed his acrobatic "Air Gait," leaping up from behind the goal and slamming
the ball in to score. Gary and Paul went on to
dominate play in the Major Indoor Lacrosse
League, Canadian box lacrosse, and the American club field game. They also started their
own retail business, GB Lax. (U.S. Lacrosse.)

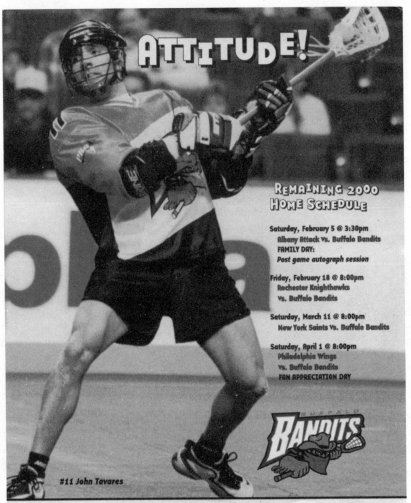

ATTITUDE!

REMAINING 2000
HOME SCHEDULE

Saturday, February 5 @ 3:30pm
Albany Attack vs. Buffalo Bandits
FAMILY DAY:
Post game autograph session

Friday, February 18 @ 8:00pm
Rochester Knighthawks
vs. Buffalo Bandits

Saturday, March 11 @ 8:00pm
New York Saints vs. Buffalo Bandits

Saturday, April 1 @ 8:00pm
Philadelphia Wings
vs. Buffalo Bandits
FAN APPRECIATION DAY

BANDITS

#11 John Tavares

For individual tickets, visit **tickets.com** (formerly Fantastix) in any Tops Friendly Markets or call toll free at
1-888-223-6000.

The Major Indoor Lacrosse League, later re-cast as the National Lacrosse League, sold the game as a commercial spectacle. This advertisement for the Buffalo Bandits showcases star scoring champion John Tavares. These semiprofessional athletes sometimes attracted crowds of more than sixteen thousand fans, but their small lacrosse paychecks led them to keep their full-time jobs as schoolteachers, police officers, and construction workers. (National Lacrosse League advertisement.)

TRIBAL LACROSSE

Even at the end of the twentieth century, "noble savage" imagery was alive and well, used now to sell T-shirts. In this advertisement from the 2001 Lax World catalog, a vividly colored Indian warrior hoists his stick in triumph while two presumably white players provide ghosted backdrop—the historical seemingly far more interesting than the contemporary. (Lax World catalog.)

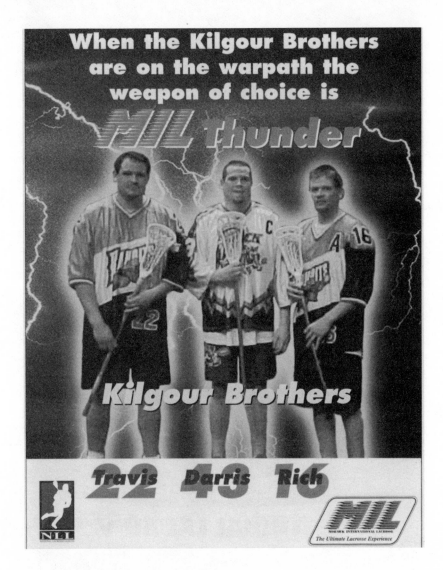

When the Kilgour Brothers are on the warpath the weapon of choice is MIL Thunder

Kilgour Brothers

Travis 22 Darris 43 Rich 16

NILL

MIL
MOHAWK INTERNATIONAL LACROSSE
The Ultimate Lacrosse Experience

Native entrepreneurs realized the commercial potential of lacrosse. Mohawk International Lacrosse manufactured synthetic playing sticks and used the celebrity athletes of indoor lacrosse to sell its products. These three brothers from the Tuscarora Reservation endorsed the company's "Thunder" stick. (Mohawk International Lacrosse advertisement.)

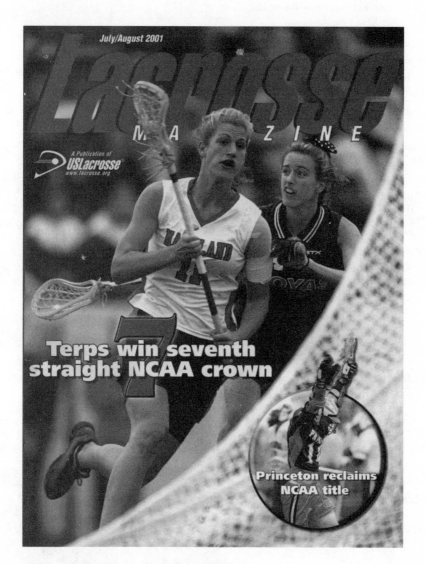

July/August 2001

Lacrosse
MAGAZINE

A Publication of
USLacrosse
www.lacrosse.org

Terps win seventh
straight NCAA crown

Princeton reclaims
NCAA title

Women's lacrosse experienced phenomenal
growth during the 1990s, due in part to the
Title IX mandates of the U.S. federal government. This *Lacrosse Magazine* cover photo
from the summer of 2001 features the University of Maryland's dominant program.
(*Lacrosse Magazine*, U.S. Lacrosse.)

In this May 31, 2001, fight between Dar Hicks of the Maple Ridge Burrards and Matthew Green of the New Westminster Salmonbellies, players invoked an old Canadian tradition. From the field contests of the late nineteenth century and the early twentieth century through the emergence of box lacrosse during the Great Depression, fighting has remained an unofficial part of the game. Some fights might result from personal feuds, but others result from the actions of "enforcers," "tough guys," and "goons." The latter type of player protects a team's shooters through physical intimidation of the opposition. Whereas fighting in a U.S. collegiate game results in immediate expulsion, Canadian box lacrosse referees send guilty parties to the penalty box for five minutes. (Paul Horn and www. Salmonbellies.com.)

By the 1990s manufacturers of consumer goods were exploiting the commercial potential of lacrosse. Companies now produce items as diverse as athletic equipment, jewelry, neckties, and blankets with lacrosse imagery. Much more recent is the use of the game to sell a class-based lifestyle. In its 2001 catalogs L. L. Bean used lacrosse sticks, roller blades, scooters, skis, and soccer balls to sell clothing to its affluent clientele. (L. L. Bean 2001 catalog.)

Simply the best fleece you'll find at these prices

Chapter 5   **The End of "The Lords of Lacrosse"?**
The Creator's Game in the Late
Twentieth Century

FOLLOWING MANY DECADES of relative continuity and stability, after 1970 the world of lacrosse underwent some of the most profound social and cultural changes it had seen since George Beers had first transformed the old Mohawk ball game into a modern sport. The guiding ethos of American lacrosse enthusiasts—which included adhering to amateurism and viewing the modern player as the symbolic descendent of the "noble savage"—had changed little from the 1890s through the crises of the 1930s and into the 1960s. Nevertheless, increasing numbers of less socially prestigious centers of higher and secondary education began supporting varsity lacrosse programs in many areas of the United States beginning in the 1970s. Moreover, the diffusion of the game from its strongholds in the Northeast throughout the rest of the country also signaled a new era. The nearly complete replacement of the traditional wooden lacrosse stick with sticks manufactured from synthetic plastics significantly increased these social and geographic developments. Indeed, the "old Indian game" was entering the era of mass culture.

The greatly diversified and expanded social composition of organized lacrosse provided for movement away from the old cultural consensus to significant fragmentation. New voices calling for alternative conceptions of the game competed with those of older traditionalists from elite universities and preparatory schools. Amateurism continued to be a prevailing ideology among most advocates, but they disagreed on who should be allowed to participate within their community. Supporters of amateur sport viewed lacrosse as their game, a sport for affluent gentlemen and women, but a growing number of suburban coaches, players, and boosters advanced their plan for general expansion down the social ladder and across North America. Many devotees scorned the professionalization and commercialization of their game because they feared the potential for chauvinism, but this did not stop entrepreneurs from attempting to develop professional versions of the sport. Many of those businessmen established ties with Canadian box lacrosse to launch their enterprises. Meanwhile, Iroquois athletes and organizers believed both forms of the game—box and field lacrosse—could provide a variety of solutions to the tensions caused by modernity's assaults on traditional culture. All of these developments threatened to topple from cultural power the few men who had controlled the sport for so many decades.

The Proliferation of Lacrosse in North America and the World after 1970

Older supporters of lacrosse witnessed unprecedented growth and expansion during the final third of the twentieth century. In terms of participation, spectatorship, and institutional support, organizers fought hard to spread their game to new enthusiasts. Their efforts increased the numbers of male and female players from youth to adult levels of play, especially in the United States; the geographic spread of the game throughout America and overseas; the diffusion of the game from affluent sporting circles to the middle and working classes and from affluent suburban neighborhoods to poor urban areas; and the emergence of larger crowds watching championship contests. Much of this enormous geographic and social expansion occurred within the college and high school ranks. The quantity of the lacrosse programs in the northeastern states certainly increased, but the game also took on greater prominence in the South, the Midwest, and the Far West. Likewise, the movement of the game from primarily elite universities and preparatory schools to less prestigious colleges and public high schools brought about significant social change. Together these trends represented a form of "democratization" that enthusiasts of other team sports had experienced in previous decades.

A brief survey of the National Collegiate Athletic Association's annual series of official lacrosse guides and the clinic notes of the United States Lacrosse Coaches Association reveals many of the geographic and socioeducational developments from the 1970s to the 1990s. Data for western collegian teams are problematic, because many were listed not as varsity squads, but rather as "clubs" in leagues affiliated with the United States Club

Lacrosse Association rather than with the NCAA or the United States Intercollegiate Lacrosse Association. Regardless, the information shows that the lacrosse community was very vibrant. The sport's intercollegiate ranks expanded by about 60 percent, from 151 programs in 1972 to 240 by 1992, with much of the growth taking place during the 1980s. The number of schools playing in the traditional "hotbed" of the game, ranging from New England and New York in the North to as far south as Maryland and Virginia, grew from 123 to 200 institutions during the same interval. Compared to the entire country, these older regions of support saw their numerical position slip proportionately, but the figures still represented between three quarters and fourth-fifths of the entire collegian lacrosse world. Some of the fastest-growing regions, however small, were actually outside the traditional areas of support. The Far West, Lower South, and Rocky Mountain regions witnessed the creation of new programs. With almost a dozen new programs joining the older, more established programs at institutions such as Syracuse and Hobart, New York state continued to have the largest number of schools supporting lacrosse. The formation of new teams at colleges in the state university system and at community colleges in areas with blossoming suburban high school programs, such as Nassau and Suffolk Counties, suggests that many institutions recognized the interests of middle-class teens headed for college. Ironically, the region with one of the slowest growth rates was Maryland.

The NCAA began to sponsor a national championship tournament in 1971. By abandoning the decades-old practice of voting for a national champion, something big-time college football chose to continue, lacrosse organizers opted for a system akin to that of basketball. Station WBAL of Baltimore televised the first NCAA championship match, Cornell's victory over Maryland, to several hundred thousand viewers in the area in and around Maryland, Delaware, Virginia, and Washington, D.C. Ten institutions monopolized the first thirty Division I championship contests. More than half came from New York (Syracuse and Cornell) and Maryland (Johns Hopkins and the University of Maryland). Other successful programs included those at Princeton and the Universities of North Carolina and Virginia. During the early 1970s championship contests drew crowds of six to seven thousand, but by the 1990s they averaged twenty to twenty-five thousand. Regular season games attracted crowds of anywhere from a few hundred to a few thousand. Spectators at the Division I "Final Four" included supporters of the participating institutions and the most loyal college lacrosse fans. According to an NCAA spectator analysis of the 1994 championship, the average adult fan had traveled 178 miles to the site. Not only did these fans represent everyone from undergraduates to retirees, but more than half were from the traditional cradles of the game: Maryland (36 percent) and New York (22 percent).[1]

The college game achieved greater national exposure in 1976 when the American Broadcasting Company's *Wide World of Sports* televised a Cornell-Maryland title rematch, with Frank Gifford and Gene Corrigan doing commentary. Other NCAA tournaments included ones for small colleges (1972–73), Divisions II and III (1974–79), Division II (1980–81, 1993–present), and Division III (1980–present). From 1972 until 1995, when it began competition as a Division I school, Hobart won sixteen small college, Division II, and Division III national championships. With growing numbers of institutions fielding teams, the tournament selection process experienced controversy. In 1996, for instance, the selection committee passed over the only undefeated Division I team in the country, from Bucknell University. Eventually the tournament implemented a system of automatic qualifiers, with conference champions receiving direct bids, beginning in 2000. The USILA also recognized the booming world of "virtual varsity" lacrosse by sponsoring the first national championship for these poorly funded collegiate club programs in 1997. Brigham Young University won the first tournament among conference champions representing almost every section of the country.

Interscholastic lacrosse grew at an even faster rate than the intercollegiate game. The number of secondary schools offering lacrosse rose 137 percent, from 337 in 1972 to 799 by 1992. In New England the number of secondary and preparatory schools increased by more than one-third, with most of this growth taking place in Massachusetts and Connecticut. Such expansion was even more pronounced in New York, New Jersey, Pennsylvania, Maryland, and Virginia, with Long Island possessing the largest local community. However, the growth in high school lacrosse slowed slightly during the 1980s. Although the expansion was greatest in the southern, midwestern, and western states, schoolboy interest also increased in the traditional region stretching from New England to Maryland. Despite the tremendous continued growth of interscholastic play in the mid-Atlantic states of New York, New Jersey, and Pennsylvania, its overall share fell to roughly two-fifths of the national total. From the wider perspective of the period from 1972 to 1992, the proportion of schoolboy programs in New England, the mid-Atlantic states, and the Upper South fell from 93.2 percent to 82.5 percent. As did the collegian game, scholastic lacrosse remained mostly an eastern phenomenon.

The worlds of intercollegiate and interscholastic lacrosse developed closer ties in the 1980s and 1990s. In contrast to their football-, basketball-, and baseball-playing peers, high school lacrosse players did not dream of professional athletic careers. Instead they viewed the game as a trendy, "cool" sport that might allow them to earn athletic scholarships and bypass the more competitive realms of football and basketball. These high school athletes realized they would not be ignored by college recruiters because of their average physical size as they might have been if they had been football or basketball prospects. Having braved the economic conditions of the 1970s, especially confiscatory taxes, inflation, and stagnant real wages, middle-class parents hoped a full or partial scholarship would make it easier to pay for a college education. The students who received scholarships would have attended four-year institutions anyway, but lacrosse lightened the financial burden. More colleges created lacrosse programs and financial aid packages as tools with which to recruit student athletes who were not talented enough to earn scholarships in the high-revenue sports. Maryland athletes were especially coveted. "The best thing lacrosse can give anybody, material-wise, is an education," one Baltimore County highway engineer and former club player commented in 1980. "Lacrosse is probably the easiest way to get a scholarship to college."[2]

The annual "meat market" of summer camps for boys and girls reinforced relationships between colleges and high schools. There were 37 such camps in 1986, but 238 in 1996. By the summer of 2000 there were 371 in twenty-seven states and the District of Columbia. Not surprisingly, the largest concentrations of camps could be found in Maryland, New York, and Pennsylvania.[3] Collegians and schoolboys—and even their female counterparts—increasingly conceptualized lacrosse as another vehicle for achieving the athletic excellence, peer acceptance, pride in school, and social mobility found among players of other more popular team sports. With NCAA championship contests attracting crowds in excess of twenty thousand, consumers purchasing "name brand" lacrosse clothing and athletic gear, and youth idolizing intercollegiate athletes, lacrosse achieved some form of egalitarianism, at least as far as colleges were concerned. The game was still less popular than the Big Three—football, baseball, and basketball—but it was hardly the elite gentleman's game of yesteryear.

The geographic origins of NCAA players demonstrate which areas of the country produced the most prized athletic talent. According to one study, the best players now came from public, suburban high schools. Few of the players at the top institutions in producing college athletes came from private schools.[4] West Genesee High School (in Onondaga County, New York) led the country, with thirty-five athletes on NCAA rosters in 1986. Counties producing the best lacrosse talent included Nassau, Suffolk, and Westchester Counties, New York; Fairfield County, Connecticut, and Baltimore County, Maryland. Among the top high school programs were those in Ward Melville and Garden City High Schools on Long Island; Yorktown High School in Westchester; and Calvert Hall, Saint Mary's, and Gilman in Baltimore County. When college recruiters looked for good athletes, they also recognized distinct regional styles of interscholastic play. Whereas players from Baltimore and other southern states started at earlier ages and could have their springtime practices and games in good weather, teams in New England and New York were forced by snow and ice to hold many practices in parking lots and games on slushy fields. These conditions allegedly produced different playing styles. Citing general player views in the mid-1990s, one observer declared: "Almost without exception, they view Upstate New York players as take-it-to-the-goal freelancers, players from Long Island as hard-nosed, no-nonsense fighters, while Baltimore—the area which receives the most 'off-the-record' criticism from non-natives—produces the best stick-handling and most team-oriented players."[5] Eventually inter-regional recruiting broke down and blurred many of these styles at the collegiate level.

Governed by the United States Women's Lacrosse Association, the women's lacrosse community continued to be quite different from the men's. By 1978 the USWLA included thirteen local associations in five districts, along with another 240 allied schools and colleges.[6] Besides the absence of time-outs and substitutes, except for injuries, the game was played on a field that lacked outlined boundaries and used twelve players instead of ten. Indeed, the game's proponents remained true to their heritage. One coach and physical education professor at Kutztown State College recalled an incident that had defined a unique quality of her sport: "During our first home game, the men's team arrived to cheer us on as we played on 'their' field which was neatly laid out with precise, white markings. As the ball went over the 'men's lines,' their goalie in a helpful gesture picked up the ball to throw to the umpire. I'm not sure who was more shocked—the women, who stopped dead in their tracks as they realized that the ball was no longer in play, or the goalie, as the other men yelled, 'Put it down! It's really not out of bounds!'"[7] Smaller than its male counterpart, the women's community followed the men's lead by creating a National Collegiate Women's Lacrosse Association tournament in 1982. The University of Maryland dominated the competition. Likewise, the College of New Jersey completely ruled a Division III tournament begun in 1985.

By the 1990s the women's game had experienced massive growth, achieving relative equilibrium with the men's at the varsity level. In 1991 there were 157 men's varsity programs, including 51 in Division I, 20 in Division II, and 86 in Division III, and 118 women's programs, including 33 in Division I, 12 in Division II, and 73 in Division III. However, many athletic directors discovered that adding a women's lacrosse team to their institutions' athletics programs would be an easy way to comply with the Title IX requirements of the federal government's gender-equity mandates for higher education. Since women's lacrosse still prohibited physical contact, a team required little in terms of equipment expenditures. By 1997 the men's varsity ranks had grown only 16 percent, to 182 programs: 54 Division I, 29 Division II, and 99 Division III. Meanwhile, the women's game grew by 53 percent to 181 teams: 56 in Division I, 18 in Division II, and 107 in Division III.[8] These numbers are deceptive, however, hiding the actual numbers of participants and teams at the college level. If varsity and "club" (nonvarsity undergraduate) programs for men are counted together, the gender disparity becomes obvious. According to a May 1999 demographic study, about 25,000 men played lacrosse for more than 400 teams (at 188 Division I–III institutions, 24 junior colleges, and more than 200 clubs) on campuses across the country. These teams had between forty-five and fifty players each, but sometimes well over sixty if there was a junior varsity program. By comparison, more than 5,500 women played on more than 240 teams (at 196 Division I–III institutions and more than 50 clubs), with an average of twenty to twenty-five players per program.[9] In other words, depending on the criteria (programs or players), the men's community was between two and four and a half times as large as the women's.

The same pattern can be found in interscholastic lacrosse. More than 15,000 girls representing 600 high schools (including 450 varsity programs) played the junior version of the women's game, with an average of twenty to twenty-five girls per program. Conversely, more than 72,000 boys representing 1,600 high schools (including 1,250 varsity programs) played lacrosse, with many teams having between thirty-five and forty boys.[10] As was the world of collegian lacrosse, the world of boys' high school lacrosse was two to nearly five times larger than the girls' community. A comparison of these college and high school data from the end of the century with data from a similar study done fifteen years earlier further demonstrates the degree of growth. According to a Lacrosse Foundation study, in 1984 there were 251 intercollegiate and 592 high school programs for men and 103 colleges and 150 high schools offering women's programs.[11] From 1984 to 1999 the male communities loomed large over the female, but the latter were catching up, as indicated by their respective growth rates: 60 percent for men's and 130 percent for women's intercollegiate programs, 170 percent for boys' and 300 percent for girls' interscholastic. Youth lacrosse for boys and girls, never a priority in previous decades, grew rapidly in the final decades of the century. By 1999 there were 76,000 boys and 27,000 girls ages five to fourteen playing in more than 4,500 programs in twenty-nine states.[12] There had only been about 20,000 youth playing in 1984, so the final decade and a half of the century witnessed a 415 percent increase in participation.[13]

Another half million children in all fifty states of the United States participated in a game called intercrosse, or "soft" lacrosse. Originating in 1986, the game was the product of the Fédération Québécoise de Crosse (FQC, the Quebec Lacrosse Federation). Reacting to the allegations that box and field lacrosse were too rough for children, FQC officials created a game utilizing safer aluminum and plastic sticks and softer rubber balls. This newest rendition of the old Indian game promoted four virtues: "the value of *movement* and activity for everyone; the value of *autonomy* and freedom for everyone; the value of *respect* for opponents; the value of *communication* with partners and opponents."[14] Noticeably absent from the core values was *competition*. The game rules made no distinctions between male and female players, and they mandated universal play for all participants and prohibited any stick or body contact. By 1991, when players from any of the twenty-two national federations gathered, contest rules required that they play on mixed rather than national teams. By removing conditions for politicization, commercialization, and national rivalry, intercrosse focused participants on athletic skills.[15] Most children in the approximately forty countries that embraced intercrosse by 1999 learned the game from physical educators.[16]

Club lacrosse also expanded in the final decades of the twentieth century. With the United States Club Lacrosse Association as a governing body since 1960, these teams included postcollegian teams of men who wanted to continue playing as they developed careers and families, but also college squads that did not hold official NCAA or USILA varsity status.[17] In 1974, for instance, the USCLA had 19 clubs in the East and another 40 collegian and postcollegian clubs in other leagues throughout the country.[18] By the mid-1990s club play had spread to thirty-two states and the District of Columbia, with 189 teams in 11 leagues, plus another 34 independent USCLA-affiliated clubs. Only three of the top ten states with clubs—Maryland, New York, and Pennsylvania—could be described as having had a significant tradition of play before 1970. With other states as geographically remote from one another as California, Illinois, and Florida, club lacrosse experienced significant geographic diffusion.[19] The largest and most prestigious club leagues—the Central Atlantic Lacrosse League and an older association directly sponsored by the USCLA—included clubs from New York, New Jersey, Pennsylvania, and Maryland, but also clubs from New England, Virginia, and even Illinois. Besides those in the mid-Atlantic area, the largest enclaves resided in the Midwest, the Far West, and the South. By 1999 there were more than 11,500 athletes, including 7,500 men and 4,000 women, playing for more than 300 postcollegiate clubs across the United States.[20]

According to a Lacrosse Foundation overview of the state of field and box lacrosse in North America, in 1984 approximately 110,000 men, women, boys, and girls played field lacrosse in the United States, from the club and intercollegiate levels down to middle school and youth leagues. In terms of family income, the average lacrosse enthusiast in the United States came from a more well-to-do background than the general population; 72 percent of participants were from families with incomes of at least $35,000 per year. One-fifth were from households making between $20,000 and $35,000, while the bottom 8 percent of participants' families made between $12,000 and $20,000 per year. In Canada approximately 17,000 box lacrosse players participated in organized play, mostly in Ontario and British Columbia. Only 1,000 men and 700 women were active in field lacrosse, with about 100,000 grammar and secondary school children participating in youth programs.[21] When these data are compared with earlier eras, it is evident that the game once known as the national game of Canada, later as the gentleman's game of the Northeast and mid-Atlantic United States, had found a new home throughout suburban America.

Unlike the American game, Canadian lacrosse did not experience continual growth. In British Columbia, for instance, the last three decades of the twentieth century witnessed a pattern of boom, slow decline, and then slow recovery in senior box lacrosse. The number of registered players jumped from 613 in 1969 to 1,316 in 1978. However, this figure declined to a low of 770 by 1986, eventually rising to 1,246 in 1999. Registration figures for "minor" youth box lacrosse paralleled those for the men's game to some degree. There were 3,370 boys registered in 1969, rising to a high of 8,360 in 1973. During the rest of the 1970s and the early 1980s, registration figures for youth plummeted to 3,030 in 1986. By 1999 there were 5,543 boys playing minor lacrosse. The number of female box and field lacrosse players was very small. In 1999 women and girls represented only 154 of 8,141 registered athletes competing in age groups ranging from "mini-tykes" to "masters."[22] The general statistics of the Canadian Lacrosse Association demonstrate significant growth in the last decade and a half of the century. The number of registered athletes throughout the dominion doubled, from 14,106 in 1986 to 29,414 in 1999. Typically 85 to 90 percent of these athletes played box lacrosse, with the rest enrolled as field players. Of course these figures do not count players who chose not to register with the CLA. The biggest spurt occurred from 1989 through 1992, when annual growth averaged between 17 and 25 percent.[23] The slow revival of the Canadian field game led the CLA to sponsor cup competition for senior women beginning in 1983 and for senior men in 1984. Teams from British Columbia monopolized both championships.

Aside from the size of the player pool and the growth rates of participation, the Canadian game continued to differ from American lacrosse in another respect. Intercollegiate and interscholastic lacrosse in the United States enjoyed various degrees of commitment from educational institutions, but the survival of a local club in Canada depended entirely upon gate revenue, local sponsorships, occasional government grants, and volunteerism. In British Columbia men such as elementary school teacher and later principal Ted Fridge provided important unpaid leadership. During the final two decades of the century he volunteered as coach, president, general manager, or commissioner of various governing bodies and clubs for referees, youth, juniors, and seniors.[24] Governments at all levels provided small grants to box lacrosse organizations, but confrontations occasionally resulted between local officials and box lacrosse promoters. For example, with twice as many youth playing softball as box lacrosse, a local parks and recreation commission in Colwood, British Columbia, replaced a boxla facility with softball diamonds in 1986. Local car dealer Robert Saunders tried, but failed, to protect his favorite pastime's playing space.[25]

To promote competition among the senior clubs, provincial leagues adopted an entry draft system during the 1970s. Following in the footsteps of major professional sports leagues, Canadian organizers believed they could facilitate parity by making the most talented junior players in a province available to all senior clubs annually, with teams making selections in the reverse order of that in which they had finished the previous season. The draft resulted in more competitive play, but the connections between locale and athlete, so important in the 1950s, were being severed. Indeed, Saint Catharines boys might wind up having to play as men somewhere else. In British Columbia the Western Lacrosse Association (WLA) began drafting players from junior clubs in 1973. Only a few years earlier, these clubs had dabbled in professional sport. In 1968 the amateur clubs in the senior Inter-City Lacrosse League collectively became the western division of the professional National Lacrosse Association. The following season, after the league had collapsed, the clubs recast themselves as the amateur WLA. These clubs assumed that they would draft a player only if they knew he would play for them and if personal and job obligations permitted him to play. Occasionally players gave general managers headaches. For instance, at the WLA's first draft the Victoria Shamrocks selected Walt Weaver of Surrey with the second pick. When Weaver balked at being selected, Victoria traded him to Vancouver, which in turn sent him to Coquitlam. He eventually landed officially where he had wanted to play all along: at New Westminster.[26] Emulating the practices of big league pro sports, these nominally amateur clubs did not have the same financial resources to make players happy who had been drafted by clubs deemed undesirable.

Box lacrosse occupied a peripheral position in Canadian sports. The way Canadians viewed their cultural heritage and contemporary consumer choices in the final decades of the twentieth century may explain this reality. According to box lacrosse historian and *Victoria Times-Colonist* sports-writer Cleve Dheensaw, it is possible that many affluent Canadians looked upon box lacrosse as part of the old Canada, one to be left in the past. Even though many British Columbia box lacrosse fans were excited about the WLA senior final between Victoria and Vancouver in 1977, by then the average "upwardly mobile" Canadian family had many sporting and leisure options from which to choose. Sitting in a hot arena did not seem attractive. The movement of ethnically diverse immigrant populations into big cities had likely reduced the possibility of any urban revival. In 1990 former player Jack Crosby highlighted the essential dilemma: "In the central city areas of Vancouver and Toronto, you get a big ethnic mix, and for some reason, that's not conducive to lacrosse." Not only were immigrants and older residents coming to dominate big cities, but box lacrosse enthusiasts had relocated elsewhere: to the suburbs of Vancouver and Toronto. "The game has followed the younger families out to the suburbs like Burnaby, Coquitlam, Richmond, Delta, Surrey, Port Coquitlam and Langley," Crosby said. A brief examination of the 1996 Canadian census certainly confirms Crosby's thesis. Many communities with senior clubs, such as Brooklin, Peterborough, and Fergus in Ontario and Maple Ridge and Victoria in British Columbia, possessed what the government called "visible minority" populations of less than 10 percent of the total population. Meanwhile, large foreign-born populations, especially Chinese and southern Asian immigrants, resided in the big cities of Toronto and Vancouver. According to *Vancouver Sun* sports columnist Archie McDonald, writing in 1986, "It may be symptomatic of this scattered country that we can't even get together on our national game."[27]

The difficulties organizers faced in promoting box lacrosse in Canada partially explains why the outdoor field version of lacrosse—the game played in the United States—became the accepted game overseas. By the end of the century, lacrosse communities existed in many countries in a variety of sizes and stages of development. By 1999 the game could be found to various degrees throughout the continent: in the United States (732,000 athletes), Canada (200,000), and Iroquoia (1,500). The largest enclaves beyond the shores of North America could be found in the two anglophone countries with lacrosse traditions dating back to the nineteenth century: England (40,000) and Australia (20,000 adults; 200,000 children playing intercrosse). Other communities could be found in Japan (14,000) and

Wales (6,000), with much smaller pockets of support in Scotland, the Czech Republic, Germany, and Sweden. Other areas with infant programs included Argentina, China, Denmark, Finland, France, Hong Kong, Ireland, New Zealand, Singapore, and South Korea.[28] Although organizers failed to convince the International Olympic Committee to include their pastime as a demonstration sport at the 1996 Atlanta Olympics, they were another step closer to transforming their game into a mainstream sport.

Regardless of problems surfacing, many American enthusiasts embraced an energetic form of proselytization. In comparison to the tours of the 1920s and 1930s, Americans journeyed overseas as teachers, not pupils. In 1980, for instance, Jackie Pitts led the U.S. women's national team on a tour of Australia and New Zealand. "The gifted should not be paid for the gift but when the opportunity arises, reach out to return the gift," Pitts said. "It is much like a seed to be sewn, cultivated and nurtured so it may not wither but flourish with continued use."[29] Following a conversation between a Johns Hopkins vice president and a Japanese graduate of the university, the Johns Hopkins men's team went to Japan several times during the 1980s to encourage growth of the game. Athletes formed a Japanese Lacrosse Association in June 1987, and some 3,000 athletes in thirty-eight men's and fifty-five women's intercollegiate programs played the game by 1991.[30] About one year after the terrorist bombing of Pan American Flight 103 over Lockerbie, Scotland, in December 1988, which had killed 270 people, including thirty-five Syracuse University students, Syracuse coach Roy Simmons, Jr., took his team to Scotland for a goodwill tour.[31] These and other energetic efforts by American enthusiasts to facilitate the international diffusion of the game led to an expansion of the number of eligible countries competing in international competition. For instance, the International Lacrosse Federation added Japan and the Iroquois Confederacy as entries to the 1990 World Games. Four years later the federation created a second tier of competition with representatives from the Czech Republic, Germany, Scotland, Sweden, and Wales.

From Wood to Plastic: Commercializing and Democratizing Lacrosse

Efforts to expand the popularity of lacrosse had to be reconciled with the availability of the equipment necessary to achieve that growth. Indeed, potential growth depended heavily on the ability of Indian wood craftsmen to meet the demand of veterans and novices requiring new sticks. Until the early 1970s, the supply of Indian-made wood sticks had limited growth due to the Indians' inability to meet all of the demands of lacrosse players in the United States and Canada. As the game steadily increased in popularity, demand for these sticks often outpaced the supply provided by stick makers. As a result, the production capacity of Indian manufacturers restricted the potential for lacrosse to achieve greater popularity among non-natives. The scarcity of sticks proved even more difficult for budding players. Although expansion among white athletes may have been limited by supply, the increasing demand by collegians and schoolboys solidified skilled employment opportunities for Native Americans for many decades. Ultimately, the nature of stick manufacturing placed significant limitations on the sport. Only the introduction of playing sticks made from synthetic materials allowed the sport to absorb many new club, intercollegiate, interscholastic, and youth teams. Over time, the so-called plasticization of lacrosse relegated the Indian craftsmen to the margins of the economic world and redefined the landscape of the game. After 1970, mass-produced sticks made of synthetic materials allowed greater numbers of athletes to participate in lacrosse and facilitated the expansion of intercollegiate and interscholastic lacrosse.

Making a wooden playing stick had been an age-old craft that had been passed down from generation to generation of Mohawks and other Iroquois peoples. Even with the Indian adoption of non-native technology— for example, metal carving and bending tools—in the nineteenth century and the early twentieth century, Indians had monopolized production knowledge. However, Anglo-Canadians had tried to commercialize the marketing of lacrosse sticks during the 1880s. Mayor, superintendent of the Cornwall Canal, and former Irish-Canadian lacrosse player Frank Lally diversified his boot and shoe business in Cornwall, Ontario, by including the sale of native-made wood lacrosse sticks.[32] The Lally family eventually monopolized the lacrosse stick market in North America. The early success of a venture between Mohawk stick maker Matty White and the Joe Lally Company led to friction between management and the native stick makers from Saint Regis. Two craftsmen in particular—Frank and Alex Roundpoint—abandoned Lally to work independently. The separation demonstrated that although Lally had capitalized on an old native craft, some Mohawks had felt they were being exploited and pursued free enterprise on

their own. The Roundpoints solidified their new business when they recruited Scottish schoolteacher Colin Chisholm to serve as business manager and part owner shortly after his arrival at the Cornwall Island School
in 1928. Chisholm practiced cultural accommodation by learning the Mohawk language during his residential tenure with a native family. Because
of this behavior, Indians trusted him to establish ties with Canadian retailers. At a teachers' conference in Toronto in June 1929, for example, he sold
store owners on the merits of Roundpoint sticks. After 1931 the new
Chisholm Lacrosse Factory competed directly with Lally for the North
American lacrosse stick market. Although the factory bore Chisholm's
name, no doubt facilitating a more favorable negotiating position for the
Indians with sporting goods distributors in Canada and America, the
teacher turned businessman recognized the indispensable role of the Mohawk stick makers. Under Chisholm the company overtook Lally's dominant market share. Lally later offered to sell his factory to Chisholm alone,
but the Scotsman balked when the Indians were excluded from the deal. Instead Chisholm waited until 1945, when Lally agreed to include Frank
Roundpoint in the transaction.[33]

Before "plasticization," the supply and nature of the basic raw material
required for lacrosse sticks had defined the production parameters of the
stick industry. After depleting the wood resources on Cornwall Island, the
Mohawk stick makers traversed the region hundreds of miles from the
reservation in search of forty-year-old hickory trees. Stick making required
a year. The stick makers took the bottom eight feet of each tree and split it
into six to ten shafts. The wood was cured outside, and then each shaft was
steamed and bent by craftsmen. After drying the sticks outside for several
months more, the Indians steamed and bent each shaft once again. Male
carvers trimmed, drilled, sanded, and shellacked each stick in the factory;
women laced them at home.[34] Even though the Mohawks used modern
tools, the careful bending of each hickory shaft precluded the complete
mechanization of the craft. According to one sporting goods executive from
Baltimore who was interviewed in 1951, an automated system could not
match a skilled craftsman: "Machines have been tried, of course, . . . but
never with any success. An automatic bending machine, for example, will
bend every stick the same amount. Due to variations in the fibers, however,
some sticks can't take as much bend as others and therefore split. The Indians seem to anticipate this danger point. They know when to stop; the

machines don't." The craftsmen's skills, their access to wood, reservation connections with urban markets, and the year-long process guaranteed Indian control over nearly every stage of production.[35]

By the mid-1960s, it is believed that the Chisholm Lacrosse Manufacturing Company factory was producing between 95 and 97 percent of all lacrosse sticks. The remainder of the market was occupied by independent stick makers or small factories at other reservations, such as the Six Nations Reserve in Ontario and the Onondaga Reservation near Syracuse. Chisholm and other manufacturers sold their sticks either directly to customers journeying to the reservations or to two sporting goods wholesalers, Bacharach Rasin of Baltimore and the W. H. Brine Company of Boston. In turn, these companies controlled the retail sale of lacrosse equipment. Monopolistic conditions in production and distribution dominated the economic world of the lacrosse stick. Because of this market situation, demand usually outstripped supply, little emphasis was placed on quality control methods or rapid innovation, and the stick makers were usually unable to meet any sharp increases in consumer demand. Since demand for sticks by players and coaches usually exceeded stick makers' supplies, there was little incentive for Mohawk craftsmen to compete with other reservation stick makers by driving down production costs and product prices through technological innovation. In other words, because lacrosse stick buyers' choices remained limited, prices for sticks were almost certainly higher than they would have been had no production monopolies existed. Making matters worse for consumers was the knowledge of many enthusiasts that sticks were in limited supply, which caused them to buy extra ones whenever they found them. As a result, the occasional buyers or customers that were farthest away from the native craftsmen may have found themselves out of the market loop.

Many Native American craftsmen took extreme pride in their work, but the stick industry was not motivated by the same forces that motivated the capitalist marketplace, such as the ability to exploit a shortage to earn greater profit by rapidly expanding production. Moreover, because the raw material of their craft was not uniform, unlike a synthetic material, the craftsmen's knowledge and skills were critical. The final products were never exactly the same; each stick had its own unique features and personality. Because no two sticks were identical, the consumer was forced to invest time in learning the nuances of a selected stick. When athletes felt satisfaction with a stick maker's work, they became loyal customers. A player's worst nightmare might be the retirement of a favorite craftsman. In 1960, for instance, the Victoria Shamrocks club wrote veteran stick maker Herb Martin of the Six Nations Reserve, pleading for new sticks: "Last year our Shamrocks had to use patched-up sticks because they wouldn't use any other make than yours."[36] Native stick makers' disinterest in the capitalist marketplace forced non-natives in both Canada and the United States to repair damaged sticks. In New Westminster, for instance, former Salmon-bellies player and firefighter Ab Brown turned his woodworking experience and workshop into a hobby repairing lacrosse sticks.[37]

Stick quality could be affected not only by the stick's material, but also by worker misbehavior. Apathy, tardiness, or alcoholism among factory employees could negatively impact the final product. Making matters worse was the difficulty stick makers sometimes had in training apprentice craftsmen. "They don't make the sticks right in the first place," Herb Martin said in 1960, explaining his inability to expand his workforce, "and in the second place they cut themselves and quit."[38] The human element greatly affected the quantity and quality of a year's batch of sticks. Naturally, the fewer sticks on the market, the greater the inconvenience to consumers, and the higher the prices. In the end, the limited number of skilled craftsmen plus the year-long production process precluded stick makers' ability to match spikes in consumer demand. Besides, because there was no massive increase in the number of lacrosse players, there was little hope that reduced prices could stimulate consumer spending and generate handsome profits. Moreover, the seasonal nature of the product, the limited regional appeal of the sport, and the remoteness of stick factories reduced the opportunity for growth in stick production. Because Native American craftsmen had no incentive to revolutionize the production process, the chance for massive production growth was remote. Therefore, Indian stick makers were never able to realize the market potential of their product.

The monopoly in distribution and the limited number of retail outlets contributed to the difficulty someone interested in lacrosse would experience in acquiring a stick. In fact, the only way for a non-native coach or player to guarantee himself a stick would be to drive dozens or even hundreds of miles by car to one of the reservations in New York, Ontario, or Quebec and buy one directly from a native craftsman. No baseball enthusiast would ever have had to make such a journey for a baseball bat. A trip by a non-native lacrosse player to the reservation in search of a wooden lacrosse stick was more akin to a baseball fan's pilgrimage to the hall of fame in rural Cooperstown, New York. A lacrosse enthusiast would return from a stick-buying trip with a sense of the history of the old Indian game. Native lacrosse stick distributors did not usually sell their product using the same themes used to sell cars, appliances, tools, clothing, and groceries. They did not emphasize convenience, the low cost of the product, or the ability of the item to enhance one's personality or convey one's social status. Instead they sometimes used the same themes employed to sell antique furniture and handmade quilts; stick ads revolved around natural materials and personal craftsmanship. Bacharach Rasin and Brine stick advertisements emphasized an age-old, romanticized link between Indian craftsmen and the natural world. In 1965, for example, Bacharach Rasin told enthusiasts it provided "the finest lacrosse sticks that nature and man can create."[39]

With the steady growth of lacrosse in the 1960s, a larger number of players relied upon the same small number of stick makers as in years gone by. Destruction of the stick makers' facilities, especially Chisholm's factory, would have been catastrophic. In 1967 Chisholm's staff of about seventy-five men and women produced 50,400 lacrosse sticks. Although Chisholm aimed for a goal of 72,000 sticks the next year, a fire destroyed the factory on June 4, 1968—ironically on the 205th anniversary of the Indian attack on Fort Michilimackinac. A heartbroken Frank Roundpoint died a month later at age sixty-eight. "Only the people in lacrosse realized how bad the stick situation was before the fire," Canadian Lacrosse Association vice president George Duddin noted after the incident. "Now it is worse." Despite the fire's destruction, workers retrieved over three quarters of the factory's sticks in progress. Chisholm also channeled new orders to independent stick makers such as Ian Williams of Six Nations, who in 1967 had made about 1,500 sticks.[40] Organized lacrosse averted a near crisis when most of the Chisholm craftsmen continued their work outside despite serious factory damage. Chisholm even secured financial assistance from the federal and provincial governments of Canada. The first native Member of the Canadian Parliament, Leonard S. Marchand of Kamloops, British Columbia, officially reopened the factory in October 1968. According to Marchand, industrialization on reserves was crucial for the future economic autonomy of Native American peoples: "The success of the lacrosse industry is proof that Indians can achieve and use their skills and traditions to help them toward independence."[41] Even though the Mohawks recreated old carving tools destroyed by the fire, they realized by the end of the 1960s that they could not keep pace with the growing demands of old and new players alike.[42] They soon faced a fundamentally different type of competition that drastically challenged the production authority of Indian stick makers.[43]

The craftsman-centered system of production seems anachronistic when it is compared to modern industrial capitalism, which relies on scientific management and mass marketing, economy of scale, mechanization of the workplace, and use of synthetic materials. Even though native stick makers enjoyed a growing demand for their work, put in long hours, and endured industrial disaster, their greatest challenge came from private American and Canadian companies that experimented with lacrosse sticks made from synthetic materials during the 1960s.[44] In 1969 a box lacrosse coach and manager from Toronto predicted that plastic would replace wood as the material of choice for sticks within two years. According to Morley Kells, "The new sticks increase the accuracy of shots and speed up the game; and they are stronger than the wooden type. But the big thing is that they will be available in quantity." Unable to control the efforts of plastics developers, the Mohawks decided to focus their attention on their more immediate problem of cultivating new sources of hickory trees.[45] The inability of Mohawk stick makers to keep pace with non-native demand, growing discontent with the quality of Indian-made sticks, and a desire for a more consumer-friendly product all converged to create a market opening for plastics developers. As the president of William T. Burnett & Company in Baltimore, former All-American lacrosse player Dick Tucker pioneered efforts in the research and development of plastics suitable for lacrosse stick production: "At the outset, it was more of a personal matter than a business venture," Murphy recalled. "We'd all played the game and, like most over-the-hill lacrosse players, we still had an ardent interest in the sport. Breakage has been a fairly common problem with lacrosse sticks, mostly in the curved, planed-down area of the stick head. We felt that if it were possible to mass-produce a more durable stick at a reasonable cost, the efforts to expand and popularize the game would be helped significantly."[46]

The plastics revolution had the potential to meet the equipment needs of a burgeoning market. In 1989 Tucker recalled, "We were working with durable urethane materials which had been used successfully in shoe soles, car bumpers, and tires. Knowing the toughness of these materials and knowing lacrosse, we felt they should make excellent lacrosse sticks."[47] By the end of the 1960s, Burnett's close relationship with the Dupont Company led to the creation of the subsidiary STX, Inc., to manage a new line of Adiprene urethane rubber stick heads mounted on ash or hickory shafts.[48] The strengths of the new sticks were obvious. Unlike the nonuniform wood stick that took an entire year to make and a long time to learn to use, its plastic counterpart was a standard, durable, and readily duplicated product that was easier to use and interchangeable with other sticks. With plastic instead of wood, supply and demand could be in equilibrium at a price most potential players could afford. Moreover, creating a factory to manufacture plastic lacrosse sticks required primarily capital investment and knowledge of plastics engineering rather than an age-old carving skill passed on from one craftsman to another. Even though plastic sticks could crack or break just as wood sticks did, it would be far easier to replace synthetic sticks from ready inventories. Whereas competition in the manufacturing of plastic sticks would spur more innovation in design and raw materials, the making of wooden lacrosse sticks lacked significant variation.

The impact of plastic sticks was immediate, expediting the social and geographic expansion of lacrosse throughout North America. Plastic sticks were easier for players learning the game and easier for manufacturers to market to consumers. The acceptance of lacrosse on cultural grounds was a separate consideration; the plastic stick could lead to greater reception of the game on material grounds. In the spring of 1971, Air Force Academy coach Major Jim Keating said the new sticks would help encourage the development of lacrosse programs among Colorado high schools: "The stick is going to be a tremendous help in promoting lacrosse in this part of the country. In trying to sell high schools on developing a lacrosse program, our efforts have been hampered by the recognition of high costs that a school might be forced to absorb because of frequent replacement of broken sticks. Now, we can recommend sticks with excellent durability and longevity and great playing qualities, too."[49] The introduction of plastic sticks irrevocably altered the flow of new sticks. No longer would the production capacity of Indian craftsmen control and limit the pace of the growth of the game. Moreover, with uniform stick quality, parity among stick buyers was achieved. Before the mass production of plastic sticks, influential coaches at universities such as Johns Hopkins and Syracuse had enjoyed early access to the best quality wood sticks. With the advent of plastic, this advantage was lost.[50] Despite the expense of the research and development of experimental molds during the 1970s and 1980s, STX and Brine revolutionized the market and soon destroyed the monopolylike power held by native producers, ironically at a time when the energy crisis of the mid-1970s was challenging the viability of many types of petroleum-based equipment. Regardless of barriers, the plasticization of lacrosse sticks allowed for greater access to the sport by less affluent enthusiasts.[51] As more people adopted the game throughout the 1970s and into the 1980s, the stick market witnessed the nearly complete replacement of wood sticks with plastic ones. By the late 1990s other companies such as Warrior Lacrosse had designed and introduced lighter sticks with titanium shafts. More competition led to greater technological innovation, and companies made efforts to use former intercollegiate stars to hawk their wares.

Even with the dominance of plastic stick manufacturers, Native American craftsmen did not disappear from the marketplace. Many box lacrosse players and proponents of the women's game remained loyal to wood. At Saint Regis, for example, Frank Benedict purchased the Chisholm factory in 1972 and renamed it the Mohawk Lacrosse Stick Manufacturing Company.[52] Benedict was not alone; stick makers in other Iroquois communities continued to ply their craft. One such native was John Wesley Patterson of the Tuscarora Reservation.[53] A graduate of Springfield College, Patterson had taught physical education in Baltimore-area high schools throughout the 1950s and 1960s. At annual coaches' meetings the Anglo-looking Patterson always concealed his native identity from other coaches, fearing racial animosity. Patterson recalled how white coaches had ridiculed Indian stick makers. "They'd say, 'these are Monday morning sticks we're getting. They're drunk all weekend and look what we get on Monday morning, nothing but junk.' . . . Being a coach, you had to be at a lot of these meetings. They would down the Indians. . . . You crawl back in your shell when you go out into the world again because 'Oh geez, if things are that bad I'd just better be quiet.'" When he retired from coaching, Patterson turned his personal stick-making hobby into a business: "I knew the Mohawks were falling apart. I knew they weren't making a quality stick."[54] Initially the business included only Patterson and his non-native wife, Carol, who also coached women's lacrosse. By the early 1990s, however, they

had a staff of fifteen to twenty and were annually producing about ten thousand sticks for a worldwide market. Patterson had successfully found a way
to combine his sense of native traditionalism with the realities of the business world. In 1997 he said, "I'm a native, but I'm also a capitalist because
I've been off the Rez."[55] Patterson's company was soon joined by other native firms such as the Mohawk International Lacrosse company, which at
the end of the twentieth century introduced to the marketplace a new line
of native-made wooden and plastic box lacrosse sticks that had the feel of
wood sticks.

Despite the efforts of Native American wood craftsmen to remain active in the stick market, molded plastic had become firmly entrenched as
the market's material of choice. Modern industrial capitalism had triumphed over a traditional native craft. Ironically, though, the plastics victory was incomplete. The synthetics revolution contributed to the massive
growth in lacrosse participation during the final two decades of the century
and created many more potential customers for wooden sticks. After all,
many veterans and novices alike might purchase wooden sticks either to use
in games or to hang on walls as they might paintings. Apparently dominating stick sales and elbowing native craftsmen to the margins of the marketplace were not enough for some manufacturers of plastic sticks. Reflecting the trend for mammoth chain stores like Wal-Mart to push small
retailers out of business, one executive of a plastic stick manufacturer offered to buy out Patterson's business in order to close its doors. Even with
the victory of plastic over wood, not all athletes celebrated material
progress. Some felt that something had been lost with the advent of modern engineering. Addressing his comments to the readers of *Lacrosse Magazine* in 1998, one former All-American attackman who had attended Cornell during the 1970s expressed his love for his wood stick, remembering, "I
looked deep within the spirit of that stick to find my game and the warrior
soul that was in me." Eamon McEneaney likened the modern plastic stick
to "disposable diapers, the aluminum bat, the fast food chain and the drive-
in movie." Making nostalgic references to a "mystical time" and an "ancient
past," he even compared breaking in a wood stick to "courting a sweet-
heart."[56] Regardless of the economic winners and losers in the stick-making
business, one reality became crystal clear: the growth and expansion of
lacrosse would not be limited by native stick manufacturers.

Blue Bloods and Blue Collars:
The Popularization of Amateur Lacrosse

Although the rise of the plastic stick abetted the social and geographic expansion of lacrosse and created the possibility of a revolution in the guiding values of the field game, many coaches and administrators remained committed to amateurism. The lack of an imposing lacrosse version of major league baseball made belief in the amateur sport seem fairly safe. The massive expansion in participation after 1970—as well as the diversification of enthusiasts in terms of gender, class, education, region, race, and nationality—provided for possible challenges to the core value system of many older supporters. Many new to the game—young boys and girls, lower-middle-class and working-class people, suburbanites, African Americans, corporations such as Toyota, and people residing in places such as California and Colorado—did not accept intact the elite amateur values of the "old Indian game." The advocates of amateur athletics continued to press their case, seeking converts outside the Northeast, among younger and socioeconomically inferior communities, and inside corporate boardrooms, but also began to understand the consequences of embracing a more inclusive ethos. Indeed, the forces of geographic diffusion, social democracy, and commercialism had the ability to decenter sport for sport's sake. By the mid-1990s calls for a national governing body in the United States aimed to control those unleashed forces and further cultivate support for lacrosse by concentrating administrative and fund-raising activities. The subtle question enthusiasts would have to answer had to do with whether they should embrace a new sporting ethos open to professionalism and commercialism, react against the social changes by purging the game of newer converts, or democratize their elite amateur ideology.

Collegian and schoolboy lacrosse were the obvious havens of amateurism, but the world of postcollegian club lacrosse reinforced the importance of that ethos. Even with the significant social and cultural changes of the 1960s, club lacrosse remained a socially exclusive activity for men who balanced their pastime against the demands of their commercial, legal, and medical vocations. The social class of the athletes, their motivations for playing, and the financial conditions that allowed clubs to field squads all point to an emphasis on amateurism. Club lacrosse of the period can be portrayed as a sport for young men aged twenty-one to thirty-five who were in the early stages of their careers. Others attended graduate school or coached high school. "Lax is not every man's game, of course," a *Forbes* magazine writer declared in 1986. "Players and fans tend to come from upper-crust East Coast families and opt for careers in finance." Although the article may have exaggerated slightly the elite social composition of players of club lacrosse, they were clearly men of affluence: "Many top college-level players wouldn't dream of accepting first jobs anywhere else but Baltimore, Boston, Washington, D.C. or, especially, New York, where the best club leagues are found. The typical club team is deep in investment analysts, traders, brokers and lending officers."[57] This community often supported campus events promoting the sport, such as the 1982 World Games at Johns Hopkins. Scanning a crowd of seven thousand fans, the *Baltimore Sun* observed how fashion revealed the crowd's social character: "Lots of yellow shirts with alligators on them. Lots of pink shirts with polo players on them. And plenty of white shirts with lacrosse emblems on them." More influential enthusiasts put aside the demands of their professions to attend the games: "The older men, the ones who just got off work at the bank, the insurance firm or the law firm, are still wearing the long-sleeve oxford cloth shirt they wore to work with their suit." Discarding a suit for bermuda shorts, the paper continued, "The result is a what the 'Dress for Success' people may call the investment-banker-at-ease-look—starch on top, bare knees on bottom."[58]

The elite disposition of club lacrosse typified class reunions as well. For instance, alumni from Johns Hopkins' undefeated national championship teams of 1947–50 assembled every year to commemorate their titles. When forty-two of them reunited in 1983, their professional development revealed their social status. Although most of the men were corporate executives or attorneys, the group included a half dozen athletic directors, lacrosse coaches, headmasters, and principals, as well as two academicians, a surgeon, a U.S. Department of Energy official, and two men who owned their own businesses.[59] Preparatory school reunions also showed the elite social status of former athletes. In October 1994 the "old boys" from the Trinity-Pawling and Phillips Andover prep schools gathered at Pawling, New York. The two schools had been named co-champions of New England in 1969, and the former school's players did not like sharing the title, especially since the schools had never played one another that season. After signing medical waivers, the aging veterans of Andover defeated the Trinity men. According to the *New York Times,* "They settled an old lacrosse score in the Hudson Valley this morning—architects in knee braces, exporters in corsets, insurance executives with reconstructed elbows, athletes whose hairlines had receded with time, even if their determination had not."[60]

A variety of factors motivated athletes to support the club game, including physical exercise and a reinvigorating "psychic income" that counterbalanced sedentary mental work. According to an international arbitrager and former Wharton School lacrosse captain, the game provided young men with access to corporations staffed by lacrosse alumni. "Players have a lot in common and can be a bit cliquey about the whole thing because they're serious about the sport and often play year-round," Donald MacLeod explained. "After college graduation, people head to big cities and use the sport as their means of gaining an introduction to the business world." Former Brown University All-American and Dean Witter investment analyst Angelo LeBosco believed this reinforcement of class cohesion did not shut out men from lower social classes: "Especially for guys who are from more modest backgrounds, tapping into the lacrosse network can make all the difference in the world for them."[61] The clubs in and around Baltimore stressed the socio-occupational benefits of the game more than did their counterparts outside Maryland. According to a computer consultant who served as president of the USCLA in 1985, former Cornell player John Phillips, Long Island athletes refrained from stressing social networking to the extent of their counterparts in Maryland. The *New York Times* distinguished these athletes from professionals: "Lacrosse players are the last of the amateur athletes. . . . They're not even playing for job development or social contact, although there's some of that in the Baltimore area."[62]

Many former collegians believed that club lacrosse provided the individual with a means to play *and* control a team sport, a unique opportunity considering the cultural dominance of professional sports in the late twentieth century. This game lacked the overt commercial inclinations of professional baseball and football, where players earned large paychecks, but had little or no formal control over the sport. At his 1984 Lacrosse Hall of Fame induction ceremony, former Cleveland Browns running back Jim Brown reported that he had found lacrosse very appealing as an athlete at Syracuse University during the 1950s. Besides engaging in varsity competition, he had also played in pick-up games with nearby Onondaga Reservation Indians. "Lacrosse is probably the best sport I ever played," Brown commented. "There was no publicity. You had to like it. There was no pressure, just great competition."[63] Many players displayed contempt for professionalism and commercialism, regardless of their status as upper-middle-class attorneys or blue-collar construction workers. However, the most vocal defenders of amateur sport, men who could most easily afford the expenses of amateur sport, were usually alumni from prestigious eastern universities and colleges who enjoyed careers in affluent occupations. In 1987 the self-proclaimed "Magazine of Executive Lifestyle," *Echelon*, described lacrosse as "a game of paradoxes—fast moving, high scoring and brutally violent, yet a gentleman's game, one still governed by time-honored concepts of fair play and sportsmanship."[64]

The women's game emphasized amateur values, and teams reinforced amateur sportsmanship with postgame fraternization. In her instructional book for girls and women, published in 1970, Anne Lee Delano of Bryn Mawr College informed athletes of their social responsibilities: "It is part of the game's unwritten rules to shake hands and introduce yourself to your opponent, and at the end of a match to shake hands once again. If you are a member of the home team, your responsibility after the game is to look after your opponent during the social occasion which should follow the match." Instead of engaging in the confrontational, boisterous behavior of their male counterparts, female athletes emphasized collegiality, respectability, and how their sport differed from the men's game. According to Delano, women's lacrosse "in its finest form suggests the grace and beauty of dance forms."[65] Despite such proclamations, women's lacrosse eventually became rougher when the growing number of new participants introduced a more competitive ethos to the sport. By the 1990s a division had emerged within women's lacrosse between those who favored retaining the ladylike qualities of the game and those who supported the more aggressive and competitive ethos found among men. The latter even argued in favor of having female players wear helmets.

Funding amateur lacrosse had long been a troubling affair. However, after 1970 three new conditions increased the cost of the sport: increased travel by postcollegian clubs, more frequent encounters with overseas opponents, and the hosting of tournaments.[66] Individual male and female athletes often paid for their own equipment, but most postcollegiate clubs and national teams held raffles, charged modest gate fees, and sought commercial sponsorships to cover travel and game expenses. Whenever an athlete accepted a roster spot on a club or national team, he or she assumed the financial burden. Regarding the women's game, Anne Lee Delano bluntly told her readers: "If you are chosen for a tour you are responsible for the expenses of your own uniform and travel, but when you arrive in a foreign country you become their guests. There is no better or easier way to become spoiled. Though expensive, it is a privilege no money can buy!"[67] Men's lacrosse was little different. In 1982, for instance, *Baltimore Magazine* observed that the elite backgrounds of many male players guaranteed the economic health of club lacrosse: "Whether a mafia or a fraternity, fueled by an alumni kinship that seems unrivaled in any other sport, this brotherhood assures the sport will never die of financial malnutrition." The prestigious schools that produced young businessmen guaranteed continuity: "Brains and money go in, brains and money come out, and as a result the local boardrooms continue to be filled with men who know the feel of a lacrosse stick. In blue-collar neighborhoods lacrosse has been viewed as an elitist sport patronized by blue bloods who wear pressed shorts and shoelaces."[68]

By the 1980s and 1990s a limited form of corporate support had become more visible, with breweries, taverns, restaurants, and sporting goods manufacturers offering funding.[69] Such patronage brought commercialization, but the lack of overt pay for play or any pressure to attract large crowds guaranteed the predominance of amateurism. By serving as the financial architect of the 1982 World Games in Baltimore, insurance guru Emil "Buzzy" Budnitz demonstrated the ability of club enthusiasts to support their game financially. A former All-American at Johns Hopkins and a ten-year veteran of the Mount Washington L.C., Budnitz served as president of the International Lacrosse Federation at the time of the Games. He helped to acquire donations of $25,000 each from six corporations, including Anheuser-Busch, Crown Central Petroleum, and the First National Bank in Baltimore. Budnitz exploited existing social networks within the business community: "You can go into almost any top corporation in Baltimore . . . and you'll find people on the board who have a lacrosse background or a son playing."[70]

After 1970 the world of amateur club lacrosse stood in contrast to the blossoming big business of professional team sports. While their version of competition lacked million-dollar player contracts, fifty-thousand-seat stadia filled with gate-paying spectators, and television audiences measured in the tens of millions, male and female club lacrosse enthusiasts played for love of the sport and for the socio-occupational benefits to be derived from the game. Ironically, many athletes represented the social class benefiting most from the commodification of culture. They knew better than anyone else how powerless the professional athlete was over his paid pastime. As a consequence, these men and women desired to retain control over their respective games. To commercialize and professionalize—and hence to popularize—lacrosse would have damaged the cultural function of the game. Besides, these athletes preferred decades-long tenures as educated white-collar workers rather than take risky gambles as highly paid professional athletes with five-year playing careers. Moreover, even though less affluent middle- and working-class lacrosse supporters possessed far fewer leisure dollars, they agreed with their well-to-do counterparts about the merits of amateur sport.

The geographic and social expansion of lacrosse after 1970 posed a variety of challenges to veteran supporters of the game. By the 1980s and 1990s, these enthusiasts faced two clear choices regarding the future of their sport: they could defend amateurism and keep the game small and elite, away from undesirables who would not appreciate a game for ladies and gentlemen, or they could spread the game as much and as far as possible, developing new comprehensive and professional systems of administration and fund-raising while controlling and defining the worldview of converts. Essentially, the lacrosse world had an undeclared cultural war on its hands. In Maryland, for instance, opinions about the future varied. Some supporters continued to defend Baltimore—that is, the elite version of the game found at Johns Hopkins, area universities, and local prep schools—as the true mecca of the sport and were happy with the status quo, but others sought further geographic and social expansion. Those with both exclusive and inclusive conceptions of the sport's future agreed that their sport should be kept amateur. The eventual winner of this cultural contest would be determined on the basis of who could best organize.

Some enthusiasts did not explicitly call for exclusivity, but offered subtle defenses of the gentleman's game. Occasionally invoking romanticized notions of yesteryear, they made nostalgic references to the old Indian ball game. In 1973 one Baltimore sportswriter expressed the belief that modern collegian teams should be judged by their expertise as defined against the chaotic qualities of the ancient game: "When seeing the game played for the first time, it is not hard to imagine Indians playing it in lieu of total war. It is still frenetic, full of fury and body contact, and punctuated by the sharp crack of clashing sticks."[71] But the message was clear: modern lacrosse expressed manly and scientific virtues. With tongue in cheek, the *Baltimore Sun Magazine* appropriated Native Americans from the past to address social anxieties in the present: "If the old Indian players could be brought back to see the champions this year they would have trouble recognizing the game they invented. If by chance they visited Wilmington, where high school girls play lacrosse but the boys do not, they would probably conclude that the women's liberation movement has gone too far."[72] Using dead Indians to critique modern social change, the writer defended the perceived nobility of veteran enthusiasts. This country club mentality bothered sportswriters and other supporters who believed the game should be made more democratic. One senior writer for *Baltimore Magazine* offered a humorous, critical examination of the relationship between social class and local lacrosse. During the summer of 1986, Ramsey Flynn attended an annual summer tournament he described as part of "an unusual rite of passage into Baltimore's social and business network." Entitled "Sticking Together," his commentary is worthy of extended quotation: "Today we will test the mettle of nearly two hundred high-school boys. Those who pass will be summarily admitted into the city's golden lacrosse network, with all of the social benefits that includes." According to Flynn, the lacrosse veterans "all come to trade tales and observe the rites as their sons don state-of-the art plastic armor." Gathered in clusters of "Kelly green and oxford blue," they observed the competition with keen interest. "You're not going to find too many people out here in *bowling shirts*," one coach told Flynn. "You know what I mean?"[73]

Observers scrutinized the young athletes for qualities useful in the business world, such as persistence and "character." While collegian scouts were evaluating talent, the athletes were establishing ties with alumni who might assist them in pursuing career opportunities. According to one broker, "A kid isn't going to get a job just because he played lacrosse, but he'll get to talk to somebody." Although this phenomenon was observed elsewhere, Flynn emphasized its prominence in Baltimore: "This facile passage from the world of lacrosse to the local business world is one that visitors find puzzling. It smacks of provincialism and inbreeding. But what the visitor doesn't understand is that Baltimore still considers itself the progenitor of lacrosse."[74] Ironically, the social and geographic expansion of organized lacrosse made the notion of Baltimore as the cultural capital of lacrosse—a view not shared by Iroquois Indians, Canadians, or enthusiasts in New York and New England—increasingly irrelevant. In contrast to their experience in earlier decades, collegian teams from Maryland won only nine of the first twenty-five title matches of the new NCAA men's Division I tournament. Moreover, Maryland's relative production of select talent had also declined significantly. In 1975, for example, about 24 percent of NCAA lacrosse players had come from Maryland. Only Nassau County in New York had produced more athletes than the city of Baltimore and Baltimore County. By 1986, however, Maryland's share of NCAA players had fallen to slightly less than 13 percent. The Baltimore area had produced the same number of players for the intercollegiate ranks, but now the three most productive counties—Nassau, Suffolk, and Onondaga—were all in New York state.[75]

This graphic decentering of Maryland lacrosse did not necessarily imply that enthusiasts in Baltimore would cease to be major movers and shakers. Flynn's analysis of the Baltimore summer league also illuminated a behind-the-scenes struggle over the present and future of the game. In his view, the older, elite traditionalists were succumbing to the numbers of less affluent enthusiasts who were calling for inclusion. Among the diverging viewpoints he had witnessed, those championing democratization had achieved victory: "There is much talk in lacrosse circles these days of redistributing the wealth. It's no secret that lacrosse in Baltimore has traditionally been a Blue Book sport. Most of the local lacrosse leaders have wanted it to grow. A minority had wanted it to grow 'only among the right people.' There was a power struggle in recent years, and the socialists won."[76] These "socialists" possessed no Marxist inclinations, and certainly did not represent any revolutionary social movement; they simply called for popularizing the sport. The ranks of the sport may have been expanding, but the traditional functions outlined by Flynn had survived. For instance, among the club players were the employees of the Alex Brown investment firm in Baltimore and bond brokers in New York City. "Thanks in part to lacrosse, the Baltimore preppies I know have managed to survive with their sense of entitlement more or less intact; for better or worse, they're not beaten down like New York preppies, who have had to compete in the remorseless meritocracy of Manhattan," John Seabrook observed in a *New Yorker* feature in 1998.[77]

Established in 1959, the not-for-profit Baltimore-based Lacrosse Foundation played a major role in breaking down social barriers. In 1983 the foundation embarked on an aggressive program of expansion. Declaring that "Youth and Lacrosse" was "The Prime Directive," the foundation-funded *Lacrosse* magazine called for activism: "The Foundation can not be a simple memorial to the few who have been recognized for their past accomplishments. It must be the spark, maybe even the fire, under an educational and promotional lacrosse movement across the country." By demonstrating "the physical and emotional values of our great game to an ever-increasing number of schools, parents and, finally, youngsters," the magazine argued, lacrosse would instill desirable qualities "for the greater good of our families and our country."[78] In other words, the masses might be taught an athletic code once only associated with the affluent. To stimulate interest, the foundation created regional chapters to supplement national promotion, improved its film and video library, expanded officiating and coaching clinics, funded injury research, sponsored an annual Hall of Fame Lacrosse Classic event, and provided greater access to its equipment loan program.[79]

During the 1980s the Lacrosse Foundation launched a youth program for urban African Americans. Created for Baltimore but then exported to other cities, the program provided equipment, uniforms, coach stipends, and playing schedules for inner-city middle school and high school teams. By 1990 some 80 percent of the six- to seventeen-year-olds in the Baltimore program were from indigent households with annual incomes of less than $10,000. More than a sports initiative, the program mandated academic and attendance standards for all athletes. The successes of the Baltimore project led to its replication in Philadelphia, Boston, Newark, and Wilmington, North Carolina. These efforts to reach out to the socially marginal demonstrated how a new generation of leaders who deemphasized the elite overtones of the game in favor of a more inclusive ethos were replacing older veterans who had played and praised the game in earlier decades.[80] One participant who had both witnessed and shaped these changes was Steve Stenersen, a former All-American player at the University of North Carolina and eventually director of the Lacrosse Foundation. In 1987 he boldly stated: "Lacrosse is no longer a sport played only by Indians and preppies."[81] Six years later, Stenersen believed that elite traditionalism had finally given way to a new way of thinking. "There was a parochialism that was present in the game in the 1950s, '60s and '70s," Stenersen observed. "There was an old guard, 'The Lords of Lacrosse,' that just didn't want the game to grow. But the sport has gone through a renaissance, nearly doubling in participation from the 1980s to the 1990s. I think that period of parochialism is over."[82] He had a most difficult job: projecting an inclusive image of the sport while not doing anything to offend elite traditionalists. Essentially, the question many organizers wrestled with was how to democratize what had been an elite cultural institution for many decades.

Two areas of social change included the slowly changing racial complexion of the game and the growing tendency of players, coaches, and fans to exhibit behavior usually associated with the larger sports world. Although the rare black athlete, such as Jim Brown, had played the schoolboy and collegian game during the 1950s, college lacrosse had long been an elite white sport with a tolerated minority of Indians. When Brown had played lacrosse during his senior year at Syracuse University, he had become the focus of attention on campus and throughout the lacrosse world. After all, he was a football All-American with a professional career ahead of him. During lacrosse season Brown defined what later became a common practice that was part of the unwritten code of black college and pro athletes: get a white girlfriend. While such a woman may have served a man like Brown as a prize, a status symbol, or a racial statement of power directed against jealous, fearful white men, this black athlete's choice of female companionship indicated the clout of his celebrity status. One day during Brown's final spring on campus, he defied spectator expectations by driving his white girlfriend around in his convertible. "I put down the top, drove to Archibald Stadium where I had a lacrosse game," Brown recalled in 1989. "All the fans were out on the road. We drove real slow, parked my car. I walked my girl to her seat in the bleachers, gave her a kiss, went down to change. Stands were so quiet you could hear time crawl."[83]

After the birth of the predominantly black Morgan State University program in 1969, intercollegiate lacrosse ceased to be racially homogeneous. In 1975 Morgan State handed top-ranked Washington and Lee its first regular season loss in three years. "They never did get over that," Morgan State coach Chip Silverman recalled. "You have to put it into perspective. A bunch of Blacks went down there and beat them at *their* game."[84] Regardless, black athletes only trickled into lacrosse, mainly because football, basketball, and baseball offered inner-city youth dreams of greater economic opportunities. "I'm sure finances and exposure had a lot to do with minorities not playing," Jim Brown observed in 1993. "When I played, I never saw another black player. The great black athletes wanted to get into the money sports."[85] One black student at Baltimore City College during the 1970s, Kurt Schmoke, eventually played for Yale, attended Oxford University on a Rhodes Scholarship, and became mayor of Baltimore.[86] Moreover, according to former All-American University of Baltimore midfielder and later Morgan State coach Sheldon Freed, black athletes felt no compulsion to try a sport "perceived as an elite, preppy sport."[87] For many years in Baltimore, older proponents of the game maintained social and racial barriers. "I didn't experience many racial slurs, but you don't have to call me names to make me feel uncomfortable," one African-American enthusiast declared in 1993. "They didn't exclude just blacks, but all minorities and poor whites, too."[88] However, by the late 1980s and 1990s black athletes had joined high school squads throughout the Northeast.[89]

Advocates of a more democratic game did not fully anticipate the consequences of their zeal. During the final two decades of the century, all sports fans found themselves bombarded with stories about multi-million-dollar contracts, a win-at-all-costs mentality, off-field criminal activities by players, boorish on-field behavior, and a growing connection between athletes and product endorsements. Organized lacrosse eventually experienced these new cultural forces. The massive expansion of the game was part of the problem. In previous decades the relatively small size of the field lacrosse community had created a world in which players might know each other throughout their interscholastic, intercollegiate, and club careers. With larger numbers of participants, the feeling of familiarity lessened. By the 1990s many coaches and sportswriters noticed a new ethic among many suburban athletes. The older aristocratic overtones of the game may have appealed to the new generation players, but many were attracted to the fast-paced tempo and roughness of the game. Their "unsportsmanlike" behaviors and attitudes included "chest-thumping," "showboating," and "trash-talking"; fistfighting and mass brawling; tantrums, whining, and disrespect for referees; intentional use of illegal equipment; overspecialization; and a heightened form of competitiveness. According to one Vermont high school coach who was interviewed for a 1995 article, "Kids come to the game with all kinds of attitude now. Some guy makes an average play and he's getting in your face. It's everywhere."[90] Another fan from New York believed lacrosse was becoming too similar to other more popular sports: "Those who think that humiliating opposing players by taunting and trash-talking is 'fun' should go play basketball."[91] Critics of the new mentality pointed to parents, who placed more pressures on coaches, as partially responsible. Some lived vicariously through their children, while the possibility of an athletic scholarship motivated others. In 1999 former Johns Hopkins lacrosse coach and athletic director Bob Scott said too many young players stressed sports at the expense of church and family: "We have pushed it too much and placed way too much emphasis on achieving greatness early."[92]

Lacrosse organizers realized that they had a crisis on their hands, one that had converged with a growing realization that their sport needed professional leadership and fund-raising to keep pace with the larger numbers of new participants and supporters. The sport had become too "popular" to continue using older models of administration. Besides, a well-managed system might bring about the marriage of the old notion of amateurism with a socially inclusive ethos. As early as 1992, both the president and the executive director of the Lacrosse Foundation proposed the idea of a national governing body in the United States. In 1994 consultant Michael Harrigan offered organizers a plan of reorganization and consolidation for more efficient administration, development, and financial planning. The new organizational paradigm called for gender-specific divisions to govern the respective versions of the sport, but all administrative, membership, marketing, communications, insurance, and fund-raising activities would be gender neutral. The men's and women's divisions would have jurisdiction over rules at the youth and club levels, but not at the interscholastic and intercollegiate levels.

The Lacrosse Foundation spearheaded these reorganization efforts. *Lacrosse Magazine* editor Keith Maynard clearly outlined the problem: "A wave of lacrosse popularity is at crest and it can carry us a long way. But if we fail to act, we might find ourselves on the back side of an ebbing swell. Or worse, the wave may crash over us while we debate philosophy and tread water." For Maynard, there was a great sense of urgency: "The resulting chaos may be difficult to recover from and could even crush us all in our present incarnations."[93] One by one, organizations voted to integrate themselves under a new governing body: U.S. Lacrosse, Inc. Formed in September 1997, it became operational the following January, with Stenersen as the interim and then permanent executive director. The first to join included the Lacrosse Foundation, postcollegian club leagues, and youth organizers; then came coaches, referees, and intercollegiate and interscholastic organizers. However, the coaches of the USILA remained outside the jurisdiction of U.S. Lacrosse. The leadership of the United States Women's Lacrosse Association remained skeptical about the new organization, some arguing that it represented both a power grab by the Lacrosse Foundation and an effort by men to seize control of the women's game. Despite passionate debate among the women, in March 1998 the USWLA's executive board voted 34–2 to join. Eventually most delegates felt comfortable with the new structure's guarantee of female control over the distinct features of the women's game. They also realized that the new organization promised greater opportunities for expansion of their game.[94]

The proponents of an amateur ethos of sport for sport's sake with a socially inclusive worldview achieved a major victory with the creation of U.S. Lacrosse. The notion of lacrosse as an exclusive game for gentlemen and ladies—the symbolic descendants of the "noble savage"—that was found only on the playing fields of elite universities and preparatory schools was dead. The coaches and athletes from suburban, middle- and working-class America simply outnumbered the old-timers who remembered when club lacrosse games played by white-collar athletes armed with wooden sticks had attracted thousands of fans. Moreover, the new leadership of organized lacrosse, led by men like Stenersen, placed a high priority on middle-class suburbanites, inner-city youth, and other sportsmen and -women who lived outside the Northeast and beyond the continent's shores. Depending on what happened in the future, this development had the potential to be one of the most important turning points in the history of lacrosse for a century and a half. However, anxieties about the paths the lacrosse community would take in the future certainly did not disappear. In 1999 *Lacrosse Magazine* editor Marc Bouchard hypothesized, perhaps too late, that the growth of the sport might lead to its adopting a sporting culture that would be indistinguishable from the cultures of all other commercialized team sports: "Will we someday romanticize about the 'good old days' when lacrosse was just a game?"[95]

Selling the Fastest Game on Two Feet:
Attempting Professional Lacrosse

The Canadian Lacrosse Association continued to administer the nominally amateur game of box lacrosse in British Columbia, Ontario, and Quebec, as it had since the 1930s. Beginning in the late 1960s, however, entrepreneurs tried to capitalize on the violent dimensions of the game and challenge Canadian governing bodies for players and spectators. With franchises in Canada and the United States, a short-lived National Lacrosse Association began play in 1968 with eight franchises: the Detroit Olympics, Montreal Canadiens, Toronto Maple Leafs, and Peterborough Lakers in the East and the Portland Adanacs, Vancouver Carlings, Victoria Shamrocks, and New Westminster Salmonbellies in the West. Most of the clubs were actually former amateur Canadian clubs that had decided to go professional. Throwing their support behind the new league in the spring of 1968, the editors of *International Lacrosse Magazine* declared: "Purists mouth the word 'professional' with the sort of distaste usually reserved for 'purse snatcher' and 'kidnapper.' Their feeling seems to be that the rape of lacrosse is imminent, spoiling it once and for all for the innocent and pure of heart." Reflecting a sense of optimism, the editors argued: "Professionalism never spoiled anything that didn't have one foot in the grave to begin with. And lacrosse has never been healthier."[96]

Unfortunately, the league folded the following March, when Montreal, Chicago, and Boston businessmen decided not to invest in existing or expansion franchises.[97] Entrepreneurs tried again a few years later, once again by heavily relying upon amateur teams turning pro. In 1972 a new National Lacrosse League came into existence that included the Brantford Warriors, Peterborough Lakers, Windsor Warlocks, and Toronto Shooting Stars in the East and the Victoria Shamrocks, Vancouver Burrards, New Westminster Salmonbellies, and Coquitlam Adanacs in the West.[98] Given the poor track record of professional lacrosse in Toronto and the summertime competition for leisure dollars, the *Toronto Sun* predicted failure: "How the heck can you expect to drag people away from their summer cottages to watch a lacrosse game in a hot arena?"[99] The prediction panned out; the hometown Shooting Stars averaged only twelve hundred fans per game, well below the twenty-three hundred needed for the franchise to break even.[100] In the span of a half decade, pro lacrosse had failed twice.

Apparently box lacrosse enjoyed intense loyalty from a segment of the Canadian population that simply could or would not support an openly professional version of the sport. In August 1973 *Maclean's* magazine captured the social, cultural, and economic essence of the game. According to former Huntsville, Ontario, player Roy MacGregor, "Lacrosse always has been town against town, not team against team. The sport is an expression of rural envy and indignation. The chippiness, the cockiness of winning and the shame of losing are perfectly matched to the rural ethos, the never-back-down way of looking at life. In a small community you never really grow out of the schoolyard. The magnitude of vanity and shame is entirely dependent on the number of people who might recognize you the next morning on the street." For MacGregor, toughness mattered more than talent. "It's a beer-drinker's game. A road trip to another town usually meant a cold case of 24 opened from the bottom to make sure cops only saw a closed top. It's a bluffer's sport. What you get away with counts more than reality."[101]

Acknowledging the limited appeal of box lacrosse, MacGregor predicted that the professional game would inevitably fail: "Lacrosse is fine for small arenas, but it's like pornography: either you can't get enough or you never want to see it. And the big cities will never find enough fanatics to fill even a medium-sized arena." In urban areas professional baseball reigned supreme during box lacrosse's summer season. While small Ontario cities such as Brantford and Windsor supported clubs, larger cities such as Toronto would not. In British Columbia, when one Vancouver club moved its home arena from "the upper-middle-class area, to the Forum, down in the workingman's haunts," as MacGregor observed, attendance increased. Even with this limited success, box lacrosse failed to capture the interest of Canadians with larger disposable incomes: "It seems people with much money to spend are using it to relax with air conditioners or get out of the city entirely rather than swelter in stuffy arenas." For those enthusiasts who did support box lacrosse, the game was more than mere entertainment. In MacGregor's view, "Lacrosse will remain a small-town game. It's ritual tribal warfare more than a game, a gut involvement more than spectator sport. The big cities want to play games; lacrosse defends the honor of a town. Big cities, it seems, have lost the passion for such pursuits."[102]

Despite early failures at pro box lacrosse, commercial ice hockey operators launched their own effort to professionalize the game in 1974 by

creating another National Lacrosse League. What motivated these businessmen was the same thing that had motivated the inventors of box
lacrosse during the Great Depression: a desire to cater to idle hockey fans
waiting for the winter. Bruce Norris, who also owned the Detroit Red Wings
and chaired the National Hockey League's board of governors, headed a
National Lacrosse League (NLL) franchise in Toronto, while Tad Potter of
the Pittsburgh Penguins operated one in Rochester.[103] Because the league's
owners believed the roughneck Canadian game would please American
hockey fans, Canadians comprised about 60 percent of all league players,
despite the fact that only two of the six franchises represented Canadian
cities. Only 30 percent of the players came from the American college ranks;
the remaining tenth came from box lacrosse clubs in upstate New York.
Some teams also recruited pro hockey players with lacrosse experience,
such as Rick Dudley of the Buffalo Sabres. Although the NLL claimed major league status, with franchises in two provinces and three states, three of
the four American franchises were actually based in southern Ontario,
earning the new circuit a reputation as a "carpetbagging" league. The
players of the Maryland Arrows, Syracuse Stingers, and Philadelphia Wings
resided in or around the Ontario cities of Oshawa, Brantford, and Peterborough, respectively. The league transported them to American cities for
"home" contests because of the unwillingness or inability of the Canadians
to abandon their full-time jobs in Ontario.[104]

Despite owners' hopes that box lacrosse would satisfy the summer ap-
petites of ice hockey fans, support for the league remained poor throughout the premier campaign. Although some owners believed franchises
needed to average 5,500 fans per game to break even, only the Philadelphia
Wings (8,737), Montreal Les Quebecois (6,934), and Maryland Arrows
(6,689) attracted sufficient crowds. Meanwhile, the dismal attendance
records of the Rochester Griffins (2,764), Syracuse Stingers (2,582), and
Toronto Tomahawks (2,102) pointed to the league's financial frailty.[105] Several familiar factors accounted for the poor attendance in Toronto: the option of watching games on local television, the lack of air conditioning in
the arena, competition from area amateur leagues, youth hockey camps,
and the tendency of affluent Canadians to take up residence at private cottages for the summer.[106] According to NLL commissioner and attorney G.
Spence Lyons, "We've talked it over many, many times and come up with a
hundred theories. One is that the sport is not socially acceptable."[107]

The NLL's relationship with Native American box lacrosse teams also explained the pro circuit's shortcomings. One year before the formation of the NLL, many of the all-native North American Lacrosse Association's reservation teams had already adopted nearby cities as their off-reservation homes to attract larger crowds. The Caughnawaga Indians moved to Montreal, the Onondaga team relocated to Syracuse, and the Tuscarora club played in Niagara Falls.[108] In Syracuse, competition between natives and the NLL resulted in a pyrrhic victory for the hometown Stingers. The owners of the 1974 Stingers—Richard and Henry Wells of the Syracuse Vending Company and dentist Arnold Baum—had sponsored a club of predominantly Onondaga Indians called the Syracuse Warriors in 1973. When the group secured the Stingers, they abandoned the Warriors and forced them out of the Syracuse War Memorial and back to their reservation dirt box facility. Despite winning the NALA title over Six Nations, the Warriors averaged only three hundred spectators during the 1974 regular season, as opposed to the three thousand they had drawn in downtown Syracuse in 1972. Warriors coach Clyde Jacques cited the uncooperative mood of Stingers management: "We could have helped each other, but they didn't want to do anything for us," Jacques said. "They called our league the beer league because we're Indians."[109]

Warriors player and NALA president Oliver Hill attacked the Stingers management in the Syracuse press in October. Believing that the NLL had tampered with "the classic game" of the Indians, Hill wrote: "Incidentally, Henry Wells . . . professes to like Indian 'boys' and to have invited Indian 'kids' to play for him because 'when it comes to athletes and women, I'm color blind.' Well as that black man said in Mississippi, 'How big do you grow "boys" around here?' Some of the 'boys' Wells was talking about are in their thirties. I only mention the remarks as a revelation of the Stinger attitude which doomed any cooperation." Hill was also critical of the NLL's style of play: "I hope you won't mind my objection to your description of 'the Stingers' faster and finesse-filled style of lacrosse' as opposed to the Warriors' 'tougher and slower version.' The Stingers are faster—but that ain't necessarily 'finesse'; we call it 'hyping the game' for people who are unsophisticated about lacrosse." The following week the Syracuse press linked poor spectator support to poor management: "The players waited for management to shape up while management waited for the fans' support and the fans waited for the players to win. And the league waited for all. Consequently, few games were won; management never got it together, and the fans never came. Then, the league said 'move.'"[110] For the 1975 campaign the Stingers became the Quebec City Caribous, while the champion Rochester Griffins were transformed into the Boston Bolts and the Tomahawks migrated to Long Island. The league folded in February 1976, despite the financial success of the Maryland, Philadelphia, and Quebec City franchises.[111]

Amid the ashes of the failed pro leagues, amateur and semiprofessional box lacrosse survived during the 1970s and 1980s at the senior and junior levels in small cities across Canada; in the less affluent suburbs of Vancouver, Victoria, and Toronto; and in Iroquois communities in New York, Ontario, and Quebec. Box lacrosse partisans maintained a sport without mass appeal. According to Canadian lacrosse historian David Savelieff, "It's not an elitist sport. . . . There aren't too many millionaires in the sport. It's a down-to-earth type of game."[112] In 1991 Canadian Lacrosse Association technical director Michael Lachappelle expressed frustration with the limited appeal of lacrosse in his country: "We also want them to learn about the game as part of Canadian history, and create players and fans. It's sad that for most people, the sum total of the history of lacrosse is that Pontiac used a lacrosse game to destroy Fort Michilimackinac."[113] By pointing to the power of mythology in twentieth-century Canada, Lachappelle was suggesting that his game had become merely part of the nation's folklore.

The Rise of the Major Indoor Lacrosse League in the Age of ESPN

Although businessmen in Canada and the United States failed to establish any long-lasting professional league during the 1970s, promoters achieved success in the next decade. A new Major Indoor Lacrosse League embraced a radically different entrepreneurial and promotional system, one based on a revolutionary single-entity ownership model. It resulted not from the efforts of box lacrosse organizers in Canada, pro hockey franchise owners, or field lacrosse enthusiasts from Baltimore, Long Island, or upstate New York, but from the efforts of promoters of mass commercial spectacles. Monster truck and rock concert promoter Chris Fritz of Kansas City conceived his plan during the early 1980s. He envisioned a new sport called "rollercross," which would combine features of box lacrosse with those of a roller derby. The science fiction film *Rollerball* (1975) had provided inspiration for Fritz. Set in the near future, the film starred James Caan and featured a sport with boisterous crowds egging on roller skaters and motorcyclists riding around a roller rink to score goals, maiming and even killing each other. Eventually Fritz settled for a type of entertainment experience that mixed box lacrosse with loud music, prize giveaways, and fan-participation halftime activities, with the game played during the winter rather than the summer.[114]

Recognizing the influence of television on sports fans, Fritz created a new type of live arena experience. Television had already affected organized professional team sports in a variety of ways since the 1960s. It had provided impetus for the formation of rival leagues, all-sports cable channels, such as the Entertainment and Sports Programming Network (ESPN), and pseudosports designed for television. More important, by televising events to millions of home viewers, networks had also changed the expectations of live spectators.[115] After all, television broadcasters showered viewers with instant replays, game statistics, and interviews with players and coaches as they watched games in the comfort of their own homes armed with refrigerators full of food and drinks. As a result, entertainment entrepreneurs felt obligated to alter the live sporting experience for spectators. The actual athletic contest became merely one component of a sports event. Although Fritz had seen few lacrosse games in his life, he joined with motor sports promoter and former Kansas City Chiefs marketing executive Russ Cline to launch an eleven-game, ten-city International Box Lacrosse Association "Super Series" tour of American and Canadian all-stars in 1985. Fritz and Cline hoped to attract field lacrosse enthusiasts, but they targeted a more general audience.[116] The relative success of the tour motivated them to create a formal league, but the numerous failures of other leagues remained in the forefront of their minds.

Fritz and Cline selected four northeastern cities to host franchises of their Eagle Pro Box Lacrosse League for their premier season, which began in early 1987. The teams were the Baltimore Thunder, Washington (D.C.) Wave, Philadelphia Wings, and New Jersey (East Rutherford) Saints. These teams played a six-game regular season and play-offs. Fritz and Cline had chosen the latter three sites because of the great potential for crossover support from ice hockey enthusiasts; only the Thunder hoped to attract field lacrosse fans. To maximize profits, Fritz and Cline introduced a single-entity ownership system whereby they owned all of the franchises. They renamed their Eagle League the Major Indoor Lacrosse League (MILL) for the second season to avoid sounding like a minor league operation.[117] They also selected new cities for expansion franchises, placed a greater emphasis on arena experience and advertisements than the actual contests, and controlled player allocation, payroll, and season length. The two owners hired local general managers to carry out daily operations, but most of the profits poured into their own coffers. They placed two franchises in traditional field lacrosse areas: Maryland (the Baltimore Thunder) and Long Island (the New York Saints). Even though these franchises won the first two league titles, respectively, neither was a consistent box office champion. Some franchises placed in hockey towns were commercially successful. In Philadelphia and Buffalo, for example, the Wings and Bandits routinely attracted crowds in excess of 15,000 and occasionally as large as 18,000 for several years. In 1993 the Bandits sold out every game at 16,325 en route to their second championship in only their second season. No American college or Canadian club could attract such crowds. However, the owners pulled the plug on teams in traditional hockey cities that were experiencing meager attendance: the teams in Washington, Detroit, Pittsburgh, and Boston. Ironically, one of the league's premier cities was Rochester, New York, home of minor league franchises in several sports, which regularly packed arenas for Knighthawks games. As a result of its various successes and failures in different markets, the league did not grow much during its first ten seasons.

Regardless of market, the MILL advertised a uniform "product" to the public, especially during the early campaigns of the league. Initially Fritz and Cline knew that their league would not receive a lucrative television contract. To attract fans they marketed their league directly to the public. "We put together a very aggressive, extensive promotion and advertising package and promoted the sport just as we would an event, as opposed to promoting it as a season," Cline said. "We made the assumption we would not get coverage."[118] Fritz and Cline portrayed their league as featuring an exciting, bone-crunching sport played to loud music. Fistfights and violent collisions took center stage. "That first year was vicious," remembered veteran goal tender Kevin Bilger. "Guys were getting boarded all over the place, and as a goalie, you were always a target."[119]

Along with the image of a roaring lion, early television advertisements featured ancient Roman gladiators followed by modern lacrosse players, each putting on protective armor. Then, over a series of cross-checks, a narrator preached that the league "makes Sunday football look like a cabbage patch picnic!" The narrator said the object of this new game was not merely victory, but survival. In 1987 Fritz and Cline spent over $1 million "on advertising aimed at blue-collar fans of ice hockey, pro wrestling and Rambo." According to Cline, "The average person thinks lacrosse is a rich kids' game. . . . We're trying to sell box to the masses as an exciting concept—an aggressively played contact sport, a working-class sport, a man's game."[120] More socially elite commentators believed the game played by the MILL differed greatly from the field game. "Unlike its blue-blooded brother," *Echelon* magazine observed, "box is billed as a brutal, working man's sport."[121] Even the radio advertisements—sounding very much like monster truck or pro wrestling ads—emphasized bone-crunching hits. According to a demographic study of MILL spectators in 1993, 52 percent of the fans possessed at least bachelor's degrees and 42 percent earned incomes of $45,000 or more; 21 percent earned at least $75,000. Compared to club lacrosse cliques in the Northeast, MILL patrons were definitely less affluent and more heterogeneous in socioeconomic status. Thirty-one percent of ticket holders possessed only grade school or high school educations, but only three percent of the people were under the age of eighteen. This discrepancy suggests that a significant number of fans worked in blue-collar or service-sector occupations.[122] These new enthusiasts might have been ice hockey fans who had not been able to pay for NHL tickets or part of a young MTV generation that was looking for a spectator experience that did not require a complete understanding of the rules of lacrosse.

As attendance increased in some cities and a base of season ticket holders emerged, the MILL began to emphasize skill as much as violence.[123] The primary catalyst for this shift from brute force to finesse was the signing of Canadian-born All-American scoring threats Gary and Paul Gait of Syracuse University. These twins from British Columbia had helped Syracuse win consecutive national titles from 1988 to 1990, dazzled crowds with their acrobatic movements and eventually played postcollegiate club field lacrosse in the United States and summer box lacrosse in Canada, opened an equipment company, and conducted youth clinics. Some fans referred to them as the "Michael Jordans" of lacrosse. Gary perfected a scoring move akin to a basketball slam dunk, leaping around from the back of the goal net without violating the crease. Copycat collegians inspired the NCAA to ban this dangerous "Air Gait" move in 1998. When the MILL assigned the Gait brothers to the Detroit Turbos for the 1991 season, the field lacrosse community took a closer look at the seemingly disreputable pro game. Aside from winning the league championship in Detroit as rookies, the Gaits increased interest in the MILL among live spectators and television audiences alike. However, the two brothers rarely stayed in the same place for very long. By the 2000 season they had moved around so often that they had played in the uniforms of six different teams, including three franchises in which they had played together as teammates. The impact of Gary and Paul Gait can be seen by examining the league's television exposure. In 1987 cable television systems in Baltimore and Philadelphia had broadcast six tape-delayed MILL games to an estimated audience of about one million people. After the Gait brothers joined the league in 1991, fifteen million people in forty-nine different television markets witnessed fourteen games. By 1992 the league had exposure in over fifty markets, with a viewership of twenty-six million.[124]

Another focal point of the Fritz and Cline ownership program was a contrived arena experience. Their focus on "game presentation" included loud music—hard rock anthems such as Queen's "We Will Rock You" for male spectators and fan-participation songs such as the Village People's "YMCA" for women, teenagers, and children—as well as orchestrated prize giveaways, halftime shows, and scantily clad cheerleaders. Drowning out many fan-initiated chants, MILL game announcers carefully directed and manipulated crowd noise, exaggerating the pronunciation of a player's name, telling people what and when to cheer, and frequently asking, "Are ya havin' fun?" The rock concert–like environment of MILL contests made it impossible for fans to hear the expected sounds of athletic contests: communication between players and coaches and fans yelling out to specific players. Eventually, in some arenas fans became complacent, speaking up only after goals, during fistfights, or whenever the announcer told them to stand up and "Make some noise!"

Field lacrosse supporters were either annoyed with the nonstop music and banter or became converts of the new hyped sporting experience. Many others simply found the MILL's version of lacrosse offensive. For example, in 1987 the editors of *Lacrosse* magazine said that the new league "often reflects the worst human elements."[125] In 1996 Syracuse University coach Roy Simmons, Jr., said, "It's a great billboard but I'm not sure it's the right message."[126] Casual spectators of the MILL's games and curious hockey enthusiasts became excited by the game atmosphere but didn't take the sport seriously, converted into lacrosse fans, or grew bored. Regardless, the inherent problems with the MILL's game presentation included the lack of any significant effort to instruct spectators about lacrosse and establish meaningful spectator-player ties. Instead the league taught people to enjoy an evening of sports entertainment. Some spectators thought the emphasis on fast tempo and violent play, loud music, and an announcer trying to manage crowd behavior made the game's athletic feats incidental to the contest. By not emphasizing fan education or promoting the sport, Fritz and Cline created an undesired consequence: for some spectators, the novelty eventually wore off. For a variety of reasons, the Buffalo Bandits had lost half of their spectators by the late 1990s. More cynical fans with a sophisticated eye for officiating could not help but think that the league manipulated the conduct and outcome of games. Pointing to inconsistent rules enforcement, fans concocting conspiracy theories said that the owners must be instructing the referees to call no penalties on teams that were down by three goals or more in the second half. Moreover, without proper rules enforcement, one *Lacrosse Magazine* columnist hypothesized, "The MILL is in danger of drifting into the twilight zone of roller derby and pro 'rasslin' (without the latter's conspicuous financial bonanza)."[127]

Aiming to avoid high player salaries, Fritz and Cline also established a system to carefully control the allocation and movement of players, basing pay on tenure in the league rather than talent, keeping the season relatively short, and limiting staff expenses by contracting ticket sales and game promotion to local arena operators.[128] Embracing incremental growth, Fritz and Cline paid all players $100 per game, regardless of performance, during the first season. They granted pay raises to players retained from season to season. Furthermore, the short regular season schedule—always a dozen or fewer games—and low pay ensured that playing lacrosse could be only a part-time occupation. Most players assented to the plan because they saw the league as an opportunity to continue their playing careers, promote the sport, and make some extra cash to supplement their full-time jobs. Perplexed by the owners' assertions that profits were small despite playing before packed crowds in Philadelphia and Buffalo, and perhaps inspired by their contemporary baseball and football brethren who had successfully negotiated for higher wages, some MILL players called for raises, merit-based pay, and individual franchise ownership to stimulate bidding wars. Although players rejected a bid to join the Teamsters' Union in 1992, they did

form their own MILL Players Association the following year. Relations between labor and management were characterized by periodic threatened
work stoppages and modest pay raises. For example, by 1996 pay had been
increased to $225 to $700 per game, depending on tenure. In the end, most
players realized that a strike was not worth the possibility of a league shut-
down.[129] They also realized that they had little authority over the game as
athletes. Fatalistic players accepted their lot. "If we go on strike," one player
observed, "they'll have 18 new players in here tomorrow."[130]

Despite meager pay increases, the brevity of the schedule guaranteed
that no player would earn a living from the MILL. On occasion the league
emphasized the notion that MILL players were "regular guys." Press coverage noted the full-time employment of many athletes. In February 1990 the
New York Times characterized the moonlighting New York Saints players
as an "assemblage of salesmen, carpenters, firefighters and investment
bankers."[131] Less than a year earlier, the *Sporting News* had described the
starting lineup of the Saints, emphasizing the social class of the white
players and the race of an Indian by asking: "What do mailman Mike Nelson, foreign bonds broker Kevin Cook, full-blooded Iroquois tribesman
Mikko Red Arrow, physical education teacher Kevin Huff, carpenter Rich
Mullen and law clerk Larry Quinn have in common?"[132] By ignoring Red
Arrow's occupation as an assistant district attorney, the paper emphasized
the age-old white fascination with the "noble savage."

Because Fritz and Cline operated the MILL as a single entity, without
competing owners' engaging in bidding wars for players, the league's pay
scale remained low. All players were temporary employees assigned to local
teams. By centralizing the ownership of teams and the direction of league
operations, the league eliminated significant disparities among teams and
promoted stable fiscal growth.[133] This monopolistic model of ownership—
clearly different from the models of Major League Baseball, the National Football League, the National Basketball Association, and the
National Hockey League—was remarkably similar to the model of "professional" wrestling organizations such as the World Wrestling Federation. Although centralized authority provided Fritz and Cline with obvious advantages, especially control of the rate of development, the system was not
without problems. After all, the owners could not possibly be sensitive to
local market conditions from their headquarters in Kansas City. In January
1995, for instance, one Blazers player told the *Boston Herald* that centraliza-

tion hindered local development: "Until the league starts selling off some franchises and gets aggressive owners, it isn't going to grow much more."[134]

With its unique blend of commercial spectacle and professional sport, the MILL relied upon an inexpensive workforce of coaches and players, centralized administrative control from a headquarters in Kansas City that was located far from its markets, and a tendency to close down any franchise that was not quickly producing profits. The unwillingness of Fritz and Cline to engage in significant market expansion, sell off franchises to individual owners, or pay players according to merit exposed the league's vulnerabilities to a challenger. During the summer of 1997 a new National Lacrosse League that had been founded by a few professional ice hockey team owners attracted Gary and Paul Gait away from the MILL by offering them five-year playing, consulting, and marketing contracts. After brief posturing by the two leagues to play separate campaigns in 1998, the MILL and NLL owners decided to avoid a head-to-head league war akin to other recent confrontations, agreeing to a merger in late July. The new league retained the NLL moniker; expanded the playing season to twelve games; revised the play-off format to grant home-field advantage to teams with better win-loss records rather than to those with the highest attendance numbers; retained franchises in most former MILL markets and added teams in Syracuse and Hamilton, Ontario; outlined vague plans for expansion elsewhere; and allowed Fritz, Cline, and a newer MILL partner each to own one of the league's franchises.[135] Franchise instability did not disappear, however; for the 1999 season the Hamilton franchise became the Toronto Rock. The immediate success of the Rock, with back-to-back titles and capacity crowds, resulted in heightened interest in the game throughout Canada. The Baltimore experiment was abandoned the following year, when the Thunder became the Pittsburgh Crossfire for a season before moving back south to become the Washington (D.C.) Power. Other hockey cities given franchises included Albany, New York, and Columbus, Ohio. After the completion of the 2001 season, the NLL decided to expand into Calgary, Vancouver, Montreal, and New Jersey.

The relative successes of the Major Indoor Lacrosse League no doubt inspired others to contemplate the possibility of succeeding with professional outdoor lacrosse. The first attempt was a disaster. In November 1987 former Adelphi player Terry Wallace convinced investors and prospective general managers of the commercial viability of his new American Lacrosse

League (ALL). The teams possessed nicknames evoking strong images of Indians and frontiersmen. Beginning in April 1988 with six franchises—the Baltimore Tribe, New Jersey Arrows, Long Island Sachems, Boston Militia, Syracuse Spirit, and Denver Rifles—the league lasted a matter of weeks. The league's general managers had not realized that Wallace intended to run the league using gate receipts to cover costs. His stated investment of $2 million had been a ruse; he had hoped to sell off the franchises and make a profit. However, a long line of creditors, including utilities and real estate agents, showed the weak foundation of the league.[136] Not for another decade was professional field lacrosse attempted again. "Body by Jake Enterprises" executive Jake Steinfeld launched an all-star Summer Showcase in the summer of 2000 to test the appeal of Major League Lacrosse (MLL), proposed for the following year. Originally from Long Island, Steinfeld had been a face-off specialist at Cortland State before establishing his California-based physical fitness empire, which included the sale of exercise merchandise, as well as television programming and personal training. Unlike any of the professional indoor leagues or the failed ALL, his new MLL enjoyed strong financial support and the endorsement of prominent field lacrosse enthusiasts.[137] The new league opened in June 2001 with six franchises: the Baltimore Bayhawks, Boston Cannons, Bridgeport (Connecticut) Barrage, Long Island Lizards, New Jersey Pride, and Rochester Rattlers. By combining recent college graduates with older players, including Gary and Paul Gait, the Lizards won the first league championship.

The massive expansion of intercollegiate and interscholastic lacrosse had produced ever-larger numbers of middle-class and working-class athletes who had little in common with enthusiasts of the gentleman's game of yesteryear. With the rise of major professional sports in general and of professional lacrosse in particular, many young collegians had begun dreaming of making money playing their favorite sport. In a feature on native and non-native lacrosse for the *New Yorker* magazine, John Seabrook placed his finger on the pulse of many young players: "Amateurism, which once served the ruling class as a way of excluding the people it didn't want to play with, now excludes the younger members of the ruling class from the ESPN sports culture that they want to belong to. The Team U.S.A. members I spoke to appeared a bit sheepish about not being able to make a living from lacrosse; not getting paid for your sport, it seems, places you lower in the status hierarchy than professional athletes."[138] Even though lacrosse organizers and coaches had fought off the culture of professionalism for decades, the late-century popularization of their sport had made it ripe for possible commercial and professional intrusion.

Playing for the Creator: Lacrosse and the Revitalization of Iroquoia

The modern sport of lacrosse had entered more fully into the larger world of mainstream American consumerism than had the old version of the game, but the old Indian game contributed to the survival of a Native American agenda. The activist pan-Indian nationalism movement of the 1960s and 1970s resulted in the extension of the game into several arenas of cultural politics, including relations between Iroquoia and the white man's world, as well as among Indians themselves. Some Iroquois peoples supported pan-Indian activities such as the American Indian Movement and attended protests at Wounded Knee II in 1973. As did most other native communities at the end of the century, the Iroquois found themselves divided into often misnamed "traditionalist" and "progressive" factions. Whereas the former wanted to achieve tribal revitalization via historical cultural institutions and systems, the latter believed that political, cultural, and economic autonomy could be realized only if native entrepreneurs exploited commercial opportunities. However much these factions warred with one another through their words or actions, they both promoted Indian sovereignty. Their leadership simply differed: "traditional" chiefs versus businessmen.

Knowing the origins of the Longhouse faith is crucial for understanding life in Iroquoia at this time. After the political devastation of the Iroquois Confederacy during the late eighteenth century, U.S. authorities had forced the Iroquois peoples onto reservations. Finding themselves no longer a dominant military power in the Northeast, the Iroquois endured alcoholism, domestic violence, confused gender roles, unstable family households, and cultural depression. In 1799 the visions of Seneca prophet Handsome Lake had led to the formation of a reformed Longhouse religion that taught Indians to reject intemperance, witchcraft, tribal infighting, sexual promiscuity, and wagering.[139] Throughout the next two centuries, natives not permanently converted to Christianity adhered to Lake's faith, a hybrid of pre–Revolutionary War Iroquois religion and the Protestant reform agenda of the Second Great Awakening. By the 1970s the Longhouse was contributing to a cultural revitalization movement. However, in reaction to the growing influence of the Longhouse on Mohawk reservations, young men on the Kahnawake Reservation advanced the paramilitary Warrior Society. This group regarded the Longhouse as a false native religion because of its indirect connection to Christianity and contended that all tribal governments were the white man's lackeys. Labeled fascist by other Indians, the Warriors possessed firearms, which made them influential players in Iroquois politics. In 1973 the Warrior Society launched an eviction campaign, telling about one thousand non-native residents to leave Kahnawake. After Mohawks occupied a particular house, Quebec Provincial Police arrived and made seven arrests. When the authorities refused to release anyone, rioting broke out, with Mohawks attacking police vehicles. Eventually both sides agreed to depart. In the settlement, twelve Mohawks accused of rioting were fingerprinted, photographed, and released. "With this final ludicrous ceremony," the local *Akwesasne Notes* commented, "the current chapter of the struggle of the Iroquois to retain some part of North America for their nations moved into the courts, hardly a place to resolve the difference between two peoples."[140] The editors also published a political cartoon depicting an Indian warrior with "Reds" across his shirt *cradling a lacrosse stick*. Inside the stick pocket was a white man about to be tossed off the reservation.

Native newspapers were not alone in recognizing the political significance of using sport to make symbolic statements. During the 1970s Indian activists protested the use of native monikers and mascots by professional sports franchises, universities and colleges, and high schools. The Cleveland Indians, Washington Redskins, and Atlanta Braves became obvious targets. Ironically, however, several box lacrosse teams representing Iroquois reservations used some of the very same names, including the Saint Regis Braves, Caughnawaga Indians, Onondaga/Syracuse Warriors, and Six Nations Chiefs. The Tonawanda Reservation near Akron used their tribal name, Senecas, for their team. The Tuscarora had turned to a weapon for their team name, the Niagara Falls Arrows; the Cattaraugus had chosen a winged creature important to the traditional Iroquois worldview for theirs, the Newtown Golden Eagles.[141] Just as some Native Americans proudly wore Kansas City Chiefs ball caps, Florida Seminoles sweatshirts, or Cleveland "Property of the Indians" T-shirts, the box lacrosse teams chose nicknames that amounted to native assertions of their authority over Indian symbols and images generated by non-natives.

Other more scholarly Indians focused on writing books that presented a modern native interpretation of the past, especially in the areas of culture, language, education, and land claims, to counter historical works produced by non-natives. By the 1970s very little had been written on the history of lacrosse. What did exist had been generated mostly by white coaches, sportswriters, and anthropologists. To challenge this trend, in 1978 the North American Indian Travelling College at Akwesasne published a book professing a "traditionalist," Longhouse-oriented view of the origins and cultural meaning of the game. The project exemplified a rare attempt to transliterate and publish part of the oral native tradition. While some natives frowned on *Tewaarathon (Lacrosse)* as a Mohawk interpretation of the origins of Iroquois lacrosse, the work is important considering the direct connection between the Mohawk ball game played in early nineteenth-century Canada and the rules outlined by George Beers. According to Mohawk researcher and writer Ernest Benedict, the project affirmed the Indians' cultural sovereignty over the sport: "Much has been written in the record books about the accomplishment of our White brothers who admired, learned and helped develop the game into its present forms, field and box lacrosse. We appreciate their contributions, but feel that we have been pushed out of the way of recognition. We will be pushed no longer."[142]

Like the accounts of other nations, the Mohawk account described the game as a gift from the Creator: "Just as a parent will gain much amusement at the sight of watching his child playing joyfully with a new gift, so it was intended that the Creator be similarly amused by viewing his 'children' playing lacrosse in a manner which was so defiant of fatigue." Lacrosse matches had served as a means "to call the Creator's attention to the efforts of the medicine people" or "to bestow honour and respect to these members living on Mother Earth who had done great things for the Nation." They had also been played "for one's personal enjoyment and physical fitness." The Mohawk researchers also emphasized the importance of community by recounting the legend of how the winged creatures (an eagle, an owl, and a hawk) had defeated the four-legged animals (a bear, a deer, and a turtle) in the original lacrosse contest. Including an illustration of an old man telling stories to children, *Tewaarathon* described said, "Our grandfathers told us that when lacrosse was a pure game and was played for the enjoyment of the Great Spirit, everyone was important, no matter how big or how small, or how strong or how weak."[143]

Besides nostalgically envisioning an ideal era, the Travelling College's account of lacrosse implicitly deemphasized the relationship between warfare and traditional ball play. Longhouse traditionalists often accused white anthropologists and coaches who described the old game as a form of war preparation of misinterpreting the Creator's game. The facts associated with the rise of the Longhouse explain this disagreement. When modern scholars assess seventeenth- and eighteenth-century ball play among the Iroquois, they do so by acknowledging the former military and diplomatic power of the Iroquois Confederacy and the role of lacrosse in maintaining this powerful geopolitical force. By the 1970s, however, Longhouse Iroquois had conceptualized lacrosse within a worldview largely informed by the code of Handsome Lake, which had been developed after the military and diplomatic demise of the confederacy. Lake had focused on improving the spiritual and social integrity of the Iroquois, not their military strength. Although this holistic faith promoted unity and reform, it minimized the Iroquois political and military hegemony that had existed prior to the War for American Independence. Any late twentieth-century acknowledgment of the military function of traditional ball play would amount to the Indians' painful concession of the fall of their once mighty league.

Despite a "traditionalist" focus on the spiritual and social aspects of ball play, the military and diplomatic purposes of the game survived well into the late twentieth century. For instance, native box lacrosse matches featured far more individual fistfights and rough play than would be found in intercollegiate or interscholastic field lacrosse. Indian teams always had "tough guys" or "goons" whose purpose was to protect a skilled player or instigate trouble. Sometimes fights took place without regard to the needs of the moment. In other words, a native player might be willing to take a five-minute penalty even though his team was already behind or short handed. The outcome of a game and an individual's pride sometimes remained separate issues. The resulting brawls not only brought cheers from spectators and teammates, but also resembled player behavior in ball play dating back centuries, when the game had functioned as a vehicle for individual feats of virility. Moreover, late twentieth-century Indian box lacrosse had functions similar to the diplomatic functions found in the eighteenth-century game. The old game had often been used to reinforce league ties and settle territorial disputes. By the early nineteenth century, with Iroquois nations facing social upheaval and confined to isolated reservations, lacrosse devolved to an intrareservation activity. However, the introduction of the modern Canadian field game toward the end of the century, the stimulus of the Carlisle team during the 1910s, and the diffusion of box lacrosse beginning in the 1930s had all led to the reestablishment of meaningful intertribal ties. Modern lacrosse allowed Mohawks, Onondagas, and Senecas to maintain national connections.

Many of these themes—stronger inter-reservation bonds, the growing voice of traditionalists, concern for domestic reform, and assertions of native sovereignty—converged in the early 1980s with the formation of a program to represent all Iroquois peoples at the highest level of lacrosse competition. Pointing to rampant poverty, juvenile delinquency, hopelessness, and the partial demise of lacrosse on some reservations, in 1983 Onondaga faith keeper Oren Lyons and Tuscarora stick maker Wes Patterson created an inter-reservation team called the Iroquois Nationals. As a teenager Lyons had quit high school and served in the U.S. Army as a paratrooper with the 82nd Airborne Division. In 1953 he had returned to the Onondaga Reservation and sold paintings of boxers to area restaurants and bars. In search of a goal tender, Syracuse University coach Roy Simmons, Sr., took the dean of admissions to a local restaurant to show him a Lyons painting of Jack Dempsey. "That got Oren into the School of Fine Arts and I got the best goalie I ever had," Simmons recalled in 1986. Throughout his playing career at Syracuse and his tenure as a commercial artist in New York City, Lyons had been learning how a Longhouse Indian could succeed in a white man's world. Roy Simmons, Jr., Lyons's teammate and eventual successor to his father as Syracuse head coach, characterized Lyons as distinct from other Indians he knew: "He was on time, he accepted discipline. Of course, he was older when he played college lacrosse. He was about 24 years old, he had a wife and baby, he'd been around. . . . But most Indian athletes are hard to read. Stoic. Never cry or admit pain. Winning and losing are not as important to them. They like to play the game, give and take licks, and when the dust settles, when it's over, just shake hands. They'll accept not being No. 1. And they'll never admit they made a mistake." Sensitive to the distinctness of native and non-native cultures and how the two related to one another, past and present, Lyons understood the uphill battle Indians faced within elite field lacrosse. "Indians are perplexing to coaches. Self-respect and individuality are very important to them. They're very sensitive, they expect rejection," Lyons explained in 1986. "You can't yell at them or they'll just 'drag up and go.' They walked out on British officers who barked orders during the Revolution, and they walk off steel when the foreman yells at them, and they'll walk off teams."[144]

Lyons's recognition of white attitudes toward Native Americans made him well suited to direct Iroquois athletic movement into a white cultural domain. Besides trying to rally Iroquoia behind their team, Lyons and Patterson believed the Nationals might create opportunities for high school graduates to obtain athletic scholarships. Several reservations provided players, coaches, support personnel, and financial resources to the Nationals, and the team appeared at the 1983 Lacrosse International at Johns Hopkins. Under the direction of Sid Jamieson, the Mohawk head coach of Bucknell University, the team included Onondaga, Tuscarora, Cattaraugus, and Akwesasne Reservation Indians. After playing in Baltimore, the Nationals served as host at the 1984 Jim Thorpe Memorial Pow-Wow Native Games held just before the Los Angeles Olympics. Capped off by contests against teams representing the United States, England, Canada, Australia, and California, the Native Games commemorated efforts to regain Jim Thorpe's lost decathlon and pentathlon medals from the 1912 Olympics.[145] The following year the team entered and toured England on Iroquois passports. Although their traveling as Iroquois rather than Americans hardly represented an international endorsement of Native American sovereignty, it was a symbolic victory for tribal traditionalists. Precedent for this incident had included Chief Levi General's trip to Switzerland on an Iroquois passport in 1926 to discuss Iroquois affairs before the League of Nations and Chief Emerson Hill's journey to Europe in 1970 as a guest of the Swedish American Indian Society and the Finnish American Indian League.[146]

Confident following the passport victory in England, the Nationals petitioned the International Lacrosse Federation (ILF) for membership. When officials examined the bid, they cited the lack of stable infrastructure as a significant team weakness. They also doubted the program's financial resources and the competitiveness of a team whose members had come from Indian reservations. Because many of the Nationals' players had come from the ranks of box lacrosse, ILF officials also questioned the ability of the Iroquois to adapt to the more genteel field game. The Canadian

Lacrosse Association had banned six native players in 1985 for attacking a white referee and forcing his hospitalization. Jurisdictional problems gave IFL delegates headaches. They were uncertain of the status of native athletes who lived within the geographical boundaries of American and Canadian governing bodies and whether they would be given the option of playing for either of the nation-states or for the Iroquois Confederacy. They were also uncertain of the status of non-Iroquois natives and whether they would be allowed to play for the Nationals and were concerned over the possibility that other lacrosse-playing non-Iroquois native peoples might demand their own separate memberships in the ILF. The Nationals, citing treaties and past relationships with the American and British governments, the lack of federal taxation on reservations, and the ability of Iroquois people to travel abroad on their own passports, based their membership claim on the argument that the Iroquois Confederacy was a sovereign entity.[147]

Although the ILF turned down the Iroquois bid to participate in the 1986 World Games in Toronto, the Nationals leadership felt confident that they could overcome the hurdles erected by ILF delegates and the lukewarm support of the Iroquois public. In an interview with *Northeast Indian Quarterly* Oren Lyons said: "We've had obstructions, and not all of them from international people. In our own communities, some people have a hard time understanding exactly what's going on." Lyons said the effort to seek international endorsement would not come to an end: "The Federation does not understand that lacrosse is an integral part of our communities; that we live, breathe and die with lacrosse in the Six Nations. They don't understand, so we're educating them and we're promoting the game. We believe the game should be played in the world Olympics and in many foreign countries. It's our game, it's our gift to humanity, and we should promote it."[148] After the Nationals had hosted a tournament in Buffalo, Lyons argued for future Iroquois inclusion in the ILF. He defended the organizational integrity of the program, pointed to the relative competitiveness of the Nationals, emphasized the Confederacy's historical relationship with the United States and England, and, most important, demonstrated how Iroquois participation would benefit white lacrosse. By referring to coverage by the *New York Times Magazine, National Geographic,* and *Sports Illustrated,* Lyons emphasized white interest in Native American cultures: "You must remember that the world is fascinated by Indians." Inclusion of an Indian team in the international federation would generate media coverage. "As an Indian Nation we attract the attention of the press, and we have utilized that attraction to promote lacrosse."[149] As for the role of the team relative to the Iroquois public, Lyons said he believed it would benefit Indian youth, generate pride within the confederacy, and allow natives to export to non-natives an important gift from the Creator.

The efforts of Lyons and other team officials paid dividends when ILF delegates voted to accept the Iroquois Nationals as the organization's fifth member at its October 1987 meeting. Officials agreed that non-Iroquois natives would be allowed to try out for the Nationals. Moreover, the ILF would accept one and only one native team as a member of the organization; there would be no Cherokee or Chippewa ILF team. Although the four national organizations did not recognize the sovereignty agenda of Iroquois traditionalists, they had made a bold statement. In the world of international sport, no native people had ever before achieved recognition as an independent entity by a governing body of modern nation-states.[150] Now nations of tens of millions of citizens would compete against a tribal alliance with tens of thousands of members—as equals. Although the Nationals did not participate in a World Games until 1990, the team challenged national teams, intercollegiate and all-star squads, and postcollegiate clubs. Sometimes the tournaments included Iroquois arts and crafts exhibitions.[151] The possibilities for cultural exchange were mutually plentiful. According to coach Jamieson, "This will provide the world with an opportunity to view another style of lacrosse, which is unique to Native Americans, and it will provide Native Americans with a special view of the game, in an educational sense, by taking the Indian kids to places that they would otherwise never see."[152] By the 1990s New York state high schools in Gowanda, Niagara-Wheatfield, Salmon River, and LaFayette had all produced a pool of Indian athletes from nearby reservations. Some of these graduates moved on to collegiate rosters at places such as Syracuse University and Nazareth College.

The competing political agendas of team officials and their funding sources made for strange bedfellows. Although many of the team's players viewed themselves as athletes prideful of their native heritage, some officials and supporters hoped for more. For example, in June 1990 Tuscarora Rick Hill declared "We thought it could help us achieve some of our political aspirations, meaning recognition as a nation."[153] However, considering the Nationals' dependence on non-native private organizations, businesses and even Hollywood celebrities, their diplomatic victory seemed incomplete. Some feared that increased costs from new obligations the team had incurred as an official ILF member might make the Nationals more reliant upon off-reservation sources of financial support. For the 1990 World Games the Grand Marnier Foundation of France supplied $35,000 worth of plane tickets for the team, while Brine Lacrosse donated equipment, shoes, and uniforms. Besides making agreements with other sports equipment and apparel companies, the Iroquois relied upon funds from a group of men who were potentially the most critical of the team's traditionalist leadership: reservation entrepreneurs. These "progressive" businessmen may have had the money to fund the Nationals, but the traditionalists viewed them as a threat to their authority. Even with such financial dependence, team officials carefully perpetuated a native identity, adopting a logo of a profiled man wearing a bald eagle headdress. According to the team secretary, "Iroquois tradition portrays the eagle as the sacred messenger of the Creator, and it is known as the protector of peace."[154] The Nationals also adopted the image of the Hiawatha wampum belt of five connected purple square figures on a clear white flag, while reservation children from the Tonawanda band of Seneca composed the team anthem. The combination of partial economic dependence on non-natives and the overt use of native symbols demonstrated the team's complex identity.

The Iroquois Nationals may not have fared well athletically at the World Games against much stronger U.S. and Canadian teams, but they piqued the curiosity of white and Aborigine spectators in Australia. According to team trainer Bill Solomon, "Everyone wants us. We've been talking to clubs about our culture. Everyone is looking for the originator of the game."[155] Much like the late nineteenth-century Mohawks who had journeyed to private clubs in England and America, these athlete diplomats sufficiently understood white fascination with their traditional culture even to make public appearances in native costume. In his Lacrosse Foundation Hall of Fame induction speech in Baltimore in 1993, Oren Lyons highlighted this sentiment among Indians. Besides thanking the foundation, family, and friends, he pointed to his status as the first Indian inducted into the hall since Leon Miller: "In the well appointed athletic facilities and locker rooms of prep, Ivy and military schools, amid the smell of stale sweat and winter green, there was an undercurrent of discussion and curiosity about the Indian lacrosse player. A myth and stereotype evolved. The im-

age of . . . a savage player of heroic courage with lethal disregard for his personal well-being, who played with skill and abandon, accepting and giving
no quarter, was created and continues to exist today. 'A savage redskin' who
lived in Indian country."[156] Ironically, although natives identified and criticized romantic stereotypes of the "noble savage," they also knew how to
capitalize on them.

Iroquois traditionalists realized that the Nationals' program served another purpose: the reassertion of a strong image of the Iroquois Confederacy in the eyes of other Indians. Directly or indirectly, the Nationals promoted the modern version of lacrosse on many other reservations. By the
1990s, for example, several native communities in the Midwest had established lacrosse programs. Oneida and Menominee Indians were playing
lacrosse in Wisconsin, while Ojibwe (Chippewa) peoples participated in
Minnesota. Although the Oneida were originally from New York and were
thus part of Iroquoia, the ancestors of the latter two peoples had played traditional ball games in the Great Lakes that had been distinct from the Iroquoian game.[157] In 1996 the under-nineteen Iroquois Nationals junior
team traveled to Denver to conduct clinics for western and southwestern
native peoples.[158] Bowing to the clout of the Iroquois Confederacy, the
National Congress of American Indians, in existence since 1944, adopted a
resolution declaring lacrosse the official sport of Native Americans. Indeed,
historically southeastern natives such as the Creek, Choctaw, and Cherokee
peoples and midwestern nations such as the Dakota and the Sac and Fox
had all embraced the modern sport, but had sometimes maintained versions of their traditional ball games.[159]

Whether or not the Nationals' athletic and cultural victories would lead
to greater inter-reservation cooperation and social reform and would minimize tribal factionalism remained to be seen. Efforts to use the game as a
vehicle for culturally revitalizing Iroquoia were being made at a time when
the economic landscape of many reservations was changing rapidly. Serious environmental problems arising from nearby factories, bridges, reser-
voirs, and dams were leading to an ongoing dispersal of young men—that
is, potential lacrosse players—throughout the northeastern United States
in search of jobs. Also, the new economic conditions were transforming
lacrosse into a contested cultural battleground between traditionalists and
progressives. Some Iroquois entrepreneurs were investing income saved

from years of dangerous construction work into new businesses. Capitalizing on the ability to engage in untaxed commerce, they were creating a variety of enterprises, ranging from restaurants and diners, gasoline stations, cigarette and fireworks stores, and casinos to operations for the illegal smuggling of narcotics, firearms, and immigrants. Businessmen on the Akwesasne Reservation, strategically located at the intersection of the New York, Ontario, and Quebec borders, were especially able to engage in these activities. What resulted from this economic revolution was the creation of a new class of relatively wealthy Indians. With attitudes reminiscent of late nineteenth-century views of industrialists as either "captains of industry" or "robber barons," most other natives viewed the entrepreneurs either as job creators and leaders of true Indian economic independence or as men just as selfish and materialistic as white businessmen. Such arguments fueled bitter factionalism.

Disagreements over gambling and confrontations between traditional and elected chiefs remained central to tribal politics. However, the conflict became violent at Akwesasne in 1990. A Mohawk civil war between those who favored and those who opposed reservation gaming resulted from the long-term environmental decay of the area. After all, the loss of native industries had forced Indians to seek other sources of employment.[160] With the passage of Public Law 100-497 by Congress in 1988, the federal government mandated state government approval of casinos on Indian reservations. However, tribal councils believed state control of gambling undermined tribal sovereignty and tribes' government-to-government relationships with Washington, D.C. Many Indians feared that the law would give state police forces an excuse to enter reservation territory and enforce gambling regulations. At Akwesasne two factions articulated opposing views on reservation gaming, but expressed the common goal of tribal autonomy. While the pro-gamers believed that casino revenue created jobs and asserted reservation sovereignty, the anti-gamers maintained that gambling benefited only the few, infected Indians with the crass materialism of the consumer culture, encouraged ties with organized crime syndicates, and invited trouble with the state. After months of fistfights, vandalism, and mysterious firebombings, the anti-gamers erected blockades at reservation entrances in March 1990. The pro-gamers escalated their attacks, filling the darkness of night with the sounds and flashes of automatic weapons' fire. After two men were discovered dead on May 1, New York State Police and Royal Canadian Mounted Police forces entered the reservation and declared the temporary imposition of martial law.

As the hatred at Akwesasne was subsiding, organizers attempted to revive box lacrosse. Besides forming a youth program, they created an Old Sticks League for men over thirty-five, with reservation gas stations and construction companies providing financial support.[161] Although organizer Ernie Mitchell said he had no altruistic motivations in reviving lacrosse, the two leagues forced many Mohawks from opposing political viewpoints to cooperate. The willingness of a diverse group of parents, athletes, businessmen, and tribal leaders to support the revival pointed to cultural solidarity. Men from opposing political viewpoints had to cooperate. Together with stick maker Frank Benedict, Ernie Mitchell's brother Mike Mitchell tried to use lacrosse to reunite the community. As Grand Chief of the Mohawk Council, Mike Mitchell survived a postwar public referendum. In June 1992 he told a *Toronto Globe and Mail* reporter, "It was a good idea starting this league. We've got guys on the same teams that were shooting at each other two years ago and now they're playing lacrosse together."[162] Even with political factionalism plaguing the Mohawks, Mitchell said the game provided for cultural unity: "But when it comes to the Old Sticks League, you have people from all different factions playing together on the same team and sitting together in the stands. . . . You have traditionalists and warriors and elected chiefs, even non-natives from Cornwall, all working together. There's no politics involved."[163] Mitchell's conceptualization of nonpartisan sport, echoed by many Indians throughout Iroquoia, affirmed that culture took precedence over politics. Indians might disagree over gambling, but lacrosse demanded consensus. The Mohawks also invoked the healing function of lacrosse. Each athlete abandoned his real-world identity and political views for sixty minutes of game time, and political opponents confronted one another on opposing teams. For men such as Chief Mitchell, a lacrosse contest allowed players to make violent statements within legitimate boundaries. "When the league started, there was still an awful lot of hatred directed at me . . . and people blamed me for a lot of things," Mitchell recalled in 1992. "I'll put it this way. Can you imagine Brian Mulroney putting on skates and playing in a hockey league somewhere and giving everyone a chance to take a crack at him?"[164]

With a lacrosse revival in motion, in 1993 stick maker Frank Benedict started a new inter-reservation box lacrosse league for the eastern reservations of the Iroquois Confederacy. The league was dubbed the Iroquois Lacrosse Association (Senior B division level), and its first campaign included competition among teams representing four reservations: the Onondaga A.C. Warriors, Kahnawake Mohawks, Kanehsatake (Oka) Eagles, and Akwesasne Thunder. The formation of the Old Sticks League had eased tensions resulting from the civil war at Akwesasne; the new ILA addressed community morale, especially among the young. By the ILA's third season, the league had expanded to seven clubs, with new teams including the Oneida Silverhawks, Tri-Town (Akwesasne) Warriors, and Long Sault (Akwesasne) Outlaws. The ideological mix of league and club officials mirrored larger political divisions among the Iroquois. Those describing themselves as traditionalists dominated the league hierarchy as well as the Onondaga, Kahnawake, and Kanehsatake clubs, while progressive businessmen sponsored the Oneida, Akwesasne, Tri-Town, and Long Sault teams. Casino operator Ray Halbritter backed the Oneida Silverhawks, while cigarette and gasoline entrepreneurs managed the three Mohawk teams. After serving jail time for a gambling conviction, Peter Burns revived the once inactive Warriors team. The divergent management groups pointed to potential politicization, but most Indian athletes and spectators viewed lacrosse through a nonpartisan lens. Akwesasne residents supported the reservation's three teams according to familial and social networks. Which team the people supported might depend on knowing a player or his family or preferring one style of play over another. Spectators sometimes supported teams on the basis of their views regarding pay for play.

Disagreement over professionalism emerged during the 1995 season, for example, when pro-gamers Fabian and Gail Hart assumed administrative and financial responsibility for the Thunder. Following the defection of some Thunder players to the new Outlaws, the Harts opened their coffers and professionalized the club by luring Native American MILL veterans to Akwesasne from the Six Nations Reserve with game stipends and promises of full-time employment during the playing season. When the unpaid Outlaws defeated the Thunder in game one of the league championship series, one spectator told the local *People's Voice,* "It really shows that the Outlaws play with their hearts and not through other people's pocketbooks."[165] Declaring the rivalry a reflection of tribal factionalism, editor Cynthia Smoke slammed league officials and the growing ethos of professionalism that she saw creeping into the ILA. "It makes you wonder what kind of Iroquois Lacrosse Association we have. One of righteousness, integrity, hardly!" Smoke declared. "It seems it's more than a lacrosse game these days. When you have the big bucks, everybody knows money talks. And when you can buy and pay players you have the team."[166] Considering Smoke's support of reservation gaming, her anti-Thunder comments highlight the primacy of professionalism rather than gambling as the divisive issue.

The bitter rivalry between the two Mohawk clubs climaxed in game two of the championship series. With the score tied at 13–13 in double overtime, referees nullified an apparent Outlaws goal because of a crease violation. As the Thunder ran with the ball back toward the Outlaws goal, debris accumulated on the floor from rowdy spectators. When a siren blew, the Outlaws thought officials had stopped play to clear the floor, but Thunder player Pete Skye scored. In retaliation, Outlaws players bloodied the head of referee Claude Giguere and sent him to the hospital.[167] An anonymous fan who had witnessed the assault urged *Indian Time* readers to provide a better atmosphere for youth: "Now I have to question whether or not I should even bring them to the games. I hear the fan's [*sic*] yelling, swearing and calling down the players. People are outside during breaks drinking alcohol. Players constantly fighting, coaches telling [their] boys 'Get him in the legs,' and the players saying 'They think this was a bad game, wait till the next one.' I was taught that a lacrosse stick is sacred, that women ain't to touch them, and yet a man can strike another man over the head with it." The writer called for a resolution: "What's wrong with you? Where's your common sense? Where's the sportsmanship? Don't you realize you are the ones that are setting the example for our future players. You are their role models."[168]

After postponing game three, the ILA forced each team to post a $5,000 bond that was forfeitable in the event of a disturbance. Although the association banned one player for life and indefinitely suspended two others, the Thunder went on to win the series. Despite disapproval from traditionalists who believed in an amateur conception of lacrosse—ironically, a conception similar to views expressed by university alumni and collegiate sportsmen—others embraced the dominant commercial view of professional sport. The Thunder captain even thanked the Harts for their "total hands-on situation" in importing their "Brothers from the West," a euphemism for their bringing in native ringers from Six Nations as well as Dean Cecconi, a white athlete from Windsor. In 1998 Thunder management engineered the entrance of the team into the Senior A division of the Ontario Lacrosse Association, where it began competing against some of the best clubs in Canada, and purchased the playing rights of non-native MILL star John Tavares from the Six Nations Chiefs.

The problems revolving around Iroquois box lacrosse reflected the dilemmas facing Iroquois society as a whole. The constant struggle between the forces of "tradition" and those of "progress"—in other words, the struggle over whether to deflect or embrace the surrounding mainstream culture—dominated life in modern Iroquoia in the late twentieth century. Natives expressed their divergent views about the future direction of their people in several ways, but perhaps none more explicit than embracing the modernized game of their ancestors. Among the western reservations of the Iroquois Confederacy, for example, Indian groups fielded teams in the Senior B-level Can-Am League. Founded in 1993, the Tuscarora Thunderhawks further demonstrate the range of native public opinion. Team general manager Ken Van Every shaped the club according to an amateur, recreational conception of the game, with sponsorship by Randy's Smoke Shop and other reservation businesses. He resisted any attempt to infuse traditional ritual—for instance, sprinkling tobacco on an open fire or praying for spiritual assistance from divine and natural powers—into the pregame preparation of the club: "When we lead our team out onto the floor, we say 'all white boys up front.' Some teams use what they call Indian medicine, burning tobacco. They try to better their team with this medicine to have their team play at perfection and ours at a so-so level where it will cause arguments amongst the players, this and that," Van Every said. "So for this to work, the Indians have to lead the way out onto the floor. So that's why we tell the white guys up front. And they're all laughing when they come out of the dressing room. They say 'you guys just gotta find the floor so come on, just come follow us.' It's just a big joke since I got the team started."[169] The ambiguity presented by Van Every's club—rejection of medicinal ritual, but celebration of a native purist view of the game—reflected the tension within many late twentieth-century Indians with regard to their lives on the reservation and the possibilities and problems presented by the outside world. For these Indians and others, box lacrosse provided a venue for exploring solutions to larger problems. Although some remained un-resolved, the forces of tradition and progress pointed to the modern ver-sion of the Creator's game as a shared but contested ground. Iroquois Indians might disagree on issues of assimilation or separation or on the means to tribal autonomy, but they agreed on lacrosse as a legitimate, authentic element of Indian culture.

In the summer of 1998 John Seabrook of the *New Yorker* traveled with the Onondaga Athletic Club and noticed some of these problems. On a bus ride to the Mohawk reserve at Kahnawanke near Montreal, Seabrook wit-nessed native players who unflinchingly accepted use of manufactured equipment, even using factory-made plastic lacrosse sticks over native-made wood sticks, but acknowledged the utility of traditional customs. One such tradition was holding "medicine games," a more spiritual three-day version of lacrosse involving many generations of male athletes. "We play the medicine game because it helps with the hunt, even if the hunt is be-hind a computer screen and the forest is in an office building," goal tender Kent Lyons told Seabrook. "Everything is a circle. Lacrosse makes the circle stronger." The Onondaga squad included both collegians and construction workers. A few even played in a band called White Boy and the Wagon Burners. During the contest with the Mohawks, the political orientation of some athletes—militant warriors on the Kahnawake squad, Longhouse conservatives playing for Onondaga—contributed to rough play. After a Mohawk player slashed one of the Onondagas' star attackmen, Onondaga coach Freeman Bucktooth sent the team's "goon" after the assailant. "He threw off one glove, grabbed the Mohawk's jersey with that hand, punched his face mask with the gloved hand until the man's helmet came off, hit him in the face a couple of times," Seabrook observed, "then pulled his jersey up over his head and slammed him down onto concrete—all in about five sec-onds." This culture of native lacrosse, where faith in the spiritual power of old customs was coupled with a willingness to resort to violence, stood in stark contrast to the culture of Baltimore lacrosse. When a member of the Iroquois Nationals punched an opponent during a 20–8 loss to the U.S. national team at Johns Hopkins in July 1998, an angry field lacrosse sup-porter yelled: "Get the animals out of the game!"[170] Clearly, a cultural di-vide remained.

The decades-long cultural and athletic renaissance of the game achieved through box lacrosse also provided the Iroquois with potential solutions to extrareservation problems, primarily how to endure difficulties with the larger non-native society surrounding them. Moreover, the symbolic victories of the Iroquois Nationals field lacrosse program and the long-term efforts of Oren Lyons eventually paid significant dividends. By achieving a limited form of sovereignty through athletics, the Iroquois Nationals recalled some of the basic purposes of native lacrosse as it was played before the military collapse of the confederacy during the late eighteenth century. As had the barnstorming teams of the late nineteenth century, these late twentieth-century Iroquois lacrosse enthusiasts recognized and capitalized on white misconceptions of the Indian world. Whether through Indians' peppering the rosters of high school or intercollegiate teams, the world cup efforts of the Iroquois Nationals, the continuation of medicine games, or the ongoing play of Iroquois box lacrosse teams and individuals, the modern version of the Creator's game reminded old and new generations of the centrality of all forms of lacrosse to Indians past and present.

Epilogue **Ground Still Contested**

North American Cultures and the
Meaning of Lacrosse

LACROSSE ENTHUSIASTS of the nineteenth and twentieth centuries never agreed how to define their game. The struggles over the sport were numerous, pitting reformers against gamblers, whites against Indians, "traditionalists" against "progressives," and even women against men. The history of lacrosse is indeed a history of contestation over culture. The struggle was and continues to be not only for power, but for authority and especially meaning. Because most coaches and athletes have cared more—at least consciously—about the game at hand on the field than about whether they had some degree of power, the cultural wars have often been fought in newspapers, convention halls, and locker rooms. Victories as indicated by the scoreboard have given rise to jubilant celebration and even nostalgic memories, but these have been short-lived achievements with little value within the larger political, social, economic, and religious spheres within which people live their daily lives. Lacrosse championships have produced accolades and trophies, but they are not entirely useful in understanding the reasons athletes, coaches, and spectators have embraced the game. Lacrosse enthusiasts have been very interested in issues related to race, class, gender, and culture—whether they have cared to admit it or not. Every rule passed, every team or player cheered, every condemnation of player behavior has been an implicit statement of cultural values.

The meanings of lacrosse are as diverse as the people who play it, but several identifiable cultural threads have been seen running through the game since the mid-nineteenth century. One such thread has been that of the socially elite gentlemen and ladies who have championed amateur sport for its own sake. When George Beers chose to standardize and codify a stick-and-ball game he had learned from Mohawk Indians near Montreal at the time of the birth of Canada, he did so for the benefit of middle-class gentlemen. By developing physical strength, self-reliance, and moral purity, he thought, these men would be able to create a hardy nation of Canadians who could conquer the cold North. Despite the eventual demise of Beers's "national game" within Canada, as social reform, nationalism, and amateurism gave way to spectatorism, commercialism, and professionalism, some Canadians transplanted this game to socially elite athletic circles in the American Northeast. From the 1880s to the 1920s lacrosse changed from a game played by clubs stocked with Canadian immigrants to a sport dominated by elite eastern universities and private clubs. The austere conditions of the Great Depression and the Second World War reinforced this gentleman's game, as both produced a recommitment to amateur ideals.

During the years between the world wars, devotees of lacrosse developed a system at preparatory schools and private academies to feed talent to the universities, colleges, and postcollegiate clubs and emphasized the transnational qualities of amateurism by confronting student athletes who represented Oxford and Cambridge. The ethos of this sport world stood in stark contrast to that of the commercial, multiclass, and democratic universe of baseball. Lacrosse supporters maintained a segregated athletic sphere that kept them separate from their socioeconomic inferiors. After World War II, intercollegiate and interscholastic lacrosse grew in numbers and scope, aided by the proselytizing Lacrosse Foundation. Although some enthusiasts called for greater geographic and social expansion, they insisted on cultural continuity with the past. By the 1960s the seemingly divergent trends of social expansion and cultural continuity had brought about a dilemma for organizers. In subsequent years the growing, diversifying group of new coaches and players made adherence to the principles of amateurism as envisioned by advocates of the "gentleman's game" rather enigmatic. In sum, the cultural thread created by George Beers in Canada and transplanted to the United States began to fray during the last quarter of the twentieth century.

An underlying theme that has contributed to the persistence of the "gentleman's game" for these many decades has revolved around the fictitious "noble savage." From the time of Beers, this creature had played a large role in the Canadian adoption of the Mohawk ball game. Many Anglo-Canadians believed that the Native American "sons of the forest" were vanishing, along with a certain manly quality that they had possessed, and they thought the adoption of an Indian game would reinvigorate Canadian manhood. Neither the Indians nor the image disappeared from the game. Romantic notions of the "red man" persisted throughout the twentieth century. Many coaches, athletes, officials, and journalists shared the conception of the modern white player as the symbolic descendent of the noble Indian warrior of the past. This mythical figure was seen as playing according to ancient instinct, savage in conduct but admirable in character. The link between the primeval Indian and the modern gentleman legitimized the rough, masculine, character-building qualities of incidental violence that occurred during matches. Complicating the matrix was the reality of competition between squads representing colleges and reservations. Whether these meetings confirmed or contradicted white preconceptions is moot, however; in either case, the image enjoyed a long career.

Another cultural thread seen running through the history of lacrosse is represented by the experiences of the people of the Iroquois Confederacy. Despite their lack of institutional authority over their ancient game as adapted by whites, their ancestors' creation of the game and their continued involvement with it calls for extended commentary. If one were to examine cross-cultural contests within the broader context of white-Indian relations, the history of lacrosse could be easily misread as a case of cultural imperialism or even cultural larceny. Such interpretations would simplistically view Indians as outnumbered, powerless, oppressed victims and whites as hegemonic thieves. They would miss the nuances that have appeared throughout the history of lacrosse. The partial exclusion of Indians from the game in late nineteenth-century Canada, the Carlisle school's efforts to anglicize Indians through use of the "gentleman's game," and the dominance of reservation teams by college programs after the First World War seem obvious evidence of white robbery from passive Indians. But this evidence ignores the complexity as well as the humanity of the experiences of generations of men who have called lacrosse "their" game. It presupposes that cultural power is more important than the meaning derived from that culture. It also assumes that native culture has always been static. A far different story emerges when we look at more than merely winners and losers.

When white Canadians adopted and formalized the Mohawk ball game during the 1860s, the two peoples had already profoundly influenced one another. These Native Americans were not the breechcloth "savages" of centuries past, completely separate from their surrounding white neighbors. As Daniel Richter has demonstrated, the peoples of the Iroquois Confederacy had experienced much acculturation well before the era of the American Revolution.[1] Whether through force or by choice, the Iroquois peoples had adapted to the new technological, economic, and political conditions of the eighteenth century. This fact should not be overlooked in light of the subsequent military collapse of the confederacy. The ball game these Indians had played among themselves during the early nineteenth century had already changed from the game played when the Iroquois had been a dominant military power, much more from the games of the precolonial era. By the middle of the next century, George Beers had modernized the acculturated game to make it palatable to middle-class Canadians. But this act of cultural appropriation did not amount to a zero-sum equation, as some twentieth-century observers might hypothesize. The white man's gain had not been simply the red man's loss. Although white clubs eventually dominated the playing of the game and white rule makers transformed the way it was played, Indians did not vanish from the game or from the American scene as many contemporary writers had theorized that they would. Instead, Iroquois athletes learned the new modern version of the game, although they never forgot how their forefathers had played the game.

The resilience of Native Americans in the face of adversity demonstrated one of the most dynamic themes of native culture throughout North America from the eighteenth century through the twentieth century: a Januslike desire to remain distinct and apart from white society, defending evolving notions of "tradition," while also aggressively trying to participate in the surrounding modern world, out of either necessity or curiosity. Even in the late twentieth century, many Indians remained perplexed at the inability of white society to understand them as a changing people who are very much a part of the modern world. In 1983, at the Conference on Indian Self-Rule at Sun Valley, Idaho, the co-founder of the Iroquois Nationals, Onondaga faith keeper Oren Lyons said: "It is a fact that a small group of people in the northeast have survived an onslaught for some 490 years. They continue their original manner of government. They also drive cars, have televisions, and ride on planes. We make the bridges that you cross over and build the buildings you live in. So, what are we? Are we traditionalists or are we assimilated? If you can get away from your categories and definitions, you will perceive us as a living and continuing society."[2]

Throughout the 1870s and 1880s, as Anglo Canadian lacrosse enthusiasts commercialized and professionalized their new sport, Iroquois Indians traveled to London, Boston, and New York City to demonstrate proudly the game of their ancestors and participate in the larger white society around them. By the second and third decades of the twentieth century, the existence of the federally run school for Indians in Carlisle inspired many young Iroquois men to renew their commitment to cross-cultural confrontations with teams representing universities and private athletic clubs. Though the best white teams usually defeated Indian squads, Iroquois athletes persisted. Caring about team victory not as the sole or even the primary purpose of competition, they took an even greater interest in lacrosse as a rite of passage to manhood. Native players wanted to maintain cultural continuity with the past, but perhaps also to vanquish white men at the latters' version of the Creator's game.

After the Second World War, Indians fully embraced a unique cultural opportunity afforded, somewhat ironically, by sport promoters in Canada. Instead of continuing to confront affluent white athletes in the "gentleman's game" of field lacrosse, they embraced the rougher, enclosed form of lacrosse known as boxla. Despite the obvious commercial origins of this game, it provided Iroquois Indians with occasions for individualized, manly confrontation. Officials and coaches of the American field game had never tolerated the individualistic "Indian style" of play or the forms of personal combat to which it sometimes gave rise. Perhaps only in centuries past, when Iroquois warriors had dominated much of the colonial Northeast and maintained their advantage as a military power in part through rough ball play, had the game strongly emphasized the importance of personal action. Canadian box lacrosse not only stressed personal action but implicitly condoned personal combat and even violence. As the modern commercial sports world proclaimed a Machiavellian faith in the creed of team victory at all costs, Indian athletes welcomed physical confrontation for the sake of physical confrontation. Over the course of the final two decades of the twentieth century, Iroquois Indians also used the game to authenticate tribal sovereignty in a world dominated by nation-states, multinational corporations, and mass consumerism by creating the Iroquois Nationals program.

Besides the gentlemanly and Native American cultural threads of lacrosse, the forces of egalitarianism and capitalism were a third thread. Beginning in the latter decades of the nineteenth century, there arose several commercial, multiclass challenges to the elite ethos of lacrosse. Players bent the rules, and speculators wagered on the outcome. Winning and money dominated their thinking. However, commercialized lacrosse in Canada never developed along the lines of baseball in America, mainly because market conditions would not support such an entity. During the twentieth century sport promoters created several professional circuits, but they usually failed. Only the organization formerly known as the Major Indoor Lacrosse League claimed long-term allegiance from anyone. Oddly enough, professional sports promoters never created a distinct, stable, cultural thread committed to multiclass commercial sport. Instead, this thread developed from within the elite game. After World War II numerous coaches and officials attempted to alter the affluent composition of the American game by exporting it to other regions and introducing it to other social classes, but these efforts never resulted in any revolution in the sport. Supporters' passion for the game and their desire to make lacrosse more acceptable to a larger audience created this more egalitarian alternative to the gentleman's game.

Ironically, the group of people who held the numerical and social expansion of lacrosse in check were Indian stick makers. The growth of the game was always limited by the production capacity of their reservation factories. Once synthetics had replaced wood as the materials of choice, by the 1970s, the elite aura of the sport was dealt a harsh blow as the floodgates to democratization were thrown open. The rise of middle-class lacrosse throughout the American Northeast and in other suburban communities across the United States weighed heavily on the ethos of the older "gentleman's game." These new supporters represented the fourth and most distinct cultural thread of the game. Many of these new enthusiasts agreed with some of the principles of amateur sport, but they were also interested in the commercial culture of mass sport. Even Hollywood began to take notice of lacrosse, making at least three films with references to the game: *Dead Poets Society* (1989), *Last of the Mohicans* (1992), and, most prominently, *American Pie* (1999). Other cultural trends adopted from the commercial world also contributed to the increased interest in lacrosse. In a June 2001 feature entitled "Little League Gets Littler," the *Wall Street Journal* examined the mind-set of many contemporary children and why they were abandoning baseball: "Raised on video games and MTV, kids today just don't have the attention span for a game that unfolds like molasses." The increased interest in lacrosse was part of a larger trend, with children taking an interest in computer and video games, "extreme" sports like skateboarding, and fast-paced but expensive sports like hockey.[3] The challenge this growing body of devotees posed to all forms of lacrosse had created a dilemma organizers were only beginning to understand. The question that organizers wrestled with was how they could manage the continual expansion of lacrosse yet limit the influence of cultural phenomena that might be judged as hostile to older conceptions of the sport. By the end of the twentieth century, the separate cultural threads of lacrosse—elite, Native American, commercial, and suburban—were pointing in different but sometimes overlapping directions. The followers of each community may have conceived the game differently from the others, but their love for the sport was the same.

Naturally the future history of lacrosse awaits to be written. No doubt the sport will continue to serve as a contested cultural battleground among the numerous constituents who organize, officiate, coach, play, support, and watch the game. Certainly many of the trends outlined in chapter 5 and in this epilogue can be projected into the twenty-first century. However, if the past century and a half is any indicator of what the future holds, the winners of any future struggle to define the sport will be those better organized and those best able to articulate their values. With the rising popularity of lacrosse at the beginning of the twenty-first century, perhaps the biggest question to be answered is whether enough current and former lacrosse players can become lacrosse "fans," in the usual commercial sense of the word, and support both Division I university programs and professional franchises by purchasing tickets, watching games on television, and buying products endorsed by star athletes. A related question is whether enough people who have never played the game, or never had a son or daughter play the game, can become lacrosse fans. As it is now, lacrosse played at the highest levels of competition comes nowhere near the popularity levels enjoyed by big-time football and baseball. After all, many National Football League and Major League Baseball franchises sell more tickets to a single game than a National Lacrosse League or Major League Lacrosse franchise sells for the whole season. However, if lacrosse devotees —native and non-native, American and Canadian, men and women— remain true to their sport's past, they will not allow the entrepreneurs to define the game completely. They can do so by continuing to support the many forms of amateur lacrosse as organizers, coaches, and players.

Appendix: All-Time Great Lacrosse Players

All–Twentieth Century U.S. Collegiate Field Lacrosse Team (compiled by Bill Tanton, Baltimore, Maryland)

Scott Bacigalupo, Princeton
Jim Brown, Syracuse
Lloyd Bunting, Johns Hopkins
Gary Gait, Syracuse
Paul Gait, Syracuse
Jimmy Lewis, Navy
Dave Pietramala, Johns Hopkins
Casey Powell, Syracuse
John Tolson, Johns Hopkins
Jack Turnbull, Johns Hopkins

All–Twentieth Century Canadian Box Lacrosse Team (compiled by Stan Shillington, Coquitlam, British Columbia)

Jack Bionda, Victoria, New Westminster Salmonbellies, Nanaimo, Portland, Brampton, Huntsville
John Davis, Peterborough and Montreal
Geordie Dean, New Westminster Salmonbellies
Wayne Goss, New Westminster Salmonbellies
John Tavares, Vancouver, Victoria, Brampton, Six Nations, Akwesasne
Lloyd Wootten, Owen Sound, Peterborough

All–Twentieth Century Combined Box and Field Lacrosse Iroquois Team (compiled by Oren Lyons, Jr., Onondaga Nation)

Frank Benedict, Mohawk

Jeff Gill, Seneca

Howie Hill, Cayuga

Oliver Hill, Sr., Oneida

Harry Isaacs, Onondaga

Lumen Jackson, Seneca

Barney Kettle, Seneca

Oren Lyons, Sr., Onondaga

Ross Powless, Mohawk

Edward Shenandoah, Onondaga

Leroy Shenandoah, Onondaga

Finn Stevens, Seneca

Angus Thomas, Mohawk

All–"National Game" Era (1880–1920) Canadian Field Lacrosse Team (compiled by Paul Whiteside, Cobourg, Ontario)

Alex Black, Cornwall

Jack Brennan, Montreal Shamrocks

Paddy Brennan, Montreal Nationals, Montreal Shamrocks

Albert Dade, Montreal Shamrocks, Montreal A.A.A., Brantford

Harry Hoobin, Montreal Shamrocks

Eduoard Lalonde, Cornwall, Montreal Nationals, Vancouver, Leaside

Eduoard L'Heureux, Sherbrooke, Montreal Nationals

Tom Paton, Montreal A.A.A.

John Powers, Ottawa, Brantford, Toronto L.C.

Charles Querrie, Toronto L.C., Toronto Tecumsehs

George Sproule, Brampton

John White, Cornwall, Toronto Tecumsehs, Leaside

All-Professional Indoor Lacrosse Team
(compiled by Tom Borrelli, Buffalo, New York)

Dallas Eliuk, Philadelphia Wings

Gary Gait, Detroit Turbos, Philadelphia Wings, Baltimore Thunder,
Pittsburgh CrosseFire, Washington Power

Paul Gait, Detroit Turbos, Philadelphia Wings, Rochester Knighthawks, Syracuse Smash, Pittsburgh CrosseFire, Washington Power

Darris Kilgour, Buffalo Bandits, Rochester Knighthawks, Albany Attack

John Tavares, Buffalo Bandits

Jim Veltman, Buffalo Bandits, Ontario Raiders, Toronto Rock

Notes

Abbreviations

The following abbreviations are used in the notes:

CSHF	Canadian Sports Hall of Fame
EPFL	Enoch Pratt Free Library
FHAJHU	Ferdinand Hamburger Archives, the Johns Hopkins University
LF	Lacrosse Foundation (now known as U.S. Lacrosse)
LOC	Library of Congress
MHS	Maryland Historical Society
NA	National Archives
NCAA	National Collegiate Athletic Association
OLA	Ontario Lacrosse Association
SUA	Syracuse University Archives
USILA	United States Intercollegiate Lacrosse Association
USMAA	United States Military Academy Archives
YUL	Yale University Library

Complete citations for official lacrosse guides published by the USILA and the NCAA can be found in the Essay on Sources following the notes.

Prologue: Contested Ground

1. Francis Parkman, *The Conspiracy of Pontiac and the Indian War after the Conquest of Canada* (Toronto: Musson Book Co., 1870), 1: 351–81.
2. Thomas Vennum, Jr., *American Indian Lacrosse: Little Brother of War* (Washington, D.C.: Smithsonian Institution Press, 1994).
3. See the introduction of Roland Marchand, *Advertising the American Dream: Making Way for Modernity, 1920–1940* (Berkeley: University of California Press, 1985).

Chapter 1: Learning from the "Sons of the Forest"

1. For a complete bibliography of Native American ball games, see the Essay on Sources following the notes.

2. Reuben Gold Thwaites, ed., *The Jesuit Relations and Allied Documents: Travels and Explorations of the Jesuit Missionaries in New France 1610–1791* (New York: Pageant Book Co., 1959), 10: 185, 187.

3. William L. Stone, *Life of Joseph Brant—Thayendanegea* (New York: Alexander V. Blake, 1838), 2: 445–49.

4. Anthony F. C. Wallace, *The Death and Rebirth of the Seneca* (New York: Alfred A. Knopf, 1973), 318–19.

5. Saint Regis Mission Records of Letters, Saint Regis Mission, as cited in North American Indian Travelling College, *Tewaarathon (Lacrosse)* (Akwesasne Reservation, 1978), 3.

6. *Wilkes' Spirit of the Times,* June 6, 1868.

7. *American Chronicle of Sports and Pastimes,* June 11, 1868, as cited in "Indian Contests, 1868," in *Sports in North America: A Documentary History,* vol. 4, *Sports in War, Revival and Expansion 1860–1880,* ed. George B. Kirsch (Gulf Breeze, Fla.: Academic International Press, 1995), 284–85, quote on 284.

8. *American Chronicle of Sports and Pastimes,* July 9, 1868, as cited in "Indian Contests, 1868," 286–87.

9. See chapter 2 of Christina A. Burr, "The Process of Evolution of Competitive Sport: A Study of Senior Lacrosse in Canada, 1844 to 1914" (master's thesis, University of Western Ontario, 1986).

10. Burr, "Senior Lacrosse in Canada," 40–41.

11. *Montreal Gazette,* July 9, 1860, as cited in Burr, "Senior Lacrosse in Canada," 46.

12. Don Morrow, "Lacrosse as the National Game," in *A Concise History of Sport in Canada,* ed. Don Morrow, Mary Keyes, et al. (Toronto: Oxford University Press, 1989), 47.

13. D. W. Gullett, *A History of Dentistry in Canada* (Toronto: University of Toronto Press, 1971), 25–27; Henry James Morgan, ed. *The Canadian Men and Women of the Time: A Hand-book of Canadian Biography* (Toronto: William Briggs, 1898), 63–64; idem, *Dictionary of Canadian Biography,* vol. 12, 1891–1900 (Toronto: University of Toronto Press, 1990), 75–77; *The Game of Lacrosse, Containing the Construction of the Crosse, Various Methods of Throwing and Catching the Ball, "Dodging," "Checking," Goalkeeping, &c.* (Montreal, 1860), as cited in *Sports in North America: A Documentary History,* vol. 3, *The Rise of Modern Sports, 1840–1860,* ed. George B. Kirsch (Gulf Breeze, Fla.: Academic International Press, 1992), 262–74.

14. W. George Beers, "Canada in Winter," *British American Magazine* 2 (1863): 166–71.

15. W. G. Beers, *Lacrosse: The National Game of Canada* (Montreal: Dawson Brothers, 1869).

16. Italics in original. *The Game of Lacrosse,* 263.

17. Morgan, *Canadian Men and Women,* 63–64; Morrow, "Lacrosse as the National Game," 49.

18. Kevin G. Jones and T. George Vellathottam, "The Myth of Canada's National Sport," *Journal of the Canadian Association for Health, Physical Education and Recreation* 41 (September–October 1974): 33–36. Morrow, "Lacrosse as the National Game," 52–55.

19. Peter L. Lindsay, "George Beers and the National Game Concept: A Behavioral Approach," in *Proceedings of the Second Canadian Symposium on the History of Sport and Physical Education* (University of Windsor, Windsor, Ontario, May 1–3, 1972), 27–44.

20. *Montreal Gazette,* June 29, 1867, as cited in Lindsay, "George Beers," 41.

21. Beers, *Lacrosse,* xv–xvi.

22. Ibid., 59.

23. *Montreal Gazette,* September 29, 1866, as cited in Burr, "Senior Lacrosse in Canada," 43.

24. Italics in original. Beers, as cited in Kirsch, ed. *Sports in North America,* 3: 263.

25. Beers, *Lacrosse,* 9.

26. Ibid., 54.

27. Ibid., 49, 50, 32–33.

28. Beers, as cited in Kirsch, *Sports in North America,* 3: 264.

29. Beers, *Lacrosse,* 21-22.

30. "William George Beers, D.D.S., L.D.S.," *Dominion Dental Journal* 13 (February 1901): 39–41.

31. "William George Beers," 39–41; Gullett, *History of Dentistry in Canada,* 43–44, 46–48, 296.

32. W. George Beers, "Annual Address Delivered before the Quebec Dental Society," *Canada Journal of Dental Science* 3 (December 1870): 38

33. As cited in Morrow, "Lacrosse as the National Game," 50.

34. As cited in ibid., 51.

35. *Montreal Gazette,* September 18, 1867, as cited in Burr, "Senior Lacrosse in Canada," 60–61.

36. See J. A. Mangan, ed., *The Cultural Bond: Sport, Empire, Society* (London: Cass, 1992); David Brown, "Canadian Imperialism and Sporting Exchanges: The Nineteen[th]-Century Cultural Experiences of Cricket and Lacrosse," *Canadian Journal of History of Sport* 18 (May 1987): 55–66; Don Morrow, "The Canadian Image Abroad: The Great Lacrosse Tours of 1876 and 1883," in *Proceedings of the Fifth Canadian Symposium on the History of Sport and Physical Education* (Toronto, August 26–29, 1982): 11–23; idem, "Lacrosse as the National Game," 58–64. For accounts of matches in Dublin, Glasgow, and Windsor, see "Tour of Great Britain, 1876," Montreal *Gazette,* May 31, 1876, as cited in Kirsch, *Sports in North America,* 4: 295–300.

37. Morrow, "The Canadian Image Abroad," 16.

38. Clipping from the *Newcastle Daily Journal,* in "Montreal Amateur Athletic Association (MAAA) Scrapbook" 15: 176, as cited in Morrow, "The Canadian Image Abroad," 16.

39. "Tour of Great Britain, 1876," 298.

40. Press clippings in "MAAA Scrapbook" 15: 124, as cited in Morrow, "Canadian Image Abroad," 13.

41. Morrow, "The Canadian Image Abroad," 22–23, 18.

42. Walter F. Willcox, ed., *International Migrations,* vol. 1, *Statistics* (New York: National Bureau of Economic Research, 1929), 636.

43. Suzanne Zeller, *Inventing Canada: Early Victorian Science and the Idea of a Trans-continental Nation* (Toronto: University of Toronto Press, 1987); Dave Brown, "The Northern Character Theme and Sport in Nineteenth-Century Canada," *Canadian Journal of History of Sport* 20 (May 1989): 47–56; Carl Berger, "The True North Strong and Free," in *Nationalism in Canada,* ed. Peter Russell (Toronto: McGraw-Hill Co. of Canada, 1966), 3–26; Stephen K. Sanderson, *Social Evolutionism: A Critical History*

(Cambridge, Mass.: Basil Blackwell, 1990); Lewis Henry Morgan, *Ancient Society; or, Researches in the Lines of Human Progress from Savagery through Barbarism to Civilization* (New York: Henry Holt, 1877).

44. On the research leading to the publication of Henry Lewis Morgan, *League of the Ho-de-no-sau-nee, or Iroquois* (Rochester, N.Y.: Sage and Brother, 1851), see Elisabeth Tooker, "The Structure of the Iroquois League: Lewis H. Morgan's Research and Observations," *Ethnohistory* 30, no. 3 (1983): 141–54. On Morgan's ethnography research club founded in 1842, see Robert E. Bieder, "The Grand Order of the Iroquois: Influences on Lewis Henry Morgan's Ethnology," *Ethnohistory* 27 (Fall 1980): 349–61.

45. On "counterrevolution" and "Canadian identity," see chapters 1, 3, and 4 of Seymour Martin Lipset, *Continental Divide: The Values and Institutions of the United States and Canada* (New York: Routledge, 1990).

46. *Montreal Gazette,* November 14, 1867, as cited in Peter Leslie Lindsay, "A History of Sport in Canada, 1807–1867" (Ph.D. diss., University of Alberta, 1969), 124.

47. *Montreal Gazette,* October 23, 1867, as cited in Lindsay, "History of Sport in Canada," 126.

48. Burr, "Senior Lacrosse in Canada," 93; Alan Metcalfe, "The Evolution of Organized Physical Recreation in Montreal, 1840–1895," in *Sports in Canada: Historical Readings,* ed. Morris Mott (Toronto: Copp Clark Pitman, 1989), 135.

49. Burr, "Senior Lacrosse in Canada," 84.

50. Ibid., 38.

51. Beers, *Lacrosse,* xiv.

52. Burr, "Senior Lacrosse in Canada," 58, 71, 106.

53. *Montreal Gazette,* July 28, 1884, as cited in Burr, "Senior Lacrosse in Canada," 66.

54. Metcalfe, "Organized Physical Recreation in Montreal," 137.

55. Nancy Pinto, "Ain't Misbehavin': The Montreal Shamrock Lacrosse Club Fans 1868 to 1884" (paper presented at North American Society for Sport History conference, Banff, Alberta, 1990), 11, 8–9.

56. Alan Metcalfe, *Canada Learns to Play: The Emergence of Organized Sport, 1807–1914* (Toronto: McClelland and Stewart, 1987), 196–203.

57. Burr, "Senior Lacrosse in Canada," 66–68, 84–85, 90.

58. "Laws of Lacrosse," in Beers, *Lacrosse,* 255–56.

59. Italics in original. Beers, *Lacrosse,* 205.

60. Burr, "Senior Lacrosse in Canada," 38–40.

61. "Laws of Lacrosse," 254.

62. Burr, "Senior Lacrosse in Canada," 76–77.

63. *Constitution of the National Lacrosse Association of Canada,* adopted 1876, in *Laws of Lacrosse and Constitution of the National Lacrosse Association of Canada,* revised and adopted on June 7, 1878 (Toronto: R. Marshall, 1878), 23, as cited in Burr, "Senior Lacrosse in Canada," 81.

64. Frank Cosentino, "A History of the Concept of Professionalism in Canadian Sport" (Ph.D. diss., University of Alberta, 1973), 37.

65. *Toronto Mail,* August 16, 1877, as cited in Cosentino, "Professionalism in Canadian Sport," 37.

66. Burr, "Senior Lacrosse in Canada," 66.

67. Metcalfe, *Canada Learns to Play,* 195.
68. Cosentino, "Professionalism in Canadian Sport," 38–39.
69. *Toronto Mail,* June 24, 1881, as cited in Cosentino, "Professionalism in Canadian Sport," 39.
70. Nancy Barbara Bouchier, "Idealized Middle-Class Sport for a Young Nation: Lacrosse in Nineteenth-Century Ontario Towns, 1871–1891," *Journal of Canadian Studies* 29 (Summer 1994): 91–95; see also idem, "'For the Love of the Game and the Honour of the Town': Organized Sport, Local Culture and Middle Class Hegemony in Two Ontario Towns, 1838–1895" (Ph.D. diss., University of Western Ontario, 1990), 300–13.
71. Bouchier, "Idealized Middle-Class Sport," 96.
72. *Woodstock Sentinel,* July 20, 1887, as cited in Bouchier, "Idealized Middle-Class Sport," 102.
73. Bouchier, "Idealized Middle-Class Sport," 102.
74. Metcalfe, *Canada Learns to Play,* 185–87.
75. Burr, "Senior Lacrosse in Canada," 90–91.
76. Metcalfe, *Canada Learns to Play,* 187.
77. Burr, "Senior Lacrosse in Canada," 65–70, 114–19.
78. Ibid., 122–24.
79. National Lacrosse Association, *Rules of Lacrosse* (Toronto: J. Ross Robertson, 1879), 5–6; Junior Lacrosse League of Montreal, *Laws of Lacrosse and Constitution of the Junior Lacrosse League of Montreal* (Montreal: Junior Lacrosse League of Montreal), 14–16; British Columbia Lacrosse Association, *Constitution and Rules of the British Columbia Lacrosse Association* (Vancouver: Evans & Hastings, 1899), 16–17.
80. *Vancouver Daily Province,* June 5, 1911.
81. Burr, "Senior Lacrosse in Canada," 134–35, 145–46, 149, 150.
82. Burr, "Senior Lacrosse in Canada," 127, 132, 184, 147–48, 137; North American Indian Travelling College, *Tewaarathon,* 50.
83. Ibid., 139.
84. *Annual Report of the Amateur Athletic Association of Canada,* 1892, as cited in Burr, "Senior Lacrosse in Canada," 140–41.
85. Burr, "Senior Lacrosse in Canada," 142–44.
86. *Toronto Globe,* April 12, 1904, as cited in Burr, "Senior Lacrosse in Canada," 143.
87. Burr, "Senior Lacrosse in Canada," 190, 191–92.
88. Ibid., 192–93, 131, 193–94, 199.
89. Ibid., 194–95, 197–98, 199–202, 200–1.
90. Ibid., 204–5.
91. Daniel Mason, "Professional Sports Facilities and Developing Urban Communities: Vancouver's Recreation Park, 1905–1912," *Urban History Review* (October 1997): 47.
92. Burr, "Senior Lacrosse in Canada," 207, 208.
93. Metcalfe, *Canada Learns to Play,* 210.
94. H. H. Roxborough, "Can Lacrosse Come Back?" *MacLean's Magazine* 42 (August 15, 1929): 38.
95. Metcalfe, *Canada Learns to Play,* 210.
96. Fred Jacob, "A Plea for the National Game," *Maclean's Magazine* 27 (May 1914): 36.
97. Ibid.
98. Roxborough, "Can Lacrosse Come Back?" 38, 36.

99. Fred Jacob, "Is Lacrosse What It Used To Be?" *MacLean's Magazine* 39 (June 15, 1926): 40.

100. Leon E. Truesdell, *The Canadian Born in the United States: An Analysis of the Statistics of the Canadian Element in the Population of the United States 1850 to 1930* (New Haven, Conn.: Yale University Press, 1943), 10.

101. Stephen Thernstrom, ed., *Harvard Encyclopedia of American Ethnic Groups* (Cambridge, Mass.: Belknap Press of Harvard University Press, 1980), 191–97; Marcus Lee Hansen, *The Mingling of the Canadian and American Peoples*, vol. 1 *(Historical)* (New Haven, Conn.: Yale University Press, 1940).

102. J. A. Hodge, Jr., "Lacrosse in the United States," *Outing* 7 (March 1886): 669.

103. David Blanchard, "Entertainment, Dance and Northern Mohawk Showmanship," *American Indian Quarterly* 7, no. 1 (1983): 2–26.

104. Hodge, "Lacrosse in the United States," 669.

105. *Spirit of the Times*, September 14, 1869, October 9, 1869, March 12, 1870, September 3, 1870, December 3, 1870; Hodge, "Lacrosse in the United States," 669.

106. See chapters 5 and 8 of Richard O'Connor, *The Golden Summers: An Antic History of Newport* (New York: G. P. Putnam's Sons, 1974).

107. *Spirit of the Times*, August 19, 1876; *New York Times*, August 17, 1876; *Spirit of the Times*, August 26, 1876.

108. Hodge, "Lacrosse in the United States," 669.

109. *New York Times*, August 24, 1878; *Spirit of the Times*, August 31, 1878.

110. See chapters 18 and 19 of Richard Slotkin, *The Fatal Environment: The Myth of the Frontier in the Age of Industrialization, 1800–1890* (New York: Atheneum, 1985).

111. "The American Lacrosse Team," *Harper's Weekly* 28 (10 May 1884): 299.

112. Hodge, "Lacrosse in the United States," 665, 670.

113. *Reports of the Proceedings of the [Boston, Mass.] City Council*, May 17, 1886, as cited in Stephen Hardy, *How Boston Played: Sport, Recreation, and Community 1865–1915* (Boston: Northeastern University Press, 1982), 141.

114. *New York Times*, September 5, 1886; *Spirit of the Times*, July 13, 1878.

115. *New York Times*, September 5, 1886; Truesdell, *Canadian Born in the United States*, 35.

116. On Wiman's life and role as an advocate of continental economic union, see Ian Grant, "Erastus Wiman: a Continentalist Replies to Canadian Imperialism," *Canadian Historical Review* 53 (March 1972): 1–20. See also W. Stewart Wallace, *The MacMillan Dictionary of Canadian Biography*, 4th ed., revised, enlarged, and updated by W. A. McKay (Toronto: MacMillan of Canada, 1978), 898; James Grant Wilson and John Fiske, eds., *Appleton's Cyclopaedia of American Biography* (New York: D. Appleton and Co., 1889), 6: 558; Henry James Morgan, ed., *The Canadian Men and Women of the Time: A Hand-book of Canadian Biography* (Toronto: William Briggs, 1898), 1093–94. For an example of Wiman's commercial unionist thought, see Erastus Wiman, "What Is the Destiny of Canada?" *North American Review* 148 (June 1889): 665–75.

117. *New York Times*, April 24, 1885, May 14, 1885.

118. Erastus Wiman, "The Canadian Club, Its Purpose and Policy, as Set Forth in the Speech of Dominion Day Dinner, July 1, 1885" (New York, 1885), 5, 7–9, 13; Truesdell, *Canadian Born in the United States*, 35.

119. *New York Times,* September 12, 1886; Grant, "Erastus Wiman," 17–19.

120. *Syracuse Journal,* July 28, 1875, July 30, 1875, August 12, 1875, August 26, 1875, July 26, 1876, August 2, 1876, October 2, 1877; Syracuse *Courier,* August 25, 1875, July 2, 1879.

121. *Syracuse Courier* and *Syracuse Journal,* March 8, 1878.

122. *Syracuse Journal,* May 29, 1878.

123. Ibid., September 2, 1875.

124. *New York World,* March 6, 1878.

125. *Spirit of the Times,* March 9, 1878, March 16, 1878.

126. *New York Times,* July 24, 1884.

127. Ibid., July 25, 1884.

128. *Spirit of the Times,* August 2, 1884.

129. *New York Times,* July 30, 1884.

130. Ibid., September 20, 1885, September 30, 1885.

131. *Spirit of the Times,* November 9, 1878.

132. *New York Times,* September 5, 1886.

133. Robert M. Utley, *The Indian Frontier of the American West 1846–1890* (Albuquerque: University of New Mexico Press, 1984).

134. Hodge, "Lacrosse in the United States," 665.

135. Blanchard, "Entertainment, Dance and Northern Mohawk Showmanship," 9–10.

136. On the Wild West Show, see L. G. Moses, *Wild West Shows and the Images of the American Indians, 1883–1933* (Albuquerque: University of New Mexico Press, 1996); Sarah J. Blackstone, *Buckskins, Bullets, and Business: A History of Buffalo Bill's Wild West* (New York: Greenwood Press, 1986); chapter 5 of Daniel Francis, *The Imaginary Indian: The Image of the Indian in Canadian Culture* (Vancouver, B.C.: Arsenal Pulp Press, 1992); Joy S. Kasson, *Buffalo Bill's Wild West: Celebrity, Memory, and Popular History* (New York: Hill and Wang, 2000); chapter 2 of Richard Slotkin, *Gunfighter Nation: The Myth of the Frontier in Twentieth-Century America* (New York: Harper-Collins, 1993).

137. *Spirit of the Times,* August 7, 1886.

Chapter 2: "King of the Field Games"

1. *New York Times,* June 21, 1879; *Spirit of the Times,* June 28, 1879.

2. *The National Cyclopaedia of American Biography* (New York: James T. White & Co., 1893; reprint, Ann Arbor, Mich.: University Microfilms, 1967), 3: 207.

3. *Spirit of the Times,* April 21, 1883, April 5, 1884, February 27, 1886, March 5, 1887, February 25, 1888, March 21, 1885, April 13, 1889.

4. William A. Davis, "The First All America Athletic Team," *Official Lacrosse Guide* 1944, 28.

5. Hodge, "Lacrosse in the United States," 670–72; *New York Times,* April 13, 1884, June 10, 1884, July 10, 1884; *Spirit of the Times,* July 12, 1884, July 19, 1884; "The American Lacrosse Team," 299; Ross MacKenzie, "Lacrosse," *Outing* 21 (October 1892): 76–80; Davis, "First All America Athletic Team," 30.

6. *New York Times,* March 22, 1886, August 8, 1886, August 9, 1886; "Lacrosse," *Harper's Weekly* 30 (August 21, 1886): 539.

7. MacKenzie, "Lacrosse," 80.

8. *Spirit of the Times,* September 16, 1882, May 29, 1886, July 26, 1886.

9. *New York Times,* July 6, 1886, July 14, 1886.

10. *Spirit of the Times,* August 7, 1886.

11. *New York Times,* January 4, 1891, January 11, 1891; *Spirit of the Times,* January 17, 1891.

12. *Spirit of the Times,* January 17, 1891; *New York Times,* January 4, 1891, February 1, 1891, February 8, 1891.

13. *New York Times,* August 27, 1892.

14. *Johns Hopkins News-Letter,* May 18, 1914.

15. *Baltimore Sun,* November 25, 1878, April 6, 1930, April 13, 1930, April 20, 1930, April 27, 1930, May 4, 1930.

16. Ibid., April 20, 1930.

17. *Lacrosse News,* December 5, 1938, 3, LF.

18. *Baltimore Sun,* April 6, 1930.

19. G. Wilson Shaffer, *Recreation and Athletics at Johns Hopkins: A One-Hundred-Year History* (Baltimore: The Johns Hopkins University Press, 1977), 5–15, 17.

20. John C. French, *A History of the University Founded by Johns Hopkins* (Baltimore: The Johns Hopkins University Press, 1946).

21. Shaffer, *Recreation and Athletics,* 1.

22. *Johns Hopkins News-Letter,* January 29, 1909.

23. Shaffer, *Recreation and Athletics,* 5.

24. *Johns Hopkins News-Letter,* June 4, 1903.

25. *The Hullabaloo* (Baltimore: Press of Guggenheimer, Weil & Co., 1898), 135.

26. *Johns Hopkins News-Letter,* January 29, 1912, June 4, 1902.

27. *The Hullabaloo* (Baltimore, 1899), 173.

28. *Johns Hopkins News-Letter,* April 30, 1909, May 24, 1909.

29. W. Oster "Kid" Norris, "A History of Lacrosse at the Mount Washington Club," in Mount Washington Lacrosse Club 1956 game program, in Mount Washington Lacrosse Team Scrapbook, MS 603, Manuscripts Division, MHS; Mark Miller, *Mount Washington: Baltimore Suburb* (Baltimore: GBS Publishers, 1980), 40, 42–43.

30. "The Mount Washington Club of Baltimore, Md.," *Illustrated Outdoor News* clipping dated May 26, 1906, in Mount Washington Lacrosse Team Scrapbook, MHS.

31. *Baltimore Sun* clipping dated July 30, 1905, in Mount Washington Lacrosse Team Scrapbook, MHS.

32. *Baltimore Sun,* May 24, 1915.

33. *Johns Hopkins News-Letter,* January 30, 1911.

34. *The Crescent Athletic Club of Brooklyn Club Book 1896* (Brooklyn, 1896), n.p.

35. *Brooklyn Eagle* clipping, March 27, 1939, in file on Crescent Athletic Club, LF.

36. *Leslie's Weekly,* as cited in "A Purely Amateur Athletic Club Team," *Crescent* 2 (June 1, 1896): 7.

37. Stuart Anderson, *Race and Rapprochement: Anglo-Saxonism and Anglo-American Relations, 1895–1904* (London: Associated University Presses, 1981).

38. Ronald A. Smith, *Sports and Freedom: The Rise of Big-Time College Athletics* (New York: Oxford University Press, 1988), 38–42, 111–14.

39. *Crescent* 2 (August 1, 1896): 6, LOC.

40. Ibid. (December 1, 1896): 11, LOC.

41. Ibid.: 16, LOC.

42. *Crescent* 2 (February 1, 1897): 20–21, LOC.

43. *New York Times*, March 12, 1897; Caspar Whitney, *Harper's Weekly* 41 (May 22, 1897): 521.

44. Whitney, *Harper's Weekly*, 521.

45. W. Stepney Rawson, "Lacrosse: How, When, and Where to See It," *Badminton Magazine of Sports & Pastimes* 6 (March 1898): 332–45, quote on 344.

46. *Crescent* 2 [3] (June 1, 1897): 16, LOC.

47. *Brooklyn Daily Eagle*, March 14, 1905.

48. "International Lacrosse: The Crescent A.C. Tour in 1897," *Official Lacrosse Guide 1922–1923* (1922), 21.

49. Undated *Brooklyn Eagle* clipping, in file on Crescent Athletic Club, LF. By the time of the forty-sixth annual lacrosse dinner held at the Crescent clubhouse in March 1938, only six men from the tour team were present. *New York Times*, March 6, 1938.

50. *Brooklyn Daily Eagle*, April 29, 1900.

51. *Hobart Herald*, March 23, 1922.

52. The 1904 games featured two Canadian teams, from the Shamrock L.C. of Winnipeg (gold) and the Mohawks of Brantford (bronze), and an American team from the Saint Louis Amateur Athletic Association. In 1908 only Canada and Britain provided teams.

53. *Crescent* 2 (January 1, 1898): 3.

54. Carroll J. Post to William C. Schmeisser, February 21, 1940, in file on Crescent Athletic Club, LF.

55. *Brooklyn Daily Eagle*, May 27, 1900, May 29, 1900, May 31, 1900, June 10, 1900, May 29, 1910, May 31, 1910.

56. Crescent Athletic Club of Brooklyn, *Annual Report 1912*, 15, 17; *Annual Report 1914*, 11, 13; *Annual Report 1915*, 11, 13; *Annual Report 1916*, 11, 13; *Annual Report 1917*, 10, 23; *Annual Report 1918*, 8, 23; *Annual Report 1919*, 6, 15.

57. *Brooklyn Daily Eagle*, June 15, 1900, May 31, 1905.

58. A. M. Learned, *Hobart College Lacrosse 75th Anniversary 1973* (Geneva, N.Y., 1973); *Hobart Herald*, June 1906, April 1908.

59. *Syracuse Daily Orange*, November 15, 1906, February 14, 1908.

60. *Baltimore Sun*, March 23, 1900.

61. *Johns Hopkins News-Letter*, April 6, 1900.

62. *Baltimore Sun*, May 5, 1900.

63. As cited in Craig E. Taylor, "Lacrosse at City College," in *One Hundred Years of the Baltimore City College*, ed. James Chancellor Leonhart (Baltimore: H. G. Roebuck & Son, 1939), 231.

64. *Johns Hopkins News-Letter*, December 21, 1906.

65. M. Howell Griswold, *Baltimore Polytechnic Institute: The First Century* (Baltimore: M. Howell Griswold, 1984), 132.

66. *Brooklyn Daily Eagle*, March 17, 1905.

67. *Andover Phillipian*, as cited in Fred H. Harrison, *Athletics for All: Physical Education and Athletics at Phillips Academy, Andover 1778–1978* (Andover, Mass.: Phillips Academy, 1983), 66–67.

68. Harrison, *Athletics for All*, 170–71.

69. *New York Times*, May 24, 1913.

70. Harrison, *Athletics for All*, 170–71.

71. Ibid., 170.

72. F. C. Alexander, "Northern Division Inter-Collegiate Lacrosse League," *Constitution, By-Laws and Playing Rules of the United States Inter-Collegiate Lacrosse League, 1910* (New York: American Sports Publishing, 1910), 9.

73. Smith, *Sports and Freedom.*

74. Steven Riess, *Touching Base: Professional Baseball and American Culture in the Progressive Era* (Westport, Conn.: Greenwood Press, 1980); Michael Oriard, *Reading Football: How the Popular Press Created an American Spectacle* (Chapel Hill: University of North Carolina Press, 1993).

75. John R. Flannery, "King of the Field Games," *Independent* 71 (July 6, 1911): 24.

76. As cited in Shaffer, *Recreation and Athletics,* 10.

77. *Johns Hopkins News-Letter,* June 4, 1903.

78. *Hobart Herald,* March 1904.

79. Frederick Weir, "Lacrosse," *Lippincott's Monthly Magazine* 49 (June 1892): 749.

80. *New York Times,* June 5, 1892.

81. *Johns Hopkins News-Letter,* January 25, 1899, February 23, 1899.

82. For a discussion of amateur athletics and the formation of social ties at universities in England, America, Germany, and other western countries, see Eric Hobsbawm, "Mass-Producing Traditions: Europe, 1870–1914," in *The Invention of Tradition,* ed. Eric Hobsbawm and Terence Ranger (Cambridge, U.K.: Cambridge University Press, 1983), 263–307, especially 291–303.

83. *Johns Hopkins News-Letter,* April 6, 1898.

84. Ibid., January 10, 1900, and October 31, 1900.

85. Ibid., May 12, 1905.

86. Ibid., April 23, 1907.

87. *Hobart Herald,* March 1904.

88. *Johns Hopkins News-Letter,* May 18, 1906.

89. "'Father Bill' Schmeisser," *Lacrosse,* lacrosse program (Hopkins vs. Maryland, Homewood, May 17, 1958), Programs, Tickets and Announcements: Lacrosse, 1926–1969, Folder 9, Box 2, Department of Physical Education and Athletics, Record Group Number 13.020, FHAJHU.

90. *Johns Hopkins News-Letter,* May 11, 1914.

91. Lewis Sheldon Welch and Walter Camp, *Yale: Her Campus, Class-Rooms, and Athletics* (Boston: L. C. Page and Co., 1899), 625.

92. *Baltimore Sun,* May 15, 1900.

93. *New York Times,* October 18, 1914.

94. See chapter 2 of James DeMuth, *Small Town Chicago: The Comic Perspective of Finley Peter Dunne, George Ade, Ring Lardner* (Port Washington, N.Y.: Kennikat Press, 1980); Grace Eckley, *Finley Peter Dunne* (Boston: Twayne Publishers, 1981).

95. *Johns Hopkins News-Letter,* May 23, 1901.

96. Caspar W. Whitney, "An Unappreciated Game," *Harper's Weekly* 38 (April 14, 1894): 349.

97. Ibid., 349.

98. H. V. Blaxter, "A Real American Game—Lacrosse," *Outing* 46 (May 1905): 223.

99. Arthur B. Reeve, "Beginnings of Our Great Games: Early Days of Tennis and Lacrosse," *Outing* 56 (May 1910): 175.

100. *Johns Hopkins News-Letter,* December 18, 1901.

101. J. Parmly Paret, *Lawn Tennis Its Past, Present, and Future to Which is Added a Chapter on Lacrosse by William Harvey Maddren* (New York: MacMillan Co., 1904), 373.

102. Paul Gustafson, "Lacrosse," in *The Book of Athletics,* ed. Paul Withington (Boston: Lothrop, Lee & Shepard, 1914), 457.

103. *Syracuse Daily Orange,* April 26, 1918.

104. Inter-University Lacrosse League of the United States, *American Lacrosse Rules* (New York: Arthur Johnson & Co., 1902), 3, 5.

105. C. E. Marsters, "Northern Division Inter-Collegiate Lacrosse League," *Constitution, By-Laws and Playing Rules of the United States Inter-Collegiate Lacrosse League, 1910,* 10.

106. "Lacrosse for the School Boys," *Official Lacrosse Guide* 1911, 63.

107. *Brooklyn Daily Eagle,* May 23, 1900.

108. *Buffalo Express,* July 2, 1901, July 3, 1901, July 4, 1901; *Buffalo News,* July 1, 1901, July 3, 1901, July 5, 1901.

109. *Brooklyn Daily Eagle,* May 19, 1905, May 21, 1905.

110. *Johns Hopkins News-Letter,* April 6, 1900.

111. *Baltimore Sun,* March 27, 1900.

112. *Hobart Herald,* July 1900, June 1903, May 13, 1911, May 18, 1912.

113. Ibid., June 1903, July 1904, July 1906.

114. *Johns Hopkins News-Letter,* February 8, 1915.

115. "Lacrosse as Played by the Indians," *Official Lacrosse Guide* 1913, 63. See also Albert B. Reagan, "Some Games of the Bois Fort Ojibway," *American Anthropologist* 21 (July–September 1919): 264–78, especially 275–76.

116. "Lacrosse as Played by the Indians," 63.

117. Raymond D. Fogelson, "The Cherokee Ball Game: A Study in Southeastern Ethnology" (Ph.D. diss., University of Pennsylvania, 1962); Kendall Blanchard, *The Mississippi Choctaws at Play: The Serious Side of Leisure* (Urbana: University of Illinois Press, 1981). In 1939 Cherokee Indians in the Smoky Mountains of North Carolina organized a team to play against white teams. See William H. "Dinty" Moore III, "Lacrosse Expansion," *Official Lacrosse Guide* 1939, 29.

118. Joseph Shacter, "Brief History of Lacrosse in the United States," *Official Lacrosse Guide* 1935, 13.

119. For overviews of the Carlisle school, see Carmelita S. Ryan, "The Carlisle Indian Industrial School" (Ph.D. diss., Georgetown University, 1962), and Pearl Lee Walker-McNeil, "The Carlisle Indian School: A Study of Acculturation" (Ph.D. diss., American University, 1979). See also Richard Henry Pratt, *Battlefield and Classroom: Four Decades with the American Indian, 1867–1904* (New Haven, Conn.: Yale University Press, 1964).

120. *Carlisle Arrow,* April 21, 1911, LOC.

121. For a cultural critique of the Carlisle football team, see Walker-McNeil, "The Carlisle Indian School," 144–48. For a more general overview of sports at Carlisle, see John Bloom, *To Show What an Indian Can Do: Sports at Native American Boarding Schools* (Minneapolis: University of Minnesota Press, 2000).

122. *Carlisle Arrow,* January 14, 1910, LOC.

123. Ibid., June 24, 1910, LOC.

124. *New York Times,* January 14, 1913.

125. Glenn S. Warner, "Lacrosse vs. Baseball: One Solution of the Summer Ball Problem," *Official Lacrosse Guide* 1914, 77, 79, 81. In another article in the annual lacrosse guide of 1922, Warner argued that baseball and lacrosse could coexist if necessary. Glenn S. Warner, "Lacrosse—The Best Spring Game for Schools and Colleges," *Official Lacrosse Guide* 1922–1923 (1922), 17.

126. *Carlisle Arrow,* May 29, 1914; Box I 1372, Publications of the Federal Government, Interior Department, 1849–, Record Group 287, NA.

127. *Carlisle Arrow,* September 15, 1911, LOC.

128. Warner, "Lacrosse vs. Baseball," 81.

129. Warner, "Lacrosse—The Best Spring Game," 15.

130. *Carlisle 1917; Being a Presentation Done in Prose and Verse Together with Illustrations of the Varied Activities of This United States Indian School Today,* LOC.

131. *Baltimore Sun,* May 7, 1910.

132. As cited in *Carlisle Arrow,* May 20, 1910, LOC.

133. As cited in *Carlisle Arrow,* April 26, 1912, LOC.

134. *Carlisle Arrow,* June 18, 1915; Box I 1373, Publications of the Federal Government, Interior Department, 1849–, Record Group 287, NA.

135. *Carlisle Arrow,* May 5, 1911, April 7, 1911, LOC.

136. *Johns Hopkins News-Letter,* May 5, 1913.

137. John R. Flannery, "Twenty Years of Lacrosse in America," *Official Lacrosse Guide* 1914, 20.

138. *Carlisle Arrow,* June 2, 1911, LOC.

139. *New York Times,* May 6, 1917.

Chapter 3: "What Are a Few Cuts . . . ?"

1. "Lacrosse Team Resolution," Folder 8, Box 1, FHAJHU.

2. Justin Cobb, "The Evolution of the Rules of Lacrosse" (master's thesis, Springfield University, 1952), 48–49.

3. "Historical Record of Championship Teams of the United States in Intercollegiate Lacrosse," *Official Lacrosse Guide* 1941, 23–24.

4. *Syracuse Daily Orange,* October 3, 1921, October 5, 1921, December 14, 1921.

5. *New York Times,* May 1, 1927.

6. Ibid., January 11, 1920; "Lacrosse in Brooklyn High Schools," *Official Lacrosse Guide* 1922–1923 (1922), 35; "Scholastic Lacrosse," *Official Lacrosse Guide* 1924, 43.

7. "Lacrosse in Brooklyn High Schools," 33; "Teams Playing Lacrosse," *Official Lacrosse Guide* 1922–1923, 41.

8. *Baltimore Sun,* March 5, 1925, March 13, 1925.

9. *Johns Hopkins News-Letter,* March 28, 1922.

10. *The Hullabaloo* (Baltimore, 1923), 265.

11. *Johns Hopkins News-Letter,* March 19, 1926.

12. Ibid., May 18, 1926, October 1, 1926.

13. Ibid., May 25, 1920, April 4, 1922, April 13, 1923.

14. Ibid., March 6, 1928.

15. *Syracuse Daily Orange,* February 17, 1925.

16. Scott D. Kimmell, "The Evolution of Army Athletics, 1890–1940," 10–11, 14–16, USMAA; "System of Intramural Athletics," *Annual Report of the Army Athletic Association, 1929,* 64–65, USMAA; *Howitzer* (West Point: United States Military Academy, 1908), 215; Joseph E. Dineen, *The Illustrated History of Sports at the U.S. Military Academy* (Norfolk, Va.: Donning Company, 1988), 272; *Annual Report of the Army Athletic Association, 1907,* 36, USMAA.

17. *Annual Report of the Army Athletic Association, 1929,* 26, 64–65, USMAA; Dineen, *Illustrated History of Sports,* 272; "Athletic Board Proceedings 1940–41," entry dated January 7, 1941, USMAA.

18. *Johns Hopkins News-Letter,* March 27, 1925.

19. *Brooklyn Daily Eagle,* June 14, 1920.

20. *Rutgers Targum,* April 29, 1924.

21. *Brooklyn Daily Eagle,* June 1, 1920.

22. *New York Evening Post,* May 1, 1919.

23. *Syracuse Daily Orange,* December 15, 1922.

24. "Lacrosse—The Game," *Official Lacrosse Guide 1922–1923,* 5; *Brooklyn Daily Eagle,* April 13, 1925.

25. *New York Evening Post,* May 1, 1919.

26. *Washington Daily Star,* April 9, 1924.

27. Clarence H. Goldsmith, "Lacrosse, the Real American Game: A Talk over the Radio from Gimbel Bros. Broadcasting Station, Philadelphia, Pa.," *Official Lacrosse Guide 1926,* 13.

28. Goldsmith, "Lacrosse, the Real American Game," 17.

29. *New York Times,* April 15, 1933, October 8, 1937; Laurie D. Cox, "Effects of the Depression on Lacrosse," *Official Lacrosse Guide 1934,* 67.

30. W. H. "Dinty" Moore, "Lacrosse Becoming Increasingly Popular," *Official Lacrosse Guide 1938,* 35.

31. *New York Times,* December 12, 1932; Laurie D. Cox, "The Evolution of the Lacrosse Rules," *Official Lacrosse Guide 1946,* 21–22; Cobb, "The Evolution of the Rules of Lacrosse," 54–62; *Syracuse Daily Orange,* March 14, 1942.

32. *New York Times,* December 14, 1932.

33. *Syracuse Daily Orange,* December 13, 1932.

34. Laurie D. Cox, "The Season of 1939," *Official Lacrosse Guide 1940,* 11; "Historical Record of Championship Teams of the United States in Intercollegiate Lacrosse," *Official Lacrosse Guide 1941,* 23–24.

35. *Syracuse Daily Orange,* May 12, 1930.

36. *New York Times,* June 15, 1940; John H. Paige, "North-South All-Star Game," *Official Lacrosse Guide 1941,* 19–20.

37. John H. Paige, "The North-South Game," *Official Lacrosse Guide 1942,* 17–18.

38. *New York Times,* April 22, 1941.

39. William A. Blower, "Prejudice in Sports," *Opportunity: Journal of Negro Life* 19 (September 1941): 260.

40. *New York Times,* April 10, 1941, April 26, 1941.

41. *Syracuse Daily Orange,* March 18, 1942, April 16, 1942, April 18, 1942, April 21, 1942, May 19, 1942; *New York Times,* February 28, 1945.

42. *Official Lacrosse Guide* 1943, iii.

43. *Official Lacrosse Guide* 1944, 12.

44. William H. Moore III, "Lacrosse Heroes in the War," *Official Lacrosse Guide* 1944, 24.

45. *New York Times*, March 13, 1943.

46. Craig E. Taylor, "Lacrosse Tops as Fitness Builder," *Official Lacrosse Guide* 1944, 32.

47. Lewis Jay Korn, "Lacrosse—A Scholastic Sport," *Scholastic Coach* 1 (February 1932): 7.

48. Caleb Kelly, Jr., interview with author, June 17, 1994, Claiborne, Md.

49. Ibid.

50. *Lacrosse* souvenir program, season 1941 (April 12, 1941, vs. Loyola), n.p., Programs, Tickets and Announcements: Lacrosse, 1926–1969, Folder 9, Box 2, FHAJHU.

51. Claxton J. O'Connor, "Scholastic Lacrosse in Maryland," *Official Lacrosse Guide* 1946, 52.

52. O'Connor, "Scholastic Lacrosse in Maryland," 51.

53. Craig Taylor, "Lacrosse Material," *Official Lacrosse Guide* 1946, 40.

54. Charles E. Marsters, "New England Prep Schools," *Official Lacrosse Guide* 1944, 49.

55. Harrison, *Athletics for All*, 252–54; *New York Times*, May 30, 1935, 24.

56. Walter S. Smith, "Scholastic Lacrosse in Central New York," *Official Lacrosse Guide* 1930, 54.

57. *Syracuse Daily Orange*, December 19, 1921.

58. *New York Times*, April 10, 1922.

59. "The Oxford-Cambridge Tour of 1922," *Official Lacrosse Guide* 1922–1923, 27, 29, 31.

60. *Syracuse Herald*, April 23, 1922.

61. *New York Times*, April 30, 1922; "The Oxford-Cambridge Tour of 1922," 31; *Crescent* 17 (June 1922): 15, file on Crescent Athletic Club, LF.

62. *Syracuse Daily Orange*, April 20, 1922.

63. *Johns Hopkins News-Letter*, April 11, 1922.

64. *Crescent* 17 (June 1922): 17, file on Crescent Athletic Club, LF.

65. *Johns Hopkins News-Letter*, May 2, 1922.

66. E. S. Barber, "International Lacrosse," *Official Lacrosse Guide* 1924, 35, 37, 39.

67. Barber, "International Lacrosse," 42.

68. Laurie D. Cox, "International Lacrosse," *Official Lacrosse Guide* 1931, 76.

69. *New York Times*, April 4, 1926, April 16, 1926, April 19, 1926.

70. *Syracuse Daily Orange*, April 17, 1926.

71. *Syracuse Journal*, April 18, 1926.

72. *Syracuse Daily Orange*, May 3, 1930.

73. *Johns Hopkins News-Letter*, April 4, 1930.

74. *New York Times*, December 10, 1934; Laurie D. Cox, "International Lacrosse for 1936," *Official Lacrosse Guide* 1936, 49.

75. Laurie D. Cox, "International Lacrosse for 1937," *Official Lacrosse Guide* 1937, 49; *New York Times*, December 7, 1936.

76. Laurie D. Cox, "The English Trip of 1937," *Official Lacrosse Guide* 1938, 47, 49.

77. Cox, "English Trip of 1937," 53, 55.

78. Martha Gable, "The Increasing Popularity of Lacrosse for Girls," *Journal of Health and Physical Education* 6 (November 1935): 31; Kathleen E. McCrone, *Playing the Game: Sport and the Physical Emancipation of English Women, 1870–1914* (Lexington: University Press of Kentucky, 1988), 137–41; S. L. Forbes and L. A. Livingston, "From

Frances Jane Dove to Rosabelle Sinclair and Beyond: The Introduction of Women's Field Lacrosse to North America," *Proceedings for the 10th Commonwealth & International Scientific Congress* (University of Victoria, Victoria, B.C., August 10–14, 1994), 83–86.

79. Joan Chrystal Burgess, "The History and Current Status of Women's Lacrosse in the United States" (master's thesis, Smith College, 1958), 18–19.

80. Ibid., 22–28; Gable, "Increasing Popularity of Lacrosse for Girls," 31.

81. Gable, "Increasing Popularity of Lacrosse for Girls," 31, 60. See also American Association for Health, Physical Education, and Recreation, *Official Field Hockey–Lacrosse Guide, with Official Rules 1941–1942* (New York: A. S. Barnes & Co., 1941).

82. See chapter 3 of Susan K. Cahn, *Coming On Strong: Gender and Sexuality in Twentieth-Century Women's Sport* (New York: Free Press, 1994).

83. G. Joyce Cran, "Lacrosse as a Game for Girls," *American Physical Education Review* 34 (November 1929): 539–40, quote on 540.

84. "More Missionaries of Sport," *Literary Digest* 117 (May 5, 1934): 34.

85. *New York Times*, April 22, 1934, October 9, 1935.

86. "Women Play Lacrosse, Rough Sport," *Literary Digest* 121 (May 16, 1936): 37.

87. Virginia Bourquardez, "Defense in Lacrosse," *Journal of Health and Physical Education* 8 (September 1937): 425, 450. See also Betty Richey, "Attack in Lacrosse," *Journal of Health and Physical Education* 8 (September 1937): 425, 450.

88. Burgess, "History and Current Status of Women's Lacrosse," 27, 30.

89. "International Lacrosse—The 1928 Olympics," *Official Lacrosse Guide* 1929, 20.

90. "Olympic Lacrosse," *Official Lacrosse Guide* 1928, 19; *New York Times*, January 20, 1928; 30 January 1928.

91. *New York Times*, June 24, 1928; "International Lacrosse—The 1928 Olympics," 21, 23.

92. "International Lacrosse—The 1928 Olympics," 23–24.

93. *Johns Hopkins News-Letter*, October 5, 1928.

94. As cited in Cox, "International Lacrosse," *Official Lacrosse Guide* 1931, 81, 85.

95. Fred I. Lorenson, "What's Wrong with Our Lacrosse?" *MacLean's Magazine* 44 (August 1, 1931): 12.

96. Ibid., 41.

97. "Lacrosse in Canada," *Official Lacrosse Guide* 1932, 65.

98. "Olympic Lacrosse," *Official Lacrosse Guide* 1931, 53, 55; *Official Lacrosse Guide* 1932, 7.

99. *Official Lacrosse Guide* 1932, 56.

100. *Baltimore Sun*, May 25, 1932; *New York Times*, May 23, 1932.

101. *New York Times*, June 12, 1932; *Baltimore Sun*, June 19, 1932, June 26, 1932; Laurie D. Cox, "Review of the 1932 Season," *Official Lacrosse Guide* 1933, 61.

102. *Baltimore Sun*, 17 July 1932.

103. W. Wilson Wingate, "Lacrosse in the Tenth Olympiad," *Official Lacrosse Guide* 1933, 68, 70; *Baltimore Sun*, August 10, 1932, August 13, 1932; *New York Times*, August 13, 1932.

104. Laurie D. Cox, "The Canadian Series for 1933," *Official Lacrosse Guide* 1934, 68–69.

105. John G. McCormack, "Indoor Lacrosse Inaugurated," *Official Lacrosse Guide* 1931, 93; *New York Times*, February 23, 1930; March 16, 1930; February 15, 1931.

106. Ted Reeve, "Box Lacrosse," *Maclean's Magazine* 44 (August 15, 1931): 7.

107. *Cornwall Freeholder* clipping dated August 1931, CSHF.

108. Ibid.

109. "The Origin of Lacrosse as Played in Canada Today," in Canadian Lacrosse Association, *Lacrosse Records and Rules of Box Lacrosse* (1950), 10–13, Saint Catharines Museum, Saint Catharines, Ontario.

110. *New York Times*, April 24, 1932, May 2, 1932, May 11, 1932.

111. *Baltimore Sun*, May 12, 1932.

112. *New York Times*, May 26, 1932.

113. Ibid., June 3, 1932.

114. *Baltimore Sun*, June 18, 1932, June 4, 1932, June 8, 1932.

115. *Syracuse Daily Orange*, January 8, 1932.

116. Laurie D. Cox, "Box Lacrosse," *Official Lacrosse Guide* 1932, 68–71.

117. Laurie D. Cox, "The Future of American Lacrosse—What?" *Official Lacrosse Guide* 1934, 11, 13, 15, 17–18.

118. Ibid., 11.

119. Harrison, *Athletics for All*, 502.

120. Cox, "Future of American Lacrosse," 13, 15.

121. See table III in Howard J. Savage, *American College Athletics* (New York: The Carnegie Foundation for the Advancement of Teaching, 1929), 140.

122. Cox, "Future of American Lacrosse," 13, 15.

123. Ibid., 15.

124. Ibid., 17–18.

125. *Syracuse Daily Orange*, April 27, 1938.

126. *New York Times*, December 10, 1939.

127. Stan Shillington, "Conflict, Chaos and Courting Judgment," British Columbia Lacrosse Association (BCLA) web-site library.

128. Stan Shillington, "Lights! Camera! Action!" BCLA web-site library.

129. Stan Shillington, "North Shore Indians—Circa 1936," BCLA web-site library; Cleve Dheensaw, *Lacrosse 100: One Hundred Years of Lacrosse in B.C.* (Victoria, B.C.: Orca Book Publishing, 1990), 48.

130. Dheensaw, *Lacrosse 100*, 48.

131. "1941–Ugly A's Win Out West," Unofficial Ontario Lacrosse Association web-site library.

132. Roy Taylor, "Lacrosse, the Original American Game," in *School Athletics in Modern Education: Wingate Memorial Lectures 1930–1931*, ed. E. Dana Caulkins (New York: Wingate Memorial Foundation, 1931), 467.

133. Joseph F. Harrigan, "Lacrosse for Schoolboys," in Caulkins, *School Athletics*, 504.

134. *New York Times*, February 24, 1940.

135. *Baltimore Sun*, April 6, 1930; W. Wilson Wingate, "Lacrosse—Oldest North American Team Game," *Official Lacrosse Guide* 1931, 60.

136. Kyle Crichton, "Murder on the Lawn," *Collier's* 94 (September 28, 1935): 38.

137. *Syracuse Daily Orange*, December 1, 1938, March 31, 1942.

138. "Women Play Lacrosse, Rough Sport," 36.

139. *Johns Hopkins News-Letter*, March 14, 1941.

140. *Syracuse Daily Orange*, May 24, 1916, April 10, 1922.

141. *Hobart Herald*, May 22, 1924, April 29, 1926.

142. *Johns Hopkins News-Letter,* April 17, 1925.

143. *Baltimore Sun,* April 19, 1925.

144. *Johns Hopkins News-Letter,* April 21, 1925.

145. *Syracuse Daily Orange,* April 12, 1930.

146. *Syracuse Post-Standard,* April 12, 1930, April 13, 1930.

147. *Syracuse Daily Orange,* May 31, 1934, May 18, 1935, May 29, 1936.

148. *Syracuse Daily Orange,* April 20, 1918, April 18, 1931.

149. H. Fenimore Baker, Jr., "The Season of 1923," *Official Lacrosse Guide* 1924, 55.

150. *New York Times,* April 4, 1926, June 12, 1927, May 6, 1928, June 10, 1928, June 16, 1929, June 8, 1930, June 21, 1932, July 12, 1940, July 26, 1940.

151. *Syracuse Daily Orange,* March 11, 1919.

152. Laurie D. Cox, "All-America Lacrosse Team, 1923," *Official Lacrosse Guide* 1924, 76.

153. *Syracuse Daily Orange,* April 17, 1931, April 16, 1932.

154. *Syracuse Post-Standard* clipping dated April 17, 1924, in vol. 4: 1924, Athletics, Dept. of Athletics, Physical Education and Recreation Records, Lacrosse, YRG 38–B-19, YUL.

155. *Hobart Herald,* April 21,1932.

156. *Syracuse Daily Orange,* April 30, 1932.

157. *New York Times,* June 9, 1926.

158. *Syracuse Daily Orange,* May 12, 1951.

159. *Syracuse Herald* clipping dated May 11, 1924, in vol 4: 1924, Athletics, Dept. of Athletics, Physical Education and Recreation Records, Lacrosse, YRG 38-B-19, YUL.

160. *Syracuse Daily Orange,* April 28, 1923.

161. Kenneth Drum, interview with author, December 28, 1994, Manlius, N.Y.

162. Albert Paige, interview with author, February 4, 1995, Syracuse, N.Y.

163. For a brief biography see Joseph H. Cash, "Louis Rook Bruce (1969–73)," in *The Commissioners of Indian Affairs, 1824–1977,* ed. Robert M. Kvasnicka and Herman J. Viola (Lincoln: University of Nebraska Press, 1979), 333–40.

164. Drum interview.

165. Laurence M. Hauptman, *The Iroquois and the New Deal* (Syracuse, N.Y.: Syracuse University Press, 1981).

166. Laurence M. Hauptman, *The Iroquois Struggle for Survival: World War II to Red Power* (Syracuse, N.Y.: Syracuse University Press, 1986), 6.

167. Shaffer, *Recreation and Athletics,* 18.

168. Howard J. Savage, *American College Athletics* (New York: The Carnegie Foundation for the Advancement of Teaching, 1929).

169. Savage, *American College Athletics,* xii; Shaffer, *Recreation and Athletics,* 33–34.

170. Savage, *American College Athletics,* xiv–xv; Shaffer, *Recreation and Athletics,* 34.

171. Savage, *American College Athletics,* xxi; Shaffer, *Recreation and Athletics,* 35.

172. Shaffer, *Recreation and Athletics,* 35.

173. *Johns Hopkins News-Letter,* March 27, 1930, April 27, 1934.

174. Ibid., March 6, 1934.

175. Shaffer, *Recreation and Athletics,* 36–39.

176. Ibid., 56–57.

177. *Johns Hopkins News-Letter,* April 27, 1934.

178. Shaffer, *Recreation and Athletics,* 40.

179. *Johns Hopkins News-Letter,* March 2, 1937.

180. Shaffer, *Recreation and Athletics,* 41.
181. *Johns Hopkins News-Letter,* March 2, 1937, March 9, 1937.
182. Shaffer, *Recreation and Athletics,* 42.
183. Ibid., 55; *Baltimore Sun,* March 10, 1940.
184. As cited in Shaffer, *Recreation and Athletics,* 55.
185. Shaffer, *Recreation and Athletics,* 57.
186. Ibid., 57–58, 60, 62–63.
187. Crichton, "Murder on the Lawn," 14, 37.
188. *Baltimore Sun,* May 19, 1930.
189. *Lacrosse* souvenir program, season 1941 (April 12, 1941, vs. Loyola), n.p., Programs, Tickets and Annoucements: Lacrosse, 1926–1969, Folder 9, Box 2, FHAJHU.
190. *Baltimore Sun,* May 10, 1935.
191. Caleb R. Kelly, Jr., "History of the Baltimore Athletic Club Lacrosse Team," 10.
192. *Baltimore Sun,* May 28, 1935.
193. As cited in Kelly, "Baltimore Athletic Club," 11.
194. *New York Times,* February 5, 1938.

Chapter 4: "Mayhem on the Lawn"

1. *Baltimore Sun Magazine,* 2 June 1946; *The Official Lacrosse Guide* (1946), 19.
2. Albert A. Brisotti, "Editorial," *The Official Lacrosse Guide* (1947), 14.
3. Albert A. Brisotti, "Editorial," *The Official Lacrosse Guide* (1948), 17.
4. *The Official Lacrosse Guide* (1949), 31; *The Official Lacrosse Guide* (1950), 21.
5. File on Syracuse University Varsity Sports, Administrative Board on Athletics, Box 3, Record Group 19, Files of Lewis P. Andreas, Director of Athletics and Physical Education, 1921–1954, Athletic Department, Office of Student Affairs and Services, SUA.
6. *The Official Lacrosse Guide* (1954), 15–16; *Syracuse Daily Orange,* May 13, 1954.
7. Earnest E. Baer, "The 1960 Collegiate Season," *The Official Lacrosse Guide* (1961), 13–15; Earnest Baer, "The 1963 Collegiate Season," *The Official Lacrosse Guide* (1964), 17; Jack Kelly, "The 1968 Collegiate Season," *The Official Lacrosse Guide* (1969), 15–16.
8. *Baltimore Sun,* June 4, 1960, June 5, 1960.
9. George Levine, "Collegiate Reviews: Rocky Mountains," *The Official Lacrosse Guide* (1960), 26–27; Robert Woodberry, "Collegiate Reviews: Rocky Mountains," *The Official Lacrosse Guide* (1961), 26.
10. *New York Times,* October 27, 1968.
11. Paul J. Truntich, "Club Lacrosse," *The Official Lacrosse Guide* (1963), 25–26; "Collegiate Reviews: U.S. Lacrosse Club," *The Official Lacrosse Guide* (1969), 27–28; "USCLA Club Reviews and Previews," *The Official Lacrosse Guide* (1970), 45–47; "Club Lacrosse (USCLA) Review-Preview," *The Official Lacrosse Guide* (1971), 45–46.
12. Johnny Jones, "Rensselaer—Home and Abroad," *The Official Lacrosse Guide* (1949), 21; Philip W. Burleigh, "Collegiate Reviews: New England," *The Official Lacrosse Guide* (1951), 29; "The Virginia Cavaliers Tour England," *The Official Lacrosse Guide* (1955), 20; Robert H. Scott, "Johns Hopkins University's 1958 England Tour," *The Official Lacrosse Guide* (1959), 31; Alexander M. Weyand and Milton R. Roberts, *The Lacrosse Story* (Baltimore: H. & A. Herman, 1965), 252–56, 268–69; I. J. Taylor, "Lacrosse in Australia," *The Official Lacrosse Guide* (1949), 22–24, quote on 23; see also

George Corrigan, "Eleven-Game Australian Tour by American Team," *The Official Lacrosse Guide* (1960), 29; *New York Times,* December 10, 1960, March 22, 1961, April 4, 1961, April 11, 1961; Earnest E. Baer, "The 1961 Collegiate Season," *The Official Lacrosse Guide* (1962), 11; E. F. Corrigan, "Eleven-Game Tour of America by Australian Team," *The Official Lacrosse Guide* (1963), 26.

13. *The History of Lacrosse at St. Paul's School* (Brooklandville, Md.: Saint Paul's School, 1965?), 10, 24.

14. Jack Schultz, "Scholastic Reviews: Metropolitan-Long Island," *The Official Lacrosse Guide* (1961), 34–35.

15. *New York Times,* June 1, 1975.

16. *International Lacrosse Magazine* 3 (Summer 1967): 4–5.

17. Charles Perkins, interview with author, June 3, 1995, LaFayette, N.Y.

18. Howard M. Fish, Jr., "Scholastic Reviews: California," *The Official Lacrosse Guide* (1960), 40; Peter T. Faulkner, "Scholastic Reviews: California," *The Official Lacrosse Guide* (1962), 32.

19. Albert W. Twitchell, comp., "Why Lacrosse?" LF.

20. Glenn N. Thiel, "Lacrosse as a High-School Sport," *Journal of the American Association for Health, Physical Education and Recreation* 22 (April 1951): 27

21. Peter David Lively, "The History of Intercollegiate Lacrosse in the Midwest" (master's thesis, Ohio State University, 1968), 49–50.

22. Albert A. Brisotti, "Collegiate Reviews: Metropolitan New York," *The Official Lacrosse Guide* (1960), 20–21.

23. James W. Carpenter, "The Development of Intercollegiate Lacrosse in the United States" (master's thesis, Kent State University, 1966), 123–24, 133–34, 140–41, 146–47.

24. Thiel, "Lacrosse as a High School Sport," 48–51, quote on 49.

25. Ibid., 48–51, quote on 50. Thiel rewrote and republished the article for another periodical a year later. See Thiel, "Lacrosse as a High-School Sport," *Journal of the American Association for Health, Physical Education and Recreation,* 26–28.

26. Twitchell, "Why Lacrosse?"; *The Official Lacrosse Guide* (1947), 25–26.

27. *History of Lacrosse at St. Paul's School,* 26, 4.

28. "Mayhem in Maryland," *Time* 49 (June 16, 1947): 71; see also W. H. Moore III, "Lacrosse from the Cradle," *The Official Lacrosse Guide* (1950), 19.

29. "Mayhem in Maryland," 71.

30. John Underwood, "Massacre on a Muddy Plain," *Sports Illustrated* 16 (April 23, 1962): 36–38, 43–44.

31. Burgess, "History and Current Status of Women's Lacrosse," 28, 32.

32. Lesley C. Wead, "Why Not Try Lacrosse?" *Journal of Health and Physical Education* 15 (December 1944): 576–77, quote on 576.

33. *Baltimore Evening Sun,* May 29, 1958.

34. Wead, "Why Not Try Lacrosse?" 576.

35. *New York Times,* March 30, 1960.

36. "The 1965 USWLA National Championships," *International Lacrosse Magazine* 1 (September–October 1965): 11–13.

37. See chapter 9 of Cahn, *Coming On Strong.*

38. *Baltimore Sun,* May 12, 1957.

39. Burgess, "History and Current Status of Women's Lacrosse," 53–55, 59–60, 66, 73–74.

40. Ibid., 55, 75–76.

41. Gretchen Schuyler, "Let's Play More Lacrosse!" *Journal of Health and Physical Education* 18 (December 1947): 718, 753, quote on 718.

42. Wead, "Why Not Try Lacrosse?" 576–77.

43. Ibid, 577.

44. Carpenter, "Development of Intercollegiate Lacrosse," 133–34, 140–41.

45. Frederic A. Wyatt, "Starting from Scratch," *The Official Lacrosse Guide* (1947), 27–28.

46. "Editorial," *The Official Lacrosse Guide* (1949), 11.

47. Milton Roberts, "The United States Lacrosse Coaches Association—What Does It Do?" *The Mentor* 6 (January 1956): 12–13, 15, quote on 12.

48. C. J. O'Connor, "The Lacrosse Boom," *The Mentor* 7 (March 1957): 16–17, 33–34, especially 16.

49. W. Kelso Morrill, *Lacrosse* (New York: Ronald Press, 1966 [copyright 1952]); G. Heberton Evans III and Robert E. Anderson, *Lacrosse Fundamentals* (New York: A. S. Barnes and Co., 1966).

50. Roberts, "United States Lacrosse Coaches Association," 12–13, 15.

51. O'Connor, "Lacrosse Boom," 17.

52. Ibid., 33–34.

53. Lively, "History of Intercollegiate Lacrosse in the Midwest," 49–50.

54. W. H. Moore, "Lacrosse: An Old Game Comes of Age," *Log's Look* 44 (April 1, 1955): 23–24; Roberts, "United States Lacrosse Coaches Association" 12–13, 15; O'Connor, "Lacrosse Boom," 16–17, 33–34.

55. Roberts, "United States Lacrosse Coaches Association," 12–13, 15.

56. "Lacrosse Capital of the Nation," *Baltimore American,* June 5, 1955.

57. Morris Touchstone, "Report of the Committee on Lacrosse Hall of Fame," December 11, 1954, in file on Lacrosse Hall of Fame—Origin, LF.

58. G. N. Thiel to Morris Touchstone, January 25, 1954, in file on Lacrosse Hall of Fame—Origin, LF.

59. G. N. Thiel to C. J. O'Connor, February 23, 1954, in file on Lacrosse Hall of Fame—Origin, LF.

60. Albert W. Twitchell to Morris Touchstone, February 12, 1957, in file on Lacrosse Hall of Fame—Origin, LF.

61. Caleb R. Kelly, Jr., "Why Keep Lacrosse in Shackles?" *The Mentor* 11 (September 1960): 6, 31–32, especially 6.

62. Caleb R. Kelly, Jr., to G. N. Thiel, March 7, 1958, in file on Lacrosse Hall of Fame—Origin, LF.

63. Milton R. Roberts, "The Lacrosse Foundation, Inc.: An Anniversary 1959–1979—Twenty Years of Progress," *Lacrosse* 2 (November 1979): 14–21.

64. "Articles of Incorporation of the Lacrosse Hall of Fame Foundation, Incorporated," May 28, 1959, in file on Lacrosse Hall of Fame—Origin, LF.

65. *Baltimore News-Post,* March 25, 1961.

66. *New York Times,* December 11, 1960, April 7, 1957; May 4, 1960; May 8, 1960.

67. Kelly, "Why Keep Lacrosse in Shackles?" 6, 31–32.

68. *New York Times,* June 12, 1966.

69. Shaffer, *Recreation and Athletics,* 81–85.

70. "Do You Know the Story of *Your* Lacrosse Hall of Fame, Its Progress to Date—Its Magnificent Future Plans? Please Read Carefully—It Includes You!" *The Official Lacrosse Guide* (1967), 6–7.

71. Roberts, "Lacrosse Foundation, Inc.," 14–21.

72. Albert A. Brisotti, "Editorial," *The Official Lacrosse Guide* (1946), 16.

73. Stephen Birmingham, *The Right People: A Portrait of the American Social Establishment* (Boston: Little, Brown and Company, 1968 [copyright 1958]), 110.

74. Albert A. Brisotti, "Don't Lose Sportsmanship," *The Official Lacrosse Guide* (1950), 18.

75. *Baltimore Sun*, May 19, 1963.

76. Gary Ronberg, "The Old Boys Are Still Best," *Sports Illustrated* 30 (March 31, 1969): 36–41, quote on 41.

77. Ronberg, "Old Boys Are Still Best," 41.

78. "Budnitz," *International Lacrosse Magazine* 2 (Spring 1966): 5–11, quote on 8.

79. Ronberg, "Old Boys Are Still Best," 36–41.

80. "The Mystique of Club Lacrosse," *Baltimore Magazine* 63 (March 1970): 21–25, 60, quote on 25.

81. For example, see G. William Domhoff, *The Bohemian Grove and Other Retreats: A Study in Ruling-Class Cohesiveness* (New York: Harper & Row, 1974), 89–90, 94–95; idem, *The Higher Circles: The Governing Class in America* (New York: Random House, 1970).

82. *Hobart Herald*, April 17, 1961.

83. Bill Tanton, "Lacrosse," *Baltimore Magazine* 60 (April 1967): 28–31, 83, quote on 29.

84. Ibid., 30, 83.

85. *Hobart Herald*, May 24, 1964, May 12, 1967, May 23, 1969.

86. John F. Steadman, "1947 Collegiate Reviews: Maryland," *The Official Lacrosse Guide* (1948), 31–35.

87. "On Sportsmanship," *International Lacrosse Magazine* 3 (Winter 1967): 7.

88. "Lacrosse Is!" *Climax* 15 (January 1969): 30–33.

89. *Hobart Herald*, April 13, 1951.

90. *Syracuse Daily Orange*, April 4, 1946.

91. *Baltimore Sun*, June 1, 1947.

92. *Baltimore Sun*, June 1, 1947.

93. "Mayhem in Maryland," 71.

94. "Mayhem on the Lawn," *Time* 65 (May 9, 1955): 63–64, 66; "Lacrosse Capital of the Nation," *Baltimore American* clipping dated June 5, 1955, in file on Lacrosse, Vertical Files, EPFL.

95. "The Great Game," *Johns Hopkins Magazine* 7 (April 1956): 7–9, 20–21; *New York Times*, June 8, 1958.

96. James H. Winchester, "Roughest Sport of Them All," *Boy's Life* (March 1962): 14–15, 71, quote on 71.

97. Avery Blake, "Fort Michilimackinac Bicentennial," *The Official Lacrosse Guide* (1964), 29.

98. "The Old Indian Game," *Popular Mechanics Magazine* 89 (March 1948): 126–30.

99. *Syracuse Daily Orange*, April 8, 1949; see also "Lacrosse Outgrows Baltimore," *Life* 32 (May 5, 1952), 165–66, 169.

100. Underwood, "Massacre on a Muddy Plain," 37; *Syracuse Daily Orange*, April 18, 1952;

"Refined *Baggataway,*" *Time* 61 (June 1, 1953): 49; see Moore, "Lacrosse: An Old Game," 23–24.

101. Alexander M. Weyand and Milton R. Roberts, *The Lacrosse Story* (Baltimore: H. & A. Herman, 1965), 5.

102. "*The Lacrosse Story* by Alexander M. Weyand and Milton R. Roberts—Financial Picture—1965 to December 31, 1971," in file on Milt Roberts, LF. During these years, total expenditures were $13,298.22, while total receipts were $9,932.86, for a net loss of $3,365.36.

103. Shaffer, *Recreation and Athletics*, 95.

104. *Syracuse Daily Orange,* May 13, 1950, May 16, 1950.

105. Ibid., May 12, 1951, May 16, 1952, April 29, 1953, May 8, 1953, April 15, 1947, May 15, 1951, April 18, 1952.

106. Ibid., May 12, 1951, May 4, 1954. May 12, 1951.

107. North American Indian Travelling College, *Tewaarathon,* 152.

108. *Syracuse Daily Orange,* May 12, 1951.

109. North American Indian Travelling College, *Tewaarathon,* 150–54.

110. John Wesley Patterson, interview with author, July 24, 1995, Tuscarora Indian Reservation, Lewiston, N.Y.

111. *New York Times,* November 14, 1936.

112. *Rochester Times-Union,* February 12, 1955.

113. "Ross Powless Guest Speech at Banquet in Fergus," unofficial OLA web-site library. Quotation marks in text added.

114. Laurence M. Hauptman, *The Iroquois Struggle for Survival: World War II to Red Power* (Syracuse: Syracuse University Press, 1986), 45–64.

115. Ibid., 85–122, 123–50, 151–78.

116. Ibid., 123.

117. Edmund Wilson, *Apologies to the Iroquois* (New York: Octagon Books, 1978 [copyright 1959]), 283–84.

118. For an overview of Mohawk steelworkers to 1959, see Joseph Mitchell, "The Mohawks in High Steel," in Wilson, *Apologies to the Iroquois,* 3–36.

119. Lilly Benedict, interview with author, August 22, 1995, Akwesasne Reservation, Rooseveltown, N.Y.

120. *Indian Time,* August 18, 1995.

121. Peter Gzowski, "How the Indians Are Leading One More Comeback for Our National Sport," *Maclean's Magazine* 77 (August 22, 1964): 47.

122. Peter Burns, interview with author, August 22, 1995, Akwesasne Reservation, Rooseveltown, N.Y.

123. See Annemarie Anrod Shimony, *Conservatism among the Iroquois at the Six Nations Reserve* (New Haven, Conn.: Department of Anthropology, Yale University, 1961), 162–65, 278.

124. Stan Shillington, "Kerry Gallagher," BCLA web-site library.

125. Stan Shillington, "Paul Parnell," BCLA web-site library.

126. "Ross Powless Guest Speech at Banquet in Fergus," unofficial OLA web-site library.

127. Don Barrie, "The Building of Miller Bowl," Peterborough Lakers web-site library.

128. "The Shape of Canadian Lacrosse," *International Lacrosse Magazine* 2 (Winter 1966): 14–18, quote on 17.

129. "1957–The Allan Fiasco," Unofficial Ontario Lacrosse Association web-site library.

130. Dheensaw, *Lacrosse 100*, 19, 23.

131. Ibid., 21.

132. Stan Shillington, "Jack Northup," BCLA web-site library.

133. "Ross Powless Guest Speech at Banquet in Fergus," Unofficial OLA web-site library.

134. *Toronto Globe and Mail*, September 2, 1989.

135. "Ross Powless Guest Speech." Misspellings in the speech were corrected by the author.

136. *Toronto Globe and Mail*, September 2, 1989.

137. Burns interview.

138. *Toronto Globe and Mail*, September 2, 1989.

139. Stan Shillington, "The National Game at Last," BCLA web-site library; Ben Holdsworth, "Our Not-so-National Sport," *Maclean's* 78 (January 23, 1965): 46; Douglas Fisher, "Our National Game That Never Was," *Canadian Geographic* 104 (December 1984–January 1985): 86.

140. Dheensaw, *Lacrosse 100*, 19.

141. Jack Kelly, "The 1967 Collegiate Season," *The Official Lacrosse Guide* (1968), 15; "United States: Winners, Yes; Champion, Maybe," *International Lacrosse Magazine* 3 (Winter 1967): 11–14, 25; "World Tournament . . . Reality at Last!" *International Lacrosse Magazine* 3 (Summer 1967): 18; Milton R. Roberts, *The Lacrosse Story 1965–1976* (Baltimore: Equitable Trust Co., 1977), 77–79.

Chapter 5: The End of "The Lords of Lacrosse"?

1. Willie Scroggs, "The View from the Inside," *Lacrosse Magazine* 18 (November–December 1994): 8.

2. "Club Lacrosse: Wild, Wonderful and Fun," *Lacrosse* 3 (July 1980): 17.

3. See the annual summer camp guides that appeared in *Lacrosse Magazine* during the 1990s.

4. Steven Kelly Luce, "The Geography of Intercollegiate Lacrosse in the United States: 1986" (master's thesis, Cornell University, 1986), 96.

5. Peter Farnsworth, "They *Really* Play Lacrosse in . . . ," *Lacrosse Magazine* 18 (May 1994): 22–24.

6. Milt Roberts, "Women[']s Lacrosse: Coming On Strong," *Lacrosse* 1 (March 1978): 13–14.

7. Susan Miller, "Women's Lacrosse: The Name's the Same," *Lacrosse* 1 (April 1978): 15, 29, quote on 15.

8. Marc Bouchard, "Growth Industry: Inside the Women's Lacrosse Explosion," *Lacrosse Magazine* 22 (May 1998): 16–19.

9. U.S. Lacrosse, Inc., *Market Research Study*, Baltimore, Md., May 1999, 8–9.

10. Ibid.

11. "1984 *Lacrosse* Magazine General Information and Projected Demographics," in file on Lacrosse, Growth & Chapters, LF.

12. U.S. Lacrosse, Inc., *Market Research Study*, 10.

13. "1984 *Lacrosse* Magazine General Information and Projected Demographics."

14. Federation internationale d'inter-crosse, "Dobry den Polska" (unpublished paper presented at the conference of the federation director in Legnica, Poland, 1991), 6, as

cited in Jean Harvey and Francois Houle, "Sport, World Economy, Global Culture, and New Social Movements," *Sociology of Sport Journal* 11 (1994): 337–55, quote on 350.

15. See also Canadian Lacrosse Association, *Inter-Lacrosse Instructional Manual* (Ottawa: Department of the Secretary of State of Canada, 1990).

16. U.S. Lacrosse, Inc., *Market Research Study,* 12.

17. *The Official Lacrosse Guide* 1972, 53; *The Official Lacrosse Guide* 1979, 61.

18. *The Official Lacrosse Guide* 1975, 50; *The Official Lacrosse Guide* 1976, 53.

19. "The Club List," *Lacrosse Magazine* 19 (November–December 1995): 53–57.

20. U.S. Lacrosse, Inc., *Market Research Study,* 10.

21. "1984 *Lacrosse* Magazine General Information and Projected Demographics."

22. British Columbia Lacrosse Association, "30 Years of Senior Lacrosse Registration" and "30 Year Registration of Minor Lacrosse," *Annual Report 1999.*

23. Canadian Lacrosse Association, "CLA Member Registrations," 1985–1989.

24. Stan Shillington, "Ted Fridge," BCLA web-site library.

25. Stephen Weatherbe, "Battle for the Box," *Alberta Report* 13 (April 7, 1986): 58.

26. Stan Shillington, "The Lacrosse Draft," BCLA web-site library.

27. Dheensaw, *Lacrosse 100,* 22, 8, 7.

28. U.S. Lacrosse, Inc., *Market Research Study,* 18–21.

29. Carole A. Wakefield, "Jackie Pitts: 'Ms. Lacrosse,'" *Lacrosse* 4 (November–December 1981): 16–17, quote on 16.

30. Yukuke Sasaki, "The History of Lacrosse in Japan," *Lacrosse* 13 (May 1989): 36–37; *New York Times,* August 27, 1989; Melissa Hendricks, "Sticks across the Sea," *Johns Hopkins Magazine* 43 (October 1991): 40–46.

31. James Hunt, "Lacrosse in a Scottish pasture," *Lacrosse* 14 (March 1990): 12–13, quote on 13. See also *New York Times,* December 25, 1989; Bud Poliquin, "'They Were Playing Lacrosse,'" *Lacrosse* 14 (March 1990): 12, 14.

32. Lally Lacrosse Company, *Illustrated Catalogue* (Cornwall, Ontario: Cornwall Standard Printing, 1902), in file on Lally Lacrosse Company Catalogue, LF.

33. North American Indian Travelling College, *Tewaarathon,* 104, 106, 109, 110–14, 116–19. Brother Alex Roundpoint died in 1934. Chisholm also remained a reservation resident until 1957, and he retired from teaching in 1967. Chisholm introduced Frank's sons Gilbert, Ronald, and Wallace into the business.

34. For overviews on the manufacture of wooden lacrosse sticks, see *Baltimore Sun Magazine,* April 15, 1951; North American Indian Travelling College, *Tewaarathon,* 127–46; Bil Lingard, "Lacrosse—The Fastest Game on Two Feet," *The Beaver* 300 (Autumn 1969): 12–16.

35. *Baltimore Sun Magazine,* April 15, 1951.

36. *Toronto Globe and Mail,* February 17, 1960.

37. Stan Shillington, "Ab Brown," BCLA web-site library.

38. *Toronto Globe and Mail,* February 17, 1960.

39. *The Official Lacrosse Guide* 1965, 6.

40. *Toronto Globe and Mail,* June 5, 1968.

41. *Cornwall Standard-Freeholder,* October 26, 1968.

42. Paul Chisholm, "The Remarkable Rebirth of Lacrosse: Will the Indians Who Invented It Be the First Victims of Its Popularity?" *Imperial Oil Review* 53 (December 1969): 22–26, quote on 23–24. See also Lingard, "Lacrosse—The Fastest Game," 12–16.

43. Chisholm, "Remarkable Rebirth of Lacrosse," 22–26.

44. For an example of Canadian experimentation with plastics, see Chisholm, "Remarkable Rebirth of Lacrosse," 22–26.

45. Chisholm, "Remarkable Rebirth of Lacrosse," 23.

46. Jack Murphy, "The Civilized Spread of a Savage Sport," *Dupont Magazine* 65 (March–April 1971): 2–5, quote on 5.

47. Bill McAllen, "STX Inc.: Big Name in Lacrosse," *Maryland Magazine* 21 (Spring 1989): 46–51, quote on 48.

48. Murphy, "Civilized Spread of a Savage Sport," 2–5; Jay Reston, "Two Companies Compete," *Lacrosse* 2 (July 1979): 20–23.

49. Murphy, "Civilized Spread of a Savage Sport," 5.

50. McAllen, "STX Inc.," 46–51.

51. Reston, "Two Companies Compete," 20–23.

52. North American Indian Travelling College, *Tewaarathon*, 123–24; Syracuse *Herald-Journal*, September 17, 1985; *Watertown Times*, April 26, 1991.

53. Carole Wakefield, "John Wesley Patterson: Yesterday's Sticks for Today's Players," *Lacrosse* 8 (March 1984): 19–23; J. F. Pirro, "An American Original: Wes Patterson's Tuskewe Krafts," *Lacrosse Magazine* 21 (September–October 1997): 16–23.

54. John Wesley Patterson, interview with author, July 24, 1995, Tuscarora Indian Reservation, Lewiston, N.Y.

55. Pirro, "An American Original," 16–23, quote on 17.

56. Eamon J. McEneaney, "The Death of the Wooden Lacrosse Stick," *Lacrosse Magazine* 22 (January–Februrary 1998): 60–61.

57. Marian L. Salzman, "The Lacrosse Connection," *Forbes* 138 (October 6, 1986): 172–73, quote on 172.

58. *Baltimore Sun*, 24 June 1982.

59. Donald T. Fritz, "Baltimore, Lacrosse, JHU and Its Incredible 1950 Team," *Baltimore Style* (February–March 1983): 42–44.

60. *New York Times*, October 16, 1994.

61. Salzman, "Lacrosse Connection," 172, 173.

62. *New York Times*, May 5, 1985.

63. Ibid., March 19, 1984.

64. Tom Callanan, "Lacrosse: A Gentleman's Battleground," *Echelon* 9 (July 1987): 60–66, quote on 60.

65. Anne Lee Delano, *Lacrosse for Girls and Women* (Dubuque, Iowa: Wm. C. Brown Co., 1970), 69, 3.

66. *New York Times*, May 29, 1977, April 6, 1980, April 10, 1983; Bob Smith, "Club Lacrosse," *Lacrosse* 1 (March 1978): 12.

67. Delano, *Lacrosse for Girls and Women*, 74.

68. Richard Kucner, "Lacrosse Evangelism," *Baltimore Magazine* 75 (June 1982): 85–89, quotes on 88. For other discussions of the elite aura of lacrosse, see Susan Watters, "The Civilized Contact Sport," *M* 3 (March 1986): 108–15; Dennis Bartel, "Bacharach Rasin: A Sports Headliner," *Maryland Magazine* 26 (March–April 1994): 40–43, 45, 47.

69. *New York Times*, April 24, 1983; Smith, "Club Lacrosse," 12.

70. Kucner, "Lacrosse Evangelism," 88.

71. Edward C. Atwater, "Lacrosse, Baltimore Style," *Maryland* 5 (Spring 1973): 16–18, quote on 16.

72. *Baltimore Sun Magazine,* April 1, 1976.

73. Ramsey Flynn, "Sticking Together," *Baltimore Magazine* 79 (October 1986): 90–91, quotes on 90.

74. Ibid.

75. Luce, "Geography of Intercollegiate Lacrosse," 60, 80.

76. Flynn, "Sticking Together," 90–91.

77. John Seabrook, "The Gathering of the Tribes," *New Yorker* 74 (September 7, 1998), 34.

78. Mickey Webster, "Youth and Lacrosse: The Prime Directive," *Lacrosse* 8 (May 1983): 43.

79. Ibid.; Don Fritz, "Happy Birthday: Lacrosse Foundation Turns 30 and Growing," *Lacrosse* 13 (April 1989): 44–47.

80. Nelson Coffin, "Lombard Becomes First Ever Inner City League Champions," *Lacrosse* 13 (September 1989): 44–45; Jamie Hunt, "Baltimore Middle School League," *Lacrosse Magazine* 18 (June 1994): 20–25; Steve Stenersen, electronic correspondence with author, July 19, 2000.

81. Callanan, "Lacrosse: A Gentleman's Battleground," 60.

82. *Baltimore Sun,* 19 May 1993.

83. Jim Brown with Steve Delsohn, *Out of Bounds* (New York: Zebra Books, 1989), 121.

84. Sam Davis, "Blacks and Lacrosse," *Metropolitan Baltimore* 7 (March 1982): 42–45, quote on 43.

85. *Baltimore Sun,* May 19, 1993.

86. Don Fritz, "Baltimore's Mayor Schmoke: Athlete, Leader, Scholar," *Lacrosse* 13 (July 1989): 34–35.

87. Davis, "Blacks and Lacrosse," 44.

88. *Baltimore Sun,* 19 May 1993.

89. Davis, "Blacks and Lacrosse," 42–45.

90. Scott Nelson, "Unsportsmanlike Conduct," *Lacrosse Magazine* 19 (May 1995): 14–21; see also John Yeager, "Good Character and the Future of the Game," *Lacrosse Magazine* 21 (April 1997): 60–63.

91. Humphrey S. Taylor, "Let's Clean Up the Language!" *Lacrosse Magazine* 20 (January–February 1996): 6.

92. "Bob Scott," *Lacrosse Magazine* 23 (May 1999): 52–53.

93. Keith Maynard, "When the Game Grows," *Lacrosse Magazine* 19 (July–August 1995): 4.

94. For an overview of the development of the national governing board, see Keith Maynard, "Report Ties Lacrosse Growth to Establishment of NGB," *Lacrosse Magazine* 19 (February 1995): 25–27; Bill Tanton, "USLCA Vote Unanimous to Move Ahead with NGB," *Lacrosse Magazine* 20 (April 1996): 36–37; Carole Kleinfelder, Steve Stenersen, *Lacrosse Magazine* 20 (May 1996): 42–43, 66; Jana M. Friedman, "Despite 'Growing Pains,' U.S. Lacrosse, Inc. Makes Progress," *Lacrosse Magazine* 21 (June 1997): 43–47; "The Dawn of a New Day," *Lacrosse Magazine* 21 (November–December 1997): 19–21; Carole Wakefield, "Vote by USWLA Exec Board a Positive Sign for Future of Women's Lacrosse," *Lacrosse Magazine* 22 (April 1998): 14.

95. Marc Bouchard, *Lacrosse Magazine* 23 (September–October 1999): 4.

96. "On All-Americans and the Pros," *International Lacrosse Magazine* 4 (Spring 1968): 7.

97. *Toronto Globe and Mail,* March 18, 1969.

98. *Toronto Star,* February 18, 1972.

99. *Toronto Sun,* February 18, 1972.

100. *Toronto Globe and Mail,* December 14, 1972.

101. Roy MacGregor, "You Have to Hate to Love Lacrosse," *Maclean's* 86 (August 1973): 14, 16.

102. Ibid., 16.

103. *Toronto Sun,* January 11, 1974; *Syracuse Post-Standard,* May 7, 1974; *New York Times,* June 16, 1974.

104. *Toronto Sun,* March 5, 1974, May 15, 1974.

105. *Philadelphia Daily News,* May 17, 1974; *Syracuse New Times,* October 20, 1974.

106. *Toronto Sun,* September 20, 1977.

107. *Toronto Globe and Mail,* August 30, 1974.

108. *Syracuse New Times,* June 14, 1973. The league included the Massena (Akwesasne) Braves, Montreal (Caughnawaga) Indians, Ottawa Rattlers, and Syracuse (Onondaga) Warriors in the east and the Akron (Tonawanda) Senecas, Hamilton (Six Nations) Chiefs, Niagara Falls (Tuscarora) Hawks, and Rochester (Newtown) Golden Eagles in the west.

109. *Syracuse New Times,* March 24, 1974, September 29, 1974.

110. Ibid., October 13, 1974, October 20, 1974.

111. *Syracuse Herald-Journal,* February 14, 1976.

112. As cited in Dheensaw, *Lacrosse 100,* 9.

113. *Toronto Globe and Mail,* June 20, 1991.

114. John Hughes, "The King of Glitz," *The Corporate Report* 13 (November 1987): 38.

115. Benjamin G. Rader, *In Its Own Image: How Television Has Transformed Sports* (New York: Free Press, 1984), 5; Richard Crepeau, "There Seems to Be No End in Sight," *Journal of Sport History* 27 (Fall 2000): 525–27; Daniel A. Nathan, "Sometimes, ESPN Seems Ubiquitous," *Journal of Sport History* 27 (Fall 2000): 528–31.

116. "A Response from the IBLA," *Lacrosse* 9 (June–July 1985): 36.

117. G. Darrell Russell, "This Season, It's Major," *Lacrosse* 11 (November–December 1987): 26.

118. Susan Biddle Jaffe, "Welcome to the Indoor League," *Lacrosse* 13 (December 1989): 22–24, article reprinted from *Business of Sports* magazine.

119. Quint Kessenich, "Behind the Scenes of Major Indoor Lacrosse League," *CrosseCheck* (1996): 8, 10, quote on 10.

120. Franz Lidz, "Thunder on the Beltway," *Sports Illustrated* 66 (March 30, 1987): 56.

121. Callanan, "Lacrosse: A Gentleman's Battleground," 60–66.

122. *Toronto Globe and Mail,* February 18, 1993.

123. *Washington Post,* April 6, 1991.

124. *Toronto Globe and Mail,* February 18, 1993.

125. "Bringing the Game Inside; or, Does Box Lacrosse Lose Something in the Translation?" *Lacrosse* 11 (April 1987): 2.

126. Quint Kessenich and Bill Tanton, "Is the MILL Good for Lacrosse?" *Lacrosse Magazine* 20 (January–February 1996): 30–31, 43, quote on 31.

127. "This Is the Way the Season Ends," *Lacrosse Magazine* 20 (June 1996): 34–35.

128. Hughes, "King of Glitz," 38.

129. *New York Newsday*, March 12, 1993, September 12, 1993; *Boston Herald*, January 24, 1995.

130. Bill Tanton, "Is The MILL Good for Lacrosse? No," *Lacrosse Magazine* 20 (January–February 1996): 31, 43, quote on 43.

131. *New York Times*, February 4, 1990.

132. "A Day in the MILL," *Sporting News* (April 3, 1989): 8.

133. Dave Burns, "Attendance Average Up for Major Indoor Lacrosse League," *Amusement Business* 101 (April 22, 1989): 16; *Toronto Globe and Mail*, February 18, 1993.

134. *Boston Herald*, January 24, 1995.

135. *Buffalo News*, July 23, 1997.

136. "The Death of Club Lacrosse—Maybe," *Lacrosse* 11 (November–December 1987): 2; Peter Lund, "One Thing Is for Sure," *Lacrosse Magazine* 23 (September–October 1999): 35.

137. Marc Bouchard, "Major League Lacrosse 'Takes It Outside,'" *Lacrosse Magazine* 23 (July–August 1999): 58–59.

138. Seabrook, "The Gathering of the Tribes," 34.

139. Anthony F. C. Wallace, "Origins of the Longhouse Religion," *Handbook of North Americans*, vol. 15, *Northeast*, ed. Bruce G. Trigger (Washington, D.C.: Smithsonian Institution, 1978), 442–65.

140. *Akwesasne Notes*, Early Winter 1973.

141. *Syracuse New Times*, June 15, 1975, May 22, 1977; *Syracuse Post-Standard*, May 14, 1977.

142. North American Indian Travelling College, *Tewaarathon*, n.p.

143. Ibid., 8, 20–26.

144. *New York Times*, June 15, 1986.

145. See "No Good Deed Goes Unpublished," *Lacrosse* 8 (November 1984): 15–17.

146. *Toronto Globe and Mail*, June 11, 1970, as cited in *Akwesasne Notes*, September 1970.

147. "Don't Bury My Stick at Wounded Knee," *Lacrosse* 9 (November–December 1985): 2.

148. "Chief Oren Lyons on Lacrosse," *Northeast Indian Quarterly* 3 (Spring 1986): 4–7, quote on 7.

149. Oren Lyons to G. F. Tillotson, October 1987, in file on Iroquois Nationals, LF.

150. *New York Times*, July 16, 1990.

151. *The People's Voice*, July 21, 1989; *Akwesasne Notes*, Late Spring 1990.

152. *People's Voice*, July 21, 1989.

153. *Syracuse Post-Standard*, June 13, 1990.

154. Rick Hill, "Challenged at Their Own Game," *Lacrosse* 7 (May 1983): 20–21, quote on 21. For a brief feature on the Nationals, see Doug George-Kanentiio, "The Iroquois Nationals: Creating a Sports Revolution for American Indians," *Akwesasne Notes* 1 (July–August–September 1995): 94–95.

155. *Syracuse Herald-Journal*, July 7, 1990.

156. Iroquois Nationals Newsletter, March 1994, LF.

157. Jeff Jenson, "The Oneida Reclaim Their Heritage through Lacrosse," *Lacrosse Magazine* 19 (April 1995): 30–33; Dan Ninham, "More Midwest Growth," *Lacrosse Magazine* 19 (May 1995): 6; Thomas Vennum, Jr., "Giving Something Back," *Lacrosse Magazine* 24 (April 2000): 6.

158. Mike Liebman, "Colorado Program Emphasizes Lacrosse's Roots," *Lacrosse Magazine* 20 (November–December 1996): 78.

159. "Lacrosse: Official Sport of Native Americans," *Lacrosse Magazine* 21 (January–February 1997): 12.

160. See Bruce Johansen, *Life and Death in Mohawk Country* (Golden, Colo.: North American Press, 1993).

161. *People's Voice,* April 26, 1991, May 18, 1992.

162. *Toronto Globe and Mail,* June 6, 1992.

163. *Cornwall Standard-Freeholder,* June 22, 1992.

164. *Toronto Globe and Mail,* June 6, 1992.

165. *People's Voice,* May 26, 1995.

166. *People's Voice,* August 18, 1995.

167. *Cornwall Standard Freeholder,* August 17, 1995, as printed in *Indian Time,* August 18, 1995.

168. *Indian Time,* August 25, 1995.

169. Ken Van Every, interview with author, August 3, 1995, Lewiston, N.Y.

170. Seabrook, "The Gathering of the Tribes," 31, 33, 36.

Epilogue: Ground Still Contested

1. Daniel K. Richter, *The Ordeal of the Longhouse: The Peoples of the Iroquois League in the Era of European Colonization* (Chapel Hill: University of North Carolina Press, published for the Institute of Early American History and Culture, 1992).

2. Testimony of Oren Lyons, taken from "Traditionalism and the Reassertion of Indianness," in *Indian Self-Rule: First-Hand Accounts of Indian-White Relations from Roosevelt to Reagan,* ed. Kenneth R. Philip (Salt Lake City: Howe Brothers, 1986), 244–46, quote on 245.

3. *Wall Street Journal,* June 15, 2001.

An Essay on Sources

SCHOLARLY STUDIES of Native American ball games are numerous. For a tribe-by-tribe overview of games, especially lacrosse or "racket," see Stewart Culin, *Games of the North American Indians* (New York: Dover Publications, 1975), 36–43, 561–616, originally published as idem, "Games of the North American Indians," in *Twenty-Fourth Annual Report of the Bureau of American Ethnology to the Smithsonian Institution, 1902–1903* (Washington, D.C.: Government Printing Office, 1907). The most comprehensive study of native stick-and-ball games in eastern North America is Thomas Vennum, Jr., *American Indian Lacrosse: Little Brother of War.* (Washington, D.C.: Smithsonian Institution Press, 1994). For a similar study of the more elaborate Mesoamerican games, see Vernon L. Scarborough and David R. Wilcox, eds., *The Mesoamerican Ballgame* (Tuscon: University of Arizona Press, 1991).

Other studies on native games include Joseph Marshall Becker, "Lacrosse: Political Organization in North America as Reflected in Athletic Competition," *Expedition* 27, no. 2 (1985): 53–56; Kendall Blanchard, "Stick Ball and the American Southeast," in *Forms of Play of Native North Americans*, ed. Edward Norbeck and Claire R. Farrer (Saint Paul, Minn.: West Publishing Co., 1979), 189–207; idem, *The Mississippi Choctaws at Play: The Serious Side of Leisure* (Urbana: University of Illinois Press, 1981); idem, *The Anthropology of Sport: An Introduction* (Westport, Conn.: Bergin & Garvey, 1995), 112–19, 172–78; Alyce Cheska, "Ball Game Participation of North American Indian Women," *Proceedings from the Third Canadian Symposium on History of Sport and Physical Education* (Halifax, Nova Scotia: Dalhousie University, August 18–21, 1974); George Eisen, "Games and Sporting Diversions of the North American Indians as Reflected in American Historical Writings of the Sixteenth and Seventeenth Centuries," *Canadian Journal of History of Sport and Physical Education* 9 (May 1978): 58–85; idem, "Early European Attitudes toward Native American Sports and Pastimes," in *Ethnicity and Sport in North American History and Culture,* ed. George Eisen and David K. Wiggins (Westport, Conn.: Greenwood Press, 1994), 1–18; Francis Eyman, "Lacrosse and the Cayuga Thunder Rite," *Expedition* 6 (Summer 1964): 14–19; Raymond David Fogelson, "The Cherokee Ball Game: A Study in Southeastern Ethnology" (Ph.D. diss., University of Pennsylvania, 1962); Maurice Jette, "Primitive Indian Lacrosse: Skill or Slaughter?" *Anthropological Journal of Canada* 13, no. 1 (1975): 14–19; Dane Lanken, "Lacrosse: 'Little Brother of War,' the Indians Called It," *Canadian Geography* 104 (November–December 1984): 36–43; Daniel Littlefield, Jr., "The Decline of the Ball Play among the Civilized Tribes," *Journal of Ethnic Studies* 4 (1975): 56–70; Eugene B. McCluney, "Lacrosse: The Combat of Spirits," *American Indian Quarterly* 1 (Spring 1974): 34–42; Michael A. Salter, "The Relationship of Lacrosse to Physical Survival among Early North American Indian Tribes," *Proceedings of the Second World Symposium on the History of Sport and Physical Education* (Banff, Alberta: May 31–June 3, 1971), 95–106; idem, "The Effect of Acculturation on the Game of Lacrosse and Its Role as an Agent of Indian Survival," *Canadian Journal of History of Sport and Physical Education* 3 (May 1972): 28–43; Herbert E. Winslow, Jr., "A History of Lacrosse as Played by the Iroquois Nation and Other Indian Nations of the Great Lakes Region 1626–1850" (master's thesis, Queens College, 1970); and Roger L. Wulff, "Lacrosse among the Senecas," *The Indian Historian* 10 (Spring 1977): 16–22.

For the most useful scholarship from the late nineteenth century, see W. M. Beauchamp, "Iroquois Games," *The Journal of American Folklore* 9 (October–December 1896): 269–77; J. N. B. Hewitt, "Iroquois Game of La Crosse," *The American Anthropologist* 5 (January 1892): 189–91; W. J. Hoffman, "Remarks on Ojibwa Ball Play," *The American Anthropologist* 3 (April 1890): 133–35; and James Mooney, "The Cherokee Ball Play." *American Anthropologist* 3 (April 1890): 104–32. The only native study of the game is North American Indian Travelling College, *Tewaarathon (Lacrosse)* (Akwesasne Reservation, 1978).

Another area of literature is that related to the nineteenth-century Canadian game. Any study of this era must begin with William George Beers, *Lacrosse, the National Game of Canada* (Montreal: Dawson Brothers, 1869).

As early as the 1860s, journalists, fans, and administrators provided historical commentary. For a contemporary journalistic history of lacrosse in Canada, see B. W. Collison and John K. Munro, "Lacrosse in Canada: Its History and the N.A.L.U.," *Canadian Magazine* 19 (September 1902): 410–26. Scholarly inquiries after the Canadian centennial include Allan Elton Cox, "A History of Sports in Canada, 1868–1900" (Ph.D. diss., University of Alberta, 1969), 135–61, 439–41; Kevin G. Jones, "Sport in Canada—1900 to 1920" (Ph.D. diss., University of Alberta, 1970), 135–61, 469–70; Peter Leslie Lindsay, "A History of Sport in Canada, 1807–1867" (Ph.D. diss., University of Alberta, 1969), 114–32, 302–04; and Thomas George Vellathottam, "A History of Lacrosse in Canada Prior to 1914" (master's thesis, University of Alberta, 1968). Subsequent studies by these former students include Peter L. Lindsay, "George Beers and the National Game Concept: A Behavioral Approach," *Proceedings of the Second Canadian Symposium on the History of Sport and Physical Education* (Windsor, Ontario: University of Windsor, May 1–3, 1972), 27–44; Kevin G. Jones and T. George Vellathottam, "The Myth of Canada's National Sport," *Journal of the Canadian Association for Health, Physical Education and Recreation* 41 (September–October 1974): 33–36; idem, "Highlights in the Development of Canadian Lacrosse to 1931," *Canadian Journal of History of Sport and Physical Education* 2 (December 1974): 31–47.

For more recent scholarship, see Cecile Marie Badenhorst, "The Geography of Sport as a Cultural Process: A Case Study of Lacrosse" (master's thesis, University of British Columbia, 1988); chapter 7 of Nancy Barbara Bouchier, "'For the Love of the Game and the Honour of the Town': Organized Sport, Local Culture and Middle Class Hegemony in Two Ontario Towns, 1838–1895" (Ph.D. diss., University of Western Ontario, 1990); idem, "Idealized Middle-Class Sport for a Young Nation: Lacrosse in Nineteenth-Century Ontario Towns, 1871–1891," *Journal of Canadian Studies* 29 (Summer 1994): 89–110; David Brown, "Canadian Imperialism and Sporting Exchanges: The Nineteen[th]-Century Cultural Experiences of Cricket and Lacrosse," *Canadian Journal of History of Sport* 18 (May 1987): 55–66; Christina A. Burr, "The Process of Evolution of Competitive Sport: A Study of Senior Lacrosse in Canada, 1844 to 1914" (master's thesis, University of Western Ontario, 1986); Alan Metcalfe, "Sport and Athletics: A Case Study of Lacrosse in Canada, 1840–1889," *Journal of Sport History* 3 (Spring 1976): 1–19; chapter 6 of idem, *Canada Learns to Play: The Emergence of Organized Sport, 1807–1914* (Toronto: McClelland and Stewart, 1987); Don Morrow,

"The Powerhouse of Canadian Sport: The Montreal Amateur Athletic Association, Inception to 1901," *Journal of Sport History* 8 (Winter 1981): 20–39; idem, "The Canadian Image Abroad: The Great Lacrosse Tours of 1876 and 1883," *Proceedings of the Fifth Canadian Symposium on the History of Sport and Physical Education* (Toronto, August 26–29, 1982), 11–23; idem, "Lacrosse as the National Game," in *A Concise History of Sport in Canada,* ed. Don Morrow et al. (Toronto: Oxford University Press, 1989), 45–68; Morris Mott, "One Town's Team: Souris and Its Lacrosse Club, 1887–1906," *Manitoba History* 1 (1980): 10–16; and Nancy Pinto, "Ain't Misbehavin': The Montreal Shamrock Lacrosse Fans 1868 to 1884" (paper presented at North American Society for Sport History conference, Banff, Alberta, 1990).

Books on twentieth-century lacrosse targeting sporting general audiences include Cleve Dheensaw, *Lacrosse 100: One Hundred Years of Lacrosse in B.C.* (Victoria, B.C.: Orca Book Publishing, 1990); Miles Harrison, Jr., and Chip Silverman, *Ten Bears* (Positive Publications, 2001), an examination of lacrosse at the historically black Morgan State University in Baltimore; Diane Hoyt-Goldsmith, *Lacrosse: The National Game of the Iroquois* (New York: Holiday House, 1998); Jim Huelskamp, *Indoor Lacrosse: The Story behind the Major Indoor Lacrosse League* (Publishing Concepts, 1992); Milton R. Roberts, *The Lacrosse Story 1965–1976* (Baltimore, Md.: The Equitable Trust Co., 1977); Darrell G. Russell, *Hotbeds for Hybrids: Lacrosse and Soccer in Baltimore* (Glen Burnie, Md.: Russell, 1978); and Alexander M. Weyand and Milton R. Roberts, *The Lacrosse Story* (Baltimore: H. & A. Herman, 1965).

Very few academic studies have been done on the American game. Several theses include James W. Carpenter, "The Development of Intercollegiate Lacrosse in the United States" (master's thesis, Kent State University, 1966); Justin Cobb, "The Evolution of the Rules of Lacrosse" (master's thesis, Springfield University, 1952); Peter Anthony Kowalski, "The History of Men's Intercollegiate Lacrosse at The Pennsylvania State University, 1913 to 1982" (master's thesis, The Pennsylvania State University, 1982); Peter David Lively, "The History of Intercollegiate Lacrosse in the Midwest" (master's thesis, Ohio State University, 1968); and Steven Kelly Luce, "The Geography of Intercollegiate Lacrosse in the United States: 1986" (master's thesis, Oklahoma State University, 1986). See also my dissertation, Donald M. Fisher, "Contested Ground: North American Cultures and the History of Lacrosse" (Ph.D. diss., State University of New York at Buffalo, 1997). Women's lacrosse has received scant attention from historians. Their work includes Catherine L. Brown, "Attitudes towards Fair Play in Women's Lacrosse" (master's thesis, Ohio State University, 1983); Joan Chrystal Burgess, "The History and Current Status of Women's Lacrosse in the United States" (master's thesis, Smith College, 1958); and S. L. Forbes and L. A. Livingston, "From Frances Jane Dove to Rosabelle Sinclair and Beyond: The Introduction of Women's Field Lacrosse to North America," *Proceedings for the 10th Commonwealth & International Scientific Congress* (University of Victoria, Victoria, B.C., August 10–14, 1994), 83–86.

Canadian fans have provided information on the World Wide Web. Some of the web sites at which this information can be found include those of the British Columbia Lacrosse Association (www.bclacrosse.com), the Peterborough Lakers (www.ptbolakerslacrosse.net), and the Unofficial Ontario Lacrosse Association (www.geocities.com/colosseum/Track/6308/index2.html).

Fiction writers have produced a number of short stories related to lacrosse: Burt L. Standish, *Frank Merriwell's Lacrosse Team, or, The Great Tustle with Johns Hopkins* (New York: Street & Smith, 1905); Don Tracy, *Second Try* (Philadelphia: Westminster Press, 1954); and Sidney Offit, *Cadet Attack* (New York: Saint Martin's Press, 1964).

Especially useful are the official publications of lacrosse governing bodies in the United States, such as the Inter-University Lacrosse League of the United States of America (IULLUSA), the United States Inter-Collegiate Lacrosse League (USILL), and the United States Inter-Collegiate Lacrosse Association (USILA): IULLUSA, *American Lacrosse Rules* (New York: Arthur Johnson and Co., 1902); USILA, *Constitution and By-Laws,* 1931; idem, *Official Lacrosse Guide* (New York: American Sports Publishing, published annually 1926, 1928–41); USILL, *Constitution, By-Laws and Playing Rules* (New York: American Sports Publishing, 1907–10); idem, *Official Lacrosse Guide* (New York: American Sports Publishing, published annually 1911, 1913–14, 1922–24); and idem, *Supplement to the Official Lacrosse Guide* (New York: American Sports Publishing, published annually 1925, 1927). The annual guides of the National Collegiate Athletic Association are also useful, including NCAA, *The Official Lacrosse Guide* (New York: A. S. Barnes and Co., published annually 1942–49; idem, *The Official Lacrosse Guide* (New York: The National Collegiate Athletic Bureau, published annually 1950–66); idem, *The Official Lacrosse Guide* (Phoenix, Ariz.: College

Athletics Publishing Service, published annually 1967–73); idem, *The Official Lacrosse Guide* (Shawnee Mission, Kan.: NCAA Publishing Service, published annually 1974–79); idem, *NCAA Lacrosse* (Mission, Kan.: National Collegiate Athletic Association, 1982); and idem, *United States Lacrosse Coaches Association Clinic* (Geneva, N.Y.: Printing Center, published annually 1982–92).

Instructional manuals written by coaches are useful in reconstructing the on-field game. The best known is Bob Scott, *Lacrosse* (Baltimore: The Johns Hopkins University Press, 1976). Others include Margaret Boyd, *Lacrosse Playing and Coaching* (New York: A. S. Barnes and Co., 1959); Herbert G. Evans and Robert E. Anderson, *Lacrosse Fundamentals* (New York: A. S. Barnes and Co., 1966); Tina Sloan Green and Agnes Bixler Kurtz, *Modern Women's Lacrosse* (Hanover, N.H.: ABK Publications, 1989); Jim Hinkson, *Box Lacrosse: The Fastest Game on Two Feet* (Radnor, Pa.: Chilton, 1975); Kelso W. Morrill, *Lacrosse* (New York: Ronald Press, 1966 [copyright 1952]); William C. Schmeisser, *Lacrosse: From Candidate to Team* (New York: American Sports Publishing Co., 1904); and Tad Stanwick, *Lacrosse* (New York: A. S. Barnes and Co., 1940).

Index

African Americans. *See* blacks

Akron Indians, 106, 174

Akwesasne Reservation Indians. *See* Saint Regis Indians

Akwesasne Thunder, 303–5

Allan, Bob, 234–35

amateurism: in Canada, 37–42, 44–47; in United States, 67–70, 156–57, 210–19, 265–77, 290. *See also* Crescent Athletic Club of Brooklyn; Johns Hopkins University; "national game," Canada's

American Box Lacrosse League, 160–61

American Lacrosse League, 289–90

Anglo-Saxonism, 76, 100–101, 142

Australia, 151, 193, 241, 254

Bacharach Rasin, 258, 260

Baltimore, Maryland, as cultural capital of lacrosse, 156, 186, 188, 198, 270–72; and cultural values learned from lacrosse, 124–25

Baltimore Athletic Club: 1878 team, 72–73; 1935 team, 186–87

Baltimore City College, origins of lacrosse at, 82–83

Baltimore Orioles, as competition with lacrosse, 124, 198

Baltimore Polytechnic Institute, origins of lacrosse at, 83

Baltimore Rough Riders, 160–61

baseball: comparisons with lacrosse, of appeal and popularity, 101, 123, 198, 208–9; —, as body developer, 136; —, cultural values of, 70–71, 86–87, 87–88, 90, 96; —, of equipment costs, 195–96; —, in high schools, 123–24; —, of historical knowledge, 97–98; —, as professional sports, 46–47, 50–51; as competitor with lacrosse, 51–52, 73, 163, 207, 240–41; as exchanged for or replaced by lacrosse, 66, 111–14. *See also* Baltimore Orioles

Beers, William George: as author of *Lacrosse: The National Game of Canada*, 25; and Canadian manliness, 26–27; as dentist and evolutionist thinker, 28–29; and early lacrosse rules, 25–26, 29–30; and health benefits of lacrosse, 28; and playing space, 27–28; and promotion of lacrosse as "national game," 26–27, 30; and scientific lacrosse, 27; and tours of British Isles, 30–32; and women's role in lacrosse, 28

Benedict, Ernest, 293

Benedict, Frank, 227, 263, 302

Bennett, James Gordon, 54

blacks: efforts to encourage play among, 273; as lacrosse players, 274; and Morgan State University lacrosse team, 274–75; and restrictions by southern schools, 133–34. *See also* Brown, Jim

box lacrosse: adoption of by Indians, 222–24, 226–28; and alcohol, 236–38, 279; and American collegians, 161; appeal of, 158–59, 239–41; and Canadian Lacrosse Association, 230–31; championships, 231; community support for clubs in

box lacrosse *(continued)*
    Canada, 233, 252–53; comparisons
        with field lacrosse, 158–59, 229–30,
        236, 252; and cultural heritage of
        Canada, 253–54; economic aspects
        of, 165, 166, 233–34, 252–53; and
        entrepreneurs, 159–60; and entry
        draft system, 253; and firefighting,
        231; growth of, 252; origins of, 157;
        and players, 159, 234–35; replacement
        of field lacrosse in Canada by, 164; role
        of professional hockey owners in,
        157–58; social aspects of, 231–39, 279;
        and spectators, 235; and violence,
        159–62, 238–39. *See also* Cox, Laurie;
        Indians; professional lacrosse; Six
        Nations Indians (Iroquois
        Confederacy)
"boxla." *See* box lacrosse
Brebeuf, Father Jean de, 17
Brine Company, W. H., 258, 260, 263,
    299
Brisotti, Albert, 135, 190, 203, 210
British lacrosse. *See* Great Britain;
    Oxbridge lacrosse
Brown, Ab, 259
Brown, Jim, 213, 267–68, 274–75
Bruce, Louis, 178
Budnitz, Emil, 212, 269
Buffalo Bandits, 284, 287
Burnett & Company, William T., 261
Burns, Peter, 228, 238, 303

Cambridge University lacrosse, 140–46
Camp, Walter, 75, 86, 94, 161
Canadian Amateur Lacrosse
    Association, formation of, 48
Canadian Lacrosse Association, 151, 166,
    230, 252, 278
Carlisle Indian Industrial School:
    adoption of lacrosse as solution to
    baseball problem, 111–14; Indian views
    of lacrosse team, 117; lacrosse players
    at, 114–15; lacrosse team and
    reservations, 119; lacrosse team as
    vehicle for positive Indian image,
    114–15; origins of, 110; white views of
    lacrosse team, 116–18
Carnegie Foundation report on college
    sports, 180

Catlin, George, 23
Cattaraugus Reservation Indians. *See*
    Seneca Indians
Caughnawaga Indians: and
    demonstration of culture, 30–31; early
    tours of United States, 57–63, 68–69;
    and Queen Victoria, 30; and tour of
    British Isles, 30–32
Chickasaw Indians, 24
Chisholm, Colin, 257, 260
Choctaw Indians, 23, 24
Claxton, T. James, 35
Cline, Russ, 283–89
club lacrosse in the United States:
    economic aspects of, 268–70; regional
    support for, 53–55, 65–66, 192–93, 251;
    social aspects of, 69–70, 192, 212, 266,
    267–68, 272–73
colleges and universities, U.S.:
    geographic origins of players, 248,
    272; growth of lacrosse in, 122, 191,
    244–45, 249; origins of lacrosse in,
    65–66, 70–71; and relations with high
    schools, 123
Cornelius, Eli, 221
Cornplanter, Edward, 106, 107–8
Cox, Laurie: and attitudes toward rough
    play, 129; criticisms of box lacrosse,
    161–64; as leader of American
    collegian lacrosse, 143; and origins of
    lacrosse at Syracuse University, 81; as
    propagator of traditions, 127; and
    relations with Indians, 170, 173–74
Cran, Joyce, 148
Creator, the, 2, 14, 16–18, 21, 293–94
Crescent Athletic Club of Brooklyn:
    amateurism of, 79; and Canadian
    clubs, 79–80; demise of as lacrosse
    power, 187; and Indians, 104; and local
    high schools, 83–84, 123, 138; as
    organizer of lacrosse, 122; origins of,
    75–76; social aspects of, 76–77; and
    spectators, 80. *See also* transatlantic
    lacrosse tours

Dominion Lacrosse Association
    (Canada), 49
Dove, Frances Jane, 147
Druid Lacrosse Club of Baltimore, 66,
    68–69, 72–73

Eagle Pro Box Lacrosse League. *See* Major Indoor Lacrosse League

Entertainment and Sports Programming Network, 283, 290

equipment: comparisons of costs with other sports, 163, 195–96; shared by institutions, 205. *See also* lacrosse stick, wood

Five Civilized Tribes, 23–24

Flannery, John R., 55, 88, 118

football: comparisons with lacrosse, 86, 87–88, 97, 191–92; connections with lacrosse, 86, 123, 129

Fort Michilimackinac Massacre: and modern lacrosse exhibition, 217; mythical depictions of, 129, 168–69, 217, 282; and Pontiac's Rebellion, 1, 20

Founders Trophy, 231

Fritz, Chris, 282–89

Gait, Gary and Paul, 285–86, 289–90

Globe Shield trophy, 45

Goertemiller, Ben, 211–12

Great Britain: comparisons of British lacrosse with American game, 77–78; origins of British lacrosse, 32; Oxbridge lacrosse, 140–46. *See also* transatlantic lacrosse tours

Great Depression, impact of, 130–34, 136–40, 165–66

hall of fame, lacrosse: in Canada, 239; in United States, 206–10

Hart, Fabian and Gail, 303–5

Harvard University: and racial controversy with Navy, 133–34; relations with high schools, 84–85

high schools: early intercity championship series, 139; as feeders to colleges and universities, 81–85; and Great Depression and World War II, 136–40; growth of lacrosse in, 123–24, 193–95, 246–47, 250; origins of lacrosse in, 81–85; and player misbehavior, 275–76; and possible college scholarships, 247; and relations with clubs, 195; and styles of play, 248; and summer camps, 247, 271

Hobart College: and Indians, 105–7; origins of lacrosse at, 81

images of lacrosse. *See* popular images of lacrosse

Indians: communities playing box lacrosse, 223–24; contests with whites, 104–8; and fighting in lacrosse, 294–95; playing tactics of, 170–73, 223; social and political problems facing, 225–26; "traditionalists" and "progressives," 291, 293, 301, 306–7; values of and motives for playing lacrosse, 61–62, 105–8, 171, 175–79, 226–28; white attitudes toward play of, 105–8, 170–75. *See also* Carlisle Indian Industrial School; Iroquois Nationals; *specific tribes*

indoor lacrosse: early commercial attempts at, 68–69; and National Guard, 158. *See also* box lacrosse; Major Indoor Lacrosse League

injuries, 94–96, 162–63, 197. *See also* violence

Intercollegiate Association, 65

Intercollegiate Lacrosse Association, 71

intercrosse, 250–51

International Freedom Festival, 241

international lacrosse: Canadian-American series of 1930–36, 151–52, 155–56. *See also* Olympics; transatlantic lacrosse tours; women's lacrosse

International Lacrosse Federation, 296–99

International Lacrosse League, 158

Irish, image of as violent, 60–61, 95–96, 129

Iroquois Confederacy, 12

Iroquois Lacrosse Association, 303–5

Iroquois Nationals: economic aspects of, 299; and International Lacrosse Federation, 296–98; origins of, 295–96; and other Indians, 300; and publicity, 297–98; and sovereignty, 296, 298–99

Japanese lacrosse, 255

Jesuits, 17–18, 22

Johns Hopkins University: alumni relations with undergraduates, 74,

Johns Hopkins University *(continued)*
92–93; amateurism at, 89, 125, 179–88;
class reunions of, 266; as cultural
leader, 87–97; and decommercializa-
tion of sport, 180–85, 218; and Indians,
107–8, 117, 118; and local children,
137–38; and local clubs, 74–75; and
local high schools, 82–83; and
Olympics, 151, 154–55; origins of
lacrosse at, 73; as producer of
intellectual leaders, 73; public image
of, 125; relations with city of
Baltimore, 124–25; and student apathy,
90–92, 126, 182; traditions at, 90–94,
125–26; use of lacrosse as advertising
mechanism, 74, 94, 124; and war
service flag, 121, 190
Jones, Con, 49

Kahnawake Reserve Indians. *See*
Caughnawaga Indians
Kelly, Caleb: and descriptions of
Baltimore, 137; and formation of
Baltimore Athletic Club, 186–87; and
hall of fame and foundation, 207,
208–9

lacrosse, as French word, 24
Lacrosse Foundation: origins of, 206–9;
as promoter of lacrosse, 273; and
support for national governing body,
276
lacrosse stick, wood: advertisement of,
260; and competition from synthetic
stick, 261–64; difficulties of buying, 53,
202–3, 260; factories for, 256–58, 260;
and Indian craftsmen, 256, 258, 264;
and limited growth of sport, 255–56;
making of, 257–59; and Montreal
Lacrosse Club, 25; selling of, 258–60
Lake, Handsome, 21, 22, 291–92, 294
Lally, Frank, 256
Lally, Joe, 152, 256–57
Lally Cup, 152, 155–56
Lalonde, Eduoard "Newsy," 44, 49
Leighten, Joseph A., 78–79, 81
Long Island, 194–95
Long Island Lizards, 290
Lyons, Ike, 174
Lyons, Jesse, 154, 179

Lyons, Oren, Jr.: and criticism of "noble
savage" imagery at hall of fame,
299–300; and criticism of stereotypes
of Indians, 311; and Iroquois
Nationals, 295–98

Maddren, William H., 74, 89–90, 100
Madison Square Garden, 159
Major Indoor Lacrosse League:
advertising of, 284–85; cities and
franchises of, 283–84; economic
aspects of, 284; and game as
entertainment experience, 282–83, 287;
influence of television on, 283, 284;
merger with National Lacrosse
League, 289; origins of, 282; and
players, 287–88; as single-entity
ownership model, 282, 288; spectators
and, 285–87
Major League Lacrosse, 290
Mann Cup, 45, 164–66, 231–34
Martin, Herb, 259
McEneaney, Eamon, 264
medicine game, 228, 306
Mesoamerican ballgames, 12
Miller, Cyrus C., 69–71, 78, 100–101
Miller, Leon, 208
Minto Cup, 45, 231
Mitchell, Mike, 302
Mohawk Civil War of 1990, 301–2
Mohawk Indians. *See* Caughnawaga
Indians; Saint Regis Indians
Mohawk International Lacrosse, 264
Montreal, Quebec: early lacrosse in,
24–25; support for lacrosse clubs by
ethnicity and religion, 43, 67
Montreal Lacrosse Club: early play with
Indians, 25; formation of, 25; as leader
within organized lacrosse, 41; and
Montreal Shamrocks, 38–39; tour of
British Isles, 30–32. *See also* Beers,
William George
Montreal Shamrocks (Lacrosse Club):
and Caughnawaga Indians, 60–61; and
championships, 36; competitive ethos
of, 36; and dispute with Toronto
Lacrosse Club, 38; and Montreal
Lacrosse Club, 38–39; social aspects of,
36
Moore, William "Dinty," 135, 208

Morgan, Lewis Henry, 33
Morrill, Kelso, 183, 204
Mount Washington Lacrosse Club: and amateurism, 211–12; controversy with Baltimore Athletic Club (1935), 186–87; origins of, 74–75; and relationship with Johns Hopkins University, 75
Myers, Howard "Howdy," 194–95

National Amateur Lacrosse Association (Canada), 43
National Amateur Lacrosse Union (Canada), 47
National Collegiate Athletic Association (United States), championship tournaments of, 245–46
"national game," Canada's: and Canadian culture, 32–34; championships and awards, 35–36, 42, 45; as commercial sport, 43–52; and community identity, 39–40, 44; early growth of, 34–35; and evolutionist thinking, 33; and World War I, 50; and gambling, 36, 40; hopes for revival of, 51–52; myth of, 26, 239–40; organizational fragmentation of, 42–43, 46–50; perceived "decline" of, 50–51, 71, 152–53; players and professionalism, 37–38, 41–42, 44–50; and restrictions on Indians, 37–38, 45; and social class, 39–41; and spectators, 35, 40–41, 44–45; spread to United States, 52–72; and support of businessmen and politicians, 35–36, 39–40, 45; transformation into modern commercial sport, 34–43; and violence, 43–44, 50–51
National Lacrosse Association (1867) (Canada): formation of, 29; name change to National Amateur Lacrosse Association, 38; restrictions on Indians, 38
National Lacrosse Association (1968) (Canada and United States), 278
National Lacrosse League (1972), 278
National Lacrosse League (1974), 279–82
National Lacrosse League (1997), 289
Native Americans. *See* Indians
New York Lacrosse Club, 67–68

Newport, Rhode Island, 53–54, 72
nicknames of teams: and Canadian cities, 44, 233; of Canadian clubs, 233–36; and frontier imagery, 290; of Indian clubs, 292–93; and New Westminster Salmonbellies, 235–36
night lacrosse, 133
"noble savage": in Canada, 27–28, 33; early imagery in United States, 98–102; and Hollywood images of Indians, 168–69, 170; origins of, 18; trophies and statues using imagery of, 102, 209–10; white players as symbolic descendants of, 215, 216, 218–19, 277
North American Indian Travelling College, 293–94
North American Lacrosse Association, 281
North Shore Indians, 166–67

O'Connor, Claxton, 204–5, 207
Oelrichs, Herman, 65, 66
Olympics: of 1904, 79, 104; of 1908, 79; of 1928, 151; of 1932, 153–55; of 1948, 193; of 1996, 255
Oneida Indians, 57
O'Neill, William T., 115–17, 119
Onondaga Reservation Indians: exhibitions in late nineteenth century, 57–59; and Hobart College, 106–7; and Syracuse University, 81, 169–76, 220–22
Oshawa General Motors Lacrosse Club, 151
Oxbridge lacrosse, 140–46
Oxford University lacrosse, 140–46

Pacific Coast Lacrosse Association, 165–66
Pan-American Exposition of 1901, 104
Parnell, Paul, 232
Patterson, John Wesley: on intertribal lacrosse matches, 224; and Iroquois Nationals, 295; as lacrosse stick maker, 263–64
Philadelphia Wings, 280, 284
Phillips Academy: origins of lacrosse at, 84; renewed interest in lacrosse at, 138; and Trinity-Pawling title match, 266–67

popular images of lacrosse: as "beer drinker's game," 279; as "cool" sport, 247; as eastern game in the United States, 205; as form of "mayhem," 217–18; as game appealing to working class, 215; as game of Canadian immigrants, 52–56; as "gentleman's game," 270–73; as historically Indian game, 163, 167–69; as inclusive sport, 274; as "intellectual game," 211; as manly game, 114, 129; as modern version of savage game, 216–18, 270–71; as "murder on the lawn," 164; as rough character-building game, 196–97; as scientific game, 60, 89, 170–72; as social mobility vehicle, 197–98, 232–33, 247; as socially elite game or "button-down sport," 212–14; as violent game, 128–29, 162–63. *See also* "national game," Canada's; "noble savage"

Powless, Gaylord, 237–38

Powless, Ross, 224, 232–33, 237

President's Cup, 231

Princeton University, origins of lacrosse at, 72

professional lacrosse, 49–50, 68–69, 278–82. *See also* American Box Lacrosse League; American Lacrosse League; International Lacrosse League; Major Indoor Lacrosse League; Major League Lacrosse; Pacific Coast Lacrosse Association

Quebec Lacrosse Federation, 250

Roberts, Milton, 2, 204, 209, 218–19

Rogers, Will, 155

Rollerball (film), 282–83

Ross, Victor, 174

Roundpoint, Alex, 256

Roundpoint, Frank, 228, 256–57, 260

rules of lacrosse: adoption of "off-sides" rule, 121; changes made during Great Depression, 131–32; and prohibitions on player behavior in Canada, 37, 43–44; and William George Beers, 25–26, 29–30

Saint Regis Indians: early tours of United States, 57, 60; and early white lacrosse, 22

Schmeisser, William C., 93–94, 126–27, 204

Schmoke, Kurt, 275

Scott, Bob, 276

Seneca Indians: at Carlisle Indian Industrial School, 116; games against white clubs, 104–8. *See also* Indians

Shaffer, G. Wilson, 180, 182–83, 185

Shamrock Lacrosse Club. *See* Montreal Shamrocks (Lacrosse Club)

Silverheels, Jay, 224

Simmons, Roy, Jr., 255, 286, 295

Simmons, Roy, Sr.: and Indians, 175–76, 221–23; and Oren Lyons, Jr., 295; as possible honorary chief, 221; and World War II, 135

Sinclair, Rosabelle, 200

Six Nations Indians (Iroquois Confederacy): lacrosse team in 1932 U.S. Olympic tournament, 154; and spread of box lacrosse among reservations, 223–34

Six Nations Reserve Indians, 104

Smith, Harry, 224

"soft" lacrosse, 250–51

"sons of the forest," 26, 29

Squamish Indians, 166–67

Steinfeld, Jake, 290

Stenersen, Steve, 273–74

stick-and-ball games, traditional: diplomatic and military aspects, 13–14, 21–22; and early influence by Europeans, 16–21; in early twentieth century, 103, 108–10; economic aspects, 16, 21; and Five Civilized Tribes, 23–24; general types, 12; of Great Lakes, 13, 109, 115; and Mesoamerican ballgames, 12–13; of Northeast, 13, 115; religious aspects, 14–15, 21; social aspects, 15–16; of Southeast, 13, 23–24, 109, 115

STX (stick manufacturer), 263

Syracuse University: lacrosse as major sport at, 123; and Onondaga Indians, 81, 169–76, 220–22; origins of lacrosse at, 81

Tavares, John, 304

television: collegian lacrosse and, 245–46; as competition with local box

lacrosse clubs in Canada, 241;
professional lacrosse and, 283
Tewaarathon (book), 293
Thiel, Glenn, 206–7
Thomas, Angus, 167
Thorpe, Jim, 110, 296
Tonawanda Reservation Indians, 106, 174
Toronto Rock, 289
tours. *See* transatlantic lacrosse tours; *specific clubs and tribes*
transatlantic lacrosse tours: American tour of 1884, 66; American tour of 1937, 146; American tours of 1950–58, 193; Canadian and Caughnawaga tours of 1867–83, 30–32; comparisons of American and British sporting values, 141–42, 144–45; Crescent tour of 1897, 76–79; Irish tour of 1886, 66–67; Oxford-Cambridge tour of 1903, 79; Oxford-Cambridge tour of 1922, 140–42; Oxford-Cambridge tour of 1926, 143–44; Oxford-Cambridge tour of 1930, 145; Syracuse University tour of 1923, 143; women's tours of 1934–36, 148–49; women's tour of 1980, 255
Tucker, Dick, 261–62
Turnbull, Jack, 135, 190, 206

United States Club Lacrosse Association, 192, 251
United States Intercollegiate Lacrosse Association: all-star game of, 133, 205–6; championship systems of, 122, 132, 192; efforts to promote lacrosse, 202; and private clubs, 122; as reorganized version of United States Intercollegiate Lacrosse League, 122
United States Intercollegiate Lacrosse League, formation of, 71
United States Inter-University Lacrosse League, formation of, 71
United States Lacrosse Coaches Association, promotional efforts of, 203–5

United States Military Academy, sports culture at, 127–28
United States National Amateur Lacrosse Association, formation of, 65
United States Women's Lacrosse Association, 147, 199
U.S. Lacrosse, Inc., 277

Vennum, Thomas, 3
violence, 59–61, 67–68, 94–96, 128. *See also* box lacrosse; injuries; "national game," Canada's

Wallace, Terry, 289–90
Warner, Glenn "Pop," 112–13, 115
Warrior Lacrosse, 263
Weaver, Walt, 253
West Genesee High School, 248
West Point, sports culture at, 127–28
Western Lacrosse Association (Canada), 253
White, Matty, 256
Whitney, Caspar, 77, 86, 98
Wild West shows, 62–63, 101
Wiman, Erastus, 56–57, 60, 66
Wingate, W. Wilson, 72–73, 168
women, as spectators, 91
women's lacrosse: British origins of, 147; and early resistance to joining U.S. Lacrosse, 277; as feminine game, 148, 149, 201–2; growth of in United States, 147, 199, 249–50; institutional support for, 200–201; movement of from Britain to United States, 147; players of, 199; unique characteristics of and comparisons with men's game, 147–48, 149, 150, 200, 248–49
World Games: countries in, 255; inclusion of Iroquois Confederacy in, 296–98; of 1982, 266, 269; origins of, 241–42
World War II, impact of, 134–36

LIBRARY
ST. LOUIS COMMUNITY COLLEGE
AT FLORISSANT VALLEY